ORGANIZED CRIME AND AMERICA
A HISTORY

Organized crime, understood in a literal sense as systematic illegal activity for money or power, is as old as the first systems of law and government and as international as trade. Piracy, banditry, kidnapping, extortion, forgery, fraud, and trading in stolen or illegal goods and services are all ancient occupations that have often involved the active participation of landowners, merchants, and government officials. Many people today, however, follow the lead of the U.S. government and American commentators and understand organized crime as being virtually synonymous with super-criminal 'Mafia-type' organizations. These are usually seen as separate entities, distinct from legitimate society but possessing almost unlimited regional, national, and even international power. In *Organized Crime and American Power*, Michael Woodiwiss argues that organized criminal activity has never been a serious threat to established economic and political power structures in the United States but rather is often a fluid, variable, and open-ended phenomenon that has, in fact, complemented those structures.

Conventional histories of the problem tend to focus on outlaws in peripheral feudal societies, most commonly Sicily, for their antecedents. Woodiwiss, in contrast, finds his antecedents in the systematic criminal activity of the powerful and respectable in those ancient and early modern societies that we usually understand to be at the centre of 'civilized' development. He examines the organization of crime in the Southern states after the American Civil War, the organized crimes of American business interests, the causes and corrupt consequences of the U.S. campaign to prohibit alcohol and other 'vices,' the elaboration of the Mafia conspiracy interpretation of organized crime, and the consequent 'dumbing of discourse' about the problem, not just nationally but internationally.

Emphasizing the importance of collaboration, as much as confrontation, between government and criminals, Woodiwiss illustrates how crime control policies based on the Mafia paradigm have not only failed to address organized criminal behaviour, but have, in many ways, proved counterproductive and damaging to individual rights and social stability.

MICHAEL WOODIWISS is a senior lecturer in the School of History, Faculty of Humanities, at the University of the West of England, in Bristol.

Organized Crime and American Power: A History

MICHAEL WOODIWISS

UNIVERSITY OF TORONTO PRESS
Toronto Buffalo London

© University of Toronto Press Incorporated 2001
Toronto Buffalo London
Printed in Canada

Reprinted in paperback 2003

ISBN: 0-8020-4700-9 (cloth)
ISBN: 0-8020-8278-5 (paper)

Printed on acid-free paper

Canadian Cataloguing in Publication Data

Woodiwiss, Michael
Organized crime and American power : a history

Includes bibliographical references and index.
ISBN 0-8020-4700-9 (bound).   ISBN 0-8020-8278-5 (pbk.)

1. Organized crime – United States.   2. Organized crime – Political
aspects – United States.   I. Title.

HV6446.W66 2001   364.1'06'0973   C2001-900832-5

The University of Toronto Press acknowledges the financial assistance to its
publishing program of the Canada Council for the Arts and the Ontario
Arts Council.

University of Toronto Press acknowledges the financial support for its
publishing activities of the Government of Canda through the Book
Publishing Industry Development Program (BPIDP).

For Ali and Laurie

What makes power hold good, what makes it accepted, is simply the fact that it doesn't only weigh on us as a force that says no, but that it traverses and produces things, it induces pleasure, forms knowledge, produces discourse. It needs to be considered as a productive network which runs through the whole social body, much more than as a negative instance whose function is repression.

Michel Foucault

He who controls the past, controls the future.

George Orwell

The struggle of people against power is the struggle of memory against forgetting

Milan Kundera

Contents

Acknowledgments

Organized Crime and American Power is the product of many years of research, and I hope I have acknowledged in the text or notes most of those who have contributed to my knowledge and understanding of the subject.

I have accumulated many personal and intellectual debts during the years spent in researching and writing this book. First, I would like to thank Hugh Brogan and Patrick Renshaw, two historians who taught me to doubt the received wisdom about the past and to respect the underdog. My first academic job was at the University of Swansea, and I must thank Craig Phelan, Phil Melling, Mike Simpson, Steve Sarson, Jim Parker, Sharon Hansard, Alan Dobson, Bev Evans, Chris Jones, David Bewley-Taylor, Jeff Newnham, Phil Lawrence, Emma Frearson, Julia Oatham, Andy Langran, Simon Morea, Heather Hughes, Colwyn Williamson, and Mike Cohen for making my time in Wales so valuable.

In addition, I must thank my colleagues in the School of History at the University of the West of England, and, in particular, June Hannan, Geoff Swain, Geoff Channnon, and Glyn Stone, for helping to create an amicable and equitable research environment. The research committee of the Faculty of Humanities also made it possible for me to travel to the United States for two American Society of Criminology conferences and thus keep in touch with the latest research. Even more importantly, I was allowed research leave in the academic year 1998–9 to write up the manuscript for *Organized Crime and American Power*.

The staff of many libraries have helped my work enormously, notably the Rare Books, Manuscripts, and Archive Section of the University of Rochester's Rush Rhees Library, the Howard-Tilton Memorial Library of Tulane University, New Orleans, the Special Collections

Department of the University of Tennessee, Knoxville, the University of Nevada, Las Vegas, and Columbia University, New York. In the United States I have also been fortunate enough to spend time in the Library of Congress and in the particularly useful John Jay College of Criminal Justice of the City University of New York. In England, I must thank the staffs of the Official Publications and the Newspapers Sections of the British Library, the University of London's United States Library, and the Bristol University Library, John Witton of the Institute for the Study of Drug Dependence, and Amanda Salter and Julie McKeane of the St Matthias Campus Library, University of the West of England. The book is extremely fortunate to have been under the supervision of Virgil Duff, Executive Editor of the University of Toronto Press, and to have been copy-edited by Kate Baltais.

I would also like to thank Soloman Hughes, Bob and Sue Morgan, Graham Barbrooke, Gerry and Alyson Dermody, Hilary Cole, Anna Kuczmierzyk, Paul Derrett, Nigel South, Nicholas Dorn, Tina Shortman, Carolyn and Steve Dougherty, Simon and Ali Edwards, the Hoyles, Davis, and Derrett families, Phil Vinall, Penny O'Hara, Stephanie Burzio, and my late stepfather, John Lawrence, for all their help and support. My mother Audrey Lawrence deserves special thanks for encouraging me and my brothers and sisters to think for ourselves. My greatest debt is to my wife Alison, for her constant love and support.

My brother Anthony Woodiwiss of the City University, London, Neil Boyd of Simon Fraser University, Vancouver, Steve Tombs of John Moore's University, Liverpool, Margaret Beare of the Nathanson Centre for the Study of Organized Crime and Corruption at York University, Toronto, and Frank Pearce of Queen's University, Kingston, Ontario, have read parts of this manuscript, and their suggestions have been enormously helpful. The original inspiration for this book was Frank Pearce's book, *Crimes of the Powerful*, and I greatly appreciate his help over the years. Any mistakes and misinterpretations in *Organized Crime and American Power* are, of course, my own responsibility.

ORGANIZED CRIME AND AMERICAN POWER

Introduction

For reasons that will soon become apparent, my understanding of the phrase 'organized crime' is literal and short – organized crime is systematic criminal activity for money or power. Organized crime, understood in this way, is as old as the first systems of law and government and as international as trade. Piracy, banditry, forgery, fraud, and trading in stolen or illegal goods and services are all ancient occupations that often involved the active participation of landowners, merchants, and government officials. More recently, corporate business interests, and public and private professionals, have also been actively involved in organized crime. While organized crime has never been exclusive to any one race, ethnic group, class, profession, or gender, many studies have shown that those with power, influence, and respectability in local, regional, national, or international society have tended to organize crime more successfully and securely than those without. Myth and misrepresentation have, however, distorted this historical record.

Variations of the phrase 'organized crime' were first used in nineteenth-century America with no fixed meaning. Depending on their political inclination, contemporaries could have applied it to the schemes of the rich or the poor. They might have read about combinations of business interests, politicians, police officers, lawyers, or professional thieves in terms suggesting their crimes were organized. Only a few would have associated organized crime almost exclusively with conspiratorial groups among foreign career criminals. Some anti-crime groups began to give the phrase a more specific meaning at the beginning of the twentieth century, making it almost synonymous with local political corruption. However, over the next fifty years or so, business groups, politicians, police officers, and lawyers were, in effect, defined out of the problem as the phrase came to have a much more limited and specific meaning. People in most countries today follow the lead of the U.S. government, in that they understand organized crime in a very restricted sense, as being virtually synonymous with super-criminal organizations such as the Mafia. These are usually seen as separate entities, distinct from legitimate society, but possessing almost unlimited regional, national, and even international power.

In this latter sense, 'organized crime' is now an integral part of the vocabulary of criminal justice across the world. Many governments are in a continuous process of devising new ways to combat what for most is a newly discovered problem. Multilateral treaties, U.N. conventions, and transnational law enforcement institutions are proliferating, and intelligence agencies once fully employed in Cold War activities now take on such presumed entities as the Mafia, the Camorra, the Yakusa, the Triads, or any others that are usually given a 'Mafia' label as identification. These groups, according to experts cited in a 1993 U.N. discussion guide, effectively constitute organized crime, since it 'consists of tightly knit, highly organized networks of operatives that pursue common goals and objectives, within a hierarchical power structure that spans across countries and regions to cover the entire world.'[1] Most popular and professional commentators follow the lead of the policy makers and use the term 'organized crime' as a synonym for gangsterism in general, or for the Mafia or Mafia-type organizations, in particular.

The consensus among most commentators suggests that the United States has had the most experience and success in dealing with the problem of organized crime. This conventional wisdom holds that organized crime first emerged as a distinctive problem there when towards the end of the nineteenth century Italian immigrants brought with them large numbers of Mafia members. Since then, according to this view, the problem has persisted broadly along the following lines: The first sustained effort at investigation of the Mafia was abruptly terminated by the murder of New Orleans Police Chief David Hennessy from New Orleans in 1890. From that time on the Sicilian-dominated organization became established in several cities. In the 1920s the Mafia grew rich and powerful during Prohibition through the sale and distribution of alcoholic drinks. After repeal of the prohibition amendment, the Mafia exploited weak and corrupt local government to expand its operations in other areas such as drug trafficking, gambling, labour racketeering, and its infiltration of the legitimate business world. In the past decade, the Mafia has been hard hit by a series of successful federal government prosecutions and has been challenged for criminal dominance by other 'cartels' or organizations 'emerging' among Chinese, Vietnamese, Colombian, Russian, and Cuban groups, plus outlaw motorcycle gangs and prison gangs. These groups compete and sometimes cooperate for control of a multitude of criminal enterprises, most notably those involving the production, importation, and distribution of heroin, cocaine, and other 'street' drugs.

Versions of this history are endlessly recycled and updated in every form of media communication. These are enlivened by often apocryphal anecdotes about career criminals such as Al Capone and Lucky Luciano and by the use of words like 'Godfather' and 'omerta' – the Mafia's code of silence.

On the foundation of this history, it is usually implied or stated by commentators or government officials that gangster organizations have gained an unacceptable level of power through violence and the ability to corrupt weak, greedy, and therefore passive public officials and otherwise respectable business people and professionals. Organized crime in this sense is a threat to rather than a part of society. Therefore, it is argued, the only answer to the problem of organized crime involves increasing the law enforcement power of every individual nation state on the U.S. model and, since many of these organizations are known to operate globally, increasing the collective power of the international community. A complex issue that should involve a thorough re-examination of each nation's laws and institutions and the constraints put upon the making of policy by commercial interests and international commitments has therefore been reduced to an easy-to-swallow package. The issue has become a simple good versus evil equation that admits only one solution – give governments more power to get gangsters or those associated with gangsters.

By providing both an explanation for the past and a justification for the present, the conventional history of organized crime as summarized above is an interpretation that fits well with the mythical past of the United States. The narrative of this mythical past is based on obstacles faced and overcome by a free and united people, and it is presented as a moral example for all the rest of the world to follow.

Most Americans, and indeed most people anywhere, now see organized crime in terms of gangsters who infiltrate and corrupt the national – even international – economic and political systems; global policy to control organized crime has evolved in response to this perception. This book argues that the current perception of organized crime is too limited, and this very limitation has led to misdirected and inadequate national and international policies to control organized crime.

Organized Crime and American Power offers a different perspective on the U.S. past and suggests that the United States can claim no legitimacy whatsoever when it comes to the analysis and control of organized crime. The nation state that has set the organized crime control agenda has a long history of protecting and sometimes even encouraging organized criminal activity. This has included the frequently criminal exploitation of indigenous peoples, African Americans, and other working peoples; the enactment of prohibitions that have fostered corruption and criminal enterprise; and the construction of a regulatory system for business that has not always considered business violations to be crimes. Indeed, from the beginning, the U.S. legal and criminal justice systems were set up in ways that showed a great deal of latitude to certain kinds of organized criminal activity.

In line with seeing organized crime as an outside threat, conventional histories of the problem tend to focus on outlaws in peripheral feudal societies, most commonly Sicily, for their antecedents. In Chapter 1 we abandon this viewpoint and consider other roots: the systematic criminal activity of the powerful and the respectable – or those on their way to power and respectability – in those societies, both ancient and early modern, that we usually associate with the centre of 'civilized' development. From earliest times, landlords, merchants, and holders of administrative and executive power have used the relative immunity that their status gave them to engage in or sponsor activity that today would be described as organized crime.

With the development of modern capitalism, opportunities proliferated for stealing land, as well as for extortion, fraud, piracy, and the smuggling of many kinds of commodities – including human beings for slave or indentured labour. Many scholars have demonstrated that organized criminal activity forms part of the history of virtually every nation and empire, including, as we shall see, Great Britain and the United States.

The American Revolution transformed the Thirteen (British) Colonies into the United States of America. In some respects the revolution represents the long and continuing effort by ordinary people to preserve individual liberties and control the aggression and greed of the powerful in society. Many revolutionary era Americans certainly felt that they were fighting against the criminal abuses of empire and for a more democratic and accountable system. The success of their efforts is perhaps best represented in the first ten amendments to the new nation's constitution, better known as the Bill of Rights. These guaranteed such essential rights and protections as the freedom of speech and religion, freedom from unreasonable searches and seizures, and the rights to privacy and fair trials. However, although the new nation's founding fathers believed and often proclaimed that they were creating the most just and perfect society on Earth – as a model for the rest of mankind to follow – the historical record does not support the rhetoric. Many Americans were denied constitutional protections, and commitments to democracy and the rule of law were frequently overridden by stronger commitments to economic development and territorial expansion.

Chapter 1 details the systematic criminal activity involved in the establishment and expansion of the United States during its first 100 years, as crime adapted to the changing organization of economic and political power. Crimes against powerless peoples such as Native Americans, African Americans, and women were frequently organized enterprises in a nation that proved to have a great tolerance for all kinds of commercial crime and large-scale official corruption. I do not make the sweeping claim that such historical processes as early capitalism, European and American expansionism, and Atlantic slavery were in themselves organized crime. Instead, my aim is simply to detail antecedents of organized crime as part of these processes.

Chapter 2 focuses on the centrality of racism in Southern organized crime, in particular, and in mainstream American thinking in general. It begins by surveying the history of systematic criminal activity aimed at African Americans from the Civil War era onwards. Many of the characteristics associated with the problem of organized crime today existed in the South after the Civil War: secrecy oaths, intimidation, the killing of witnesses, death squads, corrupt networks, and illegal enterprise. During this period, however, the knowledge that organized criminal activity in the South had directed the greatest harm at African Americans was distorted through a racist lens and was eventually lost along the way towards the reconciliation of the North and South. By the 1920s, when organized crime was first recognized as an identifiable problem in America, no commentator or government report acknowledged its contemporary or past existence in the South. Many Americans had by then been convinced that crimes committed or likely to be committed by recently arrived immigrants were more menacing than crimes committed by white Americans. In particular, after the assassinations of New Orleans Police Chief Hennessy in 1890 and New York detective Joseph Petrosino in 1909, the relatively insignificant criminal activity of Italians was magnified out of all proportion, and Mafia mythology established its roots. The idea of organized crime as a foreign import later came to provide an easy explanation for a problem that stubbornly persisted in a nation that has long prided itself on its ability to solve problems. Racism and xenophobia had thus set limits to the understanding of organized crime.

Chapter 3 begins by surveying the ruthless, often illegal, business methods used to concentrate power in U.S. commerce and industry from the late nineteenth century onwards. American businessmen in every part of the nation used bribery, corruption, and sometimes violence to break unions, beat off competition, and steal national resources. Some of the corporate empires established in this way came to dominate the core of the U.S. economy but still operated in ways that involved costly and destructive criminal activity. 'Muckraking' writers investigated and exposed these practices and, for a short while, many Americans were aware of the costs and consequences of organized business crime.

Beginning in the 'progressive era' of the early twentieth century, efforts were made to bring a new order, stability, and honesty to U.S. business and industry, and to guarantee the health and safety of workers and consumers by law. These efforts, however, did not lead to a diminution of corporate power and influence in American society, and in the long run made little impact on the extent and destructiveness of organized business crime. By a mixture of subtle and not-so-subtle actions, big business managed to render corporate criminality almost invisible.

Chapter 4 takes up a theme introduced in Chapter 2. Racism lay behind the establishment of a body of morality laws that inevitably boosted the possibilities for illegal enterprise. Between the 1890s and the 1920s hundreds of thousands of laws were added to American local, state, and federal statute books that attempted to eradicate many kinds of personal behaviour, notably sex outside marriage, gambling, drinking alcohol, and taking drugs such as heroin and cocaine. Reform groups felt that the existing local political and policing structures were too corrupt to enforce anti-vice laws, and so they set about reforming the police, primarily by insulating city police forces from local political machine bosses. During these campaigns the phrase 'organized crime' began to be used for the first time in ways that gave it a distinct meaning – gambling and prostitution operations that were protected by local politicians and public officials. Organized crime was in effect synonymous with local political corruption.

America's early twentieth-century moral reformers were successful in getting the laws they wanted on the statute books and, eventually, in ensuring that city police forces were professionalized and insulated from direct local political control. But the problem with America's moral crusade, from the beginning, was that Americans continued to buy liquor, gamble, take drugs, and fornicate whether or not they were breaking laws and despite whatever system of policing was used in the attempt to stop them. As E.R. Hawkings and Willard Waller perceptively put it in 1936, 'It happens that society has put these goods and services under the ban, but people go on producing them and people go on consuming them, and an act of legislation does not make them any less part of the economic system.'[2]

New forms of organized crime emerged as corrupt networks, often including police in the newly reformed police departments, ensured that prohibited activities continued as part of America's economic system. The effort to enforce the prohibition of alcohol ended in 1933, but supplying the demand for other prohibited goods and services gave countless opportunities to both criminal networks and freelance operators. Although local officials were clearly failing to enforce laws against gambling, prostitution, and drugs, there was no deviation from the commitment to the prohibition approach. By the middle of the twentieth century a new generation of reformers needed to explain the persistence of vice-related organized crime in a way that absolved local political and policing institutions from responsibility. Where once local corruption had been thought to be at the root of the problem of organized crime, now it was thought that a foreign conspiracy threatened American values and institutions, and the problem therefore required more federal involvement in the enforcement of vice laws.

Chapter 5 takes up this theme and examines efforts to conceptualize and combat organized crime between the 1920s and the present day, and traces the progress and implications of what amounts to a dumbing of discourse about organized crime.

All serious efforts to understand organized crime from the 1920s and early 1930s were constrained by the limits of knowledge and understanding that are discussed in the first three chapters of *Organized Crime and American Power*. Crimes against Native Americans and African Americans, and, since the end of muckraking, crimes committed by big business were not thought to be aspects of the problem. Most early efforts to describe and analyse organized crime were also constrained by both the moralism and class bias of liberal reformers and the widely held assumption that it was a problem mainly confined to city slums.[3] Despite these limitations, many early efforts to analyse or portray organized crime did at least have the merit of asking questions about U.S. laws and institutions.

By the 1920s the phrase 'organized crime' was used in several different senses, but only rarely limited to signify separate associations of gangsters. To some academics and professionals, organized crime was still virtually synonymous with local political machine corruption. To others 'organized crime' was mostly associated with certain types of criminal *activity* and was virtually synonymous with racketeering. The word 'racket' was by then well established as meaning an illegal business or fraudulent scheme. It followed that racketeering was understood to refer to such activities as dealing in stolen property, insurance frauds, fraudulent bankruptcies, securities frauds, credit frauds, forgery, counterfeiting, illegal gambling, trafficking in drugs or liquor, or various forms of extortion. It was also generally understood that criminal networks could and often did include the active involvement of police, politicians, judges, professionals such as lawyers, and ostensibly legitimate businessmen.

This perception of organized crime as systematic illegal activity and part of the social, economic, and political systems began to be supplanted in the post-Prohibition era by one that involved crude shifts of grammar and image. Among other things this new understanding of the problem of organized crime shifted attention away from defects in the system and towards the perception that organized crime was a separate association of gangsters and thereby constituted a threat to the nation's institutions. Journalists gave the illusion of historical and contemporary substance to the newly redefined problem and filmmakers provided its imagery. The consensus of opinion that emerged among politicians, law enforcement officials, and the press changed the perception of organized crime from one that demanded honest and effective local law enforcement to one that demanded much more nationally coordinated action.

The Mafia conspiracy theory gave an ethnic identification to the newly reconceptualized problem at a time, in the early Cold War years, when fear of 'un-American' thinking and behaviour was at its peak and new limits were added to the range of permissible discussion. The problem of organized crime now simply boiled down to groups of bad people who corrupted government and business. Understood in such terms, the problem of organized crime had a very simple solution: give the government more power to get the bad guys.

Federal government officials began to obtain the power they wanted to get the bad guys in the Omnibus Crime Control Act of 1968 and the Organized Crime Control Act of 1970. These gave federal law enforcement and intelligence agencies new powers that altered the commitments made to personal freedoms in the Bill of Rights. Organized crime control provisions now included forfeiture of assets, special grand juries, wider immunity provisions for compelling or persuading reluctant witnesses, extended sentences for persons convicted in organized crime cases, and the use of wire-tapping and eavesdropping evidence in federal cases. With concurrent anti-drug legislation, a far stronger policing presence was established in the United States, but it was one that so far seems to have had a far greater potential for both financial and political abuse than for successfully curbing the extent of organized criminal activity. Basically it was a good guys versus bad guys strategy that did not take account of institutional corruption and unenforceable laws. For its successful application, it thus depended on all politicians, police, prison officers, lawyers, prosecutors, and judges being honest and efficient. This clearly has never been the case, and even the selective application of the organized crime control laws since the 1970s has shown that public and private professionals are still as actively involved in organized criminal activity as they ever were.

Although a great deal of scholarship and investigative work has exposed the deceit and inadequacy of most government and popular accounts of organized crime history, popular and professional understanding of the problem is still based on the Mafia paradigm.[4] By the 1980s, however, the idea of one organization dominating organized crime had become too absurd to sustain. Mafia mythology was adapted to a new age by repeated claims that although the Mafia had once been the dominant force in U.S. organized crime, it was now being challenged by several crime 'cartels,' 'emerging' among Asian, Latin American, and other groups. Official thinking about organized crime kept to the same formula: forces outside mainstream American culture threatened otherwise morally sound American institutions.

Gary W. Potter, in his book *Criminal Organizations* (1994), described the new official consensus as the 'pluralist' revision of the alien conspiracy interpretation.[5]

The mistake that has always dogged U.S. organized crime control efforts was the misperception that organized crime was composed of conspiratorial entities that were alien and distinct from American life. A great deal of evidence suggests the opposite. High-level politicians and respectable members of business and professional communities have gained more from organized criminal activity than any other group and, for the most part, stayed out of prison. Countless scandals have indicated that the bribe and the fix are still features of the U.S. criminal justice system and the problem of police corruption is as acute as it ever was. Rackets of every variety continue to proliferate at every level of society, and even inside the prisons, gangs compete for commercial dominance in systems based on corruption and brutality. In sum, after decades of intense effort against gangsters, U.S. organized crime control measures have done little to control organized criminal activity in either legal or illegal markets.

Chapter 6 surveys organized criminal activity in the labour and corporate sectors of the U.S. economy during the second half of the twentieth century. As the economy grew and power became more concentrated in a relatively small number of corporations, labour tended to accept rather than challenge the status quo. Some, notably the giant Teamsters Union, operated corruptly and formed close alliances with racketeers. The U.S. government's response to union corruption did not work in the interests of the labour movement. Instead, it tended to weaken labour's ability to bargain with corporations, offered little support for democratic trade unionism, and neglected, in particular, protection of union welfare and pension funds from theft and fraud.

The government's response to the environmental and occupational cost of America's fast and furious economic growth and industrial production was similarly lop-sided in favour of the corporations. Federal and state governments began to enact environmental and occupational protection legislation during the 1970s, but governmental controls were evaded, often in a systematic and illegal way. The cost of different kinds of organized business crime, both in financial terms and in terms of injuries and lives lost, still exceeds that of conventionally understood organized crime and more familiar forms of criminal activity.

America's moral crusade did not end with the repeal of alcohol prohibition or a more liberal approach to gambling introduced in the 1970s. It continues with a greatly expanded national and international crusade against drugs. Chapter 7 examines the immense, violent, and treacherous trade in heroin, cocaine, marijuana, and endless combinations of synthetic substances, and the 'drug abuse industrial complex' that has emerged during efforts to control it. Profits from the manufacture, importation, and sale of illegal drugs long ago nullified the impact of honest law enforcement, while the anti-drug crusade has effectively been institutionalized as a never-ending project that seems to benefit few outside of the public and private professionals who administer it. Possibly the most disturbing development was the abuse associated with the rapid growth of the practice of asset forfeiture by local, state, and federal policing agencies. Apart from the problem of assets being seized from the innocent as well as the guilty, the vast amount of extra policing resources made possible by seizures has done little to combat drug-related organized crime and led to new forms of corruption.

Chapter 8 surveys the post–Second World War period and begins by detailing ways in which the United States has allowed and even sometimes encouraged certain kinds of organized criminal activity, if this activity advanced American foreign policy objectives. It then sketches the internationalization of the American war on drugs as U.S. diplomats successfully pressed governments around the world and international organizations such as the United Nations to follow the U.S. lead and enact measures intended to crack down on global drug use and trade. Drugs like heroin, cocaine, marijuana, and their synthetic alternatives, however, remain relatively easy to produce, process, and sell in most places in the world, and America's drug-related organized crime problems have now become global drug-related organized crime problems. Traffickers have, of course, exploited the massive increase in demand for drugs over the past forty years, but public officials and professionals such as accountants, bankers, and lawyers have also profited greatly from the illegal trade, usually at much less risk to life and liberty.

At the same time, there has been U.S.-led dumbing of global discourse about organized crime. Beginning in the 1990s, U.S. government leaders used international conferences and media outlets to help make U.S. assumptions about organized crime global assumptions. There were countless claims about supercriminal organizations constituting threats to national and international security. These forces were thought to threaten national institutions everywhere, and therefore it was argued that U.S. organized crime control techniques should be employed everywhere.

Organized Crime and American Power challenges assumptions based on a limited understanding of the U.S. experience. In the United States, organized criminal *activity* has never been a serious threat to established economic and political power structures, but more often a fluid, variable, and open-ended phenomenon that complemented those structures. This book emphasizes the importance of collaboration as much as confrontation between government and criminals, and criminal behaviour within, rather than criminal infiltration of, the various law enforcement, criminal justice, business, and political systems that make the United States work. The themes and events considered in *Organized Crime and American Power* demonstrate that corruption, social injustice, and the manipulations of knowledge and law are far more relevant to understanding the development of organized crime in the United States and elsewhere than theories involving foreign conspiracies and supercriminal organizations.

It is the contention of this book that making the term 'organized crime' synonymous with gangster or 'Mafia-type' organizations will not help in efforts to combat a problem that is indeed damaging and destructive at local, national, and international levels. This problem, however, is rarely so structured and never so separate from legitimate institutions as the usual use of the term implies. U.S. organized crime policies based on the Mafia paradigm have so far threatened civil liberties more than they threaten the multitude of frauds, evasions, shakedowns, and forms of illegal enterprise that actually do constitute organized crime in America.

Chapter 1

Old World Antecedents and the Rise of American Power

Chapter 1 surveys antecedents of organized crime from ancient times to the nineteenth century and focuses on types of criminal activity that contributed to the processes of city, state, and empire building throughout history, and, more particularly, the history of Western civilization in the New World.

Rome and the Underside of Ancient Law

Crude, unrestrained force lay behind the establishment of most early empires and states. Ancient history is littered with examples of plundering, kidnapping for forced labour, and holding populations for ransom during the state- and empire-building processes. By 1000 BC standing professional armies emerged to protect populations from invasion, preserve order internally, and when opportunities arose, attack other settlements and kingdoms. Many kingdoms and empires had laws by then, but these did nothing to restrain acquisitive rulers from attempting to seize desirable territory beyond their borders. Internally, the law served more to preserve and institutionalize the power of elites and rulers than to protect individuals in any meaningful way. In sum, as many historians have confirmed, the processes of state- and empire building were brutal and corrupt affairs that involved legitimizing theft, extortion, and murder.

According to Western legal tradition, things began to change with the Greeks and Romans. Modern laws and state institutions are often said to be the culmination of a steady progress towards civilization that began in Greece and Rome, and continued through the consolidation and expansion of European nation states from the fifteenth to the eighteenth centuries. The U.S. historian, Clinton Rossiter was one of many who emphasized this evolution. He made a list of what he called the 'the Founding Fathers of our experiment in ordered liberty,' which included Demosthenes, Cicero, Seneca, Ulpian, Gaius, Isidore of Seville, St Thomas Aquinas, Bracton, Grotius, Newton, Hooker, Locke, and Blackstone. 'It should do us good to remember at the height of our power and self esteem,' Rossiter continued, 'that our political tradition and constitutional law are late blooms on a sturdy growth more than two thousands years old and still vigorous.'[1] Karl Friedrichs developed this familiar theme in his book *The Philosophy of Law in Historical Perspective*: 'When the fathers of the American constitutions proclaimed that their constitutions were establishing governments of laws and not of men, they merely restated what Cicero had already formulated admirably well when he said, "We are servants of the law in order to be made free." [2]

But Rossiter and Friedrichs's notion of Roman freedom did not acknowledge the fact that most of those who lived in the Roman Empire were not free. The labour force that fuelled Rome's imperial expansion was either slave or half-free, recruited mainly from colonized or conquered peoples, and thus the frequent linking of Roman law to freedom can only be applied to elites.[3]

The assumption behind this type of thinking – that law lies behind civilization and is therefore an almost unquestionable force for good – does not square with the available evidence about ancient Rome. Recent scholarship has shown that systems of law developed in response to changing power relationships, rather than as part of a march towards 'ordered liberty,' and that justice was always in short supply when it was against the interests of the powerful or the soon-to-be powerful. New elites were just as likely as their predecessors to use the laws and state agencies to further their own – often criminal – interests, and if they could not get their own way legally they got their way illegally.

Criminal enterprise was itself deeply embedded in the machinery of Roman law and government, particularly during and after the rule of Tiberius (AD 14–37). There are well-documented examples of the rich and those in positions of administrative power breaking the law to cheat, intimidate, and steal from the general population and the poor in particular. The great majority of the empire's population were peasants, and if they refused to acquiesce in extortion, landlords would either use force themselves or fake evidence of an attack and then call on the military to arrest the innocent parties. Once in front of a court, the word of those of higher rank was invariably taken. On the rare occasions that this was not enough, witnesses and even judges were intimidated and, on occasion, killed. In this system of justice a class of false accusers, known as 'sycophants' in the original sense of the word, emerged and prospered. The Emperor Constantine (AD 324–337) complained about 'the accursed ruin' they caused and called them 'the one greatest evil to human life.'[4] But, in the absence of official prosecutors, 'sycophants' remained an essential part of the machinery of justice; their zeal assured by a share of property confiscated from persons convicted through their efforts. In his book *Corruption and the Decline of Rome*, Ramsey Macmullen concluded that 'the courts and jails, through "sycophants," thus served officials as a means of controlling, of bullying, and of extorting obedience and more than obedience; for governors and other officials who enjoyed rights of jurisdiction grew rich from it.'[5] In the United States, today, as we shall see in Chapter 7, there are echoes of this problem in the fast-growing business of asset forfeiture.

A succession of Roman emperors had no answer to frequent and persistent reports of systematic wrongdoing beyond increasing the number of laws and the severity of punishments. From around the third century AD scores of crimes became capital crimes. The punishment for heresy, forgery, and adultery, for example, was death, and the means of capital punishment ranged from crucifixion to being burned alive. Executions were public, designed to frighten onlookers and those in surrounding areas into good behaviour. Mercy was seen as an impediment to government advancement; ferocity was the key and advancement meant greater opportunities to profit. To administer these policies, imperial administrations needed to multiply the number of soldiers and government officials. All that this achieved, however, was a multiplication of corrupt networks exploiting the weak or the gullible. Laws were usually worded ambiguously, and thus gave almost unlimited opportunities to those appointed to interpret and enforce. Higher-ups gained most, but even lowly clerks were able to gain legal status for fees that originated in extortion. Scholarship itself became a means of extortion, particularly when it gave the appearance of legitimacy to the personal greed of government officials. Tax collectors in the western Roman provinces, for example, were known to form units of scholars and soldiers and then announce many and various new tax categories in unintelligible language to their victims.[6]

Soldiers who were known to bully, cheat, and steal from the populations they were supposed to be protecting were themselves at the mercy of their officers. 'Some,' according to a contemporary commentator, 'profit from their own staff, some from regimental rations, where the men who have vanished live on, and they can feed off the names of the dead. These are great amounts; but there are even larger gold fields, of gold that should rightly remain in the men's hands but is transferred to their commanders. So the armed forces grow poor and dispirited.'[7]

The key to all these forms of continuous criminal enterprise in the late Roman Empire was the existence of networks of accomplices with powerful connections. These not only provided any necessary force but also ensured that that those emperors not themselves involved in corrupt activities remained either oblivious or helpless. Under these circumstances extortion, intimidation, bribe taking, fraud, and illegal enterprise were pervasive and routine throughout the existence of an empire more usually praised for its achievements in promoting the rule of law and superiority to the foreign tribes or 'barbarians' that eventually brought about its demise.

Feudalism, State Building, and Organized Crime

Much of medieval European society was organized around contractual obligations, based on land. 'There was much room for complexity and ambiguity in the feudal order,' according to the historian J.M. Roberts, 'but the central fact of an exchange of obligations between superior and inferior ran through the whole structure and does more than anything else to make it intelligible to modern eyes.' Serfs were expected to obey their lords with 'fear and trembling,' while lords were expected to treat their serfs, according to 'justice and equity.'[8]

There was, of course, enormous room for abuse in such lop-sided arrangements; enough to justify the argument of one of the first authorities on modern organized crime that the feudal system was itself 'a good deal of a racket.' In an article published in the *New York Times* in 1930, Raymond Moley made it clear that the phenomenon of organized crime was 'no new type of human activity' and noted that its 'characteristics are of the same human stuff' out of which American civilization grew. He chose medieval European barons as appropriate antecedents for American racketeers:

The peasant paid over to his lord a liberal portion of his wool and vegetables and grain. In addition he agreed to lay aside the shovel and pick and take up more warlike instruments when the lord commanded. In return he was assured protection against other plundering lords and vagabonds. He purchased protection, but we may be sure not in an open market. The business of being an overlord had to be monopolistic within certain geographical limits. If the peasant refused to deal with the overload he would find himself unceremoniously driven from the neighborhood; or worse – he would find his property destroyed or taken from him, and he might in the course of events lose his life. He had to bow to the inevitable and call it providential.[9]

William of Normandy did most to establish such a system in early Britain. To gather his army to invade England at the beginning of 1066 he appealed to greed by promising land and wealth to all those who would follow him. Defeating Harold in October of the same year at the Battle of Hastings was only the beginning. He needed to defend land already conquered from hostile Welsh and northern warriors and keep the Anglo-Saxon population subdued. To accomplish this he gave away around 90 per cent of English land to fewer than 300 favoured men who were responsible for providing the new king with the services of fully equipped fighting men. The king's chief tenants, in turn, let some of their land either directly to the fighting men or to their own followers in return for their sworn loyalty and rent. They, in turn, took rents or services from the people whose land they had been given.

Elizabeth Taylor, a local historian who has made a close study of the Hereford border area between England and Wales, explained how the system was adapted to meet areas that were difficult to control:

In the Marches of Wales, as the borderland became known, an additional tool of conquest was used called the Laws of Bretuil. King William gave the difficult area of the southern March to his trusted friend William fitz Osbern ... To induce Normans and foreign mercenaries to come to a place where hard fighting rather than soft living was to be expected, the new Earl of Hereford put his earldom under the laws of Bretuil, his homeland in Normandy. Amongst other advantages, this meant that new men willing to settle in Hereford as burgesses could commit any crime for a maximum penalty of 12 pence, with only three exceptions: breaking the King's peace, house breaking, and highway robbery for which the King took the

forfeits. Any man who was willing to fight with the army only had to pay
a third of what he would have been fined for his crimes elsewhere.

Not surprisingly, the most ruthless and savage men were drawn to
Hereford and, when they had proved successful in breaking local
opposition, to other areas where people resisted.[10]

As in much of the rest of Europe where feudalism was established,
ambitious barons extorted money or goods from merchants travelling
through their lands and sometimes led or employed gangs of brigands
to plunder towns and villages. From the thirteenth century on it was
common for local lords and other persons of substance, including the
clergy, to guarantee their protection and support for known criminals.
The English House of Commons reacted to a long-established custom
when, in 1348, they petitioned Edward III to introduce legislation
intended to prevent the nobility from maintaining, whether 'privately'
or 'openly,' robbers, thieves, and other criminals on foot or on horse-
back, 'who throughout all the shires of England, go and ride on the
highway through all the land in divers places, committing larcenies
and robberies.' The new laws and others with similar intent were ineffective, and robber barons continued to commit crimes and shield
criminal activity with impunity.[11]

Until the seventeenth century, kings only differed from robber barons in that their plundering was greater. The historian Charles Tilly
has described ways in which early governments were little different
from racketeers in first acquiring their authority particularly during
wartime: 'In times of war ... the managers of full-fledged states often
commissioned privateers, hired sometimes bandits to raid their enemies, and encouraged their regular troops to take booty. In royal service, soldiers and sailors were often expected to provide for
themselves by preying on the civilian population: commandeering,
raping, looting, taking prizes. When demobilized, they commonly continued the same practices, but without the royal protection; demobilized ships became pirate vessels, demobilized troops bandits.'[12]

Early in the state-making process, kings had no choice but to share
the right to use violence with the local barons and lords and their
armed retainers. 'Disarming the great,' continued Tilly, 'stood high on
the agenda of every would-be state maker.'[13] Eventually European
governments were able to co-opt local and regional lords into more
centralized systems of power and, thus, achieve coercive monopolies
in their territories. Officialdom was extended to the local communities,

and police forces were created that were answerable to the state rather than to local power brokers.

Of course, history has never been a one-way process in favour of the powerful. In his convincing analysis of the coercive and avaricious origins of modern states, Tilly reminds us that ordinary people were not mere passive victims of the locally or nationally powerful. When they resisted vigorously, he writes, 'authorities made concessions: guarantees of rights, representative institutions, courts of appeal.'[14] It was difficult but not impossible, then as now, to hold the aggression and greed of rulers in check.

A Note on Underworlds and Conspiracy

By the nineteenth century large-scale banditry had been banished to parts of the world where state authority was still weak.[15] In the process, however, developing states tended to exaggerate the threat posed by bandits and the poor in general in order to justify boosting their relatively weak authority. To make this point Richard Cobb's study entitled *Paris and Its Provinces* includes a detailed discussion of Dinah Jacob and the *bande juive*. Dinah Jacob was a young Jewish woman, based in the area of the French-Belgian border, and married to Kotzo-Picard. In 1797 Jacob denounced her husband, father, mother, sisters, and brothers-in-law, and some eighty-one others as being part of a vast Jewish-dominated criminal conspiracy called *la bande juive*. She provided the names and addresses of the alleged conspirators and the authorities provided the arrests. The authorities then used the arrests to provide further material to strengthen and give consistency to the Jewish criminal conspiracy thesis: 'If a number of arrests were made in Amiens, then it followed that the "organisation" had its representatives there. If Jewish merchants were arrested at an inn in Tournai, where they had stopped to take some refreshment, before setting out on the next stage of their journey to Limburg, would not this then be taken as proof that the bande had agents there as well? And so on, with arrests in Reims, Valenciennes, Bethune, Ghent, Brussels, Dunkirk.'[16]

Jacob's testimony and other circumstantial evidence did not come close to justifying the state's conclusion that Kotzo-Picard and his accomplices were leaders of a vast international conspiracy. Cobb found instead that they were better described as cheap thieves, 'not above picking pockets,' who associated with other cheap thieves and 'shabby' fences.[17] The fears and fantasies of officialdom added to prejudice against Jews and elevated a group of lowly crooks to a new high status as leaders of a vast and complex underworld conspiracy. The myth of *la bande juive* thus provides a precedent for the exaggerated exploits of Murellites, Molly Maguires, and Mafiosi that, as we shall see, distracted attention away from more serious criminal activity in nineteenth- and twentieth-century America.

Although talk of underworld conspiracies was often exaggerated, there were many gangs in early modern Europe, and many did have a certain amount of organization, professional expertise, and common culture. One eigthteenth-century London gang that became known as 'The Thieves' Company' was believed to pay clerks to keep the books and divide up the profits. Another was thought to have more than a hundred members and was reported to 'have officers and treasury and to have reduced theft and robbery into a regular system.' The 'Resolution Club' was one of many to have a code of silence. Members were required if necessary to 'die mute' and to kill any, such as trial witnesses, who posed a threat to the gang.[18] Criminals even had their own language, or rather a collection of expressions that distinguished them from respectable society. A German dictionary of *Rotwelsch* or criminal slang published in 1755, for example, defined a *Wittstock* as 'someone who is neither willing nor able to learn the language of thieves, a stupid individual.' A *Kocheme* was 'an artful, crafty, and intelligent man, a member of the thieving profession' – an early 'wiseguy' in fact![19]

European Commercial Crime and the Peopling of North America

From the fifteenth-century trade and the exploitation of the Americas made the world more interdependent and led to the growth of commercial centres, such as Venice and Genoa and, later, Antwerp, Amsterdam, and London. At the same time, the world was growing more commercial, more used to the idea of employing money to make money.[20] The apparatus of modern capitalism was taking shape, and with it opportunities to make money illegally also grew – in the case of counterfeiting literally so!

Medieval Italians invented much of modern accountancy, new credit devices for the financing of international trade, limited liability to reduce the risk of investments, and banking based on bills of exchange. Edoardo Grendi's study 'Counterfeit Coins and Monetary Exchange Structures in the Republic of Genoa during the 16th and 17th Centuries' has revealed that counterfeiting was pervasive and completely integrated into the normal operations of smuggling, seign-eurial minting privileges, alchemy, and foreign trade. Goldsmiths, soldiers, convicts serving on galleys, bankers, wholesalers, grain mer-chants, butchers, millers, and especially priests specialized in counter-feit and coin-clipping operations. Aristocrats and public officials gained most from this illegal activity, however, systematically pass-ing counterfeit coins in monetary exchange markets. And, according to Grendi, the desire of many monarchs in Renaissance Europe to patronize the best alchemists merely reflects the fact that alchemy was one of the higher forms of counterfeiting. In the process of attempt-ing to dominate this early form of organized crime, early modern governments decided to classify only their competition among the lower orders as criminals.[21]

The banking supremacy of the medieval Italian cities passed briefly to Antwerp during the sixteenth century and then to Holland and Lon-don by the seventeenth century. Banks and merchant houses, followed by joint stock companies and stock exchanges, proliferated, as did new and often scandalously fraudulent schemes to mobilize and deploy money. The most notorious of these were organized by the South Sea Company and the Mississippi Company, in Britain and France respec-tively. Both were intended to exploit the potential of the New World; both with their combinations of fraud and violent coercion serve as spectacular antecedents of modern organized business crime.[22]

The South Sea Company was founded in 1711 and was well placed to exploit the high expectations that followed the Treaty of Utrecht (1713). The treaty gave British merchants the monopoly of supplying African slaves to the Spanish-American colonies and the prospect of breaking down the mercantilist barriers that protected the trade of the Spanish empire. The South Sea Company's first contract involved buy-ing slaves in Africa, taking them to Jamaica, eliminating the weakest slaves by leaving them to die on the dock, and then supplying the Spanish market with the remainder. The company expected to make so much money from this type of venture that it felt able to challenge the Bank of England as Britain's primary financial institution. In February 1720, it bribed enough members of Parliament to approve a scheme to take over the whole of the national debt in return for a payment of £7 million to the government. People rushed to invest in what must have seemed like a sure thing, and South Sea Company stock reached the untenable level of £1,050 in August. Those clever or lucky enough to do so sold their stock before this level was reached, made substantial profits, and thus avoided the ruin of many thousands after the bubble burst in September.[23]

In the meantime thousands more had invested their money in ventures other than the South Sea. Although it was illegal to float a joint stock company without a charter from the king, promoters went ahead and launched dozens of new companies in the months between February and May of 1720. Many of these turned out to be comically fraudulent, such as one that would trade in hair, 'being a commodity whose consumption is equal to, if not exceeds most of the necessaries used in dress by both sexes.' Or another that solemnly announced in the *Daily Post* of 14 June 1720: 'Proposals for raising of Two Millions for effecting the Transmutation of Fluid Mercury or Quicksilver, into a solid and malleable Body, so that 'twill spread under the Hammer, and be of equal Use, Beauty and Value with the purest standard Silver: pursuant to which, Permits will begin to be deliver'd out, and continue till completed, tomorrow being the 15th instant, at the Fountain Tavern, Stocks-Market, from the hours of 12 till 3, paying 6d. per cent, for the Permit, as a Gratuity for the Projector and Company. N.B. 'Tis demonstrable by a just calculation, that each subscriber will get above 800 per cent. When full, shall open the Books and proceed to chuse of Guvernor and Directors.'[24]

By June Parliament had passed an act declaring that companies acting without a charter would be classed as 'public nuisances' and prosecuted. Many of the wilder 'bubble' companies took their profits and disappeared. The South Sea Company survived, and by 1731 had sold around 64,000 slaves.[25]

The Mississippi bubble in France had its origins in an idea first propagated in 1697 that the Louisiana colony was rich in silver and other precious minerals. French efforts to develop mining enterprises were, however, thwarted by the English monopoly of the slave trade, and by 1717 this mass of territory extending as far west as the Rocky Mountains had yielded very little return. At this point the Scottish financier John Law stepped in and obtained a twenty-five-year lease of the territory on the condition that he agreed to settle 6,000 colonists and 3,000 slaves. Law entrusted the colony's development to Jean Baptiste Bienville, who laid the foundations of New Orleans as its capital. The main problem faced by Law and Bienville was that few French people were willing to take their chances in the New World. Settlement, therefore, had to be based on forced transportation.

Salt smugglers who had been condemned to the galley ships of the Mediterranean were the first to be transferred, followed by 300 inmates of the Bicêtre Prison whose offences ranged from begging to murder. In 1719 Law's Western company police known as *archers* began the practice of rounding up tramps, unemployed domestics, and youth thought to be delinquent. The *archers* soon became known for their corruption and casual brutality. According to Pierre Heinrich's account in *Louisiane Sous la Compagnie des Indes* (1907) they were 'not satisfied to commit a host of uncalled for deeds to collect a few francs a head granted by the Company, these improvised policemen took advantage of the occasion to enrich themselves by brigandage, robbing their captives or releasing them for ransom. Their outrages, rather enlarged by public imagination, led to frequent riots, in which a goodly number of them were killed or wounded by a furious mob.'[26]

After a slow start, Law's financial manipulations led to a massive rise in the value of company shares. In the summer of 1719 he announced that the company would pay off the French national debt of 1,500,000,000 livres. The government would then, according to the scheme, repay the money to the people from whom it had borrowed and pay the company 3 per cent interest instead of the normal 4 per cent. Law then assumed that people would use their returned money to buy shares in the company which were offered to them at less than their value. 'Thus they will be enriched,' he concluded, 'while the State is relieved.'[27]

The price of company stock rose rapidly and people from all over France and even the rest of Europe joined in a buying frenzy that saw the market price of the company rise from 300 to 18,000 livres in the space of a few months. Aristocrats gained most, but ordinary people also took opportunities to get rich quick. The bubble burst, however, because too many wanted to realize their gains and thousands were again ruined, including Law himself, who fled back to Britain. The investigation that followed treated kindly those who had been wealthy before the bubble and harshly those who had gained wealth during the speculative frenzy. Around 187 million livres in fines were levied. As Harold Perkin noted, 'The crime consisted in the fact that a great deal of money had been made by people of small account. The government declared that those must be punished who two years before had been poor, and now possessed riches above their condition ... the name of no person of rank appears among those who were fined for their good fortune.'[28]

Law's company survived and prospered without its founder by concentrating on the booming slave trade between Africa and America.

E.P. Thompson has described Britain's Whig rulers during and after

the time of the South Sea bubble as practising a sort of 'state ban-
dritry.'[29] It was, he elaborated, 'a system of nepotism, of the brutal
imposition on every branch of public service of the Whig interest, of
the purchase and intimidation of electors, of diverting public money
into private pockets, of bribes and pensions.' Justice was dispensed
mainly in the interests of property against the 'loose and disorderly
sort of people' who were thought to threaten these interests. Hundreds
of offences including the theft of goods worth 25 pence and breaking
down the mound of any fishpond became capital offences. Not surprisingly contemporaries drew attention to the lack of consistency in
the treatment of rich and poor criminals. One writer in *True Briton*,
published in the summer of 1723, for example, asked why a highway
robber 'committed, perhaps for a trifle, or the mere relief of his necessi-
ties,' would be executed, 'whilst another, who has inriched himself by
continual depredations, for a course of some years, at the expence of
his country, shall not only escape with impunity, but by the servile
herd of flatterers and sycophants, have all his actions crowned with
applause.'[30]

Corruption went from the top to the bottom of British state institutions. In London's Newgate Prison, for example, jailers extorted
money for almost every service to mitigate the horrors of being in 'hell
above ground.'[31] The prison reformer John Howard detailed these and
many other abuses in his book *The State of the Prisons* (1777). He was
also one of the first to note the importance of prisons as places of
apprenticeship for would-be professional criminals: 'In some gaols you
see ... boys of twelve or fourteen eagerly listening to the stories told by
practiced and experienced criminals, of their adventures, successes,
stratagems, and escapes.'[32]

The British state's efforts to suppress freebooters included efforts to
encourage informing, with effects as counter-productive as the Roman
sycophant system described earlier. Laws introduced from 1692
offered monetary rewards – so-called blood-money – and royal pardons for the apprehension, prosecution, and conviction of highway
robbers and other thieves. Thieves were thus set to catch other thieves,
and Jonathan Wild was the most prominent example of the symbiosis
between crime and crime control that emerged. In the early decades of
the eighteenth century, Wild simultaneously operated as the city's
most powerful fence and organizer of thieves and as London's unofficial 'thief taker' or early detective. As fence, he suggested appropriate
places to rob, provided a market for the stolen goods, and offered

police protection so that favoured thieves faced little prospect of arrest. As thief taker, he responded to periods of public outrage against burglars or highwaymen by delivering to justice those out of favour. Wild was eventually caught, convicted, and hanged. He was then succeeded by another thief taker, who was also later found to be involved in criminal enterprise. Wild and his successor can thus be seen as among those who pioneered ways to organize crime within newly formed state institutions.

As a sideline, Wild was also involved in the collusive manipulation of the system of transportation, which became an established part of the British penal system through an act of Parliament in 1717. By this act prisoners were made over by order of the court to private contractors, who sold them in the New World as virtual slave labour. Wild profited through an association with the leading private contractor, Jonathan Forward. Forward would inform Wild of any felons who had returned to England before their sentences of transportation had expired. Wild would then blackmail the transgressors, either for hush money or for the proceeds of continued criminal activity, secure in the knowledge that the government would pay the statutory £40 for their betrayal.[33]

Bernard Bailyn estimates in his book *Voyagers to the West: Emigration from Britain to America on the Eve of Revolution* that an average of about 600 English convicts supplemented the workforce in America each year between 1719 and 1772. Thousands more came from the Irish and Scottish court systems. The British government – under pressure from Forward and his fellow contractors – disallowed efforts made by colonies such as Virginia and Maryland to stem this flow of unwanted immigrants.[34]

Although many thieves, blackmailers, pimps, rapists, embezzlers, and mercenary thugs found themselves transported to America, many more were simply trivial offenders from the poorest classes. These made a significant addition to the American labour force, while the better-off criminals were often able to bribe themselves a comfortable passage across the Atlantic and secure themselves freedom on arrival to do as they pleased.[35]

The poor were also most at risk from 'crimps' and other kidnappers. The crimps helped satisfy the demand for labour in the New World, often by plying their victims with alcohol, getting them into debt, and then confronting them with the choice of debtors' prison or indentured servitude in the colonies. More systematic operations relied on inducing teenage boys in particular with tales of the land of opportunity and small amounts of money and then taking steps to prevent repudiation of the often still-informal agreements. These steps included forcible incarceration until ships were ready to sail them to America. Such episodes, as Bailyn points out, were more likely to occur when particularly heavy demands for labour in the colonies coincided with a sudden improvement in conditions in Britain.[36]

Empire Building and Organized Crime

European states modernized and extended their coercive practices as they established overseas empires and participated in piracy and the international slave trade.

American piracy had its origins in the long period of global conflict between the European powers to divide up the spoils of the New World. Motivated mainly by the prospects of seemingly unlimited supplies of gold and silver and the slave mining labour of the indigenous peoples, Spain and Portugal reached, conquered, and colonized the Americas first. Problems developed, however, as they attempted to transport their booty back to Europe. Ships laden with gold and silver could not travel fast and were easy prey for both freelance and state-sponsored pirates. The French, English, and Dutch governments soon realized that although piracy was recognized as a serious crime it was also a source of national wealth and a tactic that would weaken the Spanish and Portuguese empires.

European states created a legal fiction to rationalize the contradiction between the law and the national interest. Privateers were in effect licensed to raid the ships of rival powers, but were not permitted to plunder villages or towns or to open the captured cargo until they returned to their home ports. The reality, as William Chambliss has detailed, was at odds with these limitations.[37] Some pirates were given licence to murder, rape, plunder, and destroy as well as steal, so long as their victims lived in the territories controlled by rival powers. Pirates thus became privateers if they held letters of marque.

And it often worked the other way. Privateers became pirates when it suited their financial interest. Francis Drake, for example, made his fortune and reputation as an English national hero, by his raids on the Spanish in America. In 1572 alone, his ships carried away as much as 30 tons of gold and silver and large sums of money in ransom paid by the town of Cartagena in Panama to avoid being sacked.[38]

Piracy of this sort, according to Kenneth Andrews's account of the origins of the British Empire, was a well-protected occupation: 'Pirates could not have carried on their trade without the support of merchants, gentlemen and officials, especially admiralty officials, and measures taken against such abettors of piracy were for the most part ineffective, since all too frequently those responsible for executing the law were themselves notorious offenders. Even lord admirals – from Sir Thomas Seymour in Edward's time to the earl of Nottingham in James's – were not above conniving at acts of piracy and pocketing what amounted to bribes. Indeed, the lord admirals and their staffs were less concerned with keeping law and order at sea than with profiting directly and indirectly, from lawlessness and disorder.'[39]

There was little stigma attached to piracy in early British America for more than a century after Drake's exploits. As the colonies developed, stolen wealth often boosted the fortunes of hard-pressed local economies. Port officials in Rhode Island, New York, Virginia, Maryland, and the Carolinas were prepared to offer safety and security to pirates in return for a share in the plunder. Even governors, such as Benjamin Fletcher of New York, accepted 'gifts' of money, goods, and jewelry from a number of particularly ruthless pirates. Fletcher was eventually forced out of office in 1698, after his associations with pirates and other criminal activity were made public.

As in the case of bandits, however, when pirates became independent freebooters they became problems for states to deal with. The British began their systematic campaign to rid the seas of pirates in the early part of the eighteenth century. The Royal Navy became increasingly effective in capturing outlaw vessels and, as a result, corpses dangled in chains in British ports around the world 'as a spectacle for the warning of others.' More importantly, Parliament passed laws that allowed the death penalty to be imposed on anyone known to supply, trade, or even associate with pirates.[40] By breaking piracy's ties with legitimate society, the British virtually ended the heyday of American piracy.

The Atlantic Slave trade originated as the kidnapping of Africans by Portuguese seamen in the fifteenth century. But from around 1445 the Portuguese government decided that buying rather than stealing slaves was likely to produce more secure profits in the long run, and initiated ways of doing business with African chiefs and traders that lasted for four centuries. Africans were responsible for capturing and delivering to coastal pick-up points the great majority of slaves procured by Europeans during this time. Tribes and kingdoms were prepared to go to war or raid each other's villages in order to capture slaves to exchange for European goods and weapons. According to a contemporary observer in Africa, slaves came 'from different countries and were sold for different reasons – some as prisoners of war, some for debt, some for breaking their country's laws, and some by great men who hated them. The king of a town sells where he dislikes or fears; his wives are sold in turn by his successor. A man inveigles his brother's children into his house and sells them. The brother says nothing, but watches his opportunity and sells the children of the other.'[41]

The Portuguese were also the first to attempt to structure and collect revenue from the trade. The government gave favoured merchants licences to trade in slaves and other goods and expected to collect duties and taxes in return. The Spanish, French, Dutch, and English governments developed similar financial interests as the slave trade grew to immense proportions by the eighteenth century, mainly as it fed an insatiable demand for labour in the New World. From the beginning, captains of slave ships and naval vessels operated a variety of smuggling schemes that undermined these efforts to control the trade. They would, for example, stock more slaves than they registered and sell the surplus where they could, or enlist Africans as 'cabin boys' and sell them in America. Colonial officials tended to accept bribes and ignore offences. The South Sea Company did what it could to institutionalize such corruption and, in the words of one of its founders, to act 'as a shield for illicit trade.'[42]

There were millions of victims. No one can come close to an accurate estimate of the numbers who died in the long passage across the Atlantic, mostly through disease, but also the many who were killed if they resisted or committed suicide. As the historian Hugh Thomas concluded, both captains and merchants were, directly and indirectly, guilty of murder, for a certain number of deaths was always allowed in their calculations.[43]

Of those who did arrive in the Americas a more accurate estimate of around 10 million can be made. These should also be considered victims. The root of their problems lay in the masters' unlimited power over their lives. There was no law or impartial authority that could prevent whites killing or maiming slaves with impunity.

Smuggling, Land Theft, and Customs Racketeering in the Struggle for the Control of North America

When American colonists chose to fight a war for independence from Britain in the 1760s their leaders rationalized their rebellion in terms of Old World corruption and immorality. John Adams, the leader from Massachusetts, wrote, for example, that liberty 'can no more exist without virtue and independence than a body without a soul,' and asked what liberty can be expected to flow from 'venal' and 'effeminate' England, where 'both electors and elected are become one mass of corruption.' The theme that corruption had destroyed British vigour was constantly repeated. Alexander Hamilton of New York pictured England as 'an old, wrinkled, withered, worn-out hag.'

Benjamin Franklin echoed these thoughts and reluctantly concluded that continued union with 'rotten,' 'prodigal,' and 'foolish' Britain would ultimately poison, 'the glorious public virtue so predominant in our rising country.' Other rebellious colonial writers told Americans to look to 'our own country' for the biggest part of that liberty and freedom that remains, or is to be expected, among mankind. 'Our native country,' one wrote, 'bids the fairest of any to promote the perfection and happiness of mankind.'[44] They were all elaborating on America's most important myth, first articulated by John Winthrop early in the seventeenth century as he was leading a small band of Puritans to the New World. We must consider,' he said, that 'we shall be as a City on a Hill, the eyes of all people are upon us.' America, it was constantly repeated, was going to be a moral example to the rest of the world.[45]

Public virtue had not, however, been as predominant in America as colonial leaders were claiming. Organized criminality was prevalent in North America long before the British colonies became the United States of America at the end of the eighteenth century. Land theft, extortion, and, as we have seen, piracy, were all familiar features of the colonial experience in British America. The whole process of white settlement and economic development itself was far from being an orderly and lawful process, and it involved the subjugation and removal of the indigenous tribal population. Until recently the criminality involved in this process was denied or excused as part of the price to be paid for the advance of civilization. However, numerous historical accounts have now made it impossible to deny that these were brutal, manipulative processes that often involved activity that was criminal even by the standards and conventions of the time.

British dominance of the North American continent peaked in 1763, after the defeat of France in the French and Indian War (also known as the Seven Years War). However, problems increased for the British after this date, as attempts were made to restrict American westward expansion and undermine the relative autonomy of the colonies. These attempts coincided with the criminal abuse of power by large numbers of British officials. These restrictions and abuses helped transform thousands of loyal British subjects into active revolutionaries.

The British support of the slave trade and campaigns against piracy, detailed in the previous section, were part of a protectionist approach that also intended to exclude foreign commercial rivals from Britain's American markets. Government protection was codified by a series of Navigation Acts passed between 1651 and 1696 and produced Britain's variant of a 'mercantile' system – shorthand for restrictive and monopolistic imperial practices. Under penalty of forfeiture of ships and goods, the laws stated that all vessels importing or exporting goods to or from any English territory, must be English, with English masters, and crews that were three-quarters English. The American colonies could export only certain named products, only to each other or to England.[46]

The colonies were seen as sources of cheap food and raw materials such as rice, sugar, tobacco, and cotton, and markets for the English merchants to dominate. That, at least, was the intention. Many American merchants thought otherwise and turned to smuggling to increase their business. For much of the pre-Revolutionary War period smugglers systematically colluded with customs officials to deprive the British government of revenue from a whole range of imports, most notably tea, wine, and gunpowder.

Molasses brought in from the West Indies and distilled in small operations along the Eastern Seaboard became the basis for an industry in rum. The experience of Georgia, in particular, prefigured much twentieth-century illicit enterprise in banned substances. In 1733 Governor George Oglethorpe prohibited the importation and manufacture of rum in the colony. Rum-runners met the continuing demand, a network of salesmen emerged to distribute liquor throughout the colony, people set up illegal barrooms in homes and the back of stores, more local producers learned how to distil, and officials took bribes. Few of those involved were arrested, or if arrested, convicted. As a result of this failure the prohibition was repealed, and Georgians were again able to drink rum legally.[47]

In general, the British government's control over the colonies was confused and lax. Several government departments, including the Board of Trade, the Treasury, and the Admiralty, administered the colonies, with little coordination and much avoidance of responsibility. Officials sent to America tended to be the least capable. The chief posts in the colonial customs houses, for example, came to be sinecures, filled by placemen who remained in England and sent deputies to perform their duties. The deputies were poorly paid and rarely able to resist a bribe to ignore continual evasion of the laws of trade. The administration of Robert Warpole (1721–42) acknowledged the reality of this situation and pursued a policy of 'salutary neglect.' Ministers calculated that strict enforcement of the laws of trade would simply limit colonial purchases from England and therefore relaxed them.[48]

British rule was such that few Americans felt they were exploited or the victims of imperial abuse before the middle of the eighteenth century. The great majority of the colonial population was certainly loyal to the British cause during the Anglo-French war between 1756 and 1763. Changes in imperial policy during and after the fighting, however, ignited a sequence of events that, as we shall see, culminated in the American Revolution and the transformation of thirteen British colonies into the United States of America.

When the English first settled in what for them was the 'New World' at the beginning of the seventeenth century, they encountered a large indigenous population. Recent estimates suggest that between 8 and 12 million Native American people lived north of what is now Mexico.[49] Put bluntly, the whites wanted their land and any other sources of profit and were rarely scrupulous in the methods they employed to take it.

Warfare between whites and Native Americans began in Virginia in 1607 and continued for nearly 300 years until, in 1890, U.S. troops massacred more than 200 Sioux men, women, and children at Wounded Knee, South Dakota.[50] In the course of these three centuries of fighting, innumerable peace treaties were made and broken, usually by the whites. An early example of white treachery occurred in 1622, when a negotiator for Virginian settlers carried a butt of poisoned sack to a parley and encouraged the Natives to drink. According to his estimate, 200 died.[51]

Treachery, theft, and fraud came to characterize the whites' relationship with Natives. Traders and land agents used alcohol to befuddle the senses of their victims and make fair payment a rare event. Thousands of acres of land were, for example, traded for small quantities of tools, weapons, and beads. Alternately, whites persuaded illiterate and unrepresentative Natives to put their names to documents that fraudulently gave them title to tribal lands.[52] Troops would often, of course, be required to put down Native resistance to such deals. As Daniel Friedenberg has explained, this massive exercise in land theft created a quandary for the best legal minds in both England and its colonies: 'It is an interesting aspect of English civility that it can never nakedly despoil but must find a respectable basis for action, real estate being no exception. In fact, one might make the general statement that the codifiers of property law dealing with Indian land tussled during the first centuries of the conquest with the momentous problem of how to make legal that which was manifestly illegal; that is, how to assimilate legitimately what had been stolen.'[53]

Philosophically, the promoters of white settlement could turn to an argument first articulated by Winthrop, leader of the first migration of Pilgrims to America, and author of the idea that America should be a moral example to the rest of the world:

> That which is common to all is proper to none. This savage people ruleth over many lands without title or property; for they enclose no ground, neither have they cattle to maintain it, but remove their dwellings as they have occasion, or as they can prevail against their neighbours. And why may not Christians have liberties to go and dwell amongst them in their waste lands and woods, leaving them such places as they have manured for their corn, as lawfully as Abraham did among the Sodomites? For God hath given to the sons of man a two-fold right to the earth; there is a natural right and a civil right. The first right was natural where men held the earth in common, every man, settling and feeding where he pleased; then, as men and cattle increased, they appropriated some parcels of ground by enclosing and peculiar manurance, and this in time got them a civil right.[54]

A simplified version of this argument dominated white thinking about Natives until at least the end of the nineteenth century. Whites were civilized, Natives were savages, and whatever happened to the Natives was the price to be paid for progress.

Once white coastal settlements had been established, however, there were limits to land theft during the colonial period. Tribes to the north united to form the Iroquois League and to the south a looser Creek Confederation and were able to hold the line of white advance to the line of the Appalachians. The British government's *laissez-faire* approach to cheating and betraying the Natives changed in response to a recognition of tribal strength and, in particular, the briefly effective Pontiac's uprising in 1763.

The Ottawa chief Pontiac united northern tribes and succeeded in destroying every British post west of Niagara except Fort Pitt (now Pittsburgh) and Detroit. After seven years fighting the French for control of the North American continent, the British were not inclined to pursue a costly series of wars with the tribes and they began to seek ways to pacify and administer the interior. This involved honouring treaties, ensuring fair payment, and legal propriety for land transfers, and stemming the flow of white settlers moving west of the Allegheny Mountains. The Royal Proclamation of 7 October 1763 made this policy official. This protective legislation proclaimed 3,000 miles away in London was ignored or evaded by tens of thousands of land-hungry whites and some of the continent's leading land speculators, including Benjamin Franklin and George Washington. Those with a financial interest believed that keeping the west open for white settlement and trade was essential.[55] America was to be, as Washington put it in a letter written in 1770, 'a rising empire.'[56]

Although the proclamation remains the legal basis for Native American reserves, land claims, and Aboriginal rights in the United States and Canada, its main historical significance lies in the fact that it sharpened the desire for American independence. Restricting the areas available for white settlement and land speculation was an important contributing factor in the complex mixture of economic, political, religious, social, and ideological discontent that resulted in the American struggle for independence from Britain in the second half of the eighteenth century.

America's revolutionary leaders did not stress the desire for land. Instead, they were able to exploit the British government's inept and inflexible reaction to colonial unrest and claim that there was a conspiracy to deprive Americans of their freedoms and relative autonomy.

In the years preceding the American Revolution, members of the colonial elite were able to point to changes in imperial tax policy and numerous incidents involving the criminal abuse of power to make the argument that eventually justified the war for independence. They would eventually conclude that it was time for the colonies to unite and replace Britain as the leading power in the New World.

The ending of the British government's relaxed attitude to revenue evasion prompted early colonial resistance to imperial rule. Problems began in 1760, during the war with France, when Prime Minister William Pitt reacted to reports that some Americans were selling provisions to the enemy by ordering colonial governors to tighten up the customs service. The following year, customs officers in Boston wanting more authority, applied for writs of assistance to enable them to carry out searches for contraband. A series of court cases followed, instigated by merchants opposed to the zeal of officials carrying out the new policy. James Otis, a lawyer representing the merchants, made his name for posterity when he first articulated a theme that would eventually help unify the colonists against British rule. He portrayed his wealthy clients as defenders of the 'rights of man' against a tyrannical government that was trying to 'enslave' them. John Adams, a future president, witnessed the speech and later described its impact, 'Every man of an immense crowded audience appeared to go away, as I did, ready to take arms against writs of assistance. Then and there, was the first scene of the first act of opposition, to the arbitrary rule of Great Britain. Then and there, the child Independence was born.'[57]

The cause of American independence, of course, had deeper roots than a lawyer's defence of the rights of the privileged. But, by appealing to natural law, right and justice, and Enlightenment thinking most notably represented by John Locke, Otis had crystallized the American justification for breaking its ties with Britain fifteen years before the Declaration of Independence was signed. Governments should not exist by divine right, but should be instituted by the consent of the governed for a definite purpose, and if any particular government fails to fulfil that purpose, it should be replaced by one that will.'[58]

Otis's declaration might have featured in the stirrings of the most significant colonial revolt in modern history, but he lost the case in question. Customs officers were given the powers they wanted and, as if to confirm the lawyer's dire warnings, they abused these powers. Their duties were also expanded to include enforcement of the Sugar Act of 1764 and other revenue measures passed in 1767, and they were reorganized to become part of the newly established American Board of Customs Commissioners, with Boston chosen as its headquarters.

From then on corrupt customs officers made seizures on technicalities and pocketed the proceeds. The plundering depended greatly on a system of informers either paid by the customs commissioners or rewarded by a share in the seizures. Those who worked on board merchant vessels reported anything that might be grounds for seizure. Those who worked in the port simply reported on any gossip they might have heard from the sailors. The poor suffered more than those rich enough to afford bribery or the costs of legal action. Small boats engaged in purely local trade were seized. On larger ships, even the chests of ordinary seamen were subject to frequent searches and seizures.

Many merchants were entrapped by the technique of allowing long-established ways of doing business to continue after new laws had banned them, then suddenly cracking down and making seizures. By 1768 there were many complaints about this practice to the attorney general in England. He unambiguously condemned it, ruling that public notice should be given well in advance of any changes. Evidence suggests that the customs commissioners did not pass on this instruction to the local port officials, who continued to enrich themselves.[59]

It must have occurred to some officials that extortion from the rich was likely to yield more than extortion from the poor, and attempts were made to plunder two of the most wealthy and influential merchants in America. The first of these was Henry Laurens, probably the richest merchant in the Southern colonies. He had three ships seized in less than a year and stood to lose a large part of his fortune. Daniel Moore, collector of the port of Charleston, declared himself willing to take a bribe, but Laurens fought the seizures both in the courts and through disclosures to the press.[60] A representative comment from the *Pennsylvania Journal* summarized the growing tide of resentment against British officials and their legions of informers: 'Our property is thereby not only taken from us without our consent, but when thus taken, is applied still further to oppress and ruin us. The swarms of searchers, tide waiters, spies, and other underlings, with which every port in America now abounds, and which were unknown before the Board of Commissioners was established among us, are not it seems, quite sufficient to ruin our trade, but infamous informers, like dogs of prey thirsting after the fortunes of worthy and wealthy men, are let loose and encouraged to seize and libel.'[61]

Laurens eventually agreed a compromise settlement, but his commitment to separation from Britain was confirmed. He went on to become South Carolina's leading rebel. Since he had also made a large part of his fortune as a slave trader, however, he was one of many leading patriots who provoked Dr Johnson's famous taunt, 'How is it we hear the loudest yelps for liberty [in the American colonies] among the drivers of negroes?'[62]

The second of the rich merchants targeted by British officials was John Hancock of Boston. Hancock was an outspoken critic of British revenue policy and the board of commissioners in particular. The seizure of one of Hancock's ships, the *Liberty*, was based on the suspicion that its cargo had included large amounts of undeclared wine. The officials delayed their raid until after a new cargo of tar and oil had been loaded, thus making seizure more profitable. The informer in the case of the *Liberty* incident was a tidesman called Thomas Kirk, who claimed to have heard noises while on board the *Liberty* that might have indicated that wine was being unloaded. He was not able to give details more specific than this and had been known to perjure himself in a previous court case. He also stood to gain a share of one-third of an extremely profitable forfeiture.

Not content with the seizure of the *Liberty*, the British officials went further and filed suit against Hancock himself and five other merchants for allegedly aiding in unloading 100 pipes of wine on 9 May 1768. The case should have been tried in the regular courts of Massachusetts with a jury to decide it. Instead, the case was brought in the vice-admiralty court at Boston, without a jury, and under rules of evidence that definitely favoured the prosecution. Witnesses were examined by letter and not subject to cross-examination in court. Hancock's employees, closest relatives, and other witnesses were bullied into giving evidence against him. A tidewaiter was dismissed from his job and then offered money and his job back if he changed his testimony in ways that would help the prosecution. The proposed fines on all the defendants amounted to £54,000, and most of this was to have been divided between Governor Francis Bernard and a small number of customs officers and their informers. The case was, however, eventually dropped when the British government decided that it was likely to provoke too much unrest. Boston's residents had already shown they were ready to riot against perceived injustice.[63]

Hancock, already one of Boston's leading politicians, only gained in prestige because of his willingness to stand up to British tyranny, even if it involved the right to smuggle; he became one of the leading figures in the transition from resistance to full-blown revolution.

During the late 1760s and early 1770s newspapers, pamphlets, and committees of correspondence spread the word about the politically and criminally motivated persecutions of Laurens, Hancock, and many more. Long lists of infringements of colonial rights were made, focusing mainly on the actions of customs officers. Throughout the colonies, more and more Americans came to agree with those, such as James Otis, who were arguing that it was all more evidence of a coordinated British plot to reduce Americans to slaves. The existence of large numbers of black slaves in all thirteen colonies made whites in America acutely aware of the appalling fate that might befall them if they failed to preserve their liberties.

There was, however, more to the complaints of Otis, Hancock, and Laurens, than mere principle. They, like many other revolutionary leaders, were upper-class individuals who held the conviction that the colonies had the spiritual and physical resources to become a self-reliant, mighty New World 'empire.' These expansionists, according to Marc Egnal, 'generally agreed on a variety of issues, including the need for strengthened local sovereignty, a healthy domestic economy, thriving maritime commerce, and new land.' Expansionism in this broad sense rather than a libertarian commitment that was shared by many of those who remained loyal to Britain was behind both the Revolution and the Constitution that followed. British ineptitude, inflexibility, and corruption helped expansionists find common cause with more radical revolutionaries and a majority of ordinary Americans in the run-up to the Revolution. Most of the money and organization that sustained the movement from resistance to revolution through to the making of the Constitution came from expansionists who intended to stay in control.[64] As Francis Jennings, a leading historian of Native Americans, has put it, 'White Americans were fighting against British imperial control in the East and for their own imperialism in the West.'[65]

Colonial resistance to perceived attempts to remove their liberties initially took the form of riots and boycotts of British goods. These culminated in the Boston Tea Party of 16 December 1773, when a party of local people raided a ship owned by the East India Company and dumped its cargo of tea into the harbour. The giant company had been given privileges by the Tea Act of May 1773 that would enable it to reduce its prices and compete with smuggled tea. By threatening colonial merchants with a monopoly and smuggling rings with extinction, the Tea Act had thus united two of the strongest local interests.

The British responded harshly and, as it turned out, foolishly, to the incidents of unrest in Boston by a series of laws known as the Coercive Acts. The first act closed the port of Boston to all commerce until the dumped tea had been paid for. The second altered the government of the colony of Massachusetts, and in effect, gave the British king more power. It also forbade town meetings except for the election of town officials. The third provided that any magistrate, customs officer, or soldier indicted for a capital offence within the colony could be brought to England or Nova Scotia for trial and would therefore not have to face the probability of hostile local juries. The fourth provided for the quartering of troops in Boston whenever the governor of the colony saw fit to do so.

Although the Coercive Acts were aimed at Boston it was clear they were intended to remind all of the colonies of their subservience to the mother country. Instead, they provoked anger throughout British America and led directly to the meeting of the first Continental Congress at Philadelphia in September 1774, attended by many of the colonial elite of planters, landowners, and merchants. The Congress endorsed resistance to the Coercive Acts and demanded a colonial government that was far more responsive to American rights and priorities. The king's American subjects, according to the Congress, possessed the 'rights to life, liberty, and property,' and only their own legislatures could enact 'all the cases of taxation and internal policy,' subject to the 'veto of the crown.' The British government refused to yield on the issue of the sovereign authority of Parliament, and in February 1775, declared Massachusetts to be in a state of rebellion. The first shots in the War for Independence were fired at Lexington on 19 April.[66]

On 4 July 1776 Thomas Jefferson's Declaration of Independence of the 13 United States of America was issued. The opening of the Declaration reads:

> When in the Course of human events, it becomes necessary for one people to dissolve the political bands, which have connected them with one another, and to assume among the powers of the earth, the separate and equal station to which the laws of Nature and of Nature's God entitle them, a decent respect to the opinions of mankind requires that they should declare the causes which impel them to the separation. We hold

these truths to be self-evident, that all men are created equal, that they are endowed by the Creator with certain inalienable Rights that among these are Life, Liberty, and the pursuit of Happiness. That to secure these rights, Governments are instituted among Men, deriving their just powers from the consent of the governed. That whenever any Form of Government becomes destructive of these ends, it is the Right of the People to alter or abolish it, and to institute new Government, laying its foundation on such principles and organizing its powers in such form, as to them shall seem most likely to effect their Safety and Happiness.

The immediate intention was to articulate American grievances against the British and assure potential allies such as France that the rebels were sincere in their commitment to loosen the bonds of empire. It was a coded plea for help against what was then the world's greatest power. As Edmund Morgan points out, the immediate application of the phrase 'all men are created equal' was the assertion that Americans were entitled to 'a separate and equal station' among the nations of the earth – that Americans should have the same independence as a nation that other peoples enjoyed.[67] Jefferson as a slaveholder and a man of property did not mean the phrase to be taken literally.

Jefferson, followed in the tradition of the Enlightenment philosopher, John Locke. He felt that men should agree in a social compact to end the complete independence that existed in a state of nature and to form a society under the supervision of government, in order to protect themselves and their hard-won possessions from 'want, rapine, and force.'[68] But also in keeping with the Lockean tradition, the implied commitment to equal rights was not intended to apply to Natives, African Americans, women, and people without property. Jefferson, unlike most other revolutionary leaders, agonized about the crimes committed against the powerless but, like them, he did not propose to extend rights that would have offered them some protection. For at least the first century of the new nation's existence the excluded were vulnerable to 'want, rapine, and force,' and as we shall see, particularly vulnerable to those who were ready to combine and exploit opportunities that arose during the course of the nation's agricultural, commercial, and territorial expansion.

Power, Corruption, and Western Expansion

After a period of loose government under the Articles of Confederation, the political system of the United States was set up in 1789 following two years of deliberation at a Constitutional Convention held at Philadelphia. The delegates at Philadelphia were conscious first of the need to maintain order and unity while allowing for the development of the new nation's commercial potential. A rebellion in western Massachusetts led by Revolutionary War veteran, Daniel Shays, in 1786 was uppermost in their minds. Shays led an unarmed group of several hundred farmers, hard-pressed by a combination of low prices and high taxes, and denied the vote and the possibility of holding office by property qualifications. They briefly closed the courts in Berkshire, Hampshire, and Worcester counties, intending to prevent creditors from collecting debts. The rebellion was a mild affair that was soon put down, but it frightened the new nation's gentry elite mainly because it threatened the interests of property, and made leading patriots throughout the thirteen newly independent states aware of their vulnerability. If the individual states and the nation as a whole did not have the capacity to suppress more serious dissension, then Britain or even Spain might move in to pick up the pieces.[69]

The delegates at Philadelphia were mostly planters, merchants, creditors, or lawyers and therefore naturally favoured the interests of property. Even before Shay's rebellion, many of them had explicitly stated their loathing of leveling tendencies and their fear of the poor's potential to create disorder. They sought to design a conservative document, equipped with a system of minority checks and vetoes, which would make it easier for entrenched and wealthy interests to endure.[70] As Alexander Hamilton, one of the leading lights at Philadelphia made clear, the Constitution was not intended to be a protector of popular democracy: 'All communities divide themselves into the few and the many. The first are the rich and well-born, the other the mass of the people ... The people are turbulent and changing; they seldom judge or determine right. Give therefore to the first class a distinct permanent share in government ... Can a democratic assembly who annually revolve in the mass of the people be supposed steadily to pursue the public good? Nothing but a permanent body can check the imprudence of democracy.'[71]

Hamilton was also the delegate who best articulated the commitment to support commerce. As Hugh Brogan has noted, Hamilton was immensely exhilarated by the possibilities that he saw arising from the creation of a new nation state on a vast and virgin continent. He believed that a strong unitary American commonwealth would be most appropriate to encourage trade and industry and would also be strengthened by the new wealth it fostered. A class of wealthy merchants, financiers, and manufacturers would be linked to government by such institutional devices as a national bank, and could then use their 'energy, foresight and riches' to benefit all their fellow citizens. Hamilton cared little that such a system would be elitist and undemocratic. 'Ambition and avarice' were the most reliable pillars of the state and the art of government was to curb and guide men's fundamentally greedy appetites into useful courses so that 'private vice could be public gain.' This Founding Father, according to Brogan, was 'a prophet of capitalism and passionately believed that a political and economic system dominated by capitalists would in the end produce the greatest happiness for all.'[72]

The delegates at Philadelphia eventually agreed on a Constitution based on a balance of powers between a centralized federal government to be based in Washington, D.C. and the individual states, and between the executive, the legislative, and the judicial branches of this government. But they did not meet with immediate universal approval for their framework. Many Americans still feared that the new arrangements did not check potential despotic tendencies. In response to these doubters the first session of Congress in 1791 adopted the first ten amendments to the Constitution, which became known as the Bill of Rights. The amendments included: the freedoms of speech and religion; freedom to assemble peaceably, and to petition for redress of grievances; the right to keep arms; freedom from unreasonable searches and seizures, self-incrimination, double-jeopardy, cruel and unusual punishment, and excessive bail and fines; the rights to fair trials and procedures; and other forms of due process. The founders clearly had the abuses of power by the British in mind when they set down these rights.

They were also aware of the tendency of power to corrupt. James Madison, one of the most influential theorists among those present at Philadelphia, argued: 'in framing a government which is to be administered by men over men, the great difficulty lies in this: you must first enable the government to control the governed; and in the next place oblige it to control itself.'[73]

The separation of powers in the newly constituted United States government was intended to check and balance the untrammelled use of political authority and prevent corruption. Madison's hope was that in this system ambition would counteract ambition. However, the constitutional safeguards the framers built into the governmental structure of the United States proved inadequate to check many notable abuses. In many cases ambition has actually complemented ambition and ultimately the corrupt benefited most.

An early example of America's leniency towards corruption and its commitment to the interests of property can be found in the Yazoo land fraud case.

With the British out of the way, western land in the newly United States was up for grabs. Speculators saw numerous chances to turn relatively small investments into fortunes, but usually had to contend with conflicting titles. Individual states pointed to their colonial titles, the United States insisted that the lands belonged to the nation as a whole, and Native Americans had their own claims.

The state of Georgia claimed a mass of land that now comprises the states of Mississippi and Alabama surrounding the Yazoo River. Taking no notice of the rival claims of the Chickasaws, Cherokees, Choctaws, and Creeks who lived there, the state began distributing huge tracts of land to favoured speculators in 1789, up to 50,000 acres per person, and in one case 150 million acres. C. Peter Magrath's study entitled *Yazoo: Law and Politics in the New Nation*, has even shown that Georgia managed to distribute land that did not exist: 'While twenty-four organized counties in 1796 contained 8,717,960 acres, records in the office of the state surveyor general show that three times as much land – 29,097,866 aces – had been granted. These bogus titles were then sold to gullible purchasers in the northern states and Europe.'[74]

In 1795 four companies collaborated in a bid for the Yazoo territory, led by James Gunn, U.S. senator for Georgia. Other investors included another U.S. senator, Robert Morris of Pennsylvania (who had largely financed the American Revolution), two congressmen, the federal district attorney for Georgia, and two top state judges. Their method was simply to buy the necessary votes in the Georgia legislature to approve the bid. The usual amount was $1,000, although State Senator Thomas Whylly was offered eight to ten 'likely negroes' for his part in passing the bill and others accepted promises of land or shares. The bill disposed of the 35 million acres to the companies for $500,000, less than 1.5 cents per acre and the companies' books show that all but one of the legislators were shareholders.[75]

The corrupt implications of the deal became known in time for 'the Yazoo men' to be thrown out in the 1796 elections. The new legislature annulled the act of the previous year, but no action was taken against their predecessors beyond condemnation of their participation in the 'unconstitutional, vile, and fraudulent transaction.'[76] The companies who had paid the bribes and $500,000 for title to the Yazoo lands still profited from the deal. They had already sold their title to the land to others throughout the country, especially to the New England Mississippi Land Company. On 13 February 1796, the same day that Georgia passed the repeal act, the New England company bought most of the holdings of the Georgia Mississippi Company – around eleven million acres – for $1,138,000. The Georgia company thus made a profit of nearly 650 per cent on its original investment by selling claims to land that had been declared to be fraudulent and been reclaimed by Georgia.[77] The new buyers represented by the New England company were both large and small investors and whether they, or at least some of them, knew about Georgia's action against the frauds has never been discovered. 'It is ... difficult to believe,' according to McGrath, 'that the worldly-wise politicians and speculators of the New England Mississippi Land Company had not by February, 1796, thirteen months after the original sale, heard a single word about the fraud and the threat of repeal.'[78] Whether they were ignorant or not they were determined to make good on their investment and, on their behalf, the company lobbied Congress for restitution, claiming that Georgia's action had violated the provisions of the Constitution, forbidding states to 'impair the obligation of contract.' In 1798 the company's efforts bore some fruit when a bill was passed by Congress allowing for 'an amicable settlement' of land disputes between the United States and Georgia by providing for the United States to acquire from Georgia the entire Yazoo area. In 1800 the new administration of President Thomas Jefferson duly bought the area for $1.25 million and wanted to pay the claimants generous compensation. Congress, however, delayed payment of the claims – persuaded, at least partly, by the rhetoric of Representative John Randolph of Roanoke, Virginia, who claimed that the 'swindlers of 1795' had no title to pass on and that those who had bought shares afterwards were aware of the fraud.[79]

By that time the claimants had turned to the courts for restitution, and in 1797 they obtained a judgment from the Massachusetts Supreme Court treating the Georgia act of recission as void. They needed, however, the weight of a federal decision to bring new pressure, and this they got in the case of *Fletcher* v *Peck*, planned and staged by the New England company from 1803. In 1810 the case was decided. In the opinion of Supreme Court Justice John Marshall the

corruption surrounding the Yazoo affair did not matter, 'It was inde-
cent in the extreme to ask about corruption.' He held that the Yazoo
land grant was legally a contract and the Georgia legislature could not
constitutionally invalidate it. The historian Gustavus Myers wrote that
this was the first of a long line of court decisions 'validating grants and
franchises of all kinds secured by bribery and fraud.'[80]

After the decision the claimants could thus claim that the U.S.
Supreme Court had upheld their position and, in 1813, they renewed
their pressure on Congress for compensation. The opposition this time
was led by Representative George M. Troup who argued that the
Supreme Court decision was a feigned case worthy of no respect from
Congress. He argued that the bill if passed would 'legalize fraud and
corruption,' and described a circle of fraud and corruption 'without
parallel in history.' His efforts, however, failed and $5 million was
appropriated to reimburse the Yazoo stockholders, including the politicians and speculators of the New England Mississippi Land Company.'[81]

The affair showed not only that corruption had very little restraint
but also the length to which the new nation's leaders would go to protect the rights of property. Article 1, section 10, of the Constitution for-
bids states from impairing the obligation of contract. The Supreme
Court's decision in *Fletcher* v *Peck* provided the first great constitutional mechanism for protecting vested property rights; capitalists in
America, in effect, got legal protection from legislative interference.
Property rights and human liberty, according to the Founding Fathers,
were inseparable, and the contract clause helped to ensure that capitalism in America had very little restraint until the end of the nineteenth
century.

Howard Zinn in his book *The People's History of the United States* has
pointed out the democratic limitations of the contract clause: 'To protect everyone's contracts seems like an act of fairness, of equal treatment, until one considers that contracts made between rich and poor,
between employer and employee, landlord and tenant, creditor and
debtor, generally favor the more powerful of the two parties. Thus, to
protect these contracts is to put the great power of the government, its
laws, courts, sheriffs, police, on the side of the privileged – and to do it
not, as in premodern times, as an exercise of brute force against the
weak but as a matter of law.'[82]

In the decades before the Civil War, according to Morton Horwitz in
his book *The Transformation of American Law*, other aspects of American

law were increasingly interpreted in the courts to suit the capitalist development of the country: 'By around 1850 ... the legal system had almost completely shed its eighteenth century commitment to regulating the substantive fairness of economic exchange. Legal relations that had once been conceived of as deriving from natural law or custom were increasingly subordinated to the disproportionate economic power of individuals or corporations that were allowed the right to "contract out" of many existing legal obligations. Law, once conceived of as protective, regulative, paternalistic and, above all, a paramount expression of the moral sense of the community, had come to be thought of as facilitative of individual desires and as simply reflective of the existing organization of economic and political power.'[83]

By the end of the nineteenth century the U.S. Supreme Court had given its blessing to unchecked capitalist development in many decisions. Most notably it had interpreted the Fourteenth Amendment to the Constitution, which was intended to give civil and political rights to freed slaves, in ways that made government regulation of business activities an infringement of corporate civil rights. Criminal activity within corporations was therefore almost without risk, as we shall see in Chapter 3.

As noted earlier, the Founding Fathers of the United States were not coy about their ambitions for the newly united states. All the early U.S. presidents had the same vision; they all wanted a state that would expand in population and territory, and increase in strength and power. They agreed with George Washington's description of the United States as 'a rising empire.'

U.S. territorial expansion in the nineteenth century was impressive. In 1803 President Thomas Jefferson signed a treaty with France and secured 828,000 square miles at a cost of $15 million or around 3 cents an acre. The French leader Napoleon wanted money to continue warring against the British and abandoned his ambitions for the New World. The Louisiana Purchase doubled the national territory.

In 1819 the Spanish were 'persuaded' to cede the Floridas to the U.S. After a short and unofficial military campaign the Spanish withdrew from the North American continent. In 1846 the British ceded the Oregon territory in the Northwest and the United States could now claim territory from the Atlantic to the Pacific.

In 1845 Texas was admitted to the union. This had been Mexican territory, but the North Americans were by then strong enough to overwhelm the Mexican army. Three years later the United States and Mexico fought a brief war as a result of which the United States gained control over half a million square miles of territory that would later become the states of California, Arizona, and New Mexico.

During the course of this expansion the rights, customs, and laws of the indigenous peoples tended to be ignored. Native Americans were not included in the new constitutional arrangements; they were placed first in the category of 'foreign nations' and later 'domestic dependent' nations.

The new government claimed sovereignty over much territory, especially to the West, that they had not the strength yet to control, and initially, they had to make treaties with and respect the rights of the still-strong Native tribes. As the U.S. increased its military power the respect for Native rights diminished. Treaties were broken, more land was stolen, and tribes were forcibly removed to pockets of mainly barren lands. Although many tribes fought back and committed atrocities of their own, they could never match the firepower, unity of purpose, cruelty, and, of course, lawlessness of the whites. Government treachery allowed combinations of looters, fraudsters, bootleggers, kidnappers, and thugs to drive Natives from their lands and many fortunes were made in the process.

The largest early American fortune boosted by the use of force and fraud among the indigenous peoples was that of John Jacob Astor. Astor's well-armed and well-organized agents made immense profits for his American Fur Company selling whiskey illegally at high prices and buying furs cheaply from befuddled Natives. Another trading trick was an early example of loan-sharking that involved giving credit on such things as gunpowder, flints, knives, and tools at a rate of up to 400 per cent. When the Natives resented such robberies and injustices they could be and often were murdered. After that, as Gustavus Myers relates, 'urgent alarmist representations would be sent to Washington that the Indians were in a rebellious state, whereupon troops would be hurried forth to put them down in slaughter.'[84]

Astor protected his company's interests by holding key politicians under financial obligation. In 1812, for example, he lent a sum of $5,000 to Secretary of State James Monroe, who was experiencing financial difficulties. Monroe became president in 1817 and remained in debt to Astor until the end of his presidency. During this time Astor needed and got favours from the federal authorities in his conflicts with Indians and his attempt to monopolize the fur trade in American territory.

There is little doubt that the American Fur Company's most successful years were in the Monroe years and that Astor's hold on the president contributed to this success. Astor's technique was to hold off on charging interest, or demanding repayment while making regular demands in terms of federal government policy. As soon as Monroe left office, Astor demanded immediate settlement.[85] Having made his fortune in the West, Astor then bought vast amounts of land and property in the East. He died in 1848, unchallenged as America's richest man.[86]

Politically, the worst thing that happened to Native peoples in the early republic was the election as president in 1828 of a veteran Indian fighter, Andrew Jackson. Secure in the knowledge of presidential support for their actions and pressured by land-hungry cotton planters, the states of Georgia, Mississippi, and Alabama passed laws extending their jurisdiction over Native Americans within their borders and decreeing that tribal laws and legislative assemblies were no longer legitimate. Natives were not allowed to vote, file suit, or testify in court, but they were subject to court proceedings for debt. Effectively, whites were allowed to plunder land and anything else at will.

Federal treaties and laws gave Congress – not the states – authority over the tribes, but when Natives protested and pointed out this fact, Jackson allied himself with the states and supported removal legislation that was passed in 1830. Natives were offered money to move west of the Mississippi where they could live without state interference. The Choctaws and most of the Creeks, with regret, accepted the offer. But thousands of individual Creeks took up the provision that individuals among them might stay and select allotments. Land-grabbers then flooded the country and obtained contracts of sale. Angie Debo's book entitled *History of the Indians of the United States*, explains the significance of the land-grabbers' tactics: 'for the identical techniques were repeated many times when Indians tried to hold land by individual title ... Misrepresentation, the Indian not knowing what he was signing; the use of intoxicants; the misuse of notary seals on blank instruments, to be filled in at the swindlers' convenience; outright forgery and a specialized kind, the bribing of some subservient Indian to impersonate the owner and sign in his place; and rigged probate procedure in the state courts corrupted by the general dishonesty.'[87] Whites were able to steal not just land, but crops and livestock, and there was little the Natives could do about it.

The Cherokees put up the greatest challenge to dispossession by appealing to the U.S. Supreme Court for protection, arguing that state laws did not apply to independent tribal nations. They seemed to be vindicated in 1832 and the *Worcester* v *Georgia* decision. Chief Justice John Marshall ruled that the laws of the United States had always considered Indian nations as distinct, independent political communities, and that their territory was completely separate from that of the states. 'The whole intercourse between the United States and this nation is, by our constitution and laws, vested in the government of the United States.'[88] Georgia, Mississippi, and Alabama, in other words, had been acting illegally in extending their state jurisdictions over Native peoples.

On hearing the verdict, President Jackson reportedly said, 'John Marshall has made his decision; now let him enforce it.' The Cherokees held their ground for a few years, but still faced harassment from Georgia. Eventually resistance crumbled, they accepted pitiful compensation for their land, and joined the 'Trail of Tears' to the far west. Several thousand died through cold, hunger, and disease, and those who finally made it to the new reservations had to re-establish themselves in territory appropriately labelled on maps as the 'Great American Desert.'[89]

White citizens hunted down and murdered Native Americans everywhere, but nowhere more systematically than in California. As the western historian Richard White has detailed, the earliest Indian hunting in the state was intended to secure a labour force for California's ranches and farms. The California constitution prohibited slavery, but a state law was passed in 1850 with the deeply ironic title of, 'An Act for the Government and Protection of Indians.' This allowed the forced labor of 'loitering' or 'orphaned' Indians and was written in such a way as to enable whites to arrest any Native American not already working for whites. Whites then paid the bail of those arrested and forced them to work until they had earned enough to cover their bail or fines. There was no escape from this situation for the natives – if they attempted to leave once they had worked off their debt, they were again unemployed under the law and therefore liable for arrest. Other laws provided strict apprenticeship conditions for Natives, and taken with the 1850 law, allowed a system of peonage to develop. In northern California, peonage was transformed into something close to slavery. According to White: 'In the 1850s and 1860s white gangs raided villages, kidnapped the occupants, and sold them to farmers and ranchers. Selling human beings is no longer peonage; it is slavery. Indian women and children were particular targets. The kidnappers often killed the parents of the children they seized. When children tried to escape, whites often hunted them down and killed them. California did not repeal the law that encouraged such crime until 1863. With Indian indentures illegal, whites could not legally compel Indians to labor, and the incentive to kidnap and sell Indians vanished.'[90]

Numerous government commissions appointed to investigate Indian affairs during the nineteenth century acknowledged that white crimes against Indians far outweighed Indian crimes against whites, and that white crimes were both ruthless and systematic. In 1869, for example, a commission appointed by President Ulysses S. Grant put the crimes of whites into historical context:

> The history of the Government connections with the Indians is a shameful record of broken treaties and unfulfilled promises. The history of the border white man's connection with the Indians is a sickening record of murder, outrage, robbery, and wrongs committed by the former, as the rule, and occasional savage outbreaks and unspeakably barbarous deeds of retaliation by the latter, as the exception.
>
> Taught by the Government that they had rights entitled to respect, when those rights have been assailed by the rapacity of the white man, the arm which should have been raised to protect them has ever been ready to sustain the aggressor.
>
> The testimony of some of the highest military officers of the United States is on record to the effect that, in our Indian wars, almost without exception, the first aggressions have been made by the white man; and the assertion is supported by every citizen of reputation who has studied the subject. In addition to the class of robbers and outlaws who find impunity in their nefarious pursuits on the frontiers, there is a large class of professedly reputable men who use every means in their power to bring on Indian wars for the sake of the profit to be realized from the presence of troops and the expenditure of Government funds in their midst. They proclaim death to the Indians at all times in words and publications, making no distinction between the innocent and the guilty. They irate the lowest class of men to the perpetration of the darkest deeds against their victims, and as judges and jurymen shield them from the justice due to their crimes.

The commission then explained how a one-sided view of criminality was presented in contemporary accounts: 'Every crime committed by a white man against an Indian is concealed or palliated. Every offence committed by an Indian against a white man is borne on the wings of the post or the telegraph to the remotest corner of the land, clothed with all the horrors which the reality or imagination can throw around it.'[91]

The commission recommended that Americans should be warned of the consequences of dishonest reporting of Indian affairs and that Indians should begin to be treated fairly and justly in accordance with the laws of the United States. Few Americans, however, got to hear about the commission's views and, along with many others reflecting similar views, its report was filed and forgotten in the government's archives.

Most crimes committed against the Indians were excused as being part of the buccaneering frontier spirit associated with expansion and the spreading of 'civilization' to the west. The country's rapid development during the nineteenth century was exploited by the ruthless and corrupt, who would then piously speak of the nation's 'manifest destiny' to populate the entire continent. And as the historian Robert Wiebe has explained that portion of the stereotype defining Native Americans as savages, 'the very antithesis of a civilized people – left them helpless before the onslaught of white progress.' Whites justified their passions and interest through their elastic definitions of savagery: 'Calling the Native Americans treacherous, they cheated them. Calling them ferocious, they murdered them. Calling them barbaric, they paraded their defeated chiefs in public like freaks, then sent them off to die.'[92]

Native Americans fought on to preserve some territory and some respect for their culture, but by the end of the nineteenth century a combination of military conquest, lack of resistance to European diseases, extinction of the buffalo, and systematic criminal activity had won the West for the whites. Very little of the North American continent was left to Natives. In 1881, Natives still held 155,632,312 acres of land. By 1890, the figure was down to 104,314,349, and by 1900 to 77,865,373. The trend continued, and even accelerated, in the early years of the twentieth century.[93]

The population of Native North Americans also dwindled – from around eight to twelve million before Europeans arrived to around 200,000 at the beginning of the twentieth century. 'If they could do it, they'd take everything,' according to one Native American woman in 1906. 'The only thing they'd leave us is our appetites.'[94] The 1990 U.S. census count of two million Native Americans is testimony to the ability of the indigenous peoples to resist centuries of legal and illegal oppression.

Crime, Insecurity, and Southern Slavery

The institution of slavery became even more central to the South's economy after the invention of the cotton gin in 1793 and the greater efficiency this gave to the production of cotton. Planters wanted ever-increasing amounts of land and labour to supply foreign and north-eastern markets. The merchants and lawyers represented at Philadelphia between 1787 and 1789 reconciled any differences they had with Southern planters, and the Constitution that emerged permitted the Southern section of the new nation to maintain and develop slavery. This compromise also gave opportunities for much criminal activity directed against Africans and African Americans.

The word 'slavery' does not feature in the document, but the institution was implicitly recognized by a clause that permitted the passage of laws requiring the return of fugitives, including not only criminals but 'persons held to service.' The language was sufficiently vague to allow for a system of kidnapping of free blacks to develop. Kidnapping was a crime in most states, but it was a crime committed against black men, women, and children, and thus usually ignored by most whites in a racist society. Kidnapping became pervasive, profitable, and virtually risk-free because, as Carol Wilson has argued, 'the racism of most whites rendered it unlikely that kidnappers would be prosecuted to the full extent of the law.' Wilson identified some kidnappers of free blacks as members of professional gangs often involved in other criminal activities such as horse thieving and other forms of robbery. Some were slave catchers who hunted fugitives for slave-owner clients and sometimes claimed that free blacks were fugitives. Others were simple opportunists. Whatever their identity, their trade could be practised openly in many parts of the country; government officials were largely inactive or unconcerned and witnesses feared retribution if they spoke out. Undoubtedly violence and intimidation were features of many kidnappings, and, as always, one can only speculate how much bribe money was paid to keep government officials so passive. Wilson's research demonstrates that although blacks who lived in states bordering the Mason-Dixon line were most at risk, kidnapping was a threat to blacks throughout the nation. From the beginning of the new nation, therefore, even free American blacks did not 'enjoy the same rights, privileges, and opportunities as white Americans,' and thus were more exposed to danger and exploitation by criminals.[95]

Pressure from free blacks and abolitionists eventually succeeded in the enactment of a series of personal liberty laws, beginning with Pennsylvania's in 1825, to protect free blacks from being kidnapped as fugitives. Free blacks and abolitionists were also involved in the 'underground railroad,' by which runaway slaves were smuggled from one point to another across border states and, if necessary, across the international border to Canada. The number of successful escapes was never large, but as Charles Wiltse points out, 'the nuisance and propaganda value of the underground railroad were out of all proportion to its actual success.'[96]

At the beginning of the 1830s the institution of slavery faced two challenges. The first was from abolitionists in the North who were exposing the immorality and criminality of the slave masters to make their case. The second was the threat of slave uprisings, taken more seriously after 1831 and the small-scale but bloody rebellion led by the slave preacher Nat Turner. Southern insecurity in the face of these challenges accounts for the acceptance of a legend based around the life of a thief called John Murrell.

Murrell lived in Tennessee during the Jacksonian period. According to the legend he was an intelligent man who was raised to be a scoundrel by his unscrupulous mother. He got in trouble with the law as a young man and swore eternal vengeance against society for punishing him. He became a highwayman, a killer, a horse thief, a counterfeiter, and a slave stealer. The legend asserts, however, that his criminality became much more ambitious and threatened the entire southern social order. According to this legend, Murrell got together with hundreds of like-minded criminals in a single organization called the Mystic Clan of the Confederacy. The idea was to infiltrate the slave population and preach insurrection; then, when the time was right, Murrell would give the word for the slaves to revolt. The slaves would rise and vast armies of avenging blacks under white leadership would burn the countryside and march into cities and towns. While all this was going on, other Murrell men would be using the uprising as a diversion to rob banks and rich merchants.

As with all myths there is some substance among the nonsense. Murrell was indeed a counterfeiter, and he did steal slaves and horses. Like other slave-stealing operations, Murrell's would have been well organized, and based near a navigable river to enable the thieves to put distance between themselves and the crime relatively quickly. A slave stolen in Kentucky, for example, could be rapidly carried down the Mississippi and up the Red River to be sold in central Louisiana where dealers were unlikely to ask any questions. The rest of the legend, however, is fiction. He did not consolidate all the criminals in the South in a gigantic criminal conspiracy, or plot the overthrow of the social order. James Lal Penick's close study of the Murrell legend reveals it to be based on a single, highly unreliable source, a book by Augustus Q. Walton, published in 1835 with the lengthy title: *A History of the Detection, Conviction, Life and Designs of John Murrell, the Great Western Land Pirate, Together with his System of Villainy, and Plan of Exciting a Negro rebellion, and a Catalogue of the Names of Four Hundred and Forty Five of His Mystic Clan Fellows and Followers; and the Efforts for the Destruction of Mr Virgil A. Stewart, the Young Man Who detected Him; to which is Added a Biographical Sketch of Mr Virgil A. Stewart.*

Stewart was the man responsible for Murrell's capture and the book tells of how he infiltrated the gang and persuaded Murrell to share his secrets. He either wrote the book under the pseudonym Augustus Q. Walton, or employed someone to ghost write it. Many historians in the following century would accept it as a legitimate source of information. Murrell found his way into the *Dictionary of American Biography* and hundreds of mainstream history books as the leader of one of America's earliest crime combines. More immediately the book was calculated to appeal to the deepest fears of Southerners. Murrell had been captured, but Stewart claimed that the slave insurrection plot was still to go ahead. Whites in counties to the west and the south of the state panicked and began beating up and killing slaves who could be remotely linked to the conspiracy.

As Penick points out, all legends serve a social purpose and the legend of John Murrell was no exception. The contemporary context of the Murrell story involves Northern abolitionists who by coincidence had launched a propaganda drive against slavery in Mississippi in the same summer that Stewart's book was released. The 'Murrell conspiracy' legend became a means to attack abolitionism at its strongest point – the claim to superior morality. By using the Murrell story, Southern propagandists were able to claim that abolition was a fraud on blacks as well as whites.

Murrell was a small-time threat to the property of his neighbours who was transformed into a major threat to property and order. Such was his notoriety that some entrepreneurs got hold of his head and displayed it at fairs for 10 cents a peek. Stewart faded into obscurity, but his book survives as an early example of the *True Crime* genre with its heated exaggerations and leaps of logic.[97]

Internal kidnapping and slave stealing were not the only illegal ways in which the demand for black labour in the South was met. A form of international organized criminal activity developed when the slave trade with Africa continued long after the federal government had outlawed it in 1807. By failing to enforce the law the U.S. government effectively allowed the illegal importation of large numbers of Africans to work the South's plantations. In 1811 President James Madison acknowledged this in a message to Congress: 'It appears that American citizens are ... instrumental in carrying out a trade in enslaved Africans, equally in violation of the laws of humanity and those of their own country.'[98]

New laws were passed to suppress the illegal trade and responsibility for the enforcement of the act shifted from the Treasury to the Navy. But, despite the occasional seizure of a slaver, the government did not, however, make a serious impact on the trade. Illegal profits were shared by merchants and shipmasters on both sides of the Mason-Dixon line and the host of middlemen and corrupt local and state officials involved in the internal distribution of human contraband.

While American efforts to enforce the laws against slave trading were negligible, the British government did make a genuine effort at suppression, most notably by sending the Royal Navy to patrol the coast of Africa. By mid-century every significant maritime nation except the United States allowed the British the right to stop and search their ships for slaves. In December 1841, in response to British protests that slavers from other nations were flying the U.S. flag to avoid capture, President John Tyler rationalized the American position thus, 'American citizens prosecuting a lawful commerce in the African seas under the flag of their country are not responsible for the abuses or unlawful use of that flag by others.' Many slave ships were thus able to continue to escape search and seizure by simply running up the U.S. flag when the British approached.

Far from being intimidated by the illegality of their trade American slave ships actually became larger, secure in the knowledge that British warships were not allowed to search them. In the late 1850s when the administration of President Andrew Buchanan began to make a genuine effort to suppress American involvement in the trade it made little difference. Although the U.S. Navy succeeded in capturing many more slavers, the capture of one or even more slavers did not put its owners out of business. As Daniel P. Mannix and Malcolm Cowley have demonstrated, the owners were usually part of a syndicate 'controlling several vessels and able to reckon that the profits on two or three successful voyages more than counterbalanced the losses on four or five.' By the time of Buchanan's crackdown an adult slave could fetch around $4,000, a child $1,500, and speculators who imported slaves could expect a profit of as much as 200 per cent. Such potential for profit made possible the corruption of local, state, and national authorities and ensured that the trade continued until slavery was abolished.[99]

Crime, Commerce, and Urbanization in the New Nation

Although the United States remained primarily a rural nation populated mainly by farmers until after the Civil War, urban-based commerce and industry was gaining ground. New York, Baltimore, Philadelphia, and Boston had become large cities by the mid-nineteenth century and towns, especially in the northeast grew proportionately. At the time of the Revolution the American population as a whole was only four million, by 1860 it had risen dramatically to thirty-one million.

Since birth rates had declined, this increase can only be explained by immigration from Europe. Before 1840 the largest waves of immigrants came from Germany, Ireland, and England. Most had either enough capital to buy farms or sufficient industrial skills to set up workshops. After 1840 crop failures in Germany and the devastating famines in Ireland changed the composition of U.S. immigration greatly. Immigrants tended to be poorer and much more likely to settle in the ports where they arrived and take whatever low-paid and intermittent employment was available. Race, ethnicity, gender, and class increasingly divided the urban population. A 'respectable' class had already emerged based on property and exclusion. Below this line people were dispersed into mutually hostile groups literally fighting for territory from childhood and then ceaselessly competing for space, work, money, and self-respect.[100]

Criminal activity among government officials and 'respectable' members of society tended to be lucrative, well organized, and usually unpunished. At the federal level the most successful example was Samuel Swartwout, who as collector of customs in New York, embezzled $1,225,705.69 between 1829 and 1838. His successor Jesse Hoyt stole at a similar rate, but only lasted three years before being forced to leave his office.[101] At a local level, corruption also characterized the earliest organized police forces. An 1840 investigation into the New York police found that some officers had made as much as $50,000 in a few years by organizing crime rather than suppressing it. They were accused of prior knowledge of robberies, sharing plunder, and protecting favoured criminals. Soon afterwards, a grand jury in Philadelphia found evidence that 'police officers go bail for felons arrested by themselves; in some cases compounding felonies with thieves, and dividing the stolen property between themselves, thieves and the plundered.'[102]

The chief gainer from the illegal business of prostitution in early New York was, according to Timothy Gilfoyle's research, John Livingston, representative of one of the new nation's leading families. From 1791 until the middle of the nineteenth century Livingston bought, sold, and controlled brothels throughout the city but especially in the area of the city that became known as the Five Points. By examining landowning patterns in the heart of Five Points, Gilfoyle found that other well-known families profited from the sex trade, and that Livingston was hardly an aberration or social misfit among New York's wealthy landlords.[103]

America's respectable and governing classes may have excluded the poor, but they were happy to include the poor who became rich. John Adams, the former patriot and second American president, noted this important deviation from European class hierarchies in a letter written in 1808: 'We have one material which actually constitutes an aristocracy that governs the nation. That material is wealth. Talents, birth, virtues, services, sacrifices are of little consequence to us.'[104] The ability to make money counted far more than family or education as a means for distinguishing one man from another. And, it did not matter much how these riches were obtained. Businessmen, according to Gustavus Myers, 'did not consider it at all dishonorable to oppress their workers; to manufacture and sell goods under false pretenses; to adulterate prepared foods and drugs ... to bribe public officials and to hold up the Government in plundering schemes. These and many other practices were looked upon as commonplaces of ordinary trade.'[105]

Charles Dickens noted this tolerance for commercial crime in his book *American Notes* (1842). While travelling around the United States he found a distinctly American 'love' of 'smart dealing,' which,

> gilds over many a swindle and gross breach of trust; many a defalcation, public and private; and enables many a knave to hold his head up with the best, who well deserves a halter; though it has not been without its retributive operation, for this smartness has done more in a few years to impair the public credit, and to cripple the public resources, than dull honesty, however, rash, could have effected in a century. The merits of a broken speculation, or a bankruptcy, or of a successful scoundrel , are not gauged by its or his observance of the golden rule, 'Do as you would be done by,' but are considered with reference to their smartness ... The following dialogue I have held a hundred times: 'Is it not a very disgraceful circumstance that such a man as so-and-so should be acquiring a large property by the most infamous and odious means, and notwithstanding all the crimes of which he has been found guilty, should be tolerated and abetted by your citizens? He is a public nuisance, is he not?' 'Yes, Sir.' 'A convicted liar?' 'Yes, Sir.' 'He has been kicked and cuffed, and caned?' 'Yes, Sir.' 'And he is utterly dishonourable, debased and profligate?' 'Yes, Sir.' 'In the name of wonder, then, what is his merit?' 'Well, Sir, he is a smart man.'[106]

Cornelius Vanderbilt epitomized the type of U.S. businessman Dickens had in mind. In many ways he was the model American self-made man. He was born to a poor family in 1794. With little or no schooling he began working on the ferries between Staten Island and Manhattan, transporting passengers and freight. While still a young man he quit as an employee and began building and operating coastal steamships. By the time he was forty he was called the 'Commodore' and his ships traded at numerous cities along the east coast. To gain a fortune of around half a million dollars, Vanderbilt paid his workers minimal wages and drove out his competitors by fair means or foul. He often took the business of competing shippers by underbidding, and then, once the opposition had been driven out, he would raise his rates.[107]

Vanderbilt also increased his fortune by defrauding the government and building up a system of commercial blackmail. The fraud involved the government's payment of heavy subsidies to steamship owners for the transportation of mail. The subsidies tended to go to those, like Vanderbilt, who had corrupted postal officials and members of Congress. The system of commercial blackmail involved threatening lesser steamship operators with competition and exposure of their criminal activity. One U.S. senator specifically accused Vanderbilt of this practice: 'He is the kingfish that is robbing these small plunderers that come about the Capitol ... he says, "Fork over $56,000 a month of this money to me, that I may lie in port with my ships," and they do it.'[108]

There were many more ways to cheat in business. Ship scuttling, for example, was a common practice. Scuttling cliques or 'wrecking crews' would buy old ships cheap, repair them sufficiently to get insurance, and then load them with dummy cargoes. The ships would then put to sea and soon afterwards be wrecked. Variations on the schemes involved persuading indebted captains to wreck their own ships. Prosecutions for this type of crime were rare.[109]

Much more pervasive, however, were frauds involving counterfeit money. Until the closing decades of the nineteenth century enforcement of laws against counterfeiting was minimal and, according to David Johnson's account, it became 'a well-organized criminal activity capable of distributing its products on a national scale.' The *New York Times* estimated that nearly 80 per cent of banknotes in circulation in 1862 were counterfeit.[110] The main demand for counterfeit money came from thieves and merchants: 'Thieves bought counterfeits to pass on unsuspecting merchants, which was simply one low-risk way to earn their livings. Their efforts provided a ready market for the sale of new counterfeits. Some merchants, however, were not so unsuspecting. Peddlers, saloon owners, hoteliers, country merchants, and even factory owners created an eager pool of customers for counterfeiters. In fact, there were many entrepreneurs willing to cheat their customers or employees by giving them counterfeit money in change. Their profits were enhanced by every spurious dollar they had bought at a discount from its face value and managed to pass on the public.'[111]

Receiving stolen goods and confidence games had also become inter-state criminal activities by the Civil War. Joe Erich had reportedly become New York's most important receiver by 1855 and dealt in goods stolen anywhere in the United States. He was succeeded by, among others, John D. Grady, who only did business with the most professional thieves. He financed some particularly lucrative robberies and kept the city's police happy by informing on lesser thieves and burglars. Confidence tricksters possibly best exemplified the advantages that American mobility could have for criminals. They traveled from city to city finding dupes wherever they went and then moving on before becoming too well known by the authorities.

Legal professionals also emerged during this period to facilitate illegal enterprise. Crooked lawyers had always existed, but by the 1840s a class of bail bondsmen also appeared to ensure the rapid release of captured criminals. Pickpockets, for example, often invented false names for themselves in court cases and then paid their bondsmen fees plus enough money to cover the forfeiture of bail. They then were free to go back to work.[112]

As U.S. towns and cities grew they began to experience the problem of criminal gangs already characteristic of European cities. Philadelphia had its Buffaloes, Blood Tubs, Rugs, and Copper Heads; Baltimore its Stringers; Cincinnati its Crawfish Boys; San Francisco its Sydney Ducks and Hounds; New York its Bowery B'hoys, Plug Uglies, Highbinders, Swipers, and Dead Rabbits. These spent much of their time fighting each other over slight insults or what they considered to be territorial claims. Or they would terrorize and steal from African Americans and recently arrived immigrants.[113] From, at least the 1830s, however, gangs and gangsters were also active in city politics and in the illegal economy.

Timothy Gilfoyle's examination of gang attacks on brothels revealed several important political influences that 'ultimately signaled changes in the organization of prostitution in New York.' Thomas Hyer's gang, for example, carried out at least four attacks on brothels between 1836 and 1838. These included a gang rape for which Hyer was convicted, sentenced, and released within a year. Hyer went on to become a champion heavyweight boxer and politician, and ultimately to operate brothels, saloons, and gambling dens along Mercer Street in the two decades before the Civil War. As a politician Hyer used an alliance with the anti-immigrant Bowery B'hoy gang to intimidate opponents, guard ballot boxes, and get his voters to the polls. As a brothel operator, Hyer probably used gangsters to control his employees. Gilfoyle cited other cases and concluded that, 'Employing terror, politically-motivated gangs restructured the most highly organized forms of prostitution and established a financial foundation for the political machine for the remainder of the century.' The attacks by Hyer and other gang leaders marked a turning point. Previously women involved in the prostitution business had a large degree of control over their working lives after exorbitant rents had been paid to the likes of Livingston mentioned earlier. After the attacks the exorbitant rents continued, and large amounts in protection money to local gangsters, police, and politicians had to be added. The occasional threat of collective violence and the more constant threat of customer violence led to the need for prostitutes to employ 'pimps,' who in many cases became more exploiters than protectors.[114]

As the U.S. population increased, so did the demand for prostitution. Most women who became prostitutes did so willingly largely because the alternatives were usually long working hours for low rates of pay or dependency on a husband or father. Rape, however, was occasionally used as part of the recruiting process. Brothel keepers used either procurers or favoured customers in these assaults and could rely on public condemnation of unchaste women to keep victims under control afterwards. Such moral standards and the low age of consent in most states – ten years in New York; twelve in others – made young girls particularly vulnerable.[115]

The connections between city politicians and gangsters became closer as the nineteenth century proceeded. As in the case of Hyer and his associates the arrangement was usually reciprocal. Gangsters and the operators of illegal businesses helped win elections as campaign workers or financial contributors, or they helped to steal elections using fraud or intimidation. In return politicians used their direct or indirect influence over the police and the courts to provide virtual immunity for favoured criminals, particularly those who ran or protected gambling or prostitution enterprises, and even to eliminate petty potential rivals to established entrepreneurs.

By the final decades of the century, the political machine system had emerged in most cities. These machines were usually relatively small groups of men in the Democratic or Republican Party organizations, led by a 'boss.' Under him were district leaders who ran their own neighbourhoods, but who generally obeyed the boss when it came to citywide policies. Power was concentrated at the top, but party members at every level worked hard to get the party elected and re-elected. Their motivation was rarely more than self-interest, and this, of course, always depended on victory at election time.

Bossism was a response to the rapid development of the cities. These grew and adapted haphazardly as masses of people from every part of the world suddenly came together. U.S. cities were crowded, unhealthy, and violent. Bosses brought some order to the chaos, and in the process, accumulated power and money.

Stereotypes of the boss appeared in newspaper cartoons by the early 1870s. In these he was sometimes jovial, sometimes snarling. He often smoked cigars and wore a derby hat. He usually looked Irish and he was often portrayed with his hand in the public till, stealing public money, surrounded by dirty, snarling, thuggish-looking cronies. Like most stereotypes, as Charles Glaab and Theodore Brown have noted, these simplified a complex process.[116]

In New York the machine was almost synonymous with Tammany Hall, the title of the executive committee organization of the Democratic Party in Manhattan. Tammany was one of the first city party organizations to cultivate every neighbourhood block or faction, making its appeal as broad based as possible. It set a pattern followed by many of the other city machines, putting together coalitions of ethnic groups, such as Irish, Jewish, and Italian, as sources of electoral support.

The party machines needed and generally got the electoral support of the poor, largely because they ran a kind of informal, haphazard welfare state. They helped the unemployed find jobs, they looked after constituents who were in trouble with the law, they wrote letters for the illiterate to send back to the old country, they organized free entertainment all year round and, in winter, they provided free coal or food, if necessary. Opposition reform coalitions never matched these services.

This was a time when most migrants and immigrants came to the cities with no skills or capital. They were looking for unskilled work and the bosses had the power and ability to provide jobs. Jobs were available on the city payroll and on municipal construction projects. Public money was always being spent on schools, hospitals, libraries, courthouses, sewers, gas lines, waterworks, paved streets, and trolley lines. Private operators usually owned these utilities, but they needed to keep in with the machines and were likely to hire people recommended by the bosses. Businessmen needed the goodwill and efficiency of the city government and were ready to make deals and alliances with the machines. They tended to pay for favours as a matter of course either in cash, or in blocks of stock, or by offering tips about profitable investments.

Tammany Hall's main strategy for winning elections was the practice of doing favours for people of every sort: immigrant families, businessmen, gamblers, prostitutes, saloonkeepers, and gangsters. A favour could mean special privilege or immunity for law-breakers. In return Tammany needed votes or money for campaigns. Money came in from anyone who would benefit from a machine victory, whether legitimate or not.

Money was also required for the kind of dirty tricks that insured who won elections. The machine bought votes, employed 'floaters' to vote up to dozens of times, gangsters to stuff ballot boxes and make sure that the 'wrong' people did not vote, and, if necessary, counters to make up fictitious totals. Victory meant profits for both the politicians and the public officials they appointed. Opportunities could involve embezzlement, extortion, inside knowledge about the building of public works, and the political protection of illegal activity. It has often been said that graft was the grease that kept Tammany and other machines moving smoothly.[117]

Top politicians made the big money. In the late 1860s, for example, a ring of Tammany politicians, led by Boss William Marcy Tweed, organized a system of pay-offs, kickbacks, and bribes that was said to cost the city millions of dollars a year. Tweed and several of his colleagues were convicted, but the downfall of his ring changed nothing. Richard Croker, for example, was Tammany's boss when New York was going through its most rapid period of expansion at the turn of the century. New buildings, new services, and new mass transit systems all required massive kickbacks and bribery. Croker was not paid, but he finished up with estates, stud farms, racing stables, and a luxury hotel in an accumulation of property on both sides of the Atlantic. When a journalist asked him whether his political career was the source of his wealth he replied candidly, 'Sure I'm working for my pocket all the time, same as you.'[118]

In 1894 Croker took a trip to Europe, prompted many felt by a state investigation into New York policing, chaired by Senator Clarence Lexow. This revealed much more about lower levels of big city corruption than any previous probe had. Witnesses detailed cases that showed that police officers owed their jobs and promotions to Tammany and, in return for regular pay-offs, protected gambling, prostitution, and other illegal activities. Officers also extorted money from peddlers, storekeepers, and other legitimate businessmen who needed their cooperation to stay within municipal ordinances. Detectives allowed confidence tricksters, pickpockets, and thieves to go about their business in return for a share of the proceeds. The New York Police Department, according to one of its longest serving officers, Captain Max Schmittberger, was 'corrupt to the core.'[119]

In the following years scores of similar investigations across the country revealed that conditions were similar in many other towns and cities. This, as we shall see in Chapter 4, led some reformers and commentators to the conclusion that the police and the local politicians actually organized crime in urban America.

Breaking the Bonds of Union: The American Civil War

America's early national leaders were not the clear-eyed statesmen guiding the young republic past the shoals of foreign danger and domestic disintegration portrayed in most accounts. The union survived, as Robert Wiebe argues, only because 'too few people found compelling enough reasons during its several crises to break it.' Instead of controlling events, national leaders tended to follow the paths of least resistance and in the process turned a blind eye to the crimes of their own officials and the locally and regionally powerful.

Wiebe has described the decades immediately preceding the Civil War as 'a crisis of parallelism.' The bonds of union created in 1789 proved to be flimsy. From the Jacksonian period onwards, the union survived as one of parallel growth – North and South. The established states in the North wanted the territory acquired to the West to be organized into free-labour states. The established states to the South wanted the same territory to be organized into slave-labour states. Two systems kept together by a series of increasingly shaky compromises until the discontented Southern States decided to secede in 1861.[120] Hundreds of thousands of civilians and soldiers died to preserve the union in a conflict that settled the future of the United States. The North would not allow such a potentially powerful competitor as the Confederacy on the same continent. According to Henry J. Raymond, the editor of the *New York Times* and chairman of the Republican National Committee, by allowing secession,

> We should be surrendering to a foreign and hostile power more than half of the Atlantic seaboard, – the whole Gulf, – the mouth of the Mississippi, with its access to the open sea, and its drainage of the commerce of the mighty West, – all the feasible railroad routes to the Pacific, – all chance of further accessions from Mexico, Central America, or the West India islands, – and all prospect of ever extending our growth and national development in the only direction in which such extension will ever be possible ... What is there in our past history to lead you to consider us thus reckless of national growth and national grandeur? ... Nine-tenths of our people in the Northern and Northwestern States would wage a war longer than the war of Independence before they would assent to any

such surrender of their aspirations and their hopes. There is no nation in the world so ambitious of growth and of power, – so thoroughly pervaded with the spirit of conquest, – so filled with dreams of enlarged dominions, as ours ... in the Center and the West, this thirst for national power still rages unrestrained.[121]

After the fighting began General William Tecumseh Sherman was equally candid about American power. On one occasion, for example, he made very clear what this meant to the rebel Southerners: 'The United States has the right, and also the physical power, to penetrate to every part of our national domain ... that we will do it in our own time and in our own way ... that we will remove and destroy every obstacle, if need be, take any life, every acre of land, every particle of property, every thing that to us seems proper; that we will not cease till the end is attained; that all who do not aid us are enemies, and that we will not account to them in our acts. If the people of the South oppose, they do so at their peril; and if they stand by, mere lookers-on in this domestic tragedy, they have no right to immunity, protection, or share in the final results.'[122]

In 1864 Sherman's troops took control of the city of Atlanta and then began a march through Georgia to the sea. He had promised to 'make Georgia howl,' 'to demonstrate the vulnerability of the South and make its inhabitants feel that war and individual ruin are synonymous terms.' On the march his soldiers were told to live off the land rather than wait for supply lines to be established, and they took what they wanted and devastated the rest.[123] Fences and fields were trampled down and, according to a witness, 'the road was lined with carcasses of horses, hogs, and cattle ... that the invaders had wantonly shot down, to starve out the people.'[124] Railroad lines were torn up and homes burned in a trail of destruction fifty miles wide and 250 miles long.[125] It was total war – a demonstration of power that hastened the demoralized surrender of the Confederacy in April 1865. The world now knew that one nation was going to dominate the North American continent.

Four years of turmoil and victory in 1865 ensured that no states have seriously considered secession since. The potential of federal authority also was greatly increased, although American nation-state building was still at an early stage and the federal government's functions remained limited to protecting the rapid settlement of western territory, supporting internal improvements such as railroad construction, and the relocation of Native Americans. Most of the matters concerning the individual citizens, such as law and order, were still the responsibility of the states.

A new American order could now be constructed in which there was to be more emphasis on the control of many aspects of personal and business behaviour. In theory, this new order was to be based on free labour and free men, governed by legal and democratic principles that were guaranteed by the federal government. In practice, the United States continued to make the same compromises with local and regional elites as other great powers had made during their processes of state building. Successful criminal activity adapted to the new American order rather than challenged it.

Chapter 2

Whitewash: Racism, Xenophobia, and the Origins of 'Organized Crime' in the United States

In the immediate post–Civil War years, tens of thousands of men, organized in hundreds of different Southern localities, swore oaths demanding lifelong commitment to activity that was illegal. These men committed heinous crimes, often at night and in disguise, and they were rarely caught or punished. Their goal was to restore white rule to the South. Through their criminal activities, these men helped to create an environment with unmatched opportunities for organized racist crime to thrive. This situation persisted into the 1950s and 1960s when white supremacy was successfully challenged and finally defeated by the Civil Rights Movement. Logic and evidence would suggest that this organized crime, which kept the Southern States in its grip for almost a century, was more directly pernicious than any other contemporary variety of illegal activity; yet the South does not appear in the literature on organized crime, except as an entrance point for the Mafia. Chapter 2 offers an explanation for this omission and details other ways in which racism contributed to America's problem with organized crime in the twentieth century.

Although the 13th Amendment to the Constitution of the United States formally abolished slavery in 1865, the freedom of African Americans was almost immediately undermined by pervasive and violent criminal activity, much of which was organized for economic as well as political reasons. Until the mid-1870s, during the period known as Reconstruction, federal troops remained in the South to provide some protection for the newly freed men and women. Faced with the presence of the federal government, whites organized secret societies, such as the Ku Klux Klan, to restore white supremacy to the South.

Reconstruction was officially ended when President Rutherford Hayes ordered the removal of the last remaining federal troops in 1877. 'Home rule' returned to the Southern States. Over the following decades ways were found to institutionalize the oppression of African Americans and vigilantism, while selective law enforcement imposed a crude form of order. The South remained the nation's poorest and most backward region well into the twentieth century; nevertheless, the privileged or simply the ruthless found many opportunities for illegal enrichment.

U.S. society as a whole was transformed between the Civil War and the First World War. Railroads shrank distances between markets; agricultural, mining, and factory operations fed these markets with goods and raw materials, and jobs were created. All this prompted mass migration and immigration. Cities and towns rapidly proliferated and expanded. The nation's population nearly trebled, exceeding 100 million people by the 1920s, by which time a majority of them lived in urban areas. More than a quarter of this population increase can be accounted for by mass immigration. Around 26 million people arrived during these years. Most of these new arrivals came from Asia or the less industrialized parts of Europe, and they came because jobs were available in the rapidly expanding American economy. Of the many groups to arrive, Jews, southern Italians, and Chinese arrived in the hundreds of thousands to become factory workers, miners, and laborers, or to take any job that would give them a living. People felt confused and resentful during this disruptive period, unable to understand the forces that were transforming their lives. Many turned to simple explanations provided by those politicians, publicists, and intellectuals who argued that either these foreigners or African Americans, or combinations of both, were responsible for what seemed to be a concomitant tidal wave of crime and vice. Mafia mythology has its origins in this period. The fear of both foreigners and blacks contributed to the campaigns to prohibit drugs, alcohol, and prostitution.

Organized Crime and the Limits to African-American Freedom

From the time of Abraham Lincoln's Emancipation Proclamation in 1862, increasing numbers of black soldiers fought bravely and effectively for Northern armies, playing a significant role in the final collapse of the Confederate cause. Age-old roles were suddenly reversed when black soldiers marched through the beaten South and demanded to see the passes of white men and women. Black slavery had sustained the Southern economy and society for centuries. Blacks were considered to be chattels, beneath even the poorest white in a system dominated by a wealthy planter elite. Now this had been turned around in the space of only four years, and defeated Southern whites felt this was the ultimate humiliation. 'If I had my way,' said one Confederate soldier, 'I'd have a rope around every nigger's neck, and hang 'em and dam up this Mississippi river with them.'[1] Over the following decades the South's response to the destruction of its central economic institution was a brutal, concerted, and largely illegal effort to ensure that any role reversal was temporary and any progress for blacks halted.

Reports written in the weeks that followed the Confederacy's surrender in April 1865 indicate that from the outset many whites had no intention of respecting the rights of the newly freed men and women of the South. One witness noted that, 'Some planters held back their former slaves on their plantations by brute force. Armed bands of white men patrolled the country roads to drive back the Negroes wandering about. Dead bodies of murdered Negroes were found on and near the highways and by-paths. Gruesome reports came from the hospitals – reports of colored men and women whose ears had been cut off, whose skulls had been broken by blows, whose bodies had been slashed by knives, or lacerated by scourges.'[2]

African Americans in parts of the South away from the coasts were kept in slavery long after the official announcement of emancipation. Planters, according to another contemporary, 'endeavored and partially succeeded in maintaining between themselves and the negroes the relation of master and slave, partly by concealing from them the great changes that had taken place, and partly by terrorizing them into submission to their behests.'[3]

The first efforts by former slaves to achieve economic independence were also systematically undermined. An Army officer reported that in Texas: 'The amount of unblushing fraud and outrage perpetrated upon the negroes is hardly to be believed unless witnessed. Citizens who are esteemed respectable do not hesitate to take unfair advantage. My office is daily visited by large numbers of unfortunates who have money owing them, which they have been unable to obtain.'[4] Another report concluded that Southern whites,

> are as yet unable to conceive of the negro as possessing any rights at all.
> Men who are honorable in their dealing with their white neighbors will

cheat a negro without feeling a single twinge of their honor. To kill a negro they do not deem murder; to debauch a negro woman they do not think fornication; to take property away from a negro they do not consider robbery. The people boast that when they get freedmen affairs in their own hands, to use the classic expression, 'the niggers will catch hell.' The reason of all this is simple and manifest. The whites esteem the blacks their property by natural right, and however much they may admit that the individual relations of masters and slaves have been destroyed by the war and by the President's emancipation proclamation, they still have an ingrained feeling that the blacks at large belong to the whites at large, and, whenever opportunity serves they treat the colored people just as their profit, caprice, or passion may dictate.[5]

Despite many similar reports detailing frauds and atrocities against the freed men and women, Andrew Johnson, Lincoln's successor as president, was determined to be magnanimous in victory and allow former rebel Southerners the opportunity to re-establish their state governments as soon as possible after the war had ended. These Southerners grudgingly ratified the 13th Amendment to the Constitution that ended slavery, but more significantly passed resolutions denying the black race political, economic, and social equality, and reaffirming the belief that governments were established 'for the exclusive benefit of the white race.'[6] A series of so-called Black Codes made Southern intentions for the newly freed men and women clear. In most states ex-slaves were required to carry passes, observe curfews, and were restricted to agricultural or domestic service jobs, but were not allowed to vote, serve on juries, bear arms, or testify against white persons. Comprehensive vagrancy laws were passed under which even 'idleness' and unemployment could be interpreted as crimes and reflected a warped, authoritarian morality that, as we shall see, continued to characterize Southern race relations long after Reconstruction was over. A Florida statute was typical:

Rogues and vagabonds, idle or dissolute persons who go about begging, common gamblers, persons who use juggling, or unlawful games or plays, common pipers and fiddlers, common drunkards, common night walkers, thieves, pilferers, traders in stolen property, lewd, wanton and lascivious persons, keepers of gambling places, common railers and brawlers, persons who neglect their calling or employment, or are without reasonably continuous employment or regular income and who have not sufficient property to sustain them and misspend what they earn without providing for themselves or the support of their families, persons wandering or strolling around from place to place without any lawful purpose or object, habitual loafers, idle and disorderly persons, persons neglecting all lawful business and habitually spending their time by frequenting houses of ill fame, gaming houses or tippling shops, persons able to work but habitually living upon the earnings of their wives or minor children, and all able bodied male persons over the age of 18 years who are without means of support and remain in idleness, shall be deemed vagrants and upon conviction shall be subject to penalty.[7]

Laws such as these were usually only invoked when blacks were concerned. If convicted and unable to pay the fine imposed, unemployed blacks could be hired out as cheap or even free labour to planters or other employers.

For many in Congress, these codes were simply intended to reintroduce a new form of slavery. In response, Northern Republicans made an attempt to integrate the newly freed slaves into the mainstream of Southern political, social, and economic life. Republicans, notably the 'radicals' Thaddeus Stevens and Charles Sumner, decided that new constitutional arrangements were necessary to protect Southern blacks and codify the civil rights of Americans. In 1866, as a result of their efforts and against the wishes of President Johnson, the 14th Amendment granted black Americans the full rights of U.S. citizenship and prescribed that 'No state shall ... abridge the privileges and immunities of citizens of the United States; nor shall any state deprive any person of life, liberty, or property, without due process of law; nor deny to any person, within its jurisdiction, the equal protection of the laws.' In 1870 the 15th Amendment was ratified, giving black males the right to vote. By that time Congress had thrown out the governments of all Confederate states, except Tennessee, and organized the territory into five military districts, each under an army general. In order to be readmitted to the Union, the Southern states were required to ratify the 14th Amendment and draft new state constitutions providing for black suffrage. The period of 'radical reconstruction' lasted until the middle of the 1870s and gave African Americans the chance to make alliances with the Republican Party and enjoy a brief taste of political influence and economic opportunity. However, they soon faced an intense period of systematic political and economic terrorism, most famously practised by the Ku Klux Klan.

The Klan began innocently enough in Pulaski, Tennessee. Towards the end of 1865, six bored young men, readjusting to life after serving in the Confederate army, decided to set up some kind of club. Committees were appointed to draw up a set of rules and a ritual for the initiation of members. The name of the organization itself came from the Greek word for circle, Kuklos, perhaps suggesting the sound of 'bones rattling together.'[8]

Membership required absolute secrecy and a strange dress code. The Klan's costume consisted of a long loose-fitting robe, a white mask with holes for eyes and nose, and a hat made out of cardboard, designed to make the wearer look taller. Dressed like this, these early Klan members went out at night to play pranks on their neighbours. But innocent pranks against white people became something different when played against the newly freed slaves. Klan members came to realize the strength of fear and used it to intimidate and control their black neighbours. Word spread and Klan 'dens' began to proliferate throughout the South. Before long, the Ku Klux Klan consisted of tens of thousands of white Southerners, organized in hundreds of Southern localities – never centrally organized, but all dedicated to restore the South to its former white dominated 'glory.' Klan dens tended to be headed by the Southern elite. Planters, former generals, lawyers, merchants, shopkeepers, schoolteachers, and even ministers of churches gave respectability and legitimacy to a movement that appealed to all levels of Southern white society.

Most Klan violence was under cover of night, usually targetting blacks in isolated rural areas, and threatening or harming several on a typical night ride. Well-armed Klansmen, sometimes numbering more than a hundred, would also be prepared to cross state or county lines to carry out assignments with neighbouring Klans. Overwhelmingly, their victims were former slaves, but they were prepared to kill or maim those whites seen as aiding the cause of blacks. The aim was to keep blacks in their 'place' – economically, socially, and politically powerless.[9]

Although most historians stress the political significance of Klan terror, contemporaries were aware that economic motives were also a factor. Lewis E. Pearson of Talladega, Alabama, for example, told a Congressional committee: 'From what I have seen and heard, I have formed the conclusion that the Ku-Klux organization was formed for the purpose of controlling the negro vote and the negro labor, to prevent the free exercise, on their part, of the rights which the Federal

Government had conferred upon them. By controlling the negro's labor I mean that they intended he should work only for such persons and upon such terms as they sanctioned.'[10] A judge from the same state later confirmed Pearson's conclusions by admitting that the Klan started up when white employers, unable to 'control the labor ... through the courts,' decided to force blacks 'to do by fear what they were unable to make them do by law.'[11]

By 1871 whites in Alabama had found that their terrorism had created a labour shortage and were trying to stem migration from the state. According to Congressional testimony, more than a hundred men were killed for attempting to escape. When some blacks did manage to get out of the state, particularly to Mississippi, white gangs, including at least one deputy sheriff, crossed the state line to kidnap them and return them to work the land.[12] In a recent history of the Klan, Wyn Craig Wade has made a list of 'kluxing' cases with routine economic motives:

Aleck Stewart of Monroe County, Mississippi, was whipped by Klansmen for having the gall to sue his white employer for back wages. Jake Dannons, a successful blacksmith in Walton County, Georgia, was shot dead by Klansmen after refusing to do any more work for a white man who never paid him. Daniel Lane of Georgia was raided and whipped with hickory sticks by Klansmen after hiring a black woman to hoe his land who had earlier refused to work for a white farmer. In South Carolina, Harriet Hernandes and her child were whipped when she refused to break her labor contract with one white man to work for another. Columbus Jeter was raided after declining to buy a horse from a Klansman who wanted 20 per cent interest.[13]

There were many more cases of criminal exploitation. In Texas and Florida, whites often drove freedmen off plantations, but usually only after the harvest had been gathered. The landlords thus gained the produce of a hard year's work without effort. In other parts of the South terror was more systematically used to keep blacks on the plantations at the least possible expense to the landlords. It is clear from the accounts that the aims of many Klansmen involved replacing slavery with a system that kept the black labour force under control just as effectively. The Klan in western Alabama, for example, was led by planters who used intimidation to ensure a satisfactory work rate. Landlords had only to complain about insubordination or laziness and masked bands would arrive to punish offenders. A government official reported that the Klan always had the interests of the planter in mind: 'The Ku-Klux always remain quiet during what is called the planting season. They wanted to get the crop in the ground, and anything to punish these men they would reserve until after that was done. They would reserve the punishment so as not to interfere with the labor of the negroes.'[14]

There were also many cases involving the running and protection of criminal enterprises. In Lenoir, North Carolina, for example, a Klan-type organization known as the Constitutional Union Guard emerged in 1869 and included a deputy sheriff, a lawyer, and a prominent mill owner among its members. It represented itself as an organization to put down robbery, but as congressional testimony revealed it actually specialized in stealing horses – mainly from blacks – for sale in other counties. The group also protected illicit distilling and committed various acts of arson, murder, and extortion.[15]

In a senate committee report in 1872 it was noted that much of this criminal activity was camouflaged as part of the political campaign to 'redeem' the South from its Yankee oppressors. The point was made early in the report that 'bad men of every description take advantage of the circumstances surrounding them, and perpetuate acts of violence, from personal or pecuniary motives under the plea of political necessity.'[16] Later the report elaborated: 'Bad men, learning the strength and power of secret and disguised organizations ... have done deeds that demons would be ashamed of. These atrocities ... have very rarely had any political significance. Thirst for plunder; the gratification of private revenge or of brutal passion; the protection of illegal distilleries, or of security from detection in often extensive horse stealing operations, have been the most prominent developments.'[17]

Despite frequent Klan atrocities across the South, many African Americans did manage to take advantage of the political, economic, and educational opportunities made possible by the presence of federal troops. The main political task of white supremacists was therefore to reinstate 'home rule' by restoring the Democratic Party to power in the South. Their methods were predictably brutal and dishonest.

Violence in Louisiana, for example, escalated before elections in November 1868. An estimated 300 murders had been committed before August. At least sixty more people were killed in the city of New Orleans between 22 September and the day of the election. The great majority of all these were African Americans who supported the Republican Party.[18]

The largest single pre-election massacre was in St Landry Parish. There had been rumours of blacks organizing an armed uprising. The massacre, probably orchestrated by a Klan-type organization known as the Knights of the St Camellia, began on 28 September 1868 when twenty-nine blacks were taken prisoner, suspected of involvement in a planned uprising. The following night, whites removed all but two of these from the jail and shot them. The jailer and deputy sheriff were given advance notice of the prisoners' fate and, as they testified later, supported the vigilantes' action. After that the killing continued for days as armed whites pursued and killed armed blacks on sight. Approximately 150 black Republicans were killed. One military officer was taken out of town and shown sixteen to eighteen bodies sticking through the dirt. There were similar finds in other parts of the parish. Only blacks wearing a red string tied around their arm were relatively safe in the days following the massacre. This indicated surrender and trust in the protection of the whites.[19]

A federal report estimated the total pre-election dead at over 1,000. Ted Tunnell's study of the election returns revealed that murder was an effective campaign tactic. The Republican vote declined by tens of thousands in more than two dozen parishes. In seven parishes the Republicans received not a single vote; in nine others the combined total of votes for the Republican candidate was nineteen.[20]

Democrats also used bribery, trickery, and legal technicalities to win elections. Party workers were known to stuff ballot boxes, vote many more times than once, or pay off Republican officials to tip the balance their way. Black illiteracy was exploited to substitute worthless pieces of paper for Republican tickets. Planters warned their fieldhands that they would be out of a home and a job if they voted for the wrong side. One Tennessee planter got all his labourers together on election day, handed them all Democratic tickets, marched them to the polls, and watched them cast their ballots. In Oglethorpe County, Georgia, fraud and intimidation helped elect General Dudley DuBose, Grand Titan of the Ku Klux Klan, to Congress.[21]

Particularly chilling for the newly enfranchised black voters was a practice first noticed in Mississippi in 1868. Whites quietly but openly took down the names of blacks that voted. Compiling lists became increasingly common in Southern elections for the rest of the century. It can be safely assumed that the names on these lists were subjected to some form of 'persuasion' or worse.[22]

Black political leaders risked their lives every day and dozens were killed. Sometimes they were killed in ways that would serve as a warning to those that might emulate them. Jack Dupree, for example, who was active in Republican politics in Monroe County, Mississippi, had his throat cut and was disemboweled in front of his wife. The motive, apparently, was Dupree's reputation as a man who 'would speak his mind.'[23] Such warnings persuaded many blacks to quit politics and the neighbourhood altogether when threatened with similar fates. Eric Foner analysed the destructive impact of this type of selective killing on the political infrastructure of black communities: 'Local leaders played such a variety of roles in schools, churches, and fraternal organizations that the killing or exiling of one man affected many institutions at once. And for a largely illiterate constituency, in which political information circulated orally rather than through newspapers or pamphlets, local leaders were bridges to the larger world of politics, indispensable sources of political intelligence and guidance ... Their murder or exile inevitably had a demoralizing impact upon their communities.'[24]

Whatever the type of criminal activity involved, African Americans could expect little protection from the authorities. Many local officials were actively involved in white supremacist activity and those who were not and tried to do their jobs even-handedly could expect reprisals. Federal government protection was similarly inadequate. Despite frequent detailed reports of atrocities inflicted on black Americans, Washington made few extra troops available.

In 1870 and 1871 Congress did attempt, however, to make an impact through legislation. The Force Act, prescribed heavy penalties for anyone using force, bribery, or intimidation to prevent a citizen from voting or 'the enjoyment of any right or privilege granted or secured to him by the Constitution or laws of the United States.'[25] The Ku Klux Klan Act outlawed Klan-type organizations, gave federal courts original jurisdiction in all cases involving conspiracies or violence against the freedmen, and empowered the president to suspend habeas corpus and to declare martial law in any terrorized community.

President Ulysses S. Grant invoked the Ku Klux Klan Act towards the end of 1871, concentrating the response in South Carolina and Mississippi. Soldiers were sent into the worst affected counties and hundreds of Klansmen were rounded up to await trial. Attorney General Amos T. Akerman directed the government's legal strategy and pioneered a prosecuting technique that allowed those who confessed and identified the organization's leaders to escape without punishment. He was thus able to bring some of the organization's leaders to trial. However, the great majority of cases against Klansmen were eventually dropped. Attorneys, marshals, witnesses, and jurors were harassed and ostracized by the white communities, and several witnesses were murdered. Few long sentences were imposed, and pardons were often granted to some of the worst offenders. Despite such leniency, the federal attack seemed to break the back of this first manifestation of the Ku Klux Klan. White supremacy assumed other forms that were designed not to provoke federal intervention.[26]

Events in Louisiana illuminate both the change in strategy and the North's supine adjustment to the successful restoration of white rule. White resentment in and around the town of Colfax had been simmering away through Reconstruction as blacks gained a certain amount of social, political, and economic power from their support of the Republican Party. In April 1873 an exchange of gunfire between blacks and whites brought things to the boil. Blacks from the surrounding countryside feared reprisals and gathered in Colfax for protection. Some of them had shotguns, but they were soon confronted by a private army of more than 100 better equipped whites. On Easter Sunday, an uneven battle was followed by indiscriminate slaughter of scores of blacks. At least 105 blacks and three whites were killed, two of the whites probably by their own side.

Federal authorities brought nine men to trial under the Force Act and three were found guilty of 'violating the civil rights of Negroes.' These, however, were acquitted on appeal to the Supreme Court in 1876. According the Chief Justice Morrison R. Waite, the 14th Amendment, 'prohibits a State from depriving any person of life, liberty, or property, without due process of law; but this adds nothing to the rights of one citizen as against another.' The federal government, in other words, could protect civil rights only against their abridgement by states, not individuals. A private army of individuals had committed the massacre and therefore, in the expedient reasoning of the Court, the federal government was powerless to act.[27] The ruling ended any value of the 1870 and 1871 legislation as a deterrent to white supremacist atrocities and, with other decisions, effectively absolved the federal government from the obligation to protect the civil rights of African Americans.

The significance of these decisions was not, of course, lost on white leaders throughout the South; armed bands in the South could commit atrocities and still be virtually immune from federal jurisdiction. They took care, however, not to invite renewed federal intervention. Violence during election campaigns, for example, was usually called off several weeks before polling day. Democratic Party politicians wanted their electoral victories to appear legitimate. The irony, as the historian Michael Perman points out, was that the 'intention was to use violent and illegal means to win power legitimately.'[28]

The nature and context of white supremacist violence changed after the decline of the Ku Klux Klan. Klan terrorism had been mainly covert carried out by disguised bands of nightriders. Although many Klan members were respectable and high-ranking members of local communities they tried and usually succeeded in keeping their involvement secret. Events during and after 1873 indicated a radical change of tactics. Organized bands or paramilitary detachments now operated openly with the active support of the Democratic Party leadership. Their assaults were less on isolated individuals and more on the structures and institutions of Reconstruction government – such as the courthouses, jails, and militia units in those counties that were in Republican hands. Michael Perman reported in his book *The Road to Redemption* that a coordinated campaign of actual or threatened violence actually overthrew Reconstruction and transferred political control to an openly racist Democratic party.[29]

Reconstruction was finally abandoned in 1877 as a result of the appropriately corrupt political bargain that settled the 1876 presidential election between Samuel J. Tilden for the Democrats and Rutherford B. Hayes for the Republicans. Initially the count looked to give Tilden a narrow victory. However, the Republicans used a combination of fraud, bribery, and intimidation to swing the election towards their man. As Matthew Josephson put it, Tilden 'was overreached by superior skullduggery on the part of his opponents.'[30] With minimal protest by the Democrats, Hayes was awarded the election. The lack of protest has been convincingly explained by Southern historian C. Vann Woodward. He argued, in a thesis first articulated in 1951 and confirmed by much historical research since, that a compromise had been reached between the conservative wing of the Republican Party and the Southern Democrats. The essence of this deal was that Republicans promised the South home rule and, in return, the Democrats promised to treat blacks well.

As a result of this compromise, Hayes was inaugurated president in March 1877, and soon after removed the few remaining federal troops from the South. The following September, Hayes reassured African

Americans in a speech in Atlanta, Georgia, that 'their rights and interests would be safer' in the hands of the Southern white man than in the
care of the federal government.[31] By that time, in a pattern that continued for the next eighty years, a combination of violence, electoral
fraud, and Northern lack of interest had allowed the Democrats and
their allies to take control of every Southern State. Hayes himself
acknowledged, at least to himself, the reality of race control in the
South. In a diary entry written a year and a half after the removal of the
troops, he noted that, 'by state legislation, by frauds, by intimidation,
and by violence of the most atrocious character, colored citizens have
been deprived of the right of suffrage ... and to the protection to which
people of those States have been solemnly pledged.'[32]

Violence, therefore, combined with electoral and financial fraud,
restored white supremacist rule to the South. Systematic criminal
activity, in effect, reconstructed white domination of the Southern
political, economic, and social structure after the Civil War and made
constitutional guarantees irrelevant well into the twentieth century.

Southern History as Fiction

In the decades following Reconstruction, white supremacists refined
the use of fraud and force to preserve and maintain their political and
economic stranglehold and in the process fostered many historical and
sociological fictions to legitimize their rule. The first of these fictions
involved the interpretation of Reconstruction itself.

From the 1870s Northern and Southern attitudes to Reconstruction
coalesced around a white conservative interpretation first articulated
by James S. Pike. Pike wrote about South Carolina in 1872, in an article
entitled 'A State in Ruins,' for the *Tribune*, and argued that things had
deteriorated since the state's 'high-toned' slave-owning rulers were
removed from power after the Civil War. He described black legislators
in the Reconstruction government as a 'great mass of ignorance and
barbarism' who were led by corrupt Northern 'carpetbaggers' and 'a
few intelligent colored people.' These leaders were 'miscreants and
thieves' who fattened on flagrant corruption. The article concluded
that the 'wild crimes of Ku-Klux youth' might produce some good in
remedying this situation. In 1874 Pike elaborated on these themes in a
book entitled, *The Prostrate State*.[33]

Variations on Pike's analysis of the state of South Carolina became the basis for most scholarly, textbook, and popular analysis of Southern Reconstruction history until at least the middle of the twentieth century. According to a historical interpretation assimilated by most Americans, Reconstruction was a hopeless and corrupt failure because radical Republican Northerners were intent on punishing the South by depriving the native aristocracy of their power and status. These vindictive political leaders wanted to create a political dynasty by manipulating the ignorant, insolent, lazy, and criminally inclined blacks. The result of this political coalition between Republicans was disastrous; in the words of one historian, 'the South was now plunged into debauchery, corruption, and private plunder – government had been transformed into an engine of destruction.' The end of Reconstruction came when the decent whites united out of sheer desperation and brought an end to 'Black republican' rule. In one state after another, 'good' government was eventually restored to the South.[34]

This analysis of Reconstruction also permeated popular culture. Thomas Dixon's best-selling book *The Clansman* (1905) portrayed the Ku Klux Klan as a noble and chivalrous order which resorted to violence only to save the South from corrupt carpetbaggers and lascivious blacks. In 1915, D.W. Griffith produced a film based on the book, with the new title *The Birth of a Nation*. The film was a great success across the country and helped promote a national revival of the Klan. In the South, audiences 'wept, yelled, whooped, cheered,' and on one occasion shot up the screen in an attempt to save a young white woman called Little Sister from Gus, the black rapist.[35]

As late as 1966 an American history textbook called *The Making of Modern America* implied that Klan crime was morally justified: 'Some Southern whites, unable to improve conditions in a lawful and orderly way, decided to go outside the law.'[36] Thus, a historical framework had been constructed that effectively blamed the black victims, exonerated Klan political criminality, and obscured Klan's economic criminality. Using capital letters to emphasize the historical fraud that had been perpetrated, W.E.B. DuBois summed it up in *Black Reconstruction* (1935):

The South, finally, with almost complete unity, named the Negro as the main cause of Southern corruption. They said and reiterated this charge, until it became history: that the cause of dishonesty during Reconstruction was the fact that 4,000,000 disfranchised Black laborers, after 250 years of exploitation, had been given a legal right to have some voice in their own government, in the kinds of goods they would make and the sort of work they would do, and in the distribution of the wealth which they created.[37]

DuBois's logic, however, escaped most American whites and by the beginning of the twentieth century, Southern assumptions about African Americans had become national assumptions. The lack of any visible progress for blacks during and after Reconstruction confirmed the inferior nature of the black race in the view of a majority of whites both sides of the Mason-Dixon line. A host of 'race-thinkers' also emerged to warn Americans of the dangers presented by the freeing of a despised race and to satisfy an apparently insatiable demand among whites for information about black criminality and 'bestiality.' Abolitionist and reconstruction era evidence of organized and brutal white criminal activity was largely forgotten as whites flooded popular magazines, newspapers, scholarly journals, polemical tracts, monographs, and 'scientific' treatises with prejudiced detail on what became known as 'The Negro Problem.' Crimes committed by whites against blacks became somehow the fault of the blacks or their supporters. Crimes committed by blacks were constantly highlighted.

Organizing Crime in the New South

The massive dislocations of the war and attempt at political reform during Reconstruction scarcely disturbed the South's class structure. Southern society was still the most hierarchical in the nation, with large landowning planters at the top and masses of poor whites and blacks at the bottom. The South's economy depended on cotton as much as before the Civil War, but a slackening in world demand meant that prices fell. Agricultural overspecialization helped push the region deeper and deeper into debt, while industrialization was slow and mainly limited to parts of Tennessee, Kentucky, and Alabama.

In the New South, sharecropping replaced slavery as the predominant means of agricultural production, and in many ways, fraud and the now illegal use of force replaced the slave codes. In the sharecrop system, plantations and farms were divided up into smaller units, each worked by a black family. White landowners kept shares of the year's crops instead of paying wages or collecting rent. They also often doubled as merchants and often overcharged for the things they sold to sharecroppers, adding unreasonable interest rates for money owed. More importantly, landlords kept the books and could thus cheat the frequently illiterate cropper. According to many accounts, cheating African Americans became the norm. As late as the 1930s, Hortense Powdermaker estimated that 'not more than twenty-five or thirty per cent of the sharecroppers get an honest settlement.'[38] On each year's 'settling day' the croppers usually found themselves deep in debt. There was no choice but to pledge their labour to the landlords for another year. Those black sharecroppers fortunate enough to have honest landlords and productive strips of land only rarely succeeded in buying themselves into the independence of landownership. Intimidation and price inflation usually prevented land sales to blacks.[39]

Without the presence of federal troops, Southern blacks had very few legal protections and, instead, the law itself became an integral part of white oppression. Blacks were liable to be arrested for the most trivial of transgressions and then they would face law enforcement and court systems that were systematically biased.

Political power gave whites the opportunity to pass laws that forced blacks to accept conditions not far removed from slavery. Some laws were specifically designed to aid the planters' intention to restrict black efforts to change occupations. Such 'Anti-enticement' laws made it a criminal offence to offer employment to an individual already under contract, or to leave a job before a contract had expired. Otherwise informal agreements between planters or intermittent terror served the same purpose.[40]

Under Southern state laws and local ordinances, African Americans could be arrested for the most trivial of offences. In Selma, Alabama, for example, a journalist found a gang of black prisoners chained together and working in the street. The worst crime these had committed was 'using abusive language towards a white man.' Others were disorderly conduct, vagrancy, petty theft, and selling farm produce within the town limits.

Once arrested blacks faced legal machinery that was systematically weighted against them. White police, white lawyers, white judges, and white lawyers ensured virtual immunity for white transgressors and almost certain injustice for blacks. Police beat confessions out of them, lawyers swindled them, and magistrates, judges, and juries processed them through to peculiarly Southern and brutal systems of penal servitude.[41]

Chain gangs became familiar features of the Southern landscape. Mainly black prisoners worked for local municipalities on city streets or country roads. Conditions varied from lax to intolerable; too few records were kept to calculate the number of escapees or the number of casualties and deaths caused by overzealous guards. According to one report, many convicts simply 'disappeared as completely as if the earth had opened up and swallowed them. The very fact of their existence has been forgotten, except for the few at the humble home, who still wait and look in vain for him who does not come.'[42]

Bad as things were on the locally administered chain gangs, they were much worse on the convict lease system administered by the state in the interests of private profit. Convict leasing began soon after the end of the Civil War. Before the war there had been no black convicts in Southern state penitentiary systems; slaves had been punished by their owners. After the war, Southern states wanted to punish and control freedmen, but were not prepared to pay the costs of mass imprisonment. They therefore took to the idea of allowing businessmen to submit bids for the labour of convicted felons. The states leased convicts to the highest bidder, who was then responsible for feeding, clothing, and restraining the convicts. In return, the lessee received the right to use the convicts' labour as he wished.

To begin with the convicts were mainly leased out to plantation owners and railroad companies, but by the 1880s and 1890s more were employed in mining, especially in Alabama, Georgia, Florida, and Tennessee. Free labourers tended to be unwilling to risk their lives in Southern coal or phosphate mines, and so this new form of unfree labour offered a bonanza for capitalists. Edward Ayers has summed up the advantages: 'Labor costs were fixed and low, problems of labor uncertainty were reduced to the vanishing point, lucrative jobs could be undertaken that others would not risk, convicts could be driven at a pace free workers would not tolerate.' Convicts could be worked from dawn to dusk, for as long as it was 'light enough for a guard to see how to shoot,' every day of the year, whatever the weather, with minimal time for eating and sleeping.[43] A Southerner summed up the main difference between convict leasing and slavery in 1883, 'Before the war we owned the negroes. If a Man had a good negro, he could afford to take care of him: if he was sick get a doctor ... But these convicts: we don't own 'em. One dies, get another.'[44]

Corruption characterized the convict lease system. Party politicians took bribes from eager businessmen to vote the right way or exercise their influence. In 1882 Alabama's John H. Bankhead was described as part of a 'penitentiary ring' which was 'well organized, capable, unscrupulous, and rotten through and through and through ... The ring have shaped, moulded, framed the legislation of the session just closed.' Bankhead used his control over the lease system to build up a political machine that dominated state politics well into the twentieth century.[45] Prison officials, from the superintendents to the guards, took their share of the spoils in a system that paid everyone except those who did the work. Whippings, shootings, and the perilous and unsanitary working conditions account for a death rate of up to 40 per cent of the convicts. But no official was punished for taking bribes or for killing or maiming their charges.[46]

Convict leasing may have been accompanied by corruption and abuse but it remained a legal system of unfree labour. Peonage, the practice of holding a person to labour until a debt is paid, had been an illegal system of unfree labor since 1867 when a federal law was passed prohibiting debt servitude. By 1900, however, despite its illegality, peonage was an openly tolerated labour system in the South, accompanied by brutality, kidnapping, and corruption.[47]

Although some whites did experience peonage, many Southern blacks were particularly vulnerable to this slide back towards slavery. Denied education, susceptible to fraud by landlords or merchants, intimidated by the Klan or its successors, and threatened rather than protected by the legal system, thousands were forced by planters or other employers to work off debts that high interest rates perpetuated. Southern custom and contempt for the law overrode the federal law, and local officials could be relied on to look the other way or to pursue, capture, and return escapees. Southern states were not interested when the peonage laws were violated, and federal efforts usually failed either because blacks feared the consequences of testifying against whites, or the prejudice of juries made setting a black man's word against a white man futile.

Historians can only guess at the extent of peonage since only a few peons were brave enough to lodge complaints against their oppressors and still fewer could rely on impartial justice. In 1901 a grand jury in Anderson, South Carolina, heard charges of peonage against three of the 'largest planters and most influential men' in the county and, after an investigation indicted them for conspiracy, false imprisonment of black labourers, and assault and battery of a high and aggravated nature upon the labourers. The jury presentment 'told of illegal arrests and imprisonment, of cruel whippings, of prolonged imprisonment without even the farce of a trial, of kidnapping negroes from other counties, and even from Georgia.' Although this seemed to be clearly criminal activity, the prosecutor dropped the charges on the grounds of the unsettling effect such a case might have on the local labour situation. The planters pleaded guilty to simple assault charges for whipping their labourers and received fines of $50 each.[48]

In 1903 a series of cases in Alabama were highlighted by the Northern press and shed more light on a system that by then was well established. The New York *Evening Post*, for example, described a case involving John W. Pace. Pace had been a contractor for convict labour in Tallapoosa County since at least 1886. Because some convicts were legally on his plantation, Pace was able to supplement these with innocent black men and women. Constables kept him supplied with victims brought in on trivial charges, men supposedly on bond. Pace then forced all his labourers to work under armed guard, whether convicts or not. If Pace did not need extra labour, then constables would offer their charges to other local landowners.

Magistrates were another key part of this racket. W.D. Cosby, a rich landowner, held mock trials as justice of the peace to trick blacks into believing they had an obligation to work on Pace's plantations. In return James M. Kennedy, another justice, did the same to maintain Cosby's supply of cheap labour. Kennedy told a grand jury that 'it was sort of understood, that I was to try the men that Cosby wanted, and Cosby was to try the men that Pace wanted.' Pace pleaded guilty and was sentenced to five years in jail. After a series of legal manoeuvres, Pace was pardoned without serving any of his sentence and without having to end his business in convict labour.[49]

In Lowndes County, Sheriff J.W. Dixon had his own plantations and a reputation for killing or maiming labourers who objected to being forced to work for him. One of his victims did brave intimidation to agree to testify under federal protection. Dillard Freeman told of how he signed a contract to Dixon after the sheriff had paid his court fine. After that Freeman was beaten and dragged back to Dixon's plantation by a rope around his neck for attempting to visit his family. He was then whipped 'nigh unto death,' and chained to his bed, before being forced back to fieldwork. Freeman's testimony was recorded but no indictments were returned.[50]

Peonage was just as prevalent in other Southern states, most of whose cotton masters managed to operate their peonage systems without any serious interference from the law. Florida's turpentine companies produced their own variation. Men were taken out to camps in isolated forests, where they were obliged to buy their food and supplies from company commissaries. A worker would spend his advances on company goods marked up to 100 per cent more than their normal price. The longer a man stayed at the camp the more indebted he became. At work he was overseen by a foreman, a type described as 'the supreme authority in the camp ... To the niggers he is the law, judge, jury and executioner. If the worker tried to leave he faced arrest on some charge such as carrying a concealed weapon and faced jail unless he agreed to return to the camp.' The mounting debts of the worker were inconsequential to the bosses – they wanted the labour, and they used debt as an illegal control mechanism.[51]

Pete Daniel summed up the wider impact of peonage, it 'infected the South like a cancer, eating away at the economic freedom of blacks, driving the poor whites to work harder in order to compete with virtual slave labor, and preserving the class structure inherited from slavery days.'[52]

The story of the South after the Civil War is one of political terror, criminal exploitation, and economic stagnation. Southern industrial and agricultural development lagged far behind that of the North. It was a patchy, stunted process that ensured the prosperity of an elite of planters, merchants, and industrialists but left the great majority of black and white Southerners in debt traps and sinking deeper into poverty. The majority of Southern whites gained nothing from the criminal exploitation of blacks, but they tended to support all the legal and extra-legal constraints that kept blacks close to slavery. The most notable extra-legal constraint on blacks was lynching, which became almost a spectator sport for many whites by the end of the nineteenth century. Stewart Tolnay and E.M. Beck have identified almost 2,500 African-American victims of lynch mobs killed between 1882 and 1930 in ten Southern states. Impartial law and justice scarcely existed in the American South during this period. State and federal authorities were as negligent enforcing the laws against lynching as they were against peonage. Between 1887 and 1907 more people were lynched in the United States than were legally executed and no Southern white was convicted for his part in a lynching until 1908. Gangs of lynchers felt confident enough to brutalize and kill blacks openly, knowing that they had widespread community approval and often the connivance of local law enforcement officials. Some sheriffs willingly posed for photographs with the vigilante leaders. Hundreds of Southern whites watched shows that often included torture, dismemberment, and a share out of genitalia and other parts of the victim's body to friends and neighbours.[53]

Many blacks were lynched for alleged murder or rape. Fears of sexual contact between black males and white women were often enough to provoke mob action. Other lynchings occurred for a range of alleged offences ranging from arson or robbery to a black being 'uppity,' perhaps by smirking or a prolonged silence when spoken to by a white. At least some lynchings, however, were motivated by more than just crude ideas about popular justice or racial solidarity. Thomas Moss, Calvin McDowell, and Henry Stewart, for example, were the black co-owners of a grocery store in Memphis, Tennessee. They were lynched in August 1892 for no other known reason than their relative economic success and the business threat they constituted to a white grocer in the same neighbourhood.[54] Another victim, Will Millans, was a black coal miner in Brighton, Alabama, and one of the leaders of a strike in August 1909. After a mine was dynamited, he was lynched by a mob of whites that included at least two deputy sheriffs, despite the widespread belief that Millans had not been involved in the sabotage. Although the mine owners had most to gain from the lynching their role was not investigated in any depth.[55]

These exceptions aside, lynchings were usually spontaneous eruptions of hate rather than planned assassinations. However, in combination with countless beatings, whippings, and threats and individual acts of murder, and the lack of protection from white police forces, lynchings were part of what Eric Foner has described as a 'seamless web of oppression, whose interwoven economic, political and social strands all reinforced one another.'[56]

The complicity of local and state authorities and the hands-off approach of the federal government allowed Southern whites countless and continuing opportunities for successful and unpunished criminal activity. Neither theft nor violence against blacks was thought of as criminal. As Ned Cobb, a black farm-union organizer, put it, 'Nigger had anything a white man wanted, the white man took it.' Police protection was for whites only. As a Southern police official told police reformer Raymond Fosdick, Southern police departments had three classes of homicide before the First World War: 'If a nigger kills a white man, that's murder. If a white man kills a nigger that's justifiable homicide. If a nigger kills another nigger, that's one less nigger.' In the book *An American Dilemma* published in 1944, Gunnar Myrdal found that nothing much had changed two and a half decades later: 'Any white man can strike or beat a Negro, steal or destroy his property, cheat him in a transaction and even take his life without fear of legal reprisal.'[57]

Democratic rights did not apply to black people in the South. By 1900

Congress had repealed or the Supreme Court nullified much of the legislation designed to aid or protect black Americans. The federal government and the rest of the nation effectively acquiesced in Southern racism. They were content to look on as blacks were almost universally disenfranchised by a series of legal tricks that circumvented the 15th Amendment, the enactment of segregation or Jim Crow laws that evaded the 14th, and various other forms of force and fraud that diminished the 13th. President Teddy Roosevelt summed up the federal government's attitude to white Southern criminality best in a letter to one of the South's most persistent critics, Carl Schurz, in 1904: 'I feel just as you do on the nullification of the 14th, 15th and even 13th Amendments in the South; but as it has not as yet seemed absolutely necessary that I should notice this, I have refrained from doing so.'[58]

Roosevelt was acknowledging the strength of what became known as the 'Solid South.' For the first half of the twentieth century, the Democratic Party remained dominant in every state in the region. The only meaningful elections were the primaries, which were closed to most African Americans until the 1940s. The party ruled mainly in the interests of planters, industrialists, and other emerging business and professional groups and ensured that the South's congressional representatives would defend their peculiar sectional interests in national politics. Roosevelt and most of his successors did not dare risk alienating Southern congressmen who, through long service and seniority, had mastered the organizational and procedural structure of the U.S. Senate and House of Representatives.[59]

During the first half of the twentieth century, there was little pressure from the press or the academic community that might have shifted the national government's permissive or myopic attitude to Southern organized criminality. Cases of peonage and frauds against blacks were condemned in Northern newspapers and magazines as appalling but not as evidence of organized systems of crime which might have justified sustained federal intervention. The widespread assumption behind all this was that that 'benign neglect' was the best solution to the Southern race problem.[60]

Reflecting the same acknowledgment of Southern political realities as Roosevelt, the first national forum to consider organized crime as an identifiable problem also deliberately excluded racism from its understanding of this problem. In March 1929 President Herbert Hoover announced that former Attorney General George W. Wickersham would chair the National Commission on Law Observance and

Enforcement to investigate crime in America and make recommendations for reform of America's criminal justice and law enforcement systems. Leading African Americans made the case for a black representative to be appointed to the commission, arguing that the failure to enforce the nation's laws, especially the 14th and 15th Amendments to the Constitution, resulted in more suffering for blacks in the South than for any other single group in the nation. However, Hoover refused on the grounds that 'administrative principle' demanded that appointees to the commission must have the 'public interest' as their sole priority and he could not appoint representatives of 'any special group.'[61]

Hoover had carried several Southern states for the Republicans in the 1928 election and was unwilling to risk these inroads into previously solid Democratic support by allowing an investigation that would embarrass new converts. The Wickersham Commission focused on the nullification of the 18th or Prohibition Amendment in the North and West, and thus avoided the politically difficult task of addressing the continuing nullification of the 13th, 14th and 15th Amendments. There was thus no exposure of the ways in which African Americans were systematically robbed and cheated in the South, with the consent and often the involvement of law enforcers and criminal justice officials.

Reflecting similar evasions and omissions journalistic and academic conceptualizations of 'organized crime' in the 1920s focused on urban crime and simply did not acknowledge that organized criminality in the rural South existed. Frederic Thrasher, for example, author of the first book-length analysis of the problem in *The Gang* (1927) asserted that modern crime had only recently become 'organized and continuous.'[62] Many other writers would follow his lead and misleadingly suggest that the beginnings of 'modern' organized crime could be dated from the Prohibition era.

As we have seen, many of the violent and corrupt characteristics associated with the problem of organized crime today existed in the South that emerged after the Civil War. However, by the time organized crime was recognized as an identifiable problem in the United States, a general racist consensus ensured that no commentator made the connection. Unlike Italian-American gangsters, those involved in Southern organized crime did not engage in internecine gang warfare and very rarely finished up in prison. White criminals in the South escaped labels like 'gangsters' and 'racketeers' and many doubtless ended their days as respectable models of Southern gentility.

Racism and America's Moral Crusade

Ironically, while local, state, and national authorities allowed Southern lawlessness and systems of crime to function, both the region and the nation were looking for ways to establish a moral order in America. In a movement that gathered pace towards the end of the nineteenth century many mainly middle-class Americans had joined societies devoted to imposing virtue and abstinence on their fellows. These groups of concerned citizens lobbied in city halls, state capitals, and Washington D.C. for more laws prohibiting behaviour that they considered to be unacceptable, notably gambling, commercialized sex, drinking liquor, and the use of certain kinds of drugs. The next section examines the racism that lay behind the establishment of anti-drug and anti-alcohol laws that would have the unanticipated consequences of boosting the prospects for illegal enterprise immeasureably.

Prejudice against the Chinese was behind the earliest local, state, and national legislation prohibiting the smoking of opium during the 1880s. Propagandists, especially in the West, spoke of 'yellow fiends' or 'yellow devils' enslaving white women and children with their seductive poison. California's state legislature responded to such messages by passing laws that outlawed opium dens. In 1887 the federal government added legislation that outlawed opium importation and smoking among Chinese, but, significantly, not among white Americans.[63]

Southern propagandists soon followed suit and their concern with the 'negro problem' kept then in the vanguard of U.S. effort to legislate an end to 'vice' and 'intemperance.' Many political and religious leaders argued that allowing Southern blacks to drink alcohol or take drugs was asking for trouble; it fed their 'animalism,' and thus threatened the white race in general, white womanhood in particular, and strained relations between the races beyond endurance.

Local Southern newspapers and police officials began expressing concerns about cocaine and opiate use among blacks, in particular, and the poor in general from the late 1890s. In Tennessee, for example, the *Chattanooga Times*, reported the warnings of the local police chief: 'Before 1898 ... the negroes and the low class whites, especially women of the town, knew nothing whatever of the cocaine habit. Before that time they went to the dogs by the whiskey and morphine route, a large number of them being confirmed morphine eaters. But ... they learned a new vice – the cocaine habit – the result of which will be that if it continues many more years, we will have more lunatics on our hands than we know what to do with. The drug is far worse in its effects than either morphine or whiskey.'[64]

In May 1900 the same newspaper reported the sale of hundreds of small packages of cocaine by pharmacists and warned that the 'evil has reached alarming proportions.' The Chattanooga city council soon responded to such stories by passing a measure intended to curtail the non-medical use of cocaine and morphine, prohibiting the sale of either substance, except on a physician's prescription. Other major cities in the state soon followed Chattanooga's lead.[65]

In similar ways prejudice against blacks added fuel to the arguments of those seeking to suppress the use of cocaine nationally and internationally. In 1910, for example, the *Report on the International Opium Commission* claimed that cocaine made rapists of black males, and that blacks achieved immense strength and cunning under its influence. Dr Hamilton Wright, the man most responsible for this report and for much of the national and international anti-drug effort that followed, came to the conclusion that 'this new vice, the cocaine vice, the most serious to be dealt with, has proved to be the creator of criminals and unusual forms of violence, and it has been a potent incentive in driving the humbler negroes all over the country to abnormal crimes.'[66] Wright's most significant contribution was to help to draft and promote a bill that was passed by Congress as the Harrison Narcotic Act, which will be discussed further in Chapter 4.

Variations on the anti-drug themes were also used in the successful campaigns to prohibit alcohol in every Southern state by the First World War and by Southern representatives in the congressional debates that led to national prohibition in 1919.

Some argued that white and black mixing in the saloon would weaken the 'stronger' race and promote all kinds of vices. 'The saloon,' according to one concerned Southerner, 'is a place of rendezvous for all classes of the low and vulgar, a resort for degraded whites and their more degraded Negro associates, the lounging place for adulterers, lewd women, the favorite haunt of gamblers, drunkards and criminals. Both blacks and whites mix and mingle together as a mass of degraded humanity in this cesspool of iniquity.'[67]

Others concentrated on the need to protect white women from 'drink-crazed' black men. 'Caucasian virtue,' according to the *Atlanta Georgian* in 1906, constantly faced the peril of the 'most murderous and beastly of crimes.'[68] Two years later *Collier's Weekly* made the connection between liquor and rape explicit when it related that 'the primitive negro field hand ... pays his fifty cents for a pint of Mr Levy's gin' and 'absorbs not only its toxic heat, but absorbs also the suggestion subtly conveyed, that it contains aphrodisiacs. He sits in the road or in the ally at the height of his debauch, looking at that obscene picture of a white woman on the label, drinking in the invitation which it carries. And then comes – opportunity.'[69]

The Reverend Wilbur Fisk Crafts, president of the International Reform Bureau, even managed to use the linkage to exonerate white lynchers. He told his audience to read the accounts of lynching 'in the black belt of the United States' and ask themselves 'what devil's girdle has changed so many Negroes into sensual hyenas.' The answer, he claimed, was that 'seventy-five per cent of all liquor sales in the South Carolina's dispensaries were to Negroes.' Liquor was the cause of rape and therefore brought about the punishment: 'The souls of the black men are poisoned with alcohol and their bodies in due course drenched in petroleum and burned'[70]

Under slavery, it was argued, every plantation had been a prohibition island but the 'license' of freedom made liquor the 'the most oppressive force' in black America. The only solution for the black man's terrible biological craving for alcohol was to imitate the restrictive policies of the U.S. government towards the Indians and the European powers towards the 'inferior' peoples under their control. As a result every Southern state had prohibited alcohol by the First World War.

Once passed, however, enforcement of the Southern Prohibition laws was minimal and largely directed against blacks. The South was already by reputation the hardest-drinking section of the American nation, and it continued to be able to make this claim after the dry laws were passed.

Appropriately, it was a Southerner that introduced the first national prohibition resolution in the House of Representatives. In 1914 Richmond Pearson Hobson, a congressman from Alabama and someone who had made a lucrative career out of moral crusading, used the following theory of race to make his case: 'Liquor will actually make a brute out of a Negro, causing him to commit unnatural crimes ... The effect is the same on the white man, though the white man being further evolved it takes longer time to reduce him to the same level. Starting young, however, it does not take a very long time to speedily cause a man in the forefront of civilization to pass through the successive stages and become semicivilized, semisavage, savage, and, at last, below the brute.'[71] Hobson's resolution failed to get the necessary two-thirds majority at this time, but it helped to bring the 18th Amendment to the Constitution a step nearer. Hobson went on to bring his talents and pseudo-scientific reasoning to the crusade against drugs.

Racists such as Hobson and the others quoted were, of course, just part of America's uniquely coercive moral crusade. As we shall see in Chapter 4, business interests, church groups, and other reform groups all had their own reasons to support prohibition, and the campaigns were professionally organized by the Anti-Saloon League. The crusade's eventual success, however, would not have been possible without the South's commitment to the cause and the more general racism that pervaded all parts of the nation.

Even before the twentieth-century, moonshining, the illegal distilling of liquor, was already a minor industry in the South. In parts of Georgia, for example, government efforts against the small farmers involved in the trade were met by the rapid formation of secret societies. These killed any they suspected of informing and even, on several occasions, the government's own agents. It also transpired that not every agent had been doing his job honestly. In 1895 it was reported that some agents had brought charges against innocent people as a way of increasing their fees and had also received pay-offs for protecting illicit distillers. For a number of years, the counties of Murray and Gordon, in particular, experienced a wave of terror, betrayal, and corruption that would later be repeated nationally as a direct result of the federal prohibitions of alcohol and drugs.[72]

Organized Crime as a Foreign Import

Scapegoat explanations for the problems of the United States have long been widely accepted by a large proportion of the population, particularly explanations that pinned the blame on those at the bottom of society, especially newly arrived migrants and immigrants. Complaints about the criminal tendencies of foreigners increased in intensity during the nineteenth century and many political speeches, official reports, and magazine articles suggested that conspiracies among immigrants constituted a threat to the nation. In 1835, for example, an article in the New York *Journal of Commerce* warned: 'We have now to resist the *momentous* evil that threatens us from *Foreign Conspiracy.* The Conspirators are in the *foreign importations.* Innocent and guilty are brought over together. We must of necessity suspect them all.'[73] Two decades later the mayor of New York made a public plea to President Franklin Pierce to protect New Yorkers from 'the evil influences' of these people and their 'contaminating effect upon all those who come within the range of their depraved minds.'[74] Similar xenophobic assumptions lay behind the concept of an American 'underworld,' based more on race and ethnicity than class, which began to emerge after the Civil War during the country's first intense period of industrialization and urbanization. This is illuminated by an early example of the journalistic criminal exposé.

Edward Crapsey's book entitled *The Nether Side of New York; or the Vice, Crime and Poverty of the Great Metropolis* was published in 1872. The *New York Times'* reviewer called it an 'an astonishing revelation' and felt it was important that Crapsey had pointed out elements below respectable society 'as destructive to its existence as are the earthquake and volcano to the fair face of the earth.'[75]

Crapsey introduced several themes that would recur as the understanding of 'organized crime' was being shaped. First, was his association of the problem of crime with the masses of poor, foreign-born immigrants or black migrants then filling U.S. cities. He argued that these immigrants and migrants were the cause of New York's crime problems, partly because these groups were naturally prone to crime and 'vice.' Both xenophobia and bigotry are revealed in the following description of the Arch Block in Manhattan: 'How vile a spot can be found in the heart of a metropolis, and how bestial humanity can become, can be best seen during the early hours of any hot summer night, when Arch Block life is at its windows, in the streets, or lounging at the doors of the groggeries and groceries. Among all the thousands of human beings, of whom nearly half are negroes and the majority of the remainder Italians, there will hardly one cleanly, pleasant, humanized face. The men with few exceptions, are idlers, brawlers, thieves, or something worse than either, and the women harlots or something still less reputable.'[76]

Crapsey did not, however, suggest that immigrants and African Americans actually *organized* crime. The crime organizers in his book were receivers, confidence men, private detectives, Wall Street manipulators, and most importantly the city's leading politicians; these all exploited New York's 'diversity of races.' He claimed that New York had been largely deserted by its middle and upper classes and therefore the city, 'drifted from bad to worse, and became the prey of professional thieves, ruffians, and political jugglers. The municipal government shared in the vices of the people, and New York became a city paralyzed in the hands of its rulers ... It was the source of power and plunder. Its appointees knew its arts, and so successfully practiced them, that the whole municipality became a closed corporation of municipal rascality.'[77]

Crapsey also feared that such vices as gambling, prostitution, and drinking were becoming increasingly institutionalized, pervasive, and destructive. Card games, for example, were organized by a 'confederacy of roguery.'[78] Prostitution was not just an 'evil' that afflicted the poor but one which had 'ramifications through all circles of society, and is thus corroding where its presence is not suspected.'[79] Saloons were centres for all other vices and were thus 'the alluring doorways to moral death,' 'poisoning the whole body' of the city and they now had 'more power for evil than ever before.'[80]

The author's final prescient theme was that law enforcers were unable to match the increasing sophistication of criminals: 'Improvements in the appliances of the law for the detection and prevention of crime have not kept pace with the improved devices of the criminal to evade them.'[81]

Crapsey did not make the solutions to his lurid collection of felonies, misdemeanours, and debaucheries explicit, but the implications of his work must have been obvious to his mainly Protestant, middle-class readers. First, immigration should be curtailed. Second, city government, particularly the police and courts, should be reformed. Finally, the laws prohibiting gambling and prostitution and those regulating drinking places should be more strictly enforced. In the following decades many more middle-class Americans would be convinced by the need for action in all of these areas.

A few years after the publication of *The Nether Side* the conviction of a number of Irishmen for a series of murders in the anthracite mining area of Schuylkill County in Northeastern Pennsylvania gave some commentators the chance to give organized crime a more specific ethnic identification than Crapsey had. In 1877 F.P. Dewees published a book about these Irishmen, calling them members of the Molly Maguires, an alleged inner circle of a fraternal society of Irish immigrants, the Ancient Order of Hiberians (AOH). He made the following claim: 'The existence of a band of miscreants regularly organized for the commission of crime, extending throughout the anthracite coal-fields, had been suspected for twenty years past. Frequent and flagrant violations of laws, which, in the mode of execution and in the instruments employed, displayed organization, system, and a defined policy, induced this suspicion.'[82]

Dewees was reflecting the prosecution's case in a series of recently completed trials of alleged Mollies, which will be described in detail in Chapter 3. At this point it is enough to say that he was grossly exaggerating the degree of organization among the Mollies. The idea of organized crime as a specifically Irish import diminished almost as soon as it had achieved its purpose and the defendants had been convicted. The idea of organized crime as a specifically Italian import began to take root more successfully after a series of incidents in New Orleans in the last decade of the nineteenth century.

From the 1880s Italians were the largest ethnic group to arrive in United States and they received the most violent and abusive welcome of any of the European newcomers. Reports of beatings, shootings, and lynchings came in from all parts of the country. Instead of condemning these acts of violence committed by U.S. citizens, some politicians and commentators looked for ways to excuse them.

They achieved this most effectively by shifting attention to Italian criminality. Ordinary crimes committed in Italian neighbourhoods became more significant when the perpetrators were said to use 'stiletto knives,' and 'muskets with the barrels shortened,' to belong to a 'secret, malignant, treacherous organization of assassins.' Italians became stereotyped as particularly prone to violence, vengeance, and conspiracy.[83]

In Louisiana it was also felt by many that the new arrivals from Sicily and southern Italy were no better than blacks and should be denied the right to vote. The Homer Clipper, for example, wrote that Italians 'are corrupt and purchasable and according to the spirit of our meaning when we speak of white man's government, they are as black as the blackest Negro in existence.' The Baton Rouge Bulletin felt that 'corrupt voters – principally Negroes, Dagoes, and other irresponsible citizens' should be excluded from voter registration.[84]

The word 'Mafia' itself was first commonly used when anti-Italian feeling was at its peak following the killing of New Orleans Police

Chief David Hennessy on 15 October 1890. There had been several other unsolved assassinations of public figures in the city's recent history and no one will ever know for sure who shot Hennessy. But, two pieces of circumstantial evidence suggested that Italians may have been responsible. First, Hennessy had been investigating a commercial dispute over parts of the South American fruit trade between rival groups of Southern Italians and Sicilians at the time of the shooting. Second, on his deathbed, Hennessy was reported to have said that 'dagoes' shot him.

The city's mayor, Joseph Shakspeare, reacted to the murder by sending large numbers of police into the Italian sector. These arrested more than a hundred Sicilians and Italians and on 18 October the mayor announced:

> Heretofore these scoundrels have confined their murderings among themselves. None of them have ever been convicted because of the secrecy with which the crimes have been committed and the impossibility of getting evidence from the people of their own race to convict. Bold, indeed, was the stroke, aimed at their first American victim. A shining mark have they selected on which to write with the assassin's hand their contempt for the civilization of the new world. We owe it to ourselves and to everything that we hold sacred in this life to see to it that this blow is the last. We must teach these people a lesson they will not forget for all time.[85]

The city's police department released a list of 'assassinations, murders, and affrays committed by Sicilians and Italians' over the previous twenty-five years to add some credibility to Shakspeare's charge. When historian Humbert S. Nelli researched these murders he found no substance in the charge that they were somehow connected as Mafia executions. By comparing the list with coroners' reports Nelli found that the list 'contained errors in almost every case outlined and each error served to blacken the reputation of New Orleans Italians.'[86]

Nine Italians were placed on trial for the murder of Hennessy on 16 February 1891. After three weeks of inconsistent and contradictory testimony the jury found six of the accused not guilty and could not agree on a verdict for the remainder. Many of the city's most prominent citizens refused to accept this leniency and called for a public meeting 'to remedy the failure of justice in the Hennessy case.'[87] On 14 March speakers at this meeting urged a crowd of several thousand citizens to storm the parish prison. Prison officers decided not to resist and the shout soon went up, 'Kill the Dagoes!'[88] Eleven Italians were shot or clubbed to death, before being lynched purely for spectacle. Four of the victims had never been implicated in the Hennessy case; they happened to be Italian and unfortunate to be in the wrong place at the wrong time. None of the lynchers were brought to trial.

In the wake of the Hennessy affair many newspaper and magazine articles warned of the dangers posed by the alleged secret society while few condemned the lawless actions of the citizens of New Orleans. The Hennessy crime, according to *Harper's Weekly*, was committed by 'an oath-bound, murderous society, long formidable in Sicily, and transplanted to this country by Sicilian immigrants.' Senator Henry Cabot Lodge, writing in the *North American Review*, noted that the Mafia was 'a secret society bound by the most rigid oaths and using murder as a means of maintaining its discipline and carrying out its decrees ... It is anything but self-limited, and in a political soil like that of New Orleans it was pretty sure to extend.'[89]

In reality, the contemporary accounts grossly exaggerated the importance of Sicilian and Southern Italian crime in New Orleans. Without doubt some Mafiosi did accompany the millions of law-abiding Italian immigrants to America and some newcomers did join Mafia-type groups with initiation rituals involving finger-prickings and secrecy oaths. Organized violence, trickery, and intimidation existed in Italian-American communities, just as it did in other communities. However, it is fanciful to describe New Orleans–based, small-time criminals as members of highly structured organizations. Even banded together they were a small minority of parasitic individuals, gaining a limited degree of power and profit by preying on their neighbours. Their crimes dwindle in significance when compared with those of the white supremacists described earlier. The lynchings are better understood as examples of Southern lawlessness in a city and a region with a long-established reputation for corrupt, selective, and often non-existent law enforcement.

Despite the claims of many writers there is no convincing evidence to suggest that any of the Italians involved in the Hennessy affair went on to establish a criminal dynasty in New Orleans. Charles Matranga, who escaped the lynch mob, was widely believed to be the city's 'Mafia' leader, and still features as a kind of founding father of the American Mafia in popular crime histories.[90] David Chandler's account, for example, elevated Matranga to the position of Mafia 'Boss of Bosses' after the 1891 disputes, and suggested he held that position until 1923 before handing it over to his chosen successor, Sam Carolla.[91] Humbert Nelli's more meticulous research, however, refutes such notions by listing the mundane highlights of the rest of his life: 'Nothing occurring in the remaining fifty-two years of his life connected him to criminal activities. With his second wife, Elizabeth Hazel Dullenty, he led a quiet life as a stevedore for the Standard Fruit Company, later the United Fruit Company, until his retirement after fifty years of service in 1918 (he had started work at the age of 11). He died in 1943 at the age of 86.'[92]

At least three of the victims of the New Orleans lynch mob were Italian citizens, and the Italian government demanded both an indemnity and the prosecution of the leaders of the mob. Shortly afterwards, the Italian envoy at Washington was recalled. The press reaction to this reflected, as J. Alexander Karlin has described, 'the rising tide of fin de siècle militant American nationalism and was an important step in the previously slow road to reunion between North and South after the Civil War.'

Newspapers had misleadingly circulated rumours that the Italians were prepared to go to war on the issue. According to a poem published in the Portland *Oregonian*, for example, 'In the spring the Dago fancy / Fiercely turns to thought of war.'

The 'war scare,' once created, inspired thousands of Americans from every part of the country to volunteer for military service. A resident of Sparta, Georgia, for example, telegraphed the War Department, with the offer to raise 'a company of unterrified Georgian rebels to invade Rome, disperse the Mafia, and plant the Stars and Stripes on the dome of St Peters [sic].' The day after the announcement of the envoy's withdrawal, newspapers forgot their sectional differences with a display of national unity unknown since before the Civil War. The formerly anti-Southern Chicago *Inter-Ocean* reflected the new consensus with the announcement that an Italian attack on New Orleans would be met by 'Uncle Sam and the flag' as 'this is a Nation with a big N.' The war scare subsided when it became clear that Italy had no intention of going to war over the lynchings.[93] However, the whole series of incidents had boosted American nationalism. This fact was probably not lost on politicians who had ambitions for national office. Theodore Roosevelt, for example, called the lynchings 'a rather good thing,' and boasted that he did so at a party where there were 'various dago diplomats.'[94] Roosevelt, of course, later went on to achieve great acclaim during the war with Spain in 1898, a time of when nationalistic unity became even more focused. He became President in 1901.

The New Orleans incidents and wild jumps of imagination helped establish press and popular stereotypes that could be applied wherever Italian Americans existed and committed crimes: Italian Americans were characterized as prone to violence, vendettas, and extortion, and unwilling to cooperate with the authorities. Between the 1890s and the 1920s almost any crime committed in Italian neighbourhoods could be represented as evidence of the Mafia menace. The *New York Times*, for example, began to call for a special police force to combat what it termed 'organized crime' among the low-class Italians of the city. In 1904 such a squad was formed under the leadership of Detective Joseph Petrosino. The squad's investigations revealed that Italian gangsters victimized other Italians, but only as individuals or as part of small, unconnected groups – never as part of a large conspiracy. However, in 1909, when an unknown assassin murdered Petrosino on an investigative trip to Sicily, some contemporary commentators made the unjustifiable assumption that this was evidence of the Mafia's cohesion and awesome power.[95]

Between the 1920s and the 1940s interest in Italian conspiracies declined; reports of Mafia crime inspired little interest and proved nothing more threatening than the fact that Italian immigrant violence was almost entirely restricted to the Little Italies of a few major cities. It was not until after the Second World War that government agencies and popular writers would associate organized crime almost exclusively with Italians and look for historical justification, however inadequate, in the Hennessy and Petrosino affairs for their myopia.

Two New York journalists led the way in popularizing and adding 'history' to an idea that took root during the Cold War: the Mafia controlled organized crime in America. Jack Lait and Lee Mortimer in a book called *Chicago Confidential* (1950) and in three sequels were the first to crystallize a historical explanation for organized crime that has since been endlessly recycled. According to the formula that emerged, a secret criminal brotherhood developed in feudal Sicily, spread to New Orleans and the rest of urban America at the end of the nineteenth century, and dominated U.S. organized crime by the middle of the twentieth.

Racketeering in America, according to Lait and Mortimer, was the contribution of 'immigrant hordes' that lived 'like animals in poverty and inferiority mostly in squalid slums.'[96] The city of New Orleans, at the end of the nineteenth century, was peopled by:

> The riffraff of the Mississippi, the sailors from the swill of Europe, Cuba and South and Central America, and a wave of immigration from Italy, which formed the first Mafia on this continent, brought together three-quarters of a million of the low-bred and inter-bred scum of the world. (The city) drew the dregs of Texas, Alabama, Arkansas and Tennessee, ruffians of similar enough propensities to be assimilated in the lower layers of brawling, boozing, fornicating laborers, and loafers and illiterate Negroes, who flocked there for the fleshpots of the city, not for the hopes and aspirations of stolid North-European immigrants who set forth to the promised land of small farms, little stores and the dream of some day owning a cottage.[97]

Anecdotes and exaggerated claims about Italian-American gangsters are followed by the assertion that the Mafia is 'The super-government which now has tentacles reaching into the Cabinet and the White House itself, almost every state capital, huge Wall Street interests, and connections in Canada, Greece, China, and Outer Mongolia, and even through the Iron Curtain into Soviet Russia.'[98] The organization, they elaborated, is 'run from above, with reigning headquarters in Italy and American headquarters in New York.' It 'controls all sin' and 'practically all crime in the United States.'[99]

The authors failed to produce evidence of the Mafia as a coherent, centralized, nationwide conspiracy and instead their four collaborative books are part of a well-established racist and xenophobic tradition in American writing, as the following selections indicate: 'Bronzeville' in Chicago was described as being transformed in two decades into an area of 'filth and overcrowding' where you find 'dingy dens, depraved homosexual exhibitionism, lumber-camp licentiousness, drunkenness, dope and every sinister sign of virtually uncontrolled abandon.' They described the 'high wages for former field hands' as starting the 'Bronzeville boom with its drinking and doping and the resultant laxities that blossomed into flagrant vice' and the 'reefer parties with their dark, crowded rooms where the mixed sexes reached orgiastic stimulation.'[100] America's youth, according to Lait and Mortimer, congregate in

juke-box joints, soda-dispensaries and hot record shops, especially the latter. Like a heathen religion, it is all tied up with tom-toms and hot jive and ritualistic orgies of erotic dancing, weed-smoking and mass mania, with African jungle background.

Many music shops purvey dope; assignations. White girls are recruited for colored lovers. Another cog in the giant delinquency machine is the radio disc jockey. This character has become the high priest of this strong cult. We know that many platter spinners are hop-heads. Many others are Reds, left-wingers, or hecklers of social convention ... Through disc-jocks, kids get to know colored and other 'hot' musicians; they frequent places the radio oracles plug, which is done with design and malice, to hook juves and guarantee and a new generation subservient to the Mafia.[101]

'Degraded' Negroes and Puerto Ricans in New York were mainly 'on relief or get welfare handouts, with which they buy dope ... These animals have been fed on propaganda so long, they assume the community owes them not only a living, but junk-money.'[102]

Senator Estes Kefauver read *Chicago Confidential* while he was preparing for a nationwide congressional investigation into organized crime and was impressed enough to arrange meetings with Mortimer, and to flatter the author on the floor of the Senate, in book advertisements, and in a testimonial letter to Mortimer's boss, the publisher William Randolph Hearst.[103] As we shall see in Chapter 5, the Kefauver committee's hugely influential interpretation of organized crime was no more than a more temperate version of the conspiracy theory of the two journalists.

Literary critics reviewed the Confidential books respectfully and Americans bought these books by the hundreds of thousands. Reviewers in the *New York Times* described *New York Confidential* as 'this sprightly book,' and *Chicago Confidential* as 'a shocking social document.' The review of *U.S.A. Confidential* opened brightly by noting that 'Lait and Mortimer have been dropping lighted firecrackers down the nation's sewers for some time and by now quite a crowd has gathered to watch the excitement.'[104] All four books were repeatedly reprinted to meet the demand.

The first book-length and rather more coherent development of organized crime as a foreign import thesis was *Mafia* by Ed Reid, published in 1952. Like others that followed, Reid stripped away most of the overt racism of Lait and Mortimer's work but the framework was always directly descended from earlier less bashful racist conspiracy theories. According to Reid, 'The Mediterranean island of Sicily centuries ago gave to the world the monster known to history as the Mafia ...

The Mafiosi preyed on their own people and then on the world.'[105] Reid elaborated by including accounts of the Hennessy and Petrosino murders and concluded that the Mafia was 'history's greatest threat to morality' and 'the principal fount of all crime in the world, controlling vice, gambling, the smuggling and sale of dope, and other sources of evil.'[106]

Countless newspaper and magazine articles, books, films, and television documentaries have since repeated the same perspective on American organized crime history. The idea of organized crime as a foreign implant meanwhile could not be beaten as an easy explanation for the country's organized crime problems.

The Hennessy affair marked the genesis of a legend that still helps government officials, popular writers, and academics bypass racism in their analyses. When mainstream accounts of organized crime history feature the South, white supremacist crime is ignored. The South's main significance instead is its position as the entrance point for the Mafia into the United States. In 1972, for example, the Federal Bureau of Investigation (FBI), using its preferred term, reported that the 'the first 'family' of what has now become known as La Cosa Nostra (LCN) came from Sicily and settled in New Orleans after the Civil War. In 1979 the Select Committee on Assassination of the United States House of Representatives made a similar assertion: 'The New Orleans Mafia had been the first branch of the Mafia in America (the Sicilian La Cosa Nostra had entered the United States through the port of New Orleans during the 1880s.)'[107] A representative assertion from recent popular literature is in Stephen Fox's book entitled *Blood and Power: Organized Crime in Twentieth Century America*: 'The Mafia first surfaced in New Orleans after the Civil War.'[108] A criminology textbook, published in 1995, opened its section on the history of organized crime with the following: 'Organized crime had its origins in the great wave of immigrants from southern Italy (especially from Sicily) to the United States between 1875 and 1920.'[109]

In these ways and others to which we shall return in Chapter 5, organized crime history has been put in its own, mainly foreign compartment, far away from the 'master narrative' of American history. The idea of organized crime as a foreign import meanwhile functioned as a smokescreen for a product that was homegrown.

Chapter 3

Organized Crime and Corporate Power, 1865–1950

While the North–South conflict, as we have seen, devastated the South, the war boosted industry and agriculture in the North and West and helped the United States achieve the economic breakthrough that within a generation, made it the world's leading industrial nation. The nation's vast areas of rich agricultural land and apparently unlimited resources of raw materials were more systematically exploited after the war as modern technology evolved at just the right time to sustain a rapid rate of industrial growth. From being a land of agriculture and small workshops in 1861 the United States rapidly became a land of machines, electricity, and steel, with national and international markets. Vast amounts of foreign and domestic capital flowed into manufacturing and extractive industries in a country whose priority was always commercial and industrial growth. By the twentieth century the country outstripped all others in terms of industrial production, capital investment, and numbers of people employed in manufacturing, mining, construction, and service occupations. By the beginning of the First World War more than 30 per cent of the world's manufactured goods were made in the United States.[1]

Despite these impressive increases in productivity, conflict and a general economic instability also characterized the years between the end of the Civil War and the beginning of the twentieth century. Class conflict during these years can without much exaggeration be called a war between capital and labour. Employers typically responded to any collective pressure for higher wages or better working conditions with the lockout, the importation of strikebreakers, and physical intimidation – and in response worker violence escalated. There were also major depressions during each of the decades following the end of the war, accompanied by the collapse of many businesses.

For business leaders, the causes of their problems lay in overproduction, 'cut-throat' competition based mainly on the reduction of prices, and the inability to control an increasingly militant or unruly working class. The answer for some lay in the concentrating power by amalgamating and combining formerly competing businesses. On the one hand, it was felt that corporate dominance over finance and industry would allow for the control of production according to demand and the reduction of ruinous competition. On the other hand, large corporations would also be better able to develop more effective ways of breaking strikes and eliminating or at least controlling unions. In addition to these advantages the corporate form of capitalism would also keep the personal fortunes of capitalists safe; if their companies failed, their liability was limited to their actual investments.

For such reasons, businessmen such as Cornelius Vanderbilt and Jay Gould in railroads, John D. Rockefeller in oil, Henry Frick and Andrew Carnegie in steel, and John Pierpoint Morgan in investment banking established monopolies and oligopolies in their fields. Although they faced much economic and political opposition, a relatively small number of businessmen were able to dominate the U.S. economy by the end of the nineteenth century. Opponents castigated the ruthless and often illegal methods used to drive out competitors and trade unions and drive up profits. Supporters pointed to beneficial results of the ending of ruinous competition, such as business stability and steadily declining prices. Vanderbilt and the rest were 'robber barons' to the first group, careless of the damage they did to society. To the latter group, they were pioneering 'captains of industry' and largely responsible for America's rise to greatness.

This was, as already noted, a period of brutal class conflict in the Untied States. Both sides in U.S. industrial disputes used violence, but the employers used it more systematically and effectively, exploiting technicalities of the law to preserve their interests. Many businessmen were prepared, for example, to employ gangsters to break strikes or unions. Many unions later responded by employing their own gangsters. Once invited into the mainstream of the U.S. economy many gangsters decided to stay around and take what they could, mainly from vulnerable small business activities, union pension and welfare funds, and other industrial and commercial rackets.

Business leaders had also built up large bureaucratic structures and prepared the way for the decline of their own style of proprietary power. Although decisions and responsibilities were still concentrated at the top of corporate hierarchies, the complicated and fragmented new bureaucratic arrangements had the effect of making accountability for illegal or harmful activities far more difficult. At the same time, the new impersonal corporations proved to be just as likely to put profit ahead of the health and safety of workers, communities, and consumers as their founders.

According to Martin Sklar's book *The Corporate Reconstruction of American Capitalism*, the new corporate capitalist executives also became far more involved in institutional spheres outside of their direct economic interest than their proprietary predecessors: 'Many of them functioned on a broader social stage as leaders in commercial bodies, civic associations, reform clubs, and party politics. They were active in the institutional spheres of religion, culture, higher education, philanthropy, and organizations for inter-regional projects or development ... They were people of power, prestige, and leadership in the society at large.'[2]

These new people of power also had new ideas about the role of government. Their proprietary predecessors usually held that governments should do little more than maintain order, conduct public services at minimum cost, and subsidize business development when appropriate, but otherwise do nothing to disrupt the laws of free competition. More modern capitalists, however, expected much more government involvement in the economy and society and many became active participants in the era that would later be labelled Progressive. Business interests could not initiate or control all economic and social reform during these years but, as several historians have demonstrated, they could set outer limits on what could succeed.[3] By the time of the First World War, although mainstream American thinking had become pro-state, businessmen succeeded in ensuring that it also remained just as pro-business and dedicated to private profit as before. In the new regulated business environment, capitalism was to be checked, but not in ways that constituted any effective deterrent to organized crime activity within legal markets.

Throughout this period there was no fixed understanding of the phrase 'organized crime,' but the trend towards a reduced and compartmentalized understanding of organized crime had already begun. As we have seen, whole areas of U.S. organized crime history were unknown or unrecognized by early twentieth century Americans. Crimes against Native and African Americans were either excused or forgotten by the beginning of the twentieth century and not even the best-informed authorities on crime would have seriously considered 'the Indian problem' and 'the Negro problem' as part of the 'organized crime' problem. The systematic criminal activity of businessmen, as we shall see, was considered to be a serious problem until around the time of the First World War. After that, corporations successfully disassociated themselves from the taint of any kind of criminality.

Crime and the Rise of Big Business

After the Civil War, railroad construction accelerated and the world's most significant transportation infrastructure was established. By 1869 railroad networks linked city to city, ocean to ocean, and producers to consumers, and they kept on expanding. By sharply reducing the costs of moving goods and people, railroads opened up vast new areas to commercial farming and made the exploitation of natural resources such as coal and oil far more profitable. In the process an immense boost was therefore given to the growth of cities, most notably Chicago and Kansas City in the Midwest, and later in the century, San Francisco, Los Angeles, Portland, and Seattle on the Pacific Coast.

The construction and operation of the railroads, however, not only made America's rapid development possible, but also helped make a number of crooks spectacularly rich. Potential profits from railroading were immense, and the early battles for control of the railroads could be brutally competitive. The victors in these battles tended to be those best able to bribe, blackmail, extort, exploit, and intimidate. As noted in Chapter 1, Cornelius Vanderbilt had experience in all these techniques long before he got involved in railroads. In 1869 E.L. Godkin, the conservative editor of *The Nation*, was the first to describe Vanderbilt as the modern equivalent of 'medieval barons.' Like these he 'knew how to take advantage of lines of travel,' and 'had the heart and hand to levy contributions on all who passed his way.'[4]

Since a number of other businessmen were involved in similar activities at the same time, there were bound to be clashes. Vanderbilt won most of his business battles, but his one major defeat came in 1868 when he attempted to buy the Erie railroad and thus gain control of the lines between New York and Chicago. Three equally ruthless businessmen, Jay Gould, Jim Fisk, and Daniel Drew, opposed the Vanderbilt take-over.

Gould and Fisk were not well known at the beginning of this conflict, although Fisk had prospered during the Civil War running contraband cotton from the South through Union Army lines. Drew had by then established a reputation for cunning and ruthlessness that was almost the equal of Vanderbilt's. By refining a swindle he used in his first career as a cattle-drover, Drew is credited with the invention of a business tactic known as 'watering' stock. In his earlier career, he was thought to give large amounts of salt to his herds of cattle, then let them drink their fill just before being weighed for sale. As a railroad man, he diluted the value of stock and thus burdened his corporations with debt to beat out business competition. In the process, while Drew and his partners became much richer, railroads were left to decline, until as Myers put it, 'travel on it became a menace; one disaster followed another.'[5]

The technique was used most famously in response to Vanderbilt's attempt to buy the Erie railroad. Gould, Fisk, and Drew issued more than $50 million worth of 'watered stock,' and used this to stay in control of a majority of Erie shares. In the process they defied a court ruling by Judge George C. Barnard prohibiting them from issuing more fraudulent stock. On 11 March, the three conspirators, along with other Erie directors, needed to leave New York in a hurry to escape Barnard's jurisdiction. As Charles F. Adams narrates in his book *A Chapter of Erie* (1871):

> At ten o'clock the astonished police saw a throng of panic-stricken railway directors – looking more like a frightened gang of thieves disturbed in the division of their plunder, than like the wealthy representatives of a great corporation – rush headlong from the doors of the Erie office, and dash off in the direction of the Jersey ferry. In their hands were packages and piles of papers, and their pockets were crammed with assets and securities. One individuals bore away with him in a hackney-coach bales containing six millions of dollars in greenbacks. Other members of the board followed under cover of the night; some of them, not daring to expose themselves to the publicity of a ferry, attempted to cross in open boats concealed by the darkness and a March fog. Two directors who lingered were arrested; but a majority of the Erie Committee collected at the Erie Station in Jersey City, and there, free from any apprehension of Judge Barnard's pursuing wrath, proceeded to the transaction of business.[6]

Gould then went up to the New York State capital of Albany with

$500,000 and succeeded in bribing enough legislators to get a bill passed legalizing the fraudulent stock. Vanderbilt was also bribing legislators to defeat the bill, but not enough to succeed. One senator took $100,000 from Gould and $75,000 from Vanderbilt and held on to both amounts.[7] The criminal justice system was similarly up for sale: Judge Barnard, for example, pursued the Erie directors because he was corruptly indebted to Vanderbilt and not through any concern for upholding the law.

Charles Adams concluded his account of Erie by suggesting that the five years that succeeded the Civil War, 'have witnessed some of the most remarkable examples of organized lawlessness, under the forms of law, which mankind has yet had an opportunity to study.'[8] The stock exchange and the offices of our great corporations were, he wrote, full of thieves and conspirators against the public, and the law had become, 'a ready engine for the furtherance of wrong, and the ermine of the judge did not conceal the eagerness of the partisan.'[9]

Memoirs, credited to Daniel Drew, confirmed the essential accuracy of Adams's account and added the observations of a corporate insider or perhaps simply a perceptive ghostwriter. The law, according to Drew, 'is like a cobweb: it's made for flies and the smaller kinds of insects, so to speak, but lets the big bumblebees break through ... When technicalities of the law stood in my way, I have always been able to brush them aside easy as anything.'[10]

The same work showed how Drew or his ghostwriter had acquired a shrewd sense of what it took to become a successful business criminal. Describing the Erie War he noted:

> I began to see that it is poor policy for big men in Wall Street to fight each other. When I am fighting a money king, even my victories are dangersome. Take the present situation. I had scooped a fine profit out of this Erie deal, and it was for the most part in solid cash. But – and here was the trouble – it had all come out of one man, Vanderbilt. Naturally it had left him very sore. And being so powerful, he was able to fight back. As has been seen, he did fight back. He had put me and my party to a lot of inconvenience. That always happens when you take money from a man on your own level. On the other hand, if I had taken these profits from outsiders, it would in the aggregate have amounted to the same sum. But the losers would have been scattered all over the whole country and so wouldn't have been able to get together and hit back. A thousand dollars of my total profits would have come then out of a lumber merchant, say

in Oshgosh; five hundred dollars from a coal dealer in New Haven; eight hundred dollars from an undertaker in Ploughkeepsie; a thousand dollars or two from a doctor in Syracuse; and so on, here a little and there a little. Many drops of water make the mighty ocean, and many small profits, added together make the big profit. Thus, by making my money from people on the outside, an insider like myself could make just as much in the long run, and not raise up any one enemy powerful enough to cause him discomfort.[11]

In the end, however, there was some rough justice for Drew. He was dropped from the Erie partnership, then lost most of his money in the panic of 1873, and ended his life in poverty.[12] In the meantime Gould, and other Erie directors, continued to turn out watered stock. This time, however, they ensured that the machinery of New York law was on their side by making corrupt alliances with Judge Bernard and the boss of New York's political machine, William Marcy Tweed, who had influence over many more judges. Between 1868 to 1872, 235,000 more shares of stock were issued, and, not surprisingly, armed thugs had to be employed to prevent defrauded stockholders from examining the company's books. By the time he had finished, Gould, according to an 1879 New York State investigating committee, had made more than $12 million from his Erie frauds.[13]

Although Vanderbilt lost millions in the Erie war, these were just minor losses among many more gains. In 1869 alone he made personal profits of around $26 million by securing legislation through bribery that allowed him to issue more than $44 million of watered stock on his railroads. The illegality of these transactions was acknowledged by the 1879 New York committee, which concluded: 'It is proper to remark that the people are quite as much indebted to the venality of the men elected to represent them in the Legislature as to the rapacity of the railroad managers for this state of affairs.'[14]

There were many victims of stock manipulators and profiteers like Drew, Fisk, Gould, and Vanderbilt particularly among the farmers and small businessmen who had to pay higher rates to make up for dishonest capitalization of railroad property and small investors 'on the outside.' The Populist leader, Jerry Simpson, speaking for hard-pressed farmers in Kansas, calculated that the 8,000 miles of road in his state cost only about $100 million, whereas they were capitalized at $300 million and bonded for $300 million more. From that he argued: 'We who use the roads are really paying interest on $600 million instead of on $100 million as we ought to.' The Kansas Farmers' Alliance saw this situation as an evil 'almost beyond comprehension.'[15]

Another contemporary observer added the following sentimental example to illuminate one of the ways by which stock-watering frauds hurt innocent victims:

> A widow, having the care of a family of small children, puts her money in railway stock. She is advised to do so by the director in the railway. It is the widow's all. Soon afterward this director and a few with him, seeing the importance of their road and its capabilities, determine to secure a controlling interest in the stock for themselves, thus both increasing their investment in a profitable concern, and at the same time obtaining a power to do what they please with the road thereafter, as occasion may demand. Accordingly, their first step is to run the stock down. This they accomplish by paying agents to go to places where the stock is owned, and, by brief articles in the local newspapers, to insinuate that the road is shaky. Every little fact against the road is exaggerated ... By these means the public are soon led to believe that the road is financially a failure. Our poor widow holds on to her stock, until from par it drops to twenty-five. She is then thoroughly frightened. She hears many now say, 'Sell out your stock or you'll lose all.' So she sells her stock and loses three-quarters of her property, which even before was only enough to keep her and hers in the ordinary comforts of life. Meanwhile, our high-minded director and his partners, having brought the stock down to a low enough figure, buy it all through their agents. Soon the stock mounts to its original value, and our director has made a million dollars by the transaction. The widow is financially ruined ... This is but an instance of what is done daily by the money-magnates. The fraud takes different shapes according to circumstances, but the system of amassing lordly fortunes now in practice is essentially a fraudulent system.[16]

In addition to those ruined by what amounted to large-scale fraud were those who were killed or maimed on poorly maintained railroad equipment and minimal concern over safety. Adams, writing in 1879 described one of the most horrific train crashes:

> The train was crowded to its full capacity, and the colliding locomotive struck it with such force as to bury itself two-thirds of its length in it. At the instant of the crash a panic had seized upon the passengers, and a sort of rush had taken place to the forward end of the car, into which furni-

ture, fixtures and human beings were crushed in a shapeless, indistinguishable mass ... The [boiler] valves had been so broken as to admit of the free escape of the scalding steam, while the coals from the fire-box were scattered among the debris, and coming in contact with fluid from the broken car lamps kindled the whole into a rapid blaze ... For the severity of injuries and for the protractedness of agony involved in it, ... Crushing, scalding and burning did their work together.[17]

Twenty-nine people died and fifty-seven more were injured as a result of the 'deliberate murder' of the Eastern Railroad, in the words of the reformer Wendell Phillips. The Eastern was eventually forced to pay over half a million dollars worth of fines as compensation for its criminal negligence.

Of the principal characters in the Erie war besides Drew, Vanderbilt died in 1877, worth around $100 million. Jim Fisk's career ended in 1872 when he was shot and killed by a rival for the affections of his mistress, the actress Josie Mansfield. Jay Gould died in 1892, leaving a personal fortune of around $72 million. Less is known about the fortunes of those they bribed, but at Judge Barnard's death, $1 million in bonds and cash were found among his effects. The greatest irony, however, was in the subsequent career of Erie's outraged chronicler, Charles Francis Adams. He first became a railroad regulator for the State of Massachusetts and the most prominent advocate of the view that the large corporations should effectively regulate railroad competition themselves which would allow 'the great principle of the survival of the fittest' to be worked out. In the words of historian Edward Lustig, Adams proposed that the tasks of regulation should be mainly left to 'the captains of the private domains. The hands that inflicted the wound would be trusted to heal it.' While advocating such views Adams then became an officer in several railroad corporations, culminating in him assuming the presidency of the Union Pacific. 'By the 1890s,' Lustig continued, 'this reform Republican of 1872 was openly justifying trusts, complaining of the depredations of government, and even lending his name to legislative bribes.'[18]

Gould, Fisk, Drew, and Vanderbilt were colourful characters but their business practices were not exceptional in the 1870s and 1880s. Other businessmen were equally blatant in their corrupt activities. Bribery was seen as a normal part of doing business: 'If you have to pay money to have the right thing done,' explained Collis P. Huntington, the founder of the Southern Pacific Railroad, 'it is only right and just to do it.' Huntington had no doubt that the wheels of justice sometimes required oiling, 'I think the time well spent, when it is a man's duty to go up and bribe the judge.' Milton H. Smith, president of the Louisville and Nashville Railroad, just as casually noted that 'society, as created, was for the purpose of one man's getting what the other fellow has, if he can, and keep out of the penitentiary.' The Central Pacific Railroad even budgeted for bribery: $500,000 annually between 1875 and 1885.[19]

The most prominent among scores of scandals, involving vast amounts of money, was the 1872 Crédit Mobilier affair. Ten years earlier, Congress had entrusted to the Union Pacific, run in part by Congressman Oakes Ames of Massachusetts, the right to complete the transcontinental system from Omaha to California. In effect, the government gave Union Pacific much more. The railroad received 200 feet right of way for hundreds of miles, the privilege of using whatever wood, stone, and other materials it found nearby, gifts of alternative sections of land running twenty miles on either side of the tracks, and credits of $16,000 to $48,000 for each mile of track laid. It transpired that Ames had got such good terms for his company by spreading around $436,000 where it would 'do the most good,' meaning the most powerful politicians from both parties. These included James Garfield, a future president, the vice-president, the vice-president-elect, and numerous senators and representatives.

The promoters assigned construction of the line to a company called Crédit Mobilier, owned by top bankers like William H. Macy, top industrialists such as Cyrus H. McCormick and George M. Pullman, and, of course, the promoters themselves. Crédit Mobilier then charged Union Pacific $94 million for a road that cost about $50 million to build, leaving $44 million profit, more than half of which was in cash, for Ames and his friends. When the scam was exposed and it was revealed that the government had, in effect, built the railroad for the private profit of insiders, Ames lost his place in Congress, but kept his fortune. The other politicians involved were exonerated.[20]

There were other reasons, besides waste and corruption, for business panics and economic collapses. In particular, the race for higher productivity had costs as well as benefits. New technology demanded that factories operate nearly at capacity in order to produce goods most economically. But the more manufacturers produced the more they had to sell. To sell more, they had to reduce prices. To increase profits and compensate for reduced prices, they further expanded production and often reduced wages. To expand, they had to borrow money. To repay the loans, they had to produce and sell even more. This circular process strangled small firms that could not keep pace, and put workers in a situation of nearly constant uncertainty. The same cycle affected commerce, banking, and transportation as well as manufacturing.

As noted earlier, by the latter decades of the nineteenth century, businessmen were looking for new ways to combat the uncertainty of the boom-and-bust business cycle. Many of them turned to a centralized corporate form of business organization, pioneered by John D. Rockefeller and his Standard Oil Company.

Rockefeller during the 1870s was just one of many oilmen getting rich by exploiting the oilfields discovered in the states of Pennsylvania, West Virginia, and Ohio. Rockefeller concluded that the way to dominate the oil industry was not by producing oil but by refining and distributing it.[21] Early on he made secret deals with railroads that were in conflict with the principle of free competition because they resulted in cheaper rates for Standard Oil. This enabled Standard to undercut competitors and the ultimate aim was always to drive them out of the business.

The marketing department of Standard Oil was eventually organized to cover the whole country with the aim that Standard Oil sell all the oil sold in each area of the country. According to Ida Tarbell's exposure of the company's methods, the department organized an elaborate secret service for locating the quantity, quality, and selling price of independent shippers to forestall or meet competition. The department collected this information mainly by bribing employees of railroad companies such as freight clerks or sometimes even those employed by the shippers themselves. Tarbell detailed a case involving the latter:

in 1892 the Lewis Emory Oil Company, an independent selling concern in Philadelphia, employed a man by the name of Buckley. This man was discharged, and in September of that year he went into the employ of the leading Standard refinery of Philadelphia ... According to the affidavit made by this man Buckley, the managers of the Standard concern ... engaged him in conversation about the affairs of his late employer. They said that if they could only find out the names of the persons to whom their rival sold, and for what prices, they could soon run him out of business! And they asked Buckley if he could not get the information for them. After some discussion, one of the Standard managers said: "What's the matter with the nigger?" alluding to a colored boy in the employment of the Lewis Emory concern ... "You can tell the nigger ... that he needn't be afraid, because if he loses his position there's a position here for him."

The information was duly received, Standard Oil dispensed with the services of Buckley, and did not employ the African American after he had been discovered and sacked by Lewis Emory. People who sold information to Standard Oil were never given responsible positions. They may, as Tarbell put it, 'be shifted around to do 'dirty work," as the Oil region's phrase goes, but they are pariahs in the concern ... the Buckleys and negroes who bring him secret intelligence never get anything but money and contempt for their pains.'[22]

Having found out which dealers were buying from the independents, Standard then sought their customers by undercutting the competition. This they often did by setting up "bogus" oil companies to sell cheap oil until it could capture the independents' trade. After the rival was destroyed or brought into Standard's orbit, prices returned to their previous levels. One of Rockefeller's admirers summed up this technique: 'First, you hit your enemies in the pocketbook, hit 'em hard. Then you either buy 'em out or take 'em with you.'[23]

Standard Oil also used state legislatures to eliminate competition. By successfully opposing the right of eminent domain for pipelines in Pennsylvania, for example, the company virtually ensured that no competing pipelines could be built to link the state's oil wells with its railroads. The bribery of state senators was alleged and there was enough suspicion to justify Henry Demarest Lloyd's famous conclusion: 'The Standard has done everything with the Pennsylvania legislature, except refine it.'[24]

By the end of the nineteenth century Standard Oil had consolidated its arrangements with the railroads and new pipeline systems had been built. The company controlled up to 85 per cent of the refining capacity of the United States and most of the world market for its products.[25] Using similar combinations of legal and illegal methods, a few giant companies took control of the oil, steel, food, soap, tobacco, and other industries. 'Force and fraud,' according to Tarbell's investigation, were at the heart of Standard's rise to dominance and the same methods, she added, were 'employed by all sorts of businessmen, from corner grocers up to bankers. If exposed, they are excused on the ground that this is business.'[26]

The Myth of the Molly Maguires and the Culture of Professionalism

At the same time as Standard Oil was epitomizing the movement towards increasing corporate merger and concentration, American employers decided to exert more authority over their employee's wages, hours, and working conditions. Responding to this, trade unions organized worker resistance and the conflict that followed took decades to resolve. An early struggle involved anthracite miners and mine owners from Schuylkill County in Northeastern Pennsylvania. This was to produce the legend of the Molly Maguires and prefigure much that followed nationally.

Coal mining in Pennsylvania had increased rapidly during and immediately after the Civil War. Railroads were built to link the fields to the New York and Philadelphia markets. More money could be made from mining, more jobs were advertised, and more people came into the area to fill these jobs. The early settlers of Schuylkill County were from Ulster. English and Welsh coal miners followed later in the nineteenth century. By the 1870s, these three English-speaking Protestant groups dominated the local society and economy, owning and operating most of the mines and local shops.

As the industry developed, Southern Irish Catholics began to fill most of the jobs in the mines. If these newcomers worked at the coalface, however, they did so at some risk – coal mining was an exceptionally hazardous occupation. The death and injury rates in parts of Schuylkill County could even be compared to those of the military during combat. Mining operators and their supporters in the press tended to blame the carelessness of miners for frequent and often deadly explosions in the pits. Closer attention to detail would have revealed that inadequate ventilation and safety precautions were almost always responsible. However, most operators were not prepared to make the necessary investments and were able to avoid guilt and liability by suggesting that miners should have been more careful and prudent.[27]

One of the most destructive explosions occurred at the Avondale mine in September 1869, which had no proper procedures in place to deal with fires. One hundred and ten bodies were eventually brought out, most having been asphyxiated or killed by smoke inhalation while they waited for their delayed rescuers.[28]

In addition to the dangers of floods and explosions, miners often faced more prolonged suffering as a result of the industrial disease

known as 'miner's asthma.' In 1869 a doctor wrote: 'A peculiar asth-
matic character of cough is generally noticed; emphysema is detected
on physical exploration, and the sputa are black, often streaked with
blood. Miner's asthma is chronic bronchitis, with thickening of the air
passages, emphysema, and nervous distress in breathing. These
chronic troubles may last a lifetime, without being rapidly fatal, or necessarily so. But acute pneumonia supervenes in many cases on some
exposure and is very apt to prove fatal. If not, a chronic softening of the
lungs may occur, in other words, phthisis, which is a frequent disease
among these men, and generally an incurable one.'[29]

Mining work was also intermittent. Whenever coal markets became
glutted during this time, coal operators reacted by sacking workers or
imposing wage cuts. The operators also often required their workers to
buy overpriced goods in company stores. If workers tried organizing
strikes or boycotts, they faced the employers' tactic of 'black-listing' or
refusing to employ those thought to be potential troublemakers. The
men effectively had little freedom of speech or of action.

In response to all these problems and grievances the Workingmen's
Benevolent Association (WBA) was formed in 1868 and for the next
few years had some success, particularly in Schuylkill County, forcing some concessions from the state government and mine operators.
Until its defeat in 1875, the WBA successfully lobbied for safety legislation and hospital facilities and established a system of collective
bargaining.[30]

Franklin Gowen, as president of the local railroad company, was in
a key position to orchestrate the employers' response to the WBA. His
twin aims were to reduce competition among the smaller operators
and smash the union. Gowen controlled the railroads that got the coal
to the markets and used this control as a lever to force other mine
operators to follow his policies regarding prices, wages, and union
negotiations. With his associates he arranged for common price policies and common anti-union tactics. By the early 1870s he had dis-
creetly bought all the coal properties available and established a
virtual local monopoly. He had therefore achieved his first aim and
reduced the competition in the industry. He then turned his attention
to the WBA.

The plan was to link the union with lawlessness. During this period
street fighting and murders noticeably increased. Among the victims
were almost equal numbers of miners and mine superintendents. An
economic downturn from 1873 on led many people to fear a complete
breakdown of law and order. The newspapers made crime seem ram-

pant and then, prompted by Gowen, claimed that a secret society among Irish immigrants, known as the Molly Maguires, was responsible. The Mollies were said to control the lodges of the Ancient Order of Hiberians (AOH), a fraternal organization that had its origins in the old country.[31]

Fear of the Mollies increased after newspaper reports of more beatings and unsolved murders with such headlines as 'A Molly on the Rampage,' 'Atrocious Outrage by the Molly Maguires', 'Molly Beating,' 'Molly Coffin Notice.'[32] Franklin Gowen, in the meantime was talking up the threat of the Mollies to the press and linking them to the WBA with no supporting evidence. He told a Senate committee: 'There never, since the middle ages, existed a tyranny like this on the face of God's earth. There has never been, in the most despotic government in the world, such a tyranny, before which the poor laboring man has to crouch like a whipped spaniel before the lash.' After more of the same he made the link to the union and a demand for more government action: 'It happens that the only men who are shot are the men who dare disobey the mandates of the Workingmen's Benevolent Association. Is this to last forever? Can it be that in the Commonwealth of Pennsylvania, which has paid its taxes, is to be singled out and made subservient entirely to the dictates of the workingmen? It is, then, gentlemen, good-bye to the credit of Pennsylvania, good-bye to the coal mining and manufacturing industries. Let every man give it up and go home and be a poor man.'[33]

Gowen and his associates had realized that the defence of law and order made a better cause than union busting, and with the complicity of local police officials, he hired a secret agent called James McParlan to infiltrate the Irish community. By drinking, treating, joking, fighting, and talking about the old country McParlan gained acceptance and became a trusted and influential AOH lodge member. From 1873 he submitted reports detailing conspiratorial plans and illegal acts by what he referred to as the AOH's 'inner circle,' the Molly Maguires.[34]

The historian Anthony F.C. Wallace has examined McParlan's notes and summarized the detective's own account of the Molly Maguires. The Molly's chief function was to obtain retributive justice for members of the Irish community who had been wronged and could not get fair treatment through the court system. Retribution was most often a beating but it could include arson or murder. The Mollies were not at all well organized:

The administrative structure of the AOH, with its provision for a senior officer (the 'bodymaster'), a secretary, and a treasurer in each lodge, and its hierarchy of county, state and national delegates, gave to an amorphous collection of Irish street-gang members numbering perhaps 150 men and boys a semblance of discipline. But only a semblance: treasurers were absconding with funds, secretaries took no minutes, deputized assassins refused their assignments, and drunken Mollies fought with each other, and with the fellow-Irish Chain Gang, as enthusiastically as they beat up the Modocs, a rival Welsh gang. In spirit, however, the pattern of violence perpetrated by the AOH-affiliated Mollies was no different from the violence meted out by anonymous Irish assassins a generation earlier in the name of retributive justice.

Nothing in McParlan's notes, according to Wallace, suggests that the attacks on mine bosses and the notorious 'coffin notices' were part of a terrorist plot to take over the coal trade. Neither the notes nor any serious historical research have added any credibility to Gowen's conspiracy theory or his attempt to link the Mollies with the WBA, but his hyperbole was nevertheless effective.

In 1875, while McParlan was still undercover, there was a long strike by miners, which lasted nearly six months and was characterized by another upsurge in local violence. On the employer's side, Patrick Varry fired indiscriminately into a crowd of striking miners, leaving several wounded, but was never asked to face a trial. Another boss fired into a meeting of 100 miners, killing one. This time there was a trial, but the boss was found innocent on the ground that he had 'protected himself from the mob of assassins.' The mine operators also brought in groups of hoodlums such as the above-mentioned Modocs and the Sheet Iron Gang, to terrorize the strikers. The authorities tended to conduct cursory investigations when the bodies of radical miners were found down disused mine shafts. The unionists replied to the violence in kind, often beating and sometimes killing strikebreakers. The operators' thugs were better armed and had the support of the local police and militia. The strike was lost when the miners' union ran out of funds in 1875.[35] It was several decades before unionism of any significance returned to the Pennsylvanian coalfields.

Once Gowen and his associates had broken the strike, they set out to destroy all that remained of union strength and credibility and McParlan was the key to this. He came out of disguise the following year to become the leading state's witness during a series of trials against several AOH-affiliated Molly Maguires. The trials followed a pattern set by Gowen himself, acting as prosecuting attorney in some cases;

McParlan was the key witness, and his word was supported by a series of paid informers, who secured immunity for their own crimes. These testified that the AOH had 6,000 lodges throughout the nation and that the entire organization was 'criminal in character.' Its alleged purpose was punishment of mine owners or bosses for offending members of the order.[36]

No evidence of the existence of the Molly Maguires anywhere else in the nation was ever produced and much of this type of testimony can now be discounted as perjury. Gowen, however, took the opportunity to claim support for his conspiracy theory. He spoke of an international terrorist organization with a long history of resistance to British colonial rule that had been transplanted to Schuylkill County:

'The purpose was to make the business of mining coal in this county a terror and a fear; to secure for the leading men in this society profitable positions, and the control of large operations at every colliery. The purpose was to levy blackmail upon every man engaged in industrial disputes in this county, so that the owners, under the terror which this organization had acquired, would gladly purchase peace and immunity, by having one or two, or more of these men in prominent positions in every colliery, and employ as many of their confederates, members of this organization, as possible, to protect their property from the villainy of their own Order.'

Unless the full force of the law was employed against the Mollies, Gowen warned:

Every man of character and reputation and integrity would have been driven into other regions, and this great theatre of industry, this boundless deposit of mineral wealth with which God has blessed this region in which you live, would have been ... transformed into a desert. With these conspirators in the possession of everything that was of value, they would have driven out all honest industry, shooting down, either in the darkness of the night or in the broad daylight, as they became bolder, any man who dared oppose the dictates of their decrees ... Was there ever such an organization heard of? Search the pages of history and go back over the records of the world, and I will venture to say you will never find in any society, claiming to be civilized, such an adjudication to death, and by instruments of vengeance as ghastly and as horrible, as this society wielded for the murder of their fellow men.

His words were echoed by his assistant on the prosecution side, George

Kaercher, who claimed: 'This case involves the life or the destruction of one of the greatest criminal organizations of which any mention can be found.'[37]

No evidence presented during the trials came close to justifying the outrageous claims of Gowen and Kaercher. Wallace's examination of all the available primary sources led him to conclude: 'The reports and testimony of McParlan do not reveal a gang of professional criminals planing bank and train robberies, extorting protection money from collieries, smuggling liquor, or kidnapping for ransom. There were no rapes or beatings of women, Members showed some participation in the political process as Democrats, much of it quite irregular, with the aim of advancing the local interests of the Irish. There was apparently no AOH involvement in union activity at all.'[38] But, this did not matter to Gowen. As prosecutor, he was able to stage the trials in such a way as to link the Molly Maguires with the union. He repeatedly insinuated the false notion that Mollie violence was also union violence. After more trials and appeals twenty alleged Molly Maguires were eventually found guilty of murder and hanged. The trials cost Gowen himself more than $100,000, but the price was obviously worth paying.[39]

The historian Harold Aurand has drawn out the real significance of the Molly Maguire story when he observed:

> Historians have debated whether the Mollies were hardened criminals or innocent labor leaders; many, in the heat of the argument, have completely neglected the episode's true significance. The Molly Maguire investigation and trials were one of the most astounding surrenders of sovereignty in American history. A private corporation initiated the investigation through a private detective agency; a private police force arrested the alleged offenders; and coal company attorneys prosecuted them. The state provided only the courtroom and hangman. The fate of the Mollys taught the people of the anthracite region that the Coal and Iron police were supreme within the area.'[40]

The destruction of the union allowed the Schylkill employers to continue with their negligent attitude to the safety and welfare of their workers, as Anthony Wallace has demonstrated. On 9 May 1877, for example, a major explosion in a section of the Wadesville Shaft killed six men and injured six others. The coroner's jury reported a week later that the colliery's management had been lax and the mine inspector negligent in not enforcing the law that required operators to have proper ventilation in their mines. Later in the year the coroner indicted several of the employers and the inspector on manslaughter charges. However, the witnesses in the case decided not to repeat their earlier testimony and the trial was abandoned. The mine inspector's report for 1877 eliminated any reference to problems in the ventilation of the colliery and fire prevention procedures and predictably blamed the victims for contributory negligence.

Wallace's conclusions were: 'Accidental death and injury were a form of violence perpetrated on miners by an inept and careless organization, and that justice was arbitrarily denied ... Equal justice was a commodity in short supply, and violence in ample, in Schuylkill County in the 1870s.[41]

Corporation officials in Pennsylvania continued to find it easy to 'fix' cases for at least the next four decades. A 1910 state survey concluded that state safety inspectors were politically appointed and too few to ensure standards were met. They were not very zealous about their work and failed even to keep public records of prosecutions of safety codes violations.[42] Set in this context, Molly Maguire violence becomes less significant when set against such long-term, calculated, and better organized criminality.

After the Molly Maguire trials, Gowen left the propagation of the myth to the boss of secret agent McParlan, Allan Pinkerton. The Pinkerton Detective Agency had prospered during the 1870s and 1880s by specializing in spying on and infiltrating unions. Pinkerton published a book called, *The Molly Maguires and the Detectives*, even before all the trials were completed. This featured, according to its publicity, the exposure and destruction of a terrorist society which 'wields with deadly effect ... two powerful levers, secrecy and combination.'

In all, Pinkerton published eighteen books of this type of semifictional promotion of his agency, employing up to seven men just for the purpose of ghostwriting them.[43] In effect, he used the books to pitch his agency's services to businessmen by writing about organized rings of professional criminals: pickpockets, store robbers, hotel thieves, house breakers, confidence men, blackmailers, burglars, forgers, and counterfeiters. 'In broad daylight,' according to Pinkerton in his book *Thirty Years a Detective* (1886): 'Banks, moneyed institutions, and financial firms, have been defrauded of vast sums of money by the expert forger, the sneak-thief, and the counterfeiter. Individuals of all classes have fallen victim to the horde of dishonest men and women who infest our communities – and yet the public are [sic] unaware of the means employed to effect their ruin, or the modes by which their disasters were accomplished.'[44]

In Pinkerton's world, criminal behaviour threatened rather than characterized corporations. Skilled detectives were particularly necessary, he argued, in an era of increasing numbers of criminals whose 'modes of working and plans of operations have reached a degree of scientific perfection never before attained.' Only professional detectives in plain clothes could infiltrate 'the entire school of crime' by means of their 'superior intelligence' and thus protect the constantly threatened client.[45]

According to Burton J. Bledstein, Pinkerton was a classic example of the culture of professionalism that developed in late nineteenth-century America. This 'tended to cultivate an atmosphere of constant crisis – emergency – in which practitioners both created work for themselves and reinforced their authority over their clients.' Doctors, lawyers, criminologists, politicians, and journalists cultivated irrationality in an irrational world 'by uncovering abnormality and perversity everywhere: in diseased bodies, in criminal minds, political conspiracies, threats to national security. An irrational world, an amoral one in a state of constant crisis, made the professional person who possessed his special knowledge indispensable to the victimized client, who was reduced to a condition of desperate trust.' The culture of professionalism, Bledstein, concluded, 'bred public attitudes of passivity and submission.'[46] As we shall see, the culture of professionalism did not remain exclusively private in the twentieth century. Eventually it would permeate government service at all levels and, among other things, contribute to the process of setting limits to the understanding of organized crime.

The Origins of Industrial Racketeering

The struggle in Pennsylvania's anthracite coalfields was repeated in many other parts of the country. Most employers did not have the Irish immigrant scapegoat that Gowen used so effectively, but they used similar tactics. Strikebreakers were recruited, and protected with private armed guards. This led to bitterness, retaliation, and violence. As violence spread and local authorities failed to control it, employers became ardent defenders of law and order and property rights. If local law enforcement failed to do the job, then state or federal authorities would come in to restore order. Usually law and order was restored at the expense of the strikers and their unions.

The Pennsylvanian coal operators were not exceptional in employing gangs like the Modocs and the Sheet Irons in their disputes with trade unions, and at the same time many workers began to possess and use guns and dynamite for their own cause. These were years when U.S. industrial relations were to a great extent carried out by armed force.

To illuminate the level of systematic brutality, union official Peter J. McQuire testified before a Senate committee in 1885, that 'a man named Schleicher' armed strikebreakers during a strike of the iron moulders in Troy (New York) and told them he would pay them $15 each for every union man that they shot.' As a result two union men were shot dead and many more were injured.

After considering much more such evidence, the U.S. Industrial Commission reported in 1898: 'It is a well known fact that too often labor disputes are accompanied by violence and intimidation ... Resort to violence is especially likely to occur where employers endeavor to import considerable bodies of men from other parts of the country to take the place of the strikers ... Men of foreign birth or negroes are frequently employed, confessedly as strikebreakers.'[47]

Both sides in industrial disputes used violence, but the employers used it more systematically and effectively, most notably at Ludlow, Colorado, in April 1914. Ludlow's coal mines were dominated by the Colorado Fuel and Iron Company, partly owned by John D. Rockefeller and considered to be a Standard Oil subsidiary.

This dispute had begun the previous September, when around 9,000 miners left their company houses to establish tent colonies at the edges of the South Colorado coal-mining area. They stayed on strike for fifteen months, partly to improve pay and conditions, but mainly as a rebellion against company domination of every aspect of their lives. They wanted recognition of their union, the right to trade at stores not owned by the company, and the right to choose their own boarding places and doctors.

The mining companies imported armed thugs from Texas, New Mexico, and West Virginia, who were then deputized by local law enforcement officials. Rifle pits were dug in the hills next to mining properties, and an armoured car was brought into the action. This came to be called the 'Death Special' by the strikers.

During the first five weeks of the strike, there were thirty-eight armed clashes and eighteen deaths. On 20 April 1914 there was a twelve-hour battle when the Colorado National Guard, which was mainly composed of company men, was called in. This ended when the company's forces drenched the miners' tents with oil and set them alight. Women and children who had been hiding in pits dug under the tents for protection were trapped. The fire suffocated eleven children and two women. The miners' violent response was finally put down by federal troops after ten days of open rebellion.

A military commission investigated the disaster and found that, 'the tents were not all of them destroyed by accidental fire. Men and soldiers swarmed into the colony, and deliberately assisted the conflagration ... Beyond a doubt it was seen to intentionally that the fire should destroy the whole of the colony ... Men and soldiers seized and took from the tents whatever appealed to their fancy ... clothes, bedding, articles of jewelry, bicycles, tools, and utensils ... cans of oil found in the tents were poured unto them and the tents lit with matches.'[48]

In January of the following year Rockefeller was called to testify about the massacre at U.S. Commission on Industrial Relations hearings and accepted only limited responsibility for the actions of Colorado Fuel and Iron. He strongly denied charges that he exercised absolute control over Colorado's coal industry and claimed that as a director he did not shape the firm's managerial policies and rather concentrated on financial affairs. At later hearings evidence was produced that showed that the multimillionaire was in much closer contact with the management that he had maintained and had also used his influence on the state governor Elias M. Ammons to allow the militia to aid the strikebreakers. This move signalled an escalation of violence in the dispute.[49]

The Ludlow massacre and Rockefeller's complicity provoked the opposition of some of the major newspapers and the anger of protestors who picketed Standard's New York headquarters. Rockefeller took this bad publicity seriously enough to hire the best publicity agents to project a more positive image for his companies and to make large philanthropic gestures. However, to many radicals the whole affair revealed the source of many of America's worst problems: too much private economic power in too few hands.

In the early years of industrialization the official police forces were almost irrelevant, although industrial conflict in the United States involved many kinds of criminal activity. Few businessmen considered the official police forces as organized or reliable enough to protect their interests. Instead, private police were thought to be more cost-effective in protecting property and breaking strikes.

The Pinkerton Detective agency's reputation grew as a result of the Molly Maguire trials, and for the next two decades the Pinkertons supplied guards for industrial plants and organized teams of strikebreakers when necessary. They began to lose their good name in the 1890s, when reports of their indiscriminate shooting of strikers and their families were circulated.

The Pinkertons then moved more into the private, non-labour, detective work for which they became more famous, but other professional strikebreaking organizations were ready and able to take their place and pick up any business the corporations offered them. James Farley headed one of these. He had at least 400 fighters available on short notice to break strikes in many major cities. Farley's stated policy was to import hard-core men to the scene of the strike and to keep them there until the job was safe for non-professional strikebreakers. He made a reported $1 million from breaking strikes between 1904 and 1914.[50]

Farley was one of numerous middlemen between the corporations and local gangsters, such as Paul Kelly in New York and 'Umbrella' Mike Boyle in Chicago. The latter got his name by visiting local bars and collecting protection money in an upturned umbrella. The gangsters were used to mix in with the strikers and provoke disturbances. The disturbances produced anti-strike court injunctions, and then state troops would be brought in to restore order, effectively ending the strike.

Paul Kelly was actually an Italian named Paolo Vaccarelli; he decided to give himself an Irish name because the New York police were mainly Irish and were less likely to interfere with one of their own. He was a leading figure among the city's street gangsters. By 1919 Kelly had changed from strikebreaker to union organizer without changing his methods or his allegiance to self-interest. He became a leader of the International Longshoremen's Association and pioneered some of the extortions, kickbacks, and rackets that characterized the New York waterfront throughout the twentieth century.[51]

From the beginning of the twentieth century, more unions made alliances with gangsters. 'Dopey Benny' Fein, for example, became the chief provider of thugs for the International Ladies Garment Workers' Union in New York. When strikes were called outside his own neighbourhood he called on support from the gangs that operated in the appropriate territory such as the 'Hudson Dusters' in the Upper West Side and the 'Gas House' combinations from around East 35th Street.

'Dopey Benny,' who had begun his career robbing drunks as a 'lush worker,' soon proved he was capable of business organization. To minimize disputes over money, for example, he had a standard scale of prices: The price for raiding and wrecking a small manufacturing plant was $150. At this figure 'Dopey Benny' was to provide all the gangsters necessary to complete the job. The price for raiding and wrecking the largest of the shops in the clothing and needle trades was $600. For shooting a man in the leg or the arms or 'clipping his ear off' (a favourite device of intimidation employed by the gangsters), the price ranged from $600 up, according to the importance of the man shot or maimed. For invading a factory for the purpose of throwing an objectionable manager or foreman down an elevator shaft or breaking his arm or thumb, the price was $200. A complete 'knockout' or murder of any individual of 'ordinary importance' cost $200. Even when confined to jail for his activities on behalf of the unions, 'Dopey Benny' demanded a salary of $25 a week for his period of incarceration.[52]

In 1915 Fein was arrested and this time the unions refused to pay his bail. As a result he felt double-crossed and decided to tell all about his career and his partners in crime. As a result of his confession, he received a light sentence for extortion. Although more than thirty of his associates were arrested, none of them ever faced trial.[53]

For a number of reasons gangsters have also played a significant part in the development of the New York construction industry from the beginning of the twentieth century. Building work is often seasonal and unpredictable. The interests of contractors, subcontractors, and supply dealers often conflict. Stoppages and strikes can paralyze building projects at crucial times. Such factors combine to make the construction industry a breeding ground for both union and business corruption.

Samuel Parks was the dominant figure in the New York building trades at the turn of the century. After years as an itinerant labourer, Parks was employed by the George A. Fuller Construction Company. At the same time he became the chief business agent of the Housesmith's, Bridgemen's, and Structural Iron Workers' Union. Both union and company paid him until his death. As union man, he engineered a revival and reunification of most New York building trades locals; as company man he helped keep the Fuller Construction Company virtually strike free during a period of industrial turmoil.

If violence was the best way to get results, then Parks used violence. He once said that he would rather fight than eat, and had a simple remedy for those who hesitated about joining the union: 'Some did not believe that unions were good for them and I gave them a belt on the jaw. That changed their minds.' A beating was then followed by Parks standing on his opponent's face. Other dissenters were dealt with by a standing 'entertainment's committee.'

Parks also got results for his men. He succeeded in raising the daily wage of ironworkers, for example, from $2.50 to $4.50, putting them up with the highest paid craftsmen, and gaining loyalty through results as much as by intimidation. But Parks worked for himself first, taking bribes from Fuller and other large concerns to keep them free from industrial conflict, and extorting payments from smaller concerns. On one occasion he demanded money from the Hecla Iron Works to 'make things easy over here.' When the president of the company asked what he should do, Parks replied, 'I'm it, you pay me. I don't care a damn for the union, the president of the union, or the laws of the country. You can go back to work when you pay Sam Parks $2,000.' The company paid, but also informed the district attorney, beginning years of legal difficulty for Parks that only ended with his death in 1904.[54]

After Parks's death, the larger building firms organized themselves into the New York Building Trades Employers Association (BTEA) to gain greater control over the industry, using union officials like Robert Brindell to establish a less volatile but equally corrupt system. An investigative committee found that BTEA operated as 'a mere cover for price-fixing, restriction of output or division of territory and for the practice of many other devices that had for their purposes the exaction of tribute from owners, builders and contractors.' BTEA recognized Brindell's importance as head of the Carpenters' Union and they became allies to keep smaller competitors and rival unions out of the business.

Brindell had helped 'rationalize' a previously unorganized state of affairs, using his control over the supply of labour to take his share. He made himself the highest paid union official in the United States and also extorted money from construction contractors, principally through the sale of 'strike insurance.' If a contractor failed to pay off to Brindell's satisfaction, some pretext could be fabricated on which to call a strike.

Brindell played a key part in the establishment of a system that operated in the building trades of New York and other cities throughout most of the twentieth century – systematic bribery and extortion backed up by violence if necessary. He was convicted for extortion in 1921 and his days as an industrial racketeer were effectively over. But there were many more like him to take his place.[55]

The dominant labour organization by the end of the nineteenth century was the American Federation of Labor (AFL), headed by Samuel Gompers. Gompers and the rest of the AFL leadership undoubtedly knew about their violent and corrupt members, but resisted reform. Gompers depended on the support of corrupt union bosses to remain leader of the AFL. The leaders of the building trades' unions, like Parks and Brindell, were the most notorious racketeers in the labour movement, but they also ran the most powerful labour organizations in the country. As Harold Seidman points out in his book entitled *Labor Czars*:

> No matter how grave might be the abuses, Gompers would not countenance any interference by city, state, or federal authorities in matters affecting labor unions, even though the A. F. of L. had shown itself powerless to put its house in order. He would also do nothing to reform the stacked constitutions, which were ... the chief source of the autocratic power of the labor czars. He would not force union officials to keep accounts so that the rank and file might have some way of checking up on expenditures. To Gompers the only cure was the 'evolution and enlightenment' of the labor movement. In other words Gompers would do nothing to wipe out the abuses of the labor racketeers.[56]

The problem, according to labour historian Philip S. Foner, was the lack of union democracy: 'When unions become dictator-run bureaucracies and the membership, in effect, lose their democratic right to decide union policies, then the door is open to all forms of racketeering.'[57] As we shall see, all forms of industrial racketeering increased from the 1920s, usually to the advantage of management.

Muckraking Business Criminality and the Limits of Regulation

Despite the efforts to stigmatize foreigners as prone to criminal conspiracy, Americans in the nineteenth century and until the second half of the twentieth century would not have had any fixed understanding of the phrase 'organized crime.' Indeed, until that time many would have been as likely to associate organized criminality with the schemes and practices of the rich rather than the poor and to look for coordinated criminal activity among native-born businessmen rather than groups of foreigners finding their way in a strange new land.

Howard Crosby, the director of the newly formed Society for the Prevention of Crime, was one of the earliest to reflect these views, writing in 1883. In an article called, 'The Dangerous Classes,' Crosby concluded that 'the rich and powerful classes in the community' had made and maintained 'a system of plunder and oppression of the poorer classes and of the public generally.' He went on: 'Prices are made, not through the natural laws of supply and demand, but by 'corners' and conspiracies. Fair competition, which is the life of trade, is utterly crushed by this money-swollen monster. A few monopolize the entire trade of any given article by reason of their money-power, remorselessly destroying any one who dares even to glean in the field they have made their own by robbery.'

The sense that the real problem of crime and corruption stemmed from the top of the economic and social order continued to grow with rising working-class and farmer militancy towards the end of the nineteenth century. Henry Demarest Lloyd crystallized these feelings in 1894 in his book *Wealth against Commonwealth* in which he wrote a scathing exposé of the Standard Oil Company. His conclusions were: 'If our civilization is destroyed, it will not be by ... barbarians from below. Our barbarians come from above. Our great money-makers ... are gluttons of luxury and power, rough, unsocialized, believing that mankind must be kept terrorized. Powers of pity die out of them, because they work through agents'[58]

The new American order came under increased scrutiny and criticism at the turn of the nineteenth and twentieth centuries. And many more writers described and denounced the systematic criminal activity of the powerful. These writers included Ida Tarbell, Lincoln Steffens, Upton Sinclair, Ray Stannard Baker, and Samuel Hopkins Adams, and they showed in graphic detail how the practices of big business and their allies in politics were corrupt, destructive, and often illegal. Although President Theodore Roosevelt labelled them 'muckrakers' in a 1906 speech and considered them to be 'friends of disorder,' both he and his successors, William Howard Taft and Woodrow Wilson, were forced to respond to the avalanche of disclosure.

Fraud, larceny, bribery, and exploitation on an immense scale were revealed in many businesses including oil, meat, sugar, railroads, and life insurance. The case against big business criminality was made in popular magazines like *McClure's, Hampton's, Harper's Weekly, Collier's,* and *Success,* and in novels such as Upton Sinclair's *The Jungle* (1906), and to a lesser extent in the popular newspapers of the day run by E.W. Scripps, Joseph Pulitzer, and William Randolph Hearst. Even the new medium of film contributed such productions as *The Usurer* (1910), *One Is Business, The Other Crime* (1912), *What Is to Be Done?* (1914), *The High Road* (1915), *The Italian* (1915), and the filmed version of *The Jungle* (1914). All of these implicitly or explicitly attacked big business criminality.[59]

Muckrakers were able to use government statistics to find danger in many business practices and to call for these practices to be criminalized. More than 1.5 million wage-earners were children, for example. Children worked in garment sweatshops, flour mills, foundries, cotton mills, and many other industries. Pay was minimal and working conditions lacked even basic safety precautions – many died in fires, were mangled by machinery, worked standing in several inches of water, or froze to death in delivery vans.[60]

Safety was no better for older workers. In the nation's industry as a whole U.S. Bureau of Labor experts estimated that at the turn of the century industrial accidents killed 35,000 workers each year and maimed 500,000 others. Over 3,000 or nearly 25 per cent of recent immigrants employed at the Carnegie Steel Works in Pittsburgh were killed or injured each year between 1907 and 1910. The U.S. Geological Survey reported in 1908 alone that 3,125 coal miners in the previous year were killed and 5,316 had been injured. The survey explained, however, that the figures did not give 'the full extent of the disasters, as reports were not received from certain States having no mine inspectors.'[61] The overall accident rate in U.S. coal mines in the period between 1900 and 1906 was almost four times that of France and twice that of Prussia.[62] As one study concluded, 'Speed-ups, monotonous tasks, and exposure to chemical toxins, metallic, and organic dusts, and unprotected machinery made the American workplace among the most dangerous in the world.'[63]

A tragedy at a New York factory graphically illustrated the lack of safety standards. As described by Nell Irvin Painter: 'On March 25, 1911, a fire broke out in the Triangle Shirtwaist Company on the top floor of the Asch building in Washington Square. Although the factory was new and reputedly fireproof, careless maintenance, and the practice of locking doors and windows – supposedly to prevent employees from leaving the factory or stealing – transformed the burning building into an inferno. Either women remained trapped in the building to suffocate or burn to death or they jumped nine floors to death on the pavement. The Triangle fire took the lives of 146 women.'[64] One fireman told of the horror of the girls leaping to their deaths: 'They hit the pavement just like hail. We could hear the thuds faster than we see the bodies fall.'[65]

Government and press investigation found the factory owners and their insurance company responsible and found that the procedure and practice of the New York City fire and building departments was, to say the least, inadequate. No one, however, was convicted on criminal charges. Soon after the fire the National Association of Manufacturers financed a film, called *The Crime of Carelessness* (1912). In a manner that became familiar, the film shifted attention away from employer neglect of factory safety laws by showing how a sweatshop blaze similar to the Triangle fire was caused by a careless, cigarette-smoking employee.

Less dramatic than unsafe working conditions but even more costly in terms of lives lost were occupational diseases. Painters, printers, linotypers, plumbers, tinsmiths, electricians, workers in storage battery factories, cut glass workers, pottery workers, and workers in white lead factories were far more liable to die from work-related diseases than their equivalents in Europe. These workers often worked with poisonous substances in poorly-ventilated conditions because, as William Ludlow Chenery put it in his exposé in the *Independent*, 'cheapness of production' is 'our American industrial ideal rather than the welfare of the workers or of the community.'[66]

Workers could and did turn to the courts for compensation under employers' liability laws. Corporations then responded by boosting their legal representation so that when cases were brought against them the odds would be in their favour. Corporation lawyers, for example, would exonerate employers from liability in worker compensation claims even when they were clearly at fault for the deaths or injuries of employees. A study published in 1910 showed that widows and children bore the entire income loss in more than half of all work-accident fatalities in Allegheny County, Pennsylvania, resulting not only in 'hardship alone' but hardship as 'an outcome of injustice.' A negligent employer could rely on lawyers to claim that his maimed or dead employee was himself or herself negligent, or had assumed the risk by taking the job, or that a co-worker was at fault.[67]

In 1906 Upton Sinclair's book *The Jungle* informed millions of Americans that not only workers were at risk from the new mass production methods. The book was a novel, but based on close observation and detailed research. In it Americans read about how their food was prepared and the rotten conditions in the Chicago meat-packing plants. The passages that follow brought home graphically the threat posed to consumers by the new methods for preparing food for the mass market: 'It seemed that they must have agencies all over the country, to hunt out old and crippled and diseased cattle to be canned. There were cattle that had been fed on "whisky-malt," the refuse of the breweries, and had become what the men called "steerly" – which means covered with boils. It was a nasty job killing these, for when you plunged your knife into them they would burst and splash foul-smelling stuff into your face; and when a man's sleeves were smeared with blood, and his hands steeped in it, how was he ever to wipe his face, or to clear his eyes so he could see?' In another passage, Sinclair described the ingredients of Durham's canned goods, 'which had become a national institution':

> the things that went into the mixture were tripe, and the fat of pork, and beef suet, and hearts of beef, and finally the waste ends of veal when they had any. They put these up in several grades and sold them at several prices; but the contents of the cans all came out of the same hopper. And then there was 'potted game' and 'potted grouse' and 'devilled ham' – devyled, as the men called it. 'De-vyled' ham was made out of the waste ends of smoked beef that were too small to be sliced by the machines; and also tripe, dyed with chemicals so that it would not show white; and the trimmings of hams and corned beef; ... and finally the hard cartilaginous gullets of beef, after the tongues had been cut out. All this ingenious mixture was ground up and flavored with spices to make it taste like something. Anybody who could invent a new imitation had been sure of a fortune from old Durham ... but it was hard to think of anything new in a place where so many sharp wits had been at work for so long; where men welcomed tuberculosis in the cattle they were feeding, because it made them fatten more quickly.

Sinclair's account then detailed the condemned meat industry:

> People believed that government inspectors protected them from diseased meat but they did not understand that for the inspection of meat to

be sold in the city and State the whole force in Packingtown consisted of three henchmen of the local political machine! ... one of these, a physician, made the discovery that the carcasses of steers ... contained ptomaines, which are deadly poisons, were left upon an open platform and carted away to be sold in the city; and so he insisted that these carcasses be treated with an injection of kerosene – and was ordered to resign the same week! So indignant were the packers that they went farther, and compelled the mayor to abolish the whole bureau of inspection; so that since then there has not been even a pretence of any interference with the graft. There was said to be two thousand dollars a week in hush-money from the tubercular steers alone; and as much again from the hogs which had died of cholera on the trains, and which you might see any day being loaded into box cars and hauled away to place called Globe, in Indiana, where they made a fancy grade of lard.[68]

The journalists Charles Edward Russell and Samuel Merwin substantiated Sinclair's charges that the meat packers themselves controlled government inspection of the meat industry. The 'inspectors' were political pawns who usually only saw the livestock before slaughter and preparation. Nevertheless, newspaper and magazine advertisements reassured consumers that the product had been 'government inspected.'[69]

Government investigation and legislation followed exposure. President Roosevelt set up a special inquiry into the Chicago meat-packing industry, which confirmed the essential truth of the descriptive passages in *The Jungle*. The workers most at risk in Sinclair's novel were recently arrived Lithuanians, and the fact that immigrants faced greater dangers than native-born workers was confirmed in other muckraking pieces. In 1911, for example, Arno Dosch contributed an article for *Everybody's Magazine* entitled 'Just Wops' and included the following dialogue with a manager's assistant of a construction company about a recently excavated railroad cut:

'To think,' I exclaimed, 'that not a man was killed.' 'Who told you that?' asked the young assistant.
'Why, it's here in this report sent to the newspapers by your press agent. He makes a point of it.'
The young assistant smiled. 'Well, yes. I guess that right,' he replied. 'There wasn't anyone killed except just wops.'
'Except what?'

'Wops. Don't you know what wops are? Dagos, niggers, and Hungarians
– the fellows that did the work. They don't know anything, and they
don't count.'

The accident rate for non–English-speaking workers in many industries was frequently twice that of the rest of the workforce, and employers were doubtless aware that language problems would make it far
more difficult for the victims' families to press for compensation.[70]

An unprecedented rush of legislation at state and federal levels followed the exposures of child labour, unsafe working conditions, poisonous food products, and other industrial hazards. Although each
statute carried with it some form of criminal sanction for violation, the
results were mixed because many business interests found ways to circumvent these laws or to use them to their own advantage.

The threat to the health of consumers was taken most seriously.
However, as the cases of the Pure Food and Drug Act and the Meat
Inspection Act of 1906 indicate, this was because business interests
feared loss of profits more than the loss of lives. After *The Jungle*'s disclosures had triggered a 50 per cent drop in sales and threatened meat
packers with the loss of their European markets, the giant packing concerns expediently came out in favour of meat inspection, and pressured for the act to be passed. The meat packers had discovered, along
with other corporations, that government regulation could work in
their favour. As the criminologist James Coleman explained: 'Not only
did meat inspection offer the best way of restoring public confidence in
the product, but the costs of maintaining adequate sanitation were a
much greater burden on small meat packing firms and thus helped the
large corporations to consolidate their control over the market.'[71]

On child labour, most Northern and Western states had prohibited
the employment of children under fourteen by the second decade of
the twentieth century. Southern states were, however, much slower to
inconvenience employers, and they were aided in this by a series of
Supreme Court decisions that held federal legislation on this matter
unconstitutional. The census of 1920 found that more than one million
children between the ages of ten and fifteen were employed mainly in
agriculture, manufacturing, the street trades, and industrial home-
work. Ten years later a presidential conference on the problem found
that most state laws were seriously defective and rarely enforced with
any degree of honesty or efficiency. Many employers thus considered

that the profits from cheap child labour were worth the minimal risk of inspection.[72]

The record on health and safety at work was also patchy. The exposures of the dangers of unsafe working conditions and occupational diseases again led many states to adopt reform measures and accident frequency rates did decline in the following decades. The measures included new mine and factory safety laws, inspection requirements, and employer liability and workmen's compensation laws.[73] Workers could expect limited compensation in the case of injury so long as they accepted that their employers had not been at fault. And as Joseph A. Page and Mary Win O'Brien concluded in their book entitled *Bitter Wages* (1973):

> The emergence of workmen's compensation did not mark any revolutionary change in values, nor did it signal the end of the ascendancy of property rights over human rights. Though the humanitarian aspects of the new statutes were often proclaimed, the truth of the matter was that workmen's compensation made excellent business sense, and for that reason powerful business interests backed its adoption. Dissatisfaction with existing methods of work-accident compensation had reached such a level that some reform was inevitable. Businessmen feared the liberalization of employer's liability laws, which would have limited the employer's common-law defenses and made it much easier for injured workers to recover full compensatory damages. Workmen's compensation would be much less costly to industry, particularly because state legislatures would be relatively easy to manipulate, and thus compensation benefits could be kept at a low level.[74]

The federal government also proved to be slow or unwilling to protect workers whether from occupational diseases or contributory negligence on the part of employers. Despite the exceptionally poor safety record of the U.S. mining industry, the Federal Bureau of Mines, which was created in 1910, was not given any powers of compulsion. And, despite increasing awareness of the cost in lost lives of occupational diseases, the U.S. government was at least six years behind European governments in banning the use of white phosphorus in the manufacture of matches. As we shall see in Chapter 6, it was even more inadequate in its response to the use of other toxic substances in the workplace.[75]

Two decades of reform, however, had ensured that health and safety laws were on the statute books. The challenge for many business interests was how to break these laws and stay out of prison.

Big Business and the End of Muckraking

As indicated by the discussion of Upton Sinclair and other muckrakers, informed American opinion was never more conscious of the cost and the consequences of organized business crime than at the beginning of the twentieth century. Following in the tradition of Henry Demarest Lloyd, many writers found that America's barbarians came from above.

Lincoln Steffens in *The Shame of the Cities* (1904) revealed corrupt alliances between business and politics at a local level. He detailed different types of corrupt activity in six major cities, beginning with St Louis. St Louis exemplified 'boodle' where public franchises and privileges 'were sought, not only for legitimate profit and common convenience, but for loot.' The results were 'poorly-paved and refuse-burdened streets,' and public buildings such as the city hospital that were firetraps in a city that boasted of its wealth. Steffens found that 'the big businessman' was the chief source of corruption in every city he visited: 'I found him buying boodlers in St Louis, defending grafters in Minneapolis, originating corruption in Pittsburgh, sharing with bosses in Philadelphia, deploring reform in Chicago, and beating good government with corruption funds in New York. He is a self-righteous fraud, this big businessman ... it were a boon if he would neglect politics.'[76]

David Graham Phillips most dramatically illustrated corrupt alliances between business and politics at a national level in a series of articles for *Cosmopolitan Magazine*. In 'The Treason of the Senate,' Phillips focused on Senator Nelson W. Aldrich's role at the centre of a powerful clique of conservative Senators and big business interests. Phillips described Aldrich as the 'chief agent of the predatory band which was rapidly forming to take care of the prosperity of the American people' and the 'permanent and undisputed boss' of 'the obsequious servants of corruption' in the senate. 'To relate the treason in detail,' he wrote,

> would mean taking up bill after bill and going through it, line by line, word by word, and showing how this interpolation there or that excision yonder meant millions on millions more to this or that interest, millions

on millions less for the people as merchants, wage or salary earners, consumers; how the killing of this measure meant immunity to looters all
along the line; how the alteration of the wording of that other "trifling"
resolution gave a quarter of a cent a pound on every one of hundreds of
millions of pounds of some necessary of life to a certain small group of
men; how this innocent looking measure safeguarded the railway barons
in looting the whole American people by excessive charges and rebates.
Few among the masses have the patience to listen to these dull matters –
and, so "the interests" and their agents have prosperity and honor instead
of justice and jail.

No railway legislation that was not either helpful to or harmless against
"the interests"; no legislation on the subject of corporations that would
interfere with "the interests", which use the corporate form to simplify
and systematize their stealing; no legislation on the tariff question unless
it secured to "the interests" full and free license to loot; no investigation of
wholesale robbery or of any of the evils resulting from it – there you have
in a few words the whole story of the Senate's treason under Aldrich's
leadership, and of why property is concentrating in the hands of the
few.[77]

Few informed Americans would have disagreed with Phillip's analysis. Washington Gladden, for example, one of the leaders of the social
gospel movement, reflected widespread concern about what he called
'predatory wealth' and elaborated on this in his autobiography published in 1909: 'It is impossible to deny the existence of a considerable
class of persons who have obtained great wealth by predatory methods, by evasion and defiance of the law, by the practices of vast extortions, by getting unfair and generally unlawful advantages over their
neighbors, by secret agreements, and the manipulation of railway and
government officials ... by manifold arts that tend to corrupt the character and destroy the foundations of the social order.'[78]

The academic who came closest to articulating a new understanding
of modern crime based on the avalanche of evidence of business
wrongdoing was Edward A. Ross in his book *Sin and Society* (1907).
Ross argued that lawless and destructive business practices had created a need for a redefinition of ideas about crime. The typical new
criminal of industrial society was, for Ross, one who prospered by
destructive 'practices which have not yet come under the ban of public
opinion.' Although Ross shared many of the race and class assumptions of his academic contemporaries, he also felt that the new type of

criminal was far more dangerous than 'his low-browed cousins' or the 'plain criminal.' The newcomer, according to Ross, 'sports the livery of virtue and operates on a Titanic scale' and occupies 'the cabin rather than the steerage of society.' Because 'patent ruffians' were 'vermin' and confined to the 'social basement' they had few opportunities to damage society. Big business 'criminaloids,' on the other hand, were 'beasts of prey' who could 'pick a thousand pockets, poison a thousand sick, pollute a thousand minds, or imperil a thousand lives.' Modern crime was based on betrayal rather than aggression, and monstrous treacheries exist on all levels of modern life: 'Adulterators, peculators, boodlers, grafters, violating the trust others have placed in them.'[79]

By pointing out that the sins of modern industrialists were more destructive than more familiar older forms of crime, Ross was thus attempting to broaden the definition of crime. Big business 'criminaloids' robbed and killed on a much grander scale than ever witnessed before, but 'so long as morality stands stock-still in the old tracks, they escape both punishment and ignominy ... The man who picks pockets with a railway rebate, murders with an adulterant instead of a bludgeon, burglarizes with a "rake-off" instead of a jimmy ... does not feel on his brow the brand of a malefactor ... Like a stupid, flushed giant at bay, the public heeds the little overt offender more than the big covert offender.'[80]

Ross's recommendations to address organized business crime involved making directors individually accountable for 'every case of misconduct of which the company receives the benefit, for every preventable deficiency or abuse that regularly goes on in the course of business.' 'Strict accountability,' he continued would send flying the figure-head directors who, when the misdeeds of their protégés come to light, protest they 'didn't know.' It will bar buccaneering insiders from using a group of eminent dummies as unwitting decoys for the confiding investor or policyholder. It will break up the game of operating a brigand public service company (owned by some distant "syndicate") from behind a board of respectable local "directors" without a shred of power. And, accountability should be enforced by the reality of prison rather than the 'flea-bite' deterrent of fines. 'Never will the brake of the law grip these slippery wheels until prison doors yawn for the convicted officers of lawless corporations.'[81]

In the following decades there were far fewer indictments of what is now known as corporate crime and violence. Lawyers and other business representatives colluded with government legislators and regulators and continued to help many corporations circumvent or ignore much of the legislation passed to protect workers and consumers. A new class of industrial psychologists emerged and tended to find the causes of work place injuries and deaths in the defects or carelessness of individual workers rather than factors that affected profitability, such as rate of production or adequate safety devices and adequate lighting. Corporate violators were occasionally discovered but rarely faced more than the 'flea-bite' deterrent of fines. Organized business crime continued to cause the death and injury of many hundreds and thousands of Americans.

For all the revulsion at the criminal and destructive practices of big business, the period of Progressive reform did not lead to a diminution of corporate power and influence in American society. On the contrary, as the words and actions of the two most notable progressive presidents demonstrate, corporations remained privileged players in American society permitted to commit what for individuals would be criminal acts.

Despite President Theodore Roosevelt's reputation as a 'trust buster' or anti-big business crusader, he actually initiated only a few selective anti-trust prosecutions during his time in office against what he called 'bad' corporations such as Standard Oil, whose directors he privately described as 'the biggest criminals in our country.'[82] He was much more amenable to those he called 'good' corporations. On one occasion, as the historian Gabriel Kolko indicates, his naive faith in the integrity of executive officers of 'good' corporations even allowed him to be the unwitting participant in a transaction that has all the appearances of a gigantic fraud. In 1907 Roosevelt approved U.S. Steel's takeover of Tennessee Coal and Iron for $45 million, after taking the word of Elbert H. Gary and Henry C. Frick of the larger company that the smaller company was not even worth that amount. The president promised he would not initiate an anti-trust prosecution against U.S. Steel and kept his word despite the fact that a little investigation would have shown that the Tennessee company was actually worth $180 million.[83] The following year Roosevelt again acted improperly by responding to pressure from companies in the electrical supply business in an attempt to stall a Justice Department investigation of their price-fixing activities. On this occasion his attorney general tactfully persuaded him that the investigation should go on.[84]

William Howard Taft, who succeeded Roosevelt as president, was more consistent in his attitude to anti-trust proceedings. During his four-year term there were twice as many prosecutions under the Sherman Anti-Trust Act as the Roosevelt administration had brought in eight years. Those indicted included such giants as the General Electric Company, the American Sugar Refining Company, the International Harvester Company, and U.S. Steel. In the case of the latter Taft incurred Roosevelt's anger by ignoring the earlier deal. The prosecution of Standard Oil was also brought to a successful conclusion in 1911. 'No disinterested mind,' according to the judge's summary in the case, 'can survey the period in question (since 1870) without being irresistibly drawn to the conclusion that the very genius for commercial development and organization ... soon begat an intent and purpose to exclude others ... from their right to trade and thus accomplish the mastery that was the end in view.'[85] As a result of this decision, Standard was broken up into five companies.

The system of informal detentes had broken down. According to Frank Pearce's study of anti-trust legislation, corporations soon realized their precarious position in relation to the federal and state governments. 'Woodrow Wilson,' Pearce wrote, 'shared their concern, and during his presidency the legal situation was radically modified. Legislation was passed making regulation a Federal responsibility, and creating agencies responsive to the interests of big business.'[86]

Wilson, who took office in 1912, used different terminology, but essentially his views were as favourable to corporations as those of Roosevelt. The proper policy of government, according to Wilson before he took office, was to regulate business practices so as to prevent the misuse of corporations and market power by individuals and to make guilt and punishment for unfair methods and unreasonable restraint of trade individual rather than corporate. In the case of wrongdoing, he announced, 'we will ... find the officer who ordered that thing done, and we will indict him not as an officer of the corporation but as an individual who used that corporation for something that was illegal.'[87] A great deal of evidence indicated that business crime depended on collusion, corruption, and corporate policy to exclude competition and trade union activity. Crime, in other words, that was organized. President Wilson here was not even allowing for the possibility of the existence of organized business crime. It was an assumption that lay behind much government policy during his and succeeding administrations.

In January 1914, as president, Wilson announced a new program of business reform by telling Congress that his administration's policy towards business would be based on collaboration not confrontation: 'What we are purposing to do ... is, happily, not to hamper or interfere with business as enlightened businessmen prefer to do it, or in any sense to put it under the ban. The antagonism between business and government is over ... The Government and businessmen are ready to meet each other half way in a common effort to square business methods with both public opinion and the law.'[88]

The result was the passage of the Federal Trade Commission Act in September of that year. It established a Federal Trade Commission to regulate business activities, authorized to investigate the activities of all corporations engaged in interstate commerce and to act against those that employed unfair methods of competition. The following month a related measure was passed that was intended to strengthen existing anti-trust legislation. The Clayton Act prohibited certain business practices including price discrimination that tended to lessen competition or promote monopoly.[89]

From then on, as Wilson intended, there was a shift towards closer cooperation between government and the corporations that accelerated under the emergency conditions of the First World War. Industry was organized and disciplined as never before to meet the emergency and industry leaders were brought into close and regular contact with their counterpart congressional committees and executive agencies. The end of the war established the practice of regular formal consultation and massive informal collusion between government and big business.

By the time Wilson took office, the age of muckraking was over. Many of the magazines that had publicized the crimes of big business found themselves faced with crippling libel costs or forced out of business in other ways. In 1910, *Hampton's*, for example, had run a series of articles on the rise and illegal practices of the giant New York, New Haven, and Hartford railroad, despite receiving threats of reprisals. From that time on, as the historian Louis Filler narrates, the owner Benjamin Hampton was a marked man: 'Spies ferreted their way into his offices, and one in the accounting department found the opportunity to copy out the entire list of Hampton's stockholders. Each stockholder was separately visited and regaled with stories of how Hampton was misusing company funds. Wall Street agents of the railroad made extraordinary bids for the stock in order to indicate it was losing value.'

Hampton, recognizing the threat, convened a committee of stock-holders and received endorsements for $30,000. These were then taken to the bank and accepted. Hampton was able to draw money on them until, the following day, he was ordered to return the money and take back the notes from the bank. 'Such banking practice was illegal,' Filler continued, 'but the manager of the bank told Hampton that he was powerless to do anything else; "downtown" people were giving the orders, and he had to take them.' The downtown people he was refer-ring to were associated with J.P. Morgan, the most powerful invest-ment banker in the United States:

> Hampton now tried and failed to float a loan. One banker who declared that he would stand by Hampton in his crisis, whether the 'Morgan Crowd' willed it or not, was forced to stop his transactions and was him-self forced out of business within several months.
>
> Within ten days Hampton had to turn his affairs over to his lawyers. Facing receiverships, he chose what seemed the lesser of two evils; he relinquished the magazine to a group of promoters who offered impres-sive introductions and gave promises that the magazine would be fully supported. In a few months Hampton became convinced that the new owners had no intention but to loot the magazine. He was later told by the bookkeeper that they abstracted $175,000 from the property, and then took the books down to the East River and threw them from a bridge.[90]

Other muckraking outlets were also destroyed or their editors expe-diently turned away from exposing the corporations towards safer subjects. The muckrakers themselves either had to go along with the pro-business tide, or publish privately and lose circulation as in the case of Upton Sinclair, or look for careers outside journalism. After almost two decades of exposing the crimes of the powerful things were back as they were at the turn of the century when, E.W. Scripps, founder of the first modern newspaper chain declared: 'The press in this country is so thoroughly dominated by a wealthy few ... that it cannot be depended upon to give the mass of the people that correct information concerning political, economical and social subjects which it is necessary that the mass of people shall have in order that they vote ... in the best way to protect themselves from the brutal force and chica-nery of the ruling and employing classes.'[91]

The First World War also marked the end of an era of radical film-making. According to the film historian Steven Ross, big business interests had begun to dominate the movie industry by this time and did not tolerate productions that were overtly critical of the business system. Instead, as Ross argued, 'Hollywood's emphasis on consumer fantasies marked a conservative retreat from the far more serious and ideological diverse treatments of class conflict that characterized pre-war filmmaking.'

Ross also shows how censorship at local, state, and federal government levels added to the more conservative trend in filmmaking. During the war, for example, George Creel's Committee on Public Information, urged studios to produce cheerful films that presented the 'wholesome life of America' in order to counter 'enemy propaganda' that publicized 'news of strikes and lynchings, riots, murder cases, graft prosecutions, and all the public washings of the Nation's dirty linen.'[92]

By the end of the First World War, crime commissions had been set up to put pressure on the police and the courts to enforce laws against any crimes that adversely affected the interests of property. They collected facts and expert opinion on aspects of the crime problem and issued reports and statements to the media to win support for specific recommendations to improve the efficiency and honesty of criminal justice and law enforcement.[93] The most influential of these was the Chicago Crime Commission (CCC) which was set up by local businessmen after a successful bank robbery in 1917. It was described by its first director, Henry Barrett Chamberlin, as 'an organization of bankers, business and professional men who are applying modern business methods to correct a system which has, through inertia, been allowed to grow up in the departments of state and municipal government having to do with the prevention, apprehension, prosecution, and punishment of crime and criminals ... The Chicago Crime Commission is purely and simply an organization of business men determined to do its duty, without fear or favor, to the end that organized crime in Chicago is destroyed.'[94]

Because the CCC, like other commssions, was funded by business it did not see business crime as organized crime. Crime commissions in general tended to ignore organized criminality within legal markets and focus public attention on organized criminality in illegal markets such as alcohol during Prohibition and gambling after the repeal of the 18th Amendment.

From the second decade of the twentieth century to the late 1960s 'investigative' reporting meant, for the most part, exposing soft targets

and inventing threats in ways that would often benefit and rarely challenge the interests of corporate America. Ways were found to excuse or
ignore business criminality or explain it as a deviation from normal
practice. Even when big business criminality was too blatant to ignore,
the business class and their allies in the press found ways to ensure
that the status quo was not unduly disturbed.

In the early 1920s, for example, a series of scandals during the
administration of President Warren Harding revealed that politicians
and businessmen were as involved in organized criminal activity as
ever before. Millions of dollars were effectively looted from the public
treasury. But, as Frederick Lewis Allen noted, the harshest condemnation during the Harding scandals was reserved for those who insisted
on bringing the facts to light. Senators Thomas Walsh and Burton K.
Wheeler, who led congressional investigations into Harding-era corruption, were called 'the Montana scandalmongers' by the *New York
Tribune* and 'assassins of character' by the *New York Times*.'[95]

The background and response to a major disaster at Gauley Bridge,
West Virginia demonstrate that the press was equally as protective of
business interests when it came to health and safety violations. In 1929
the New Kanawha Power Company – a Union Carbide subsidiary –
chose the Rhinehart-Dennis Construction Company as the subcontrac-
tor to build a tunnel near Gauley Bridge. Rhinehart-Dennis recruited a
mainly black and unskilled workforce for the task who were desperate
for work during the Depression and began the construction of the
tunnel in 1930. According to Joseph Page and Mary-Win O'Brien's
account, working conditions strained credulity:

> Gasoline-powered trains filled the tunnel with carbon monoxide, poison-
> ing the workers and making them drowsy. The dust was often so thick that
> workers couldn't see ten feet in front, even with the headlights of a train ...
> Though West Virginia mining law required a thirty-minute wait after blast-
> ing, workers were herded back into the tunnel immediately after a blast.
> The foremen at times had to beat them with pick handles to get them to
> return. The silica content of the rock being blasted was extremely high.
> Though New Kanawha Power warned its engineers to use masks when
> entering the tunnel, no one ever told the workers to take precautions.
>
> Increasing numbers of workers became progressively shorter of breath
> and then dropped dead. Rhinehart-Dennis contacted with a local under-
> taker to bury the blacks in a field at fifty-five dollars per corpse. Three
> hours was the standard elapsed time between death in the tunnel and

burial. In this way, the company avoided the formalities of an autopsy and death certificate. It was estimated that 169 blacks ended up in the field, 2 or 3 to a hole.

An estimate of the project's final human cost put it at 476 dead and 1,500 disabled. Senator Rush Dew Holt of West Virginia called it, 'The most barbaric example of industrial construction that ever happened in this world. That company well knew what it was going to do to these men. The company openly said that if they killed off those men there were plenty of other men to be had.'

Some survivors took Rhinehart-Dennis and New Kanawha to court to sue for negligence, but the cases were sabotaged by public and private corruption in West Virginia. The chief of West Virginia's Mines Department testified that he had observed no dust in the tunnel in 1930 or 1931, although he had written letters to the company in 1931 urging them to do something about the dust condition. One of the jurors was found out to be riding home every night in a company car and there were many more rumours of jury tampering. Eventually, 167 of the suits were settled out of court for $130,000, with one-half going to the workers' attorneys. One of the workers' law firms was later found to have accepted a $20,000 side-payment from the companies. No punitive action was ever taken against Rhinehart-Dennis, New Kanawha Power, or Union Carbide.

Throughout the affair the national press was almost as unconcerned about the dead workers as the companies. It took five years from the time construction began for the press to take notice and then it was just a temporary flurry of interest.[96] In the wake of the Gauley Bridge slaughter, business leaders showed more concern about the possible cost of a toughened up regulatory response than the loss of life caused by unsafe working practices. Soon after Congress investigated the affair in 1936, a group of industrialists and scientists met to discuss the problem. From this meeting came the Air Hygiene Foundation, later renamed the Industrial Hygiene Foundation (IHF). IHF's function, according to Daniel Berman in his book *Death on the Job*, was to forestall massive claims for occupational disease compensation. The IHF's public relations campaigns were successful in helping to curb any increase in claims and any unwanted government regulation. It became 'a permanent and important part of the compensation-safety apparatus, specializing in debunking the seriousness of occupational health problems.'[97]

Business Racketeering and Labour Corruption

Although the 1920s has the reputation for being a prosperous decade most American workers experienced poor wages and appalling, often dangerous, conditions. Efforts to organize the mass production industries such as car manufacturing and steel failed. The vast majority of workers – nearly 90 per cent – thus remained unorganized and most employers wanted to keep it that way, using both legal and illegal tactics in the process.

With the encouragement of pro-business Republican administrations and a series of Supreme Court decisions, business stepped up efforts to break unions where they existed and to maintain the effectively non-union open shop where they did not. In 1922 the Railway Labor Board ordered a wage cut and 400,000 workers responded with a walkout. Attorney General Daugherty then ordered a court injunction prohibiting all strike activity on the grounds that it violated both anti-trust and transportation laws. 'So long and to the extent that I speak for the government of the United States,' Daugherty declared, 'I will use the power of the government to prevent the labour unions of the country from destroying the open shop.'[98] The Supreme Court had already upheld the 'yellow-dog' contract that banned workers from joining a union as a condition of employment, declared it illegal to organize a boycott in favour of union recognition, and drastically limited picketing and other union rights. Employers were thus still at liberty to use any means including violence, intimidation, spying, and blacklisting to forestall any chance of having to face collective bargaining.

The practice of the 'special deputy' system was one anti-union tactic among many. Coal managers in Logan, West Virginia, for example, paid the county over a $100,000 a year in the early 1920s for the purpose of hiring extra anti-union deputy sheriffs and justices of the peace. Sheriff Don Chafin testified in 1921 that after a decade of holding various country offices, his official salary was only $3,500. His personal wealth, however, was about $350,000 and included many coal holdings. Under his control were up to forty-six active deputies, many of who drew salaries from both the county and the coal operators and about 500 more who could be drawn on in times of emergency. Chafin effectively used beatings or the threats of beatings to keep union organizers out. When he left office he became a partner in a coal company and achieved millionaire status.[99]

A similar deputy sheriff system was in operation in Harlan County, Kentucky, until the mid-1930s. Coal operators and their allies there used bombing, kidnapping, and the assassination not only of organizers but also of sympathetic law enforcement officers to keep out the United Mine Workers. A large number of the deputies had been convicted of various felonious charges ranging from murder to carrying concealed weapons. Eventually the federal government stepped in to protect the civil liberties of unionists since, as in many other areas, the local authorities were largely beholden to the companies.[100]

In larger cities the balance of power also heavily favoured employers during conflicts with labour. During a 1927 dispute between the Pittsburgh Coal Company and the United Mine Workers, for example, employees were illegally evicted from company houses and two deaths resulted from the action of the company police. In the first, two company policemen beat a striker to death in the police barracks, even after being warned by a company doctor of the likely consequences of too severe a beating. They received short prison sentences. In the second, another company policeman and a mine superintendent were convicted of felonious homicide when they shot an unarmed shopkeeper for expressing sympathy for the strikers.[101]

Henry Ford was the most prominent U.S. businessman to employ gangsters in the battle against unions. For years Ford ensured uninterrupted assembly lines and ever-increasing productivity by keeping its Detroit workforce powerless and unorganized. The company used both the stick and the carrot to keep unions out. It usually paid better to work for Ford, but the stick was often literally the stick wielded by thugs and gangsters, or fists, or lengths of rubber hoses and, sometimes, guns. As late as 1940 the National Labor Relations Board described Ford methods as 'organized gangsterism.'[102]

The man who ran the violent side of Ford's operation was Harry Bennett, head of the company's 'service department.' Bennett was an ex-boxer who had risen from the bottom to the top of the corporation's hierarchy within a decade of the First World War. In the process, he organized many acts of violence, most often against workers who complained about pay and condition-. As an expert in intimidation, he used Ford money to locate and recruit like-minded people.

In Prohibition-era Detroit, Ford's favoured racketeer was Chester LaMare. Bennett gave LaMare a Ford car showroom for use as his headquarters and the concession for supplying fruit to the Ford factory

canteens. LaMare was assassinated in 1931, but Ford continued to deal
with such local gangsters as Anthony D'Anna, who was a part-owner
of Detroit's principal haul-away business, the E. and L. Transport
Company. When a Senate committee questioned Bennett about these
relationships in 1950, he claimed no knowledge of them and had no
documents to refer to since he kept 'no files, records, or memoranda of
any kind.'[103]

While gangsters functioned as little more than strong-arm men in
industrial disputes involving large corporations, they had more opportunities to exploit both management and labour in smaller-scale industries. Many businessmen, especially in the service trades, had
welcomed gangster involvement as a solution to the problem of price-
cutting and cut-throat competition. These, according to a 1927 report
by the Chicago Employers' Association (CEA), 'desiring to create a
monopoly in their particular field engage men whose very names
strike terror in the hearts of the timid to organize an association of pro-
prietors in their line. In soliciting members the organizers make vague
reference to the possibility of damage to property and persons, and to
prevent which the association is being organized. If the proprietor does
not join quickly his plant is bombed, windows broken, stench bombs
exploded on his premises, employees assaulted, or perhaps called on
strike.'[104]

Six years later, another CEA study, this time written by Gordon
Hostetter and T.Q. Beesley, noted that at least thirty-seven of the city's
important service industries could be characterized as rackets. These
included laundry, barbers, building material, paving, coal, food distribution, garages, long-distance hauling, ash and garbage removal, railway express, florists, janitors, window washers, oil wagon drivers,
electrotyping, interior decorating, and photographic trades. This 'vast
system of criminal racket control,' they estimated, cost the people of
the city 'more than one hundred millions of dollars per year in inflated
prices for services and commodities within the city, unnecessary over-
head costs in doing business, high insurance rates, property damage,
costly police protection and legal services.'

Hostetter and Beesley's study was entitled 'Twentieth Century
Crime' and demonstrated that Chicago racketeering consisted of five
distinct but interdependent elements: business, labour unionism, politics, lawyers, and criminals. The rackets structure had benefits for all
five units. Businessmen wanted monopolies in their trades or services,

control of their labour force, the power to fix prices in their favour, and control over the enactment or application of regulatory laws. The corrupt leader of organized labour also wanted to control the labour force for 'this insures to the treasury the dues of all men of that trade ... 'Moreover, it enables him to manipulate his man forces to the advantage of his co-conspirators, the businessman or the politician or both, and to the discomfiture and disadvantage of businessmen who dare to assert independence of the racket.'

Politicians gained through 'campaign contributions, organization work, and votes at election time, and frequently also [through] participation in the profits of the conspiracy.' Gangsters found 'lucrative employment to bomb; to commit arson; to slug, maim and kill; to terrorize an entire community into staying away from the poll at election time.'

The most damning comments in Hostetter and Beesley's study were reserved for lawyers. These not only charged high fees to guide, protect, and counsel racketeers before the courts and in the realm of politics, but probably also constituted 'the most important cog in the machinery of crime.' The lawyer 'has twisted and distorted the law to suit the purposes of a criminal clientele. He has subverted the dignity of habeas corpus. He has made the "continuance" in criminal cases anathema to complainants and a solace to the criminals. He is the godfather of every criminal gang worthy of mention in America. He devises the clever legal instruments that constitute the charters of rackets ... Some rackets have had their very genesis in legal quarters, and yet the profession of lawyers appears to be without facilities of inquiry and discipline for such members, or if such facilities exist they seem to have atrophied years ago.' Hostetter and Beesley made it clear that lawyers were employed to exploit loopholes and legitimize and front operations, activities that without the protection of legal smokescreens would be recognized as simple extortion.

Although businessmen, labour leaders, and lawyers constituted the framework of racketeering, according to Hostetter and Beesley, out-and-out criminals were beginning to take control. From control of competition and prices, 'racketeering has broadened into a vast system of exploitation for the enrichment of a criminal class.' 'Twentieth Century Crime' was written principally as a warning to small businessmen, particularly in the service industries. The root cause of the racketeering problem, according to Hostetter and Beesley's analysis was 'cut-throat' competition. This problem had been largely eliminated in the centre of the economy by the rise of the giant corporations but small business-men by contrast were still 'beset by the problem of the ever-present price reductionist.' Small businessmen therefore found racketeering acceptable as a way of stabilizing prices.

By undermining the political principles of freedom of opportunity that originally made possible their entrance into the field of business, these businessmen, according to Hostetter and Beesley, contributed to 'the creation of a criminal overlordship and the final breakdown of ordered security' ... To them it does not matter that they trample upon human rights which have been established step by bitter step through the centuries in the common man's emergence from serfdom. In fact, after a period they become serfs indeed in the harshest sense of the word, because once part of the racket, they are beyond the pale of help. Being equally culpable, with the criminal, before the law, they can do nothing but bear the impositions the racket places upon them.'

As representatives of the CEA, Hostetter and Beesley's concern for the businessmen was, of course, to be expected. Underpinning their work was a long-standing business complaint against anti-trust laws: 'It is a fact, however, that many sections of business, being unable under the law to organize themselves for rational control of competition, have developed a positively criminal philosophy, and have created an economic monstrosity the acts of which have run the whole scale of crime.'[105]

Other commentators reiterated variations on the same theme. Murray I. Gurfein, in an early attempt to define organized crime, called the racketeer 'a natural evolutionary product of strict laissez faire' and blamed the government's hands-off approach to business during the 1920s for the problem.[106] Similarly, the influential columnist Walter Lippmann noted that employers 'faced with the constant threat of cut-throat competition' were likely to employ gangsters to drive competitors from the field. He again suggested that the insecurity of highly competitive capitalism was the root cause of the problem.[107]

In the progressive tradition all of these commentators were more concerned with waste and disorganization than exploitation and none of them noted that racketeering damaged the interests of workers more than any other groups. In all the industries listed by Hostetter and Beesley, workers could be driven to work harder and longer at low rates of pay because if they failed to deliver they would be sacked and then placed on a blacklist. If workers complained about their situation they could expect a beating or worse. Gangster-dominated unions supported rather than fought exploitative systems. The workers, in other words, not the businessmen, were the modern-day serfs.

In 1933 the New Deal government of Franklin D. Roosevelt began to address the problems of industrial disorganization thought to lie behind racketeering and other labour-management problems. The National Industrial Recovery Act (NIRA) set up committees usually dominated by business representatives to draw up codes to regulate the terms upon which business was to be conducted. 'Usually without direct price-setting,' according to Paul Conkin, 'most industry codes achieved the same result indirectly by limiting production, preventing price cutting, and forbidding unfair competition.' Business effectively gained the right to regulate prices through trade associations, without fear of anti-trust suits under the Sherman Act. In exchange labour gained minimum wage and hours standards, and under Section 7a, the right to organize.

Although the Supreme Court declared NIRA unconstitutional in 1935, it had established trends in industry that persisted. Most businessmen felt that the stability its codes had brought to industry was preferable to previous conditions and their provisions were largely retained by new collective bargaining agreements. Union rights were strengthened by the National Labour Relations Act of 1935. This guaranteed the right of collective bargaining by a union chosen by a majority of employees, legalized collective action such as strikes and boycotts, and by a code of fair practices outlawed such traditional weapons as the company union, blacklist, and yellow-dog contract.[108] In the new context of American industrial relations, racketeering began to change. Whereas previously businessmen invited racketeers in to reduce the wastes of competition, now the only useful service performed by racketeers for business was labour control and, even this would in time become outdated.

After the New Deal had ushered in extensive government regulation and a turning away from *laissez-faire*, racketeers thus became more like parasites than useful servants. As a result, both business and unions put pressure on authorities to act and stamp out industrial racketeering. The response, however, was patchy. In Manhattan, special prosecutor Thomas E. Dewey investigated and secured convictions in the poultry and restaurant rackets and began an investigation into the garment trucking rackets which eventually broke the power of Lepke Buchalter and Jacob Shapiro and led to the former's execution for murder in 1944. Although Dewey's action against industrial extortionists was excessively praised in the press at the time, it did little to protect New York unions and small businesses from gangsters in the long term.[109]

At least an effort had been made in New York. In Chicago, many successful rackets operated with the approval and sometimes the active involvement of officials in the state attorney's office, represented in the 1930s by Thomas C. Courtney and his chief investigator Dan Gilbert. The earliest suggestion that Courtney's use of his office was an abuse of power came in an article in the *Chicago American*, on 22 March 1934. The newspaper declared that Courtney's real job should be state's attorney and not 'industrial dictator.' The article then cited a recent case in which Courtney had 'marshaled squads of police against a certain coal merchant because he would not deal with the unions organized by Mr Courtney with the notorious "Lefty" Lynch.' Lynch was the head of the Chicago Teamsters Union whose qualifications for the job included a conviction for murder. A contemporary journalist summed up Lynch's union as no more than a 'strong-arm' racket working with the employers' association and against the rank-and-file.[110]

During these years gangsters such as Frank Nitti, Murray Humphries, Jack Guzik, and others took over many unions often with Courtney and Gilbert's approval. Employers paid off gangster-controlled unions handsomely in return for low wage settlements, and gangsters also gained opportunities to loot union funds, which were not protected by local, state, or federal legislation.

Courtney kept his job as state's attorney until 1942 despite widespread awareness of his complicity in the city's racketeering. In 1940, for example, Frank J. Loesch, president of the Chicago Crime Commission, had told a radio audience: 'Few labour crimes have been solved in Chicago because of the close association between labour gangsters and law enforcement agencies. A real state's attorney could either jail, electrocute or drive these labour goons from our gates. A fearless, courageous and honest State's Attorney could accomplish that feat and the war on crime would be over.'[111] In 1942, however, Courtney was rewarded for his public service with a judgeship.

Chief Investigator Gilbert held his position until 1950 and prospered as a middleman in Chicago's political-criminal-business networks. His official duty was to gather evidence for criminal prosecutions of felonies, but crime writer Ovid Demaris described his actual role more accurately:

He worked as a labour organizer for the syndicate in a score of unions: he kept an eye on the gambling and handbook joints. He was a wheelhorse for the Democratic party – when Courtney was elevated to the bench he raised $30,000 from among the hoodlum element for the campaign of William Touhy. He visited the Criminal Courts Building almost daily, where he wandered in and out of courtrooms and chambers, conferred with runners, fixers who worked directly with judges, and bondsmen, spending considerable time in Felony Branch, where tens of thousands of felonies are reduced to misdemeanors each year. He was interested in vending machines, jukeboxes, slot machines and a variety of vices including prostitution.[112]

Gilbert survived a minor setback in 1938 when he was indicted by a federal grand jury for participating in a racket to maintain a high price for milk in Chicago, which was set by the big distributors. He was charged with using 'unlawful threats, intimidation and acts of violence' against the drivers of the milk wagons of independent distributors, and with preventing 'the delivery of daily supplies of meat, bread, bakery goods, vegetables and other foods to places of business served by the independent distributors' who refused to maintain trust prices for milk.' However, the indictment was quashed.[113]

In 1950 Gilbert testified before the Kefauver Committee and admitted to a net worth of about $360,000 and a yearly income of around $42,000 from his stocks and bonds. He told the committee that he was a very lucky gambler and that this explained his wealth. During the hearings the newspapers finally got hold of the Gilbert story and dubbed him 'the world's richest cop' after Gilbert had been playing a crucial role in racketeering operations for eighteen years. Soon after the hearings he retired from Chicago politics and moved to California.[114]

The best known Chicago example of the breed of criminal defence lawyers excoriated by Hostetter and Beesley in their analysis of racketeering was Abraham Teitelbaum. In 1939 the Chicago Restaurant Association (CRA) hired Teitelbaum at an annual retainer of $125,000, as a 'labour relations expert.' The association, which had been formed in 1914 to keep unions out of the restaurant business, had found that its members were suddenly being subjected to a series of beatings, bombings, and strikes. These just as suddenly stopped as soon as Teitelbaum had worked out a compromise. The owners paid union initiation fees and dues for a limited number of employees, who were not consulted and rarely knew that they had become members of a union. Such arrangements usually lasted for years, and dues were collected on members who had changed jobs, left the state or country, or even died. It made no difference to either party in the deal, because the union was no more than a 'paper' organization. The restaurant owners contributed to a 'voluntary fund' for use during regular labour disputes and, as a result, Teitelbaum was always able to arrange settlements before expensive strikes occurred. In 1951 some restaurateurs revealed the complicity of the Chicago police and the state attorney's office in all this, but their complaints were ignored. Most restaurant owners probably calculated that Teitelbaum's retainer worked out much cheaper than paying fair wages to their employees.[115]

Criminal officials like Gilbert and criminal professionals like Teitelbaum flourished because of their local power and influence and the reluctance of federal authorities to interfere in what were still considered to be local matters. Although anti-racketeering laws passed in 1934 had significantly broadened the legal basis for federal jurisdiction, they were rarely used. One exception involved the movie industry and the uncovering of an extortion racket whose origins could be traced to a meeting in 1933 between Willie Bioff and George E. Browne.

Bioff, otherwise known as William Berg, Henry Martin, Harry Martin, and Mr Bronson, had been part of a protection racket involving kosher butchers, and Browne was a business agent of the International Alliance of Theatrical Stage Employees (IATSE), which represented movie projectionists and allied workers. They decided to combine and concentrate on Browne's union.[116]

Early in 1934 they approached the head of a movie theatre chain, Barney Balaban, with a demand that he restore a pay cut imposed on IATSE members in 1929. Balaban took the hint that it would be cheaper to pay them off than to restore the pay cut, and parted with $20,000. Several years later Bioff testified, 'The restoration of the pay cut was forgotten. We were not interested in that then or at any other time. We didn't care whether wages were reduced or raised. We were interested only in getting the dough, and we didn't care how we got it.' The welfare of the workers always came a distant second to opportunities to extort money from them in dues, initiation fees, and 'assessments.' For almost a year IATSE members were assessed 2 per cent of their earnings for no particular reason.[117]

A short time after their initial coup Browne and Bioff were 'invited' to meet Frank Nitti, Louis Campagna, Paul DeLucia, and Frank Rio and other top Chicago gangsters. They were told to surrender at least 50 per cent of their take from future extortions, the scope of which would be vastly increased after Browne had won the presidency of the union.

In June 1934 Browne was elected president of IATSE unopposed. Two of his rivals for the post had decided not to contest the election after receiving death threats, and dozens of gangsters from around the nation circulated among the electing delegates at the union's convention in Kentucky just to make sure. Bioff was immediately appointed Browne's 'personal representative.' Soon after the election, Tom Maloy, the business manager of the Motion Picture Operators Union Local 110 in Chicago, and Clyde Osterberg, a IATSE union dissident, were murdered, as the way was cleared for the future extortions.[118]

In Chicago Browne and Bioff expanded their operations when they collected $100,000 from movie theatre chains by threatening to force them to hire two projectionists for each theatre instead of one. When asked later by a grand jury whether it was necessary to have two projectionists in a booth, Bioff replied, 'To be honest with you I never was inside a booth. I wouldn't know.'[119] After that they varied their techniques; threatening to strike, raise wages, and cut hours but always in the end being prepared to accept large payments to guarantee labour peace. The Loew's theatre chain, for example, paid out $150,000 in 1935 for 'strike prevention.'

IATSE were actually more interested in breaking strikes than winning them. In 1937, for example, a coalition of Hollywood painters, plumbers, grips, draftsmen, and others called themselves the Federated Motion Picture Crafts (FMPC) and went on strike. IATSE called in scores of San Francisco and Chicago thugs who experienced no difficulty getting gun permits from the Los Angeles Police Department. The FMPC responded by recruiting some tough longshoremen from the port of San Pedro. The battles between the two sides lasted six weeks with several killed and many more injured. The strike was broken after Bioff had issued thousands of IATSE union cards to anyone who wanted to walk through the picket lines. Soon after the ending of the strike Bioff also received a cheque for $100,000 from Joseph Schenck, president of the Motion Picture Producers Association and chairman of Twentieth Century Fox. Schenck first called it a friendly loan, then later claimed that he was forced to pay this amount to secure labour peace. Others called the money a bribe by the producers to keep the union docile. Either way both the strike and the FMPC were broken, with only the painters among the strikers gaining something for their efforts. They held out for a 20 per cent increase in wages and literally beat off attempts to break them. 'We had organized thugs going after us,' according to the painters' leader Herb Sorrell, 'but in many respects we out-thugged the thugs.'[120]

Arrangement between gangsters and studio bosses had been made at least a year before the strike. In 1936 Bioff had visited Joe Schenck's brother Nicholas, who was president of the Loew's theatre chain and founder of Metro-Goldwyn-Mayer. Bioff suggested that a system of massive yearly payments would save movie bosses much more. Bioff, according to Schenck, told him, 'We will close down every theatre in the country. You couldn't take that. It will cost you many millions of dollars over and over again. Think it over.'[121]

Schenck decided to pay, as did Sidney Kent of Twentieth Century Fox, and Leo Spitz of RKO Pictures Corporation. These major companies agreed to pay $50,000 a year in an arrangement that was meant to continue indefinitely. Schenck and Kent made their first payment in a room in the Hotel Warwick, New York. The racket, however, started to come apart in 1941, when Browne and Bioff were tried and found guilty of extortion and conspiracy. Bioff was sentenced to ten years in prison, Browne to eight.

In 1943 Bioff decided to inform on his Chicago gangster backers. Frank 'The Enforcer' Nitti shot himself rather than face trial, but a number of top gangsters were convicted by Bioff's testimony: Louis Campagna, Phil D'Andrea, Frank Maritone, Charles Gioe, and John Rosselli were convicted of conspiracy to extort more than $1 million from the movie studios and sentenced to ten years imprisonment and fines of $20,000 each.

The racketeers that Bioff helped put into prison were released almost as soon as they had served the minimal one-third of their ten-year sentences, despite their reputation as dangerous criminals. In 1946 a federal prosecutor had sent a memorandum to Tom Clark the Attorney General of the United States, which stated: 'The convicted defendants are notorious as successors to the underworld power of Al Capone. They are vicious criminals who would stop at nothing to achieve their ends. The investigation and prosecution were attended by murder, gunplay, threatening of witnesses, perjury.'

On 13 August 1947 the three members of the federal parole board voted to release the movie racketeers on parole. The release of the gangsters was considered so urgent that there was not time to make the customary investigations of the parole advisers. Virgil Peterson, director of the Chicago Crime Commission at the time, wrote an account of the deals made by the gangsters' attorneys that resulted in such rapid and lenient treatment. In particular, Peterson implicated Maury Hughes and Paul Dillon, both of whom had high level connections in the Truman administration, in the release of the gangsters. These had 'actively worked on their behalf as paid legal advisers.' Gangsters, like corporations before them, had worked out that it pays to have friends in the right places.[122]

Of the co-conspirators, Louis Campagna and Phil D'Andrea died of old age in the mid-1950s, Charles Gioe and Frank Maritote were murdered, and only John Rosselli would have much future significance. After his short spell in federal prison Rosselli returned to Hollywood to part-produce several popular movies, including *T-Men* and *He Walked by Night*, both made in 1948. Thus, in another ironic twist a gangster was involved in the production of films that glorified the government's action against crime.[123]

Bribery, fraud, and various forms of intimidation have been constants in U.S. industrial and business life, but murder has been reserved for special cases, such as Peter Panto. In 1939 Panto, a young refugee from Fascist Italy, had been causing problems on the Brooklyn waterfront by leading rank-and-file opposition to the locals of Joe Ryan's International Longshoreman's Association (ILA) and, in particular union kickback and extortion rackets. Panto wanted an honest union that represented waterfront workers, but the ILA was a union that only represented its officials, who made cozy deals with the employers. Longshoremen had packed into neighbourhood halls to hear Panto attack collusion and corruption. Then in July 1939 Panto suddenly disappeared. His body was found a year later in a New Jersey lime pit. Resistence to the ILA persisted but in an atmostphere of terror and intimidation.[124]

The port of New York during the 1930s and 1940s was the richest in the world. Each year, cargoes worth between $15 and $16 billion passed across its piers, including more than a third of the country's foreign trade and about half of the furs, jewels, watches, and other luxuries. One in ten New Yorkers were employed in port or ancillary occupations. The fictional corrupt union boss, Johnny Friendly, in the 1954 film *On the Waterfront* used appropriate imagery when he demanded his cut of 'the fattest piers in the fattest harbor in the world.' His real-life counterparts were similarly much more interested in self-enrichment than participating in honest collective bargaining. A stevedoring contractor explained the bargaining process as one of calling in Ryan 'once a year or so,' and asking, 'Joe, how much of a raise do you need to keep the boys in line?'[125]

The ILA was, in effect, a company union run by gangsters. It made no pretence of maintaining a strike fund, because its function was to prevent the men organizing and to break strikes. The union gangsters only drew a nominal salary from the treasury – they were regularly paid off by the companies and allowed to operate any pierside rackets they chose. These included wage kickbacks, numbers, bookmaking, and larger scale operations such as hijacking cargo and taking exorbitant fees for the loading and unloading of pierside motor trucks. On all but a few piers gangsters hired longshoremen on a casual basis, because gangsters had demonstrated to the stevedoring firms that they made the most efficient foremen.

The only way longshoremen could improve pay and conditions was through 'wildcat' industrial action. Beginning in the late 1930s with Panto and his supporters and continuing through to the 1950s, rank-and-file movements of longshoremen fought both the bosses and the gangster union of ILA president Joseph P. Ryan. The gangsters used violence or murder to maintain the status quo, while politicians ensured, through either corruption or inertia, that the normal rules governing law and order did not apply. The occasional gesture by the law enforcement agencies was treated with contempt. Conscientious police and prosecutors were rare in waterfront areas, and if necessary cases could be 'fixed' through political influence or by terrorizing or murdering witnesses. The longshoremen had no protection from the law and, according to a 1949 grand jury report, were reduced to a form of 'hopeless peonage.'[126]

Howard Kimeldorf described the methods of the gangsters as 'selective terrorism:' 'Dissidents were routinely "dumped," or worse. In one case, two rank-and-file activists were found murdered, gangland style, in different parts of the city only hours after meeting with Communist leader Sam Madell. No one was safe, not even women party members, who were routinely roughed up by Ryan's "organizers" whenever they tried to distribute literature on the docks. Nor were left-wingers the only targets. Organizers with the anti-communist Association of Catholic Trade Unionists, reactionary Teamster bosses, and even rival ILA leaders were all victimized by waterfront thugs.'[127]

The waterfront murders that appeared on the record were only a small percentage of the actual total. A Roman Catholic Priest, Father John Corridan, testified that not all accidents on the docks were accidents; heavy dockside paraphernalia provided plenty of opportunities for planned mishaps. Corridan also knew of policemen who were aware of murders that went down on the record as heart attacks. Rank-and-file strikes were crushed with systematic brutality as Joe Ryan's 'goon squads' administered beatings while the police looked on.

The employers used Ryan and his gangster allies to keep the workforce cheap and docile and to keep profits healthy. The great wealth of waterfront interests effectively ensured that no politician interfered with this situation. Every year through the 1930s, 1940s, and into the 1950s, the Joseph P. Ryan Association gave a testimonial dinner that dramatized the corrupt complicity of business, union, criminal, and political interests. William McCormack, a friend of Ryan's and the businessman generally considered to be the most powerful single individual on the waterfront, usually held the title of chairman of the committee on arrangements for the annual dinner. Ryan and McCormack presided over a gathering of district attorneys, judges, magistrates, state legislators, city councilmen, police, bankers, shipping and stevedoring entrepreneurs, AFL functionaries, usually the mayor, and always waterfront gangsters.[128] Not all those attending the functions were corrupt, but by being there they were accepting political realities and the corrupt conditions on the waterfront which fostered racketeering.

Despite the prevalence of gangsters in the ILA, IATSE, and other unions, the 1930s were good years for American labour. Changes in the law brought in with the New Deal gave workers the legal right to belong to unions and they joined in the millions. In 1932 less than three million Americans belonged to unions, by 1940 there were more than ten million. All these members paid union dues and each week millions of dollars went into union treasuries. Most of this wealth went towards building up the political and economic strength of the labour movement. However, a proportion of this wealth would be redirected into the pockets of the corrupt and, as Alan Block has concisely described, a transformation in the nature of racketeering took place:

In the early decades of urban unionism, the essence of racketeer activity lay in utilizing violent skills to control locals in order to hold down labour costs for employers. Commanding membership monies became another benefit. Once locals were seized by gangsters, they sold out the rank-and-file with sweetheart contracts for bribes and/or used the threat of strikes and unionization to extort monies from industry bosses. That sort of criminality lasted a long time but was eventually merged with, and then supplanted, in the decades after World War II, by the lure of welfare and pension funds piling up in union coffers. Nothing better illustrates this than the International Brotherhood of Teamsters, whose contracts became stronger and stronger ... The better the benefits, the more there was to steal or embezzle. This gave racketeers an incentive to leave behind old-fashioned sweetheart contracts.[129]

The career of Teamster leader Jimmy Hoffa and the alliances he made with gangsters to counter America's anti-union orthodoxy, illuminates the complexities involved in this process. Hoffa had joined the Teamsters Union in 1932 as a young man and soon proved himself to be an effective organizer. Based in Detroit, Michigan, he helped organize workers in warehouses and local cartage companies, and then, crucially, the long-haul truck drivers. By the 1940s his power was statewide, and by the 1950s he was head of the most powerful national union in America. Long-distance trucking by that time had successfully competed with the railroads for long-haul freight, helped by the federal government's creation of a new interstate highway system in the 1950s. Teamsters became key workers, transporting the growing volumes of consumer goods nationwide, while Hoffa and his fellow negotiators ensured that union members got increasingly better deals from their employers. From the beginning, however, organizing them was a struggle. According to Hoffa's account,

In the early days every strike was a fight ... I was in a lot of fights, got my head broke, got banged around. My brother got shot. We had a business agent killed by a strikebreaker ... Our cars were bombed out ... Cars would crowd us off the street ... They hired thugs who were out to get us, and Brother, your life was in your hands every day. There was only one way to survive – fight back. And we used to slug it out on the streets. They found we didn't scare ... The police were no help. The police would beat your brains out for even talking union. The cops harassed us every day. If you went on strike you got your head broken ... Once I was in jail eighteen times within twenty-four hours. That was the Crowley-Miller strike of 1939. Every time I showed up on the picket line, I got thrown in jail. Every time they released me, I went back to the picket line; eighteen times in one day, it happened. But we stayed on the picket line for a year and a half, and we won the strike.[130]

Just as the employers he faced brought in strike-breaking goon squads, Hoffa decided early on that to compete in U.S. industrial disputes it was necessary to have as much muscle as the other side. In 1941 he visited and, presumably, enlisted the support of several Detroit gangsters, including Santo Perrone, 'Scarface Joe' Bommarito, and Frank Coppola. From then on he developed contacts with gangsters around the country, including John Dioguardi and 'Crazy' Joe Gallo in New York, Tony Provenzano in New Jersey, and Sam Giancana in Chicago.

In 1959, he told an interviewer, 'Twenty years ago, the employers had all the hoodlums working for them as strikebreakers. Now we've got a few and everybody's screaming.'[131] He believed that the police were either ineffective or collaborating with gangsters and so, he explained in another interview, 'These [gangsters] are the people you should know if you're going to avoid having anyone interfere with your strike. And that's what we know them for. I can pick up the phone in Detroit and call anybody and have a meeting with them ... We make it our business, and the head of any union who didn't would be a fool. Know who are your potential enemies and know how to neutralize 'em.[132]

The connections with gangsters and crooks, however, went deeper. In the late 1940s the Teamsters union established the Central States Health and Welfare Fund for its members. All contracts now would require employers to pay a certain amount every month into the fund that would be used to cover hospital treatment and death benefits for union members. Insurance companies found themselves in competition for the right to manage these potentially enormous sums of money.

At this time Paul 'Red' Dorfman was head of the Chicago Waste Handlers' Union. A former boxer, Dorfman had assumed the leadership of the union in 1940 on the night he paid his first dues and with no experience of work in the industry. This rapid elevation had closely followed the murder of its founder and secretary-treasurer, and Dorfman's subsequent career was also accompanied by a string of unsolved murders and beatings. A Teamster official later described Dorfman as the 'kind of guy who'd walk in and throw two bullets on a guy's desk and tell him, "The next one goes into your fuckin' head."'[133]

Hoffa met Dorfman in 1949 and offered his stepson, Allen Dorfman, the multimillion dollar Central States Health and Welfare business. The younger Dorfman had no experience in insurance, no office, and no money. Despite this he rapidly set up the Union Casualty Company and got the Teamsters' account. During the 1950s Dorfman helped establish the fund's lending policy, which was, according to a government study, to make 'very large real estate loans to high risk ventures.' Parties to the loan transactions – recipients, brokers, attorneys, and accountants – were identified as being gangsters or associates of gangsters. According to an estimate reported in the study, 30 per cent of the fund's real estate loans were delinquent.[134]

The unfortunate fact about many of those involved in the American labour movement was that they were in it for the money. Most of the plundering was from the workers' welfare and pension funds and involved a certain amount of finesse in disguising the disappearing money. John T. O'Brien, secretary-treasurer of Teamsters Local 710, organized a much more blatant system by simply taking nearly a quarter of his members' monthly dues and dividing it up with the president and vice-president of the local. O'Brien's total income from the local between 1952 and 1958 was nearly half a million dollars, and this was without the money he made through a financial interest in the Dearborn Insurance Agency. Dearborn was a company owned by an insurance broker called Harland H. Maris and happened to be the recipient of numerous excessive commissions paid for by Teamster Local 710 funds. In 1959, after listening to testimony revealing the ways O'Brien and other corrupt union officers operated, Senator Frank Church declared that they had reversed the Robin Hood story: 'Instead of robbing the rich and giving it to the poor, they are robbing the working people and making themselves rich.' He added that 'these men are not labor union leaders at all. They are capitalists, and they are the capitalists and exploiters in the same tradition as the robber barons of old.'[135]

'What Church sensed, and aptly noted,' according to Alan Block and William Chambliss, 'was the triumph of capitalism as unregenerate greed at the very core of one of America's largest trade unions.' It was case of 'organized labor as organized crime.'[136]

Big Business and the Obscuring of Organized Crime

As we have seen, awareness of the fraudulent and often destructive activities of corporations had declined since the muckraking era. This was partly the result of the government's extreme reluctance to treat business crimes as real crimes and commit resources capable of achieving genuine enforcement. During the administration of the first Roosevelt, for example, the Antitrust Division of the Justice Department took on the might of the corporations with a staff of five lawyers and four stenographers. By the time of Franklin Roosevelt, the staff was much larger, but the reluctance to treat business crimes as real crimes was still there. According to an analogy used by the division's leader, Thurman Arnold, its task was to act continuously to keep open the flow of commerce – like a traffic policeman at a busy intersection maintaining the flow of traffic.[137]

Business helped maintain this lenient approach partly by exerting more direct and indirect influence on the communications media. The effects of the increasing concentration of media ownership were noted by two contemporary sociologists, Robert Merton and Paul Lazerfield: 'Since the mass media are supported by great business concerns geared into the current social and economic system, the media contribute to the maintenance of that system. This contribution is not found merely in the effective advertisement of the sponsor's product. It arises, rather, from the typical presence in magazine stories, radio programs and newspaper columns of some element of confirmation, some element of approval of the present structure of society. And the continuing re-affirmation underscores the duty to accept.'

By the Second World War, according to Merton and Lazerfield, the press functioned in three main ways. First, to decide which are the legitimate subjects of public discussion. Second, to enhance the authority of and bestow prestige on those persons, organizations, and social movements deemed desirable by its editors. Finally, to reaffirm existing social norms and to expose deviance.[138] In this context it was far less likely that the powerful in society would be portrayed as criminally deviant. There were, of course, criminal businessmen, but these were seen as exceptional and deviant individuals in a fundamentally sound system.

According to Ruth Vesey's recent study of Hollywood, filmmakers also operated under codes and policies geared towards conveying messages that supported the existing public and private distribution of power. It was Hollywood policy to ensure 'the general probity of onscreen public officials, as well as the benevolence of cinematic bankers, lawyers, doctors, teachers, social workers, newspapermen, and police. Where villainous professionals were depicted at all, they were shown to be renegades, soon pulled back into line by bosses or colleagues; "compensating characterizations" were designed to counter hostile reactions to the depiction of professional irresponsibility. In general, both public administration and private enterprise were shown to be motivated by altruism, and the benefits of capitalism were not subject to challenge.'[139] Given such compliant media it is not surprising that corporate interests were able to keep much systematic and damaging illegal activity effectively hidden from public view.

Amid the pro-business consensus there was, however, one significant academic dissenter. In his book entitled *White Collar Crime* (1949), Edwin H. Sutherland of Indiana University made the most ambitious attempt to uncover business criminality since the muckraking era. Sutherland began this work by dismissing the idea that mass immigration was the cause of America's crime problems. Sutherland stressed instead crimes that were committed by those in positions of power in corporations. The powerful were exploiting the very immigrants who were supposed to be the main source of the problem, paying them wages below permissible limits, making them work in unsafe working conditions, and illegally breaking their unions. According to Sutherland, 'The present-day white collar criminals are more suave and less forthright than the robber barons to the last century but not less criminal. Criminality has been demonstrated again and again in reports of investigations of land offices, railways, insurance, munitions, banking, public utilities, stock exchanges, the petroleum industry, the real estate industry, receiverships, bankruptcies, and politics.'[140] Sutherland argued that 'persons of the upper socioeconomic class engage in much criminal behavior; that this criminal behavior differs from the criminal behavior of the lower socioeconomic class principally in the administrative procedures which are used in dealing with the offenders; and that variations in administrative procedures are not significant from the point of view of causation of crime.'[141]

He documented cases of bribery, fraud, embezzlement, antitrust violations, false advertising, and theft of trade secrets by such major corporations as Armour and Company, Swift and Company, General Motors, Sears Roebuck, and Westinghouse. In the steel and automobile industry he found evidence that corporations were often ready, willing, and able to use violence to win industrial disputes or break unions. In the mid-1930s, for example, he pointed out that Republican Steel spent $79,712 on 142 gas-guns with 6,714 shells and grenades, while the whole of the Chicago Police Department felt it needed to buy only thirteen gas-guns and 757 shells and grenades. He demonstrated that there were forms of corporate violence other than strike-breaking, using Union Carbide, Rhinehart-Dennis, and the Gauley Bridge disaster as his main examples. Finally, he showed that the U.S. 'free enterprise' system was a misnomer since practically all large corporations engaged in illegal restraint of trade.[142]

Sutherland found that the criminality of the corporations, like that of professional thieves, was persistent, extensive, usually unpunished, most often deliberate, and involved the connivance of government officials or legislators. It was, in sum, organized. He elaborated:

> Organization for crime may be either formal or informal. Formal organization for crimes of corporations is found most generally in restraint of trade, as illustrated by gentlemen's agreements, pools, many of the practices of trade associations, and cartels. Formal organization is found, also, in conferences of representatives of corporations on plans regarding labour relations. They are organized formally also for the control of legislation, selection of administrators, and restriction of appropriations for the enforcement of laws which may affect themselves. While some associations have developed codes of business ethics and many of the representatives have been sincere in their formulation of such codes, the actual effect of the codes is not different from what it would have been if the codes had been written by men with their tongues firmly in their cheeks.
>
> The informal organization for crimes by corporations consists in consensus among businessmen. While businessmen, with consensus, give lip service to free competition and free enterprise, they also, with consensus, practice restraint of trade. They are not willing to bear the burdens of competition or to permit the economic system to regulate itself in accordance with the laws of supply and demand, but they adopt the method of industrial planning and manipulation. While corporations seldom insist that their advertising agencies engage in misrepresentation, they reward the agencies which increase sales with little regard for the honesty of the methods which are employed. They have high degree of consensus regarding the patent laws, as restrictions which are to be disregarded or circumvented.[143]

Sutherland was aware of the problems involved in the exposure and prosecution of the crimes of the powerful. Newspapers, for example, were unlikely to highlight violations of regulatory laws, since this might prompt an investigation into their own illegal working practices. Judges were unlikely to impose long prison sentences on people from their own social class.

Just before publication he was made even more aware of the difficul-

ties of 'whistle blowing' on the powerful in America by his publisher's
reluctance to allow the naming of the guilty corporations in case they
took court action. The publisher, Dryden Press, had been advised by its
counsel that it would be liable for damages because the book called
certain corporations "criminal" although they had not been dealt with
under criminal statutes. Sutherland had insisted that the white-collar
behaviours he detailed were criminal rather than civil offences and
that the persons who committed them ought to be punished as
severely as persons who committed personal or property crimes. However, Sutherland finally agreed to drop the corporate names, after more
pressure from his university's administrators. The book appeared in a
form that would not offend the corporate criminals involved.[144]
Although *White Collar Crime* has now been read by generations of criminology students, its impact was thus massively reduced by what
amounted to a form of censorship.

Until the 1960s and 1970s few criminologists chose to risk their
careers by stepping outside the prevailing pro-business consensus and
exposing pervasive organized crime in business. Two exceptions were
Frank Hartung and Marshall Clinard. In 1950 Hartung reported on
patterns of fraud in the wholesale meat industry in Detroit during the
Second World War. Clinard studied wartime violations of the rules of
the Office of Price Administration. In his book entitled *The Black Market*
(1952), he demonstrated that the assumption that the black market was
primarily the result of the entrance of shady or gangster elements into
U.S. business was a misconception. The big manufacturers and suppliers gained most from wartime violations and any racketeers involved
simply engaged in the wholesale black marketing of U.S. wartime
business in general.[145]

Sutherland, Hartung, and Clinard might have demonstrated that
organized crime permeated the top of the U.S. economic structure at
least as much as the bottom but the point would have been lost on
most people by the late 1940s. It was considered almost unpatriotic to
challenge the integrity of the U.S. economic system during the first two
decades of Cold War against communism at home and abroad.

By the 1940s Sutherland was also exceptional in pointing to robber
baron activity as the appropriate antecedent for organized crime.
Many more academics now glossed over the ruthless and often illegal
methods of late nineteenth-century businessmen and emphasized their
contribution to the making of the United States. Historians were now
more likely to describe the Vanderbilts, Rockefellers, and Goulds as

'industrial statesmen' who guided the nation to its prominent position among other nations. Past abuses were dismissed as relatively minor transgressions along the way to greatness, respectability, and responsibility.

Despite Sutherland's work, organized business crime had become almost invisible by mid-century. Big business had become 'domesticated,' to use Richard Hofstadter's term. Most Americans by then accepted modern corporations as largely benevolent forces in the economic world. Corporate officials were now thought to be 'socially responsible' even by former critics such as New Dealer Adolph Berle who at the beginning ofthe 1930s had demanded new forms of public control over corporate power to check their criminality.[146]

Barbarians in the new corporate liberal order would be seen as coming from below, and new antecedents for organized crime would have to be found. In the meantime, taking the spotlight off organized business crime did not diminish its destructive impact.

Chapter 4

America's Moral Crusade and the Organization of Illegal Markets, 1789–1950

Throughout most of American history, moral reformers were mainly white Anglo-Saxon Protestant Americans who shared a commitment to make their country efficient, productive, and ordered. With this end in sight they succeeded in placing many laws on the nation's statute books that prohibited various kinds of personal behaviour. Prohibition laws were meant to end or at least drastically curtail activities that were thought to be harmful, such as gambling, prostitution, drinking alcohol, and taking certain kinds of drugs. By the end of the Progressive era the laws were in place, and it was felt improving policing and court procedures would solve any problems about enforcement and compliance.

The hopes of reformers that moral reform laws and honest and effective law enforcement would eradicate the 'vices' of millions of Americans proved to be misplaced. Instead, the laws fostered, facilitated, and sustained an illegal economy that was far more destructive and corrupting than any that existed in more tolerant societies. Prohibiting disapproved goods and services failed to prevent people producing and consuming them. Networks began to multiply to supply the rapidly expanding illegal markets. In effect, the laws only changed the way business in these prohibited areas was conducted and only succeeded in opening up new fields of criminal enterprise.

The Business and Rhetoric of Moral Reform

Moral crusading in the United States began with the new nation. Clergy from every denomination were agreed that morality was essential to the very survival of the Republic and that the best way to achieve this was to mobilize ordinary people in the cause of virtue. New reform institutions and moral societies were formed in ambitious attempts to imbue their fellow citizens with 'correct moral principles.' Reformers felt that by suppressing such 'vices' as gambling, drinking, Sabbath-breaking, and prostitution, they would address the sources of poverty, crime, and other social evils.[1]

From the 1820s more business interests joined the moral reform movement which then became more professional and systematic in its efforts. Merchant-led 'antipauperism' societies in New York, Baltimore, and Philadelphia, for example, began to divide their cities into districts and hire agents to gather detailed information on the vices that were thought to underlie most poverty. Reform leaders would then use this information to argue for stricter legal control of vice and intemperance.

By the middle of the nineteenth century, many state legislatures had responded to pressure by passing anti-gambling, anti-prostitution, and other laws thought desirable by the reformers. As we have seen in Chapter 1, however, few city governments consistently directed their police to enforce these laws. The politicians, in effect, licensed vice, enabling entrepreneurs to build up bookmaking, lottery, and policy syndicates, operate strings of gambling houses, or run houses of prostitution. Enforcement in some parts of the cities was purely for show or to crack down on those operators who failed to pay enough protection money.

By the end of the nineteenth century moralists could see that their efforts had thus far failed. Evidence of moral decline was everywhere, especially in the cities. New styles of clothing, 'suggestive' dances, 'titillating' movies, and 'salacious' stage productions were all examples of the 'deadly moral poison' sapping America's strength or were seen as the 'germs of licentiousness' contaminating national morality. Illegal gambling houses, from the lavish to the most basic, operated in every city, and turned 'promising young men' into 'slothful idlers.' The use of alcohol and other drugs was said to have reached 'epidemic' proportions. Countless books were turned out predicting degradation and disgrace for the country's youth if exposed to liquor, in particular. Boys were doomed to be profligates and degenerates, and girls would inevitably meet with seduction and 'white slavery.' One book entitled *Horrors of the White Slave Trade* claimed, 'The saloon is the arch destroyer of men, the brothel the arch destroyer of women. A sort of hellish blood-relationship exists between them' and added that 'liquor and lust' were 'the Devil's Siamese twins.'[2]

Frightened by the apocalyptic, racist, and xenophobic messages of moral propagandists detailed in Chapter 2, many more middle-class and Protestant Americans began to take part in local, state, and national campaigns to impose common standards of behaviour on the country's multinational and multiracial population. Anti-vice, anti-drug, and anti-alcohol societies mushroomed across the country. These lobbied energetically at local, state, and national levels for more laws prohibiting activities deemed to be unacceptable and for more agencies capable of real enforcement. The idea was to dispel half-measures involving the regulation of demoralizing activities such as gambling, commercialized sex, the drinking of liquor, and recreational drug use, and eradicate these activities completely.

American moralists had the advantage of being united, well organized, and obsessive while their opponents were divided, usually uninterested, and easily characterized as the representatives of almost unbounded evil. By the beginning of the 20th century moralists had the finance and organization, as well as the commitment to persuade and cajole enough people to ensure that virtue and abstinence became official policy at every level of American government.

Business interests provided the crucial financial backing and political pull in the campaigns that put morality on the statute books. Working-class morality and abstinence made dollar-sense. Drinking, gambling, prostitution, and drug-taking were seen as diverting wages from the purchase of manufactured goods; if wages were not spent on wasteful activities there would be less demand for wage rises. Alcohol decreased work efficiency at a time when most managers were searching for ways to get more productivity out of their workers. Business interests also used their alliance with prohibitionists and America's preoccupation with vice and crime to divert the reform element from attacks on corporate corruption and other economic evils. Finally, businessmen believed that the way saloons had become the focus of working-class political and economic activity was simply not in their interests. It was unacceptable to them that labour unions were using the saloons to recruit and organize workers.[3]

No moral reform organization was better financed than the Anti-Saloon League. By 1919 about 14,000 U.S. businessmen had contributed funds, including sizeable and regular support from John D. Rockefeller Jr. After the Ludlow massacre Rockefeller felt the need to contribute more funds to Colorado's drive to prohibit liquor. After one $10,000 contribution he was assured that Prohibition was crucial in maintaining 'the peace and order of the state against anarchy and red revolution.' And when the national Prohibition Amendment was first submitted to the states a league representative wrote him these thanks: 'In light of what your money made possible ... we trust that you will feel repaid for your investment.'[4]

On a smaller scale, business fortunes also found drug control an attractive investment. In 1912, for example, the lawyers for Mrs William K. Vanderbilt were casting around for an issue to boost her image and found that the repression of narcotic drugs fit the bill. Mrs Vanderbilt then organized anti-narcotics committees, led marches up and down Fifth Avenue, and with the help of unlimited funds, launched telegram and letter campaigns to lawmakers in Albany, New York, and Washington, DC on the theme that helpless people of the lower classes needed protection from 'this poison.' These campaigns helped towards the enactment of the Western world's first repressive anti-narcotic law. The Towns-Boylan Act became effective 1 July 1914 and provided for substantial penalties for all non-medicinal trafficking and use of drugs. The aim of this, in part, was to force addicts to receive treatment, because as, Charles Towns, one of the sponsors of the act, put it, 'it takes only five or six days to cure a drug fiend in hospital.'[5]

The Harrison Narcotic Act was also passed in 1914. Although the intention of the act was chiefly to prohibit the use of drugs for recreational purposes, Treasury agents exploited an ambiguity in the wording of the act to prohibit opiates and other drugs totally. They began an intense campaign to prevent doctors from treating drug users, resulting in some 3,000 doctors serving penitentiary sentences between 1914 and 1938. Doctors were thus effectively prohibited from dispensing heroin or morphine to addicts or to ease the pain of the terminally ill despite representations from the medical community that these drugs were most effective in doing so. Drug control thus became a police problem rather than a medical problem in the United States and addicts began to search for illegal sources of supply. American dollars began to fuel the national and international drug traffic.[6]

Campaigners in the Progressive era wasted no time trying to communicate or compromise with their opponents, they used 'sets of stereotypes' to confront their opponents or, to borrow another phrase from the historian Robert Wiebe, 'frozen images that were specifically intended to exclude discussion.'[7] These techniques were particularly noticeable in the campaigns against 'white slavery' and liquor, and they anticipated the 'sets of stereotypes' and 'frozen images' used in more recent campaigns against drugs and organized crime.

During the 'white slave' hysteria of the early twentieth century, many reformers called for tougher government action against what was thought to be a massive national and international trade in women and girls forced into prostitution. Theories purporting to explain the white slave trade saw the problem as one big conspiracy. Edwin W. Sims, the U.S. attorney in Chicago led the way in 1909 when he claimed: 'The legal evidence thus far collected establishes with complete moral certainty these awful facts: That the white slave traffic is a system operated by a syndicate which has its ramifications from the Atlantic seaboard to the Pacific ocean, with "clearing houses" or "distribution centers" in nearly all of the larger cities; that in this ghastly traffic the buying price of a young girl is from $15 up and that the selling price is from $200 to $600 ... that this syndicate ... is a definite organization sending its hunters regularly to scour France, Germany, Italy and Canada for victims; that the man at the head of this unthinkable enterprise it [sic] known among his hunters as "The Big Chief."'[8]

The same year an article in the magazine *Outlook* pleaded with the U.S. government to 'prevent the importation of vice' explaining: 'Unfortunately the government does not realize the powers of the strongly entrenched syndicate, with its many agents abroad and distributed in the various cities, with large financial backing, which imports immigrant girls and sells them from city to city, and has not provided adequate machinery to reach this all-powerful combine.'[9]

Federal legislators responded to such pressure by framing a bill that was intended 'to put a stop to a villainous interstate and international traffic in women and girls.' The bill's sponsor, Representative James R. Mann, emphasized its importance with a claim that was not considered to be absurd at the time: 'The white-slave traffic, while not so extensive, is much more horrible than any black-slave traffic ever was in the history of the world.' His colleague, Edward R. Saunders of Virginia, spoke of 'conditions of restraint, and compulsion, which have been aptly, and universally styled, "white slavery"' and paraphrased the claims made earlier by Sims that 'an organized society exists both in this country, and abroad, formed for no other purpose than to exploit innocent girls for immoral purposes. This syndicate had headquarters and distributing centers in New York, Chicago, San Francisco, Denver, and many other American cities.' Representative Gordon J. Russell made it clear that any that voted against the bill were on the side of 'the whoremongers and the pimps and the procurers and the keepers of bawdy houses. Upon that other side you would find all those who hate God and scoff at innocence and laugh at female virtue.' Given the temper of the times it was not surprising that there was little opposition to the bill and President William H.Taft signed it into law in 1910.[10]

Most of the claims made about the centralized structure of white slavery were found to be bogus, but that was not the point.[11] A sinister force had been identified and therefore tough government action had to destroy it. The passage of the Mann Act was thought to have struck the deathblow against the white-slave combine detailed by U.S. Attorney Sims and others. However, since no such coherent organization existed, there was no way that the Mann Act could make a significant impact on the extent or control of prostitution. Although the abduction of girls and women into forced prostitution was a significant problem then as now, it did not at any time sustain prostitution. Few genuine white slavers were convicted and certainly none connected to the mythical international syndicate.

The Mann Act's greater long-term significance lay in the increasing powers it gave to a newly formed investigative agency in the Department of Justice, the Bureau of Investigation set up in 1908 and later renamed the Federal Bureau of Investigation (FBI). According to Max Lowenthal, 'The enforcement of the Mann Act began the transformation of the Justice Department's police bureau from a modest agency concerned with the odds and ends of Federal law enforcement to a nationally recognized institution, with agents in every State and every large city.'[12]

President Theodore Roosevelt had set up the Bureau of Investigation in 1908 and enforcement of the Mann Act was one of its first major responsibilities. The Mann Act was thus notable as a landmark in the federalization of American law enforcement, but it made only a marginal impact on commercialized sex in the United States.

In a process similar to that in the white-slave hysteria, prohibitionists also used 'frozen images' to exclude rational discussion of alcohol control. They tended, for example, to lump the many thousands of breweries, distilleries, and saloons together and refer to them as the 'Liquor Power.' This, according to the Reverend Mark Matthews, the nation's most prominent Presbyterian, was 'the most fiendish, corrupt and hell-soaked institution that ever crawled out of the slime of the eternal pit.'[13] Josiah Strong's verdict after detailing cases of bribery and corruption in his book called *Our Country* (1886) was that the cities were already under the heel of the liquor power. He warned that the liquor power would get even more opportunities to paralyze and cor- rupt government when the cities with their rapidly expanding popula- tions came to dominate the whole nation politically. He drew an unjustified distinction between the methods of the liquor power and other businesses, and then claimed: 'Such a powerful organization, resorting to such unscrupulous methods in the interests of legitimate business – mining, railroading – would be exceedingly dangerous in a republic; and the whole outcome of this traffic, pushed by such wealth, such organized energy and such means, is the corrupting of the citizen and the embruting of the man.'[14]

In 1914, during the same debate on a national prohibition amend- ment that included Hobson's racist exposition quoted in Chapter 2, Representative Clyde Kelly of Pennsylvania claimed that Congress should pass the prohibition resolution because of the very forces against it: 'The allied powers that prey, the vultures of vice, the corrupt combinations of politics, the grafters and gangsters, the parasites that clothe themselves in the proceeds of a woman's shame, the inhuman ones that bathe themselves in the tears of little children, the wastrels who wreck and ruin material things while they contaminate child- hood, debauch youth, and crush manhood; the plunder-laden ones who fatten themselves upon the misery and want and woe that their own greed has created, the Hessians in the black-bannered troop whose line of march is over wrecked homes and broken hearts and ruined lives.'[15] The arguments of those that opposed the amendment seemed weak by comparison!

By 1918 the 18th Amendment prohibiting the manufacture, trans- portation, sale, or importation of intoxicating liquor within the United States had received the required support to be added to the Constitu- tion. The following year the Volstead Act was passed, providing for the enforcement of Prohibition and thus the final link in the legislative chain of America's moral reform program was in place. A host of entrepreneurial opportunities in the illegal economy thus became available just as the dominance of big business was restricting them in the legal economy.

Organized Crime, Machine Corruption, and the Progressive Legacy

Adding laws to the statute books was just one aspect of America's moral reform movement. Many reformers had little faith in the ability of the existing structure of policing and criminal justice to accomplish the task of enforcing any laws, let alone the laws that banned vice and intemperance. Early conceptualizations of organized crime were made at a time when the professional and business classes were dissatisfied with existing forms of crime control, which they felt allowed both professional thieves and vice entrepreneurs to flourish and gave the working classes too much access to power.

In the cities, the boss or political machine system was thought to be the primary obstacle to moral reform and good government. Reformers concentrated on the connections between politicians, police, and illegal enterprise to highlight the corruption of boss rule in their campaigns to clean up city government and during these campaigns variations on the phrase 'organized crime' began to be used more frequently. In 1895, for example, the Reverend Charles Parkhurst described a police captain in New York who tolerated illegal gambling operations as one factor in 'a colossal organization of crime.' He contended that the police represented 'organized municipal criminality,' the machine, 'the organization of crime.' Parkhurst was by then president of the New York Society for the Prevention of Crime, which described itself in its 1896 annual report as 'a small, compact body, completely organized for offensive operations and thoroughly committed to a policy of exposing and breaking down official misconduct and organized crime.'[16] This was perhaps the first time reformers had used the phrase 'organized crime' in a way that gave it a distinct meaning – gambling and prostitution operations that were protected by public officials.

During the following decades the society often by-passed the police in its zeal to close down brothels and gambling houses in working-class and immigrant areas of the city, such as the Bowery, the Lower East Side, and Greenwich Village.[17]

Parkhurst had replaced Howard Crosby as president of the Society for the Prevention of Crime in 1891. He stirred life into the organization, largely by getting the support of wealthy business interests. It was therefore probably not a coincidence that he also dropped his predecessor's critique of big business noted in Chapter 3. Instead, as he made plain in his most famous sermon, Parkhurst's 'dangerous classes' were Tammany Hall politicians: 'There is not a form under which the devil disguises himself that so perplexes us in our efforts ... as the polluted harpies that, under the pretense of governing the city,

are feeding day and night on its quivering vitals. They are a lying, per-
jured, rum-soaked and heinous lot.'[18] Other commentators began to
take the lead of Parkhurst's organization and use the phrase 'organized crime' as almost synonymous with the municipal corruption that
protected vice and intemperance.

Parkhurst and his anti-crime organization displayed a bias that put
them in the racist tradition discussed at the end of Chapter 2. Their
most common targets among ethnic groups were Italians and eastern
Europeans. As an example of this bias, the first book on Parkhurst's
crusade against Tammany, published in 1894 and written by one of the
society's former detectives, Charles W. Gardner, included the following
description of a raid on a gambling club in Little Italy: Seated on the dirt
floor, four men were playing cards. They were Italians from Calabria,
swaggering brigands, with gold rings in their ears, ready to cut your
throat for a shilling. On the benches sat swarthy ruffians from Lom-
bardy, scowling at our intrusion. The spawn of the criminal world of
Italy hated representatives of free American institutions it seemed.'[19]

Three years later, the attorney for the society, Frank Moss, wrote
about the arson-for-profit specialists in the Jewish ghetto in New York
as typical of what he saw as the inherent moral depravity of the Jews.[20]

Throughout these and other contemporary writings was the
assumption that the 'foreign element' was much more likely than
native-born Americans to succumb to the bribery and corrupt promises of machine politicians. Those wishing to reform criminal justice,
such as Roscoe Pound, one of the most influential jurists of the early
twentieth century, also shared this assumption. Reform was necessary,
he argued in 1912, because the current system was outdated 'in a heter-
ogeneous community, divided into classes with divergent interests,
which understand each other none too well, containing elements ignorant of our institutions.' Referring to the immigrant ghettoes, he continued that this was especially true of a community 'where the
defective, the degenerate of decadent stocks, and the ignorant or enfee-
bled victim of severe economic pressure are exposed to temptations
and afforded opportunities beyond anything our fathers could have
conceived.'[21]

Both Pound and Parkhurst pitched their messages at the white middle classes. Parkhurst referred to them in his book entitled *Our Fight
with Tammany* (1895) as 'the self-respecting elements in the community'
or 'men with intelligence.' Pound, reflecting Social Darwinist thinking,
referred to them as 'the fit.' From the perspective of Parkhurst, Pound,

and other elite reformers the only hope for improved municipal conditions was to take power away from the machines and their 'unfit' constituents.[22]

Parkhurst advocated a solution to the problem of the police protection of vice and crime that would also be taken up by many twentieth-century reformers. First of all, he suggested in an article written in 1894, remove policing from the hands of the politicians: 'The sooner we get rid of the whole system of police commissioners, the better; such a system affords a nest for all sorts of political machinations to breed in, and, by distributing responsibility, makes it impossible definitely to locate responsibility ... A good deal of the present difficulty in dealing with our police department lies in the fact that, corrupt though it be in its entire animus and working, everybody in it hides behind everybody else, and it is next to impossible to pin obligation anywhere.'[23]

It was an early call, in other words, for the police to be organized as a profession, independent of local politics. Other reformers would elaborate and refine Parkhurst's observations into a coherent program of police reform based on the emerging consensus about what constituted organized crime.

In 1909 New York's former commissioner of police Theodore A. Bingham wrote an article for *McClure's* magazine in 1909 called 'The Organized Criminals of New York.' He was mainly referring to politically protected gamblers and brothel operators. He detailed aspects of his term of office involving what he called 'an aggressive campaign against the criminal centers of the city' and an attempt to 'compel the body of men under me – against its old custom and obvious self-interest – really to enforce the law.' The campaign targeted the Lower East Side of Manhattan where 'the criminals of New York City naturally gravitate, and, for that matter, many from all over the country. They lie there, not in any loose mass, but thoroughly organized, financially, politically, and legally, for offence and defense.'

Bingham claimed that his efforts successfully cleaned up several politically protected gambling houses, brothels, and saloons 'as they had never been cleaned up before.' Mayor George McClellan then suddenly removed him from office 'due to political or other pressure.'[24] Bingham's implication was that the pressure had come from the political-criminal alliance although the pressure might equally have come from downtown Jews angered by an earlier suggestion by Bingham that Jews were at the heart of this alliance. In any event Bingham's solution to the centralized underworld was to centralize the police department and remove it from the type of political interference that stymied tougher law enforcement.

In 1921 Pound crystallized the reform argument when he concluded that the administration of justice had nearly collapsed and was not able to perform its basic task of punishing criminals and preventing crime. The problem, he wrote, was threefold: 'men, machinery, and environment.' And, most importantly, he suggested the way forward for the next generation of law enforcement and criminal justice professionals. According to Pound, the administration of justice demanded better-qualified personnel, changes in the structure of agencies to remove obstacles to speedy justice, and finally, eliminating the corrupting influence of the political environment.[25]

As has already been made clear, there was undoubtedly substance to the charges of Parkhurst, Bingham, and Pound – politicians and police had been protecting different forms of organized criminality since the beginning of the Republic. But they misrepresented the degree of centralized control in vice operations. Timothy Gilfoyle has noted, for example, that 'Tammany Hall's relationship with the underground economy rested upon the actions of individual members. No directives came from the general committee of the hall ... Relations between Tammany and the prostitution business were informal and fluid, varying according to the neighborhood and the individual leader.'[26] When eventually old-style machines like Tammany disappeared from the U.S. political scene, other informal and fluid relationships ensured that prostitution and other protected criminal activity did not.

In the first half of the twentieth century, anti-vice and anti-crime efforts at the local level focused on a long and often frustrating campaign to reform and professionalize U.S. city police forces. To make significant structural changes, however, reformers needed to win city elections consistently and this proved difficult, at least in cities with firmly established political machines such as Chicago, New York, Boston, and Philadelphia.

To begin with the machines lost a few electoral battles, but usually they regained power after ineffectual periods of reform government. For the most part the machines kept the votes of the poor and the working classes. They were thrown out at regular intervals, usually after a graft scandal. Reformers came in and rarely lasted for more than one term of office. Basically this was because they catered to a middle-class constituency and hardly attempted to get poorer people on their side. Tammany and other machines continued to win elections because, as we have seen in Chapter 1, they acted as a kind of personalized welfare state when there was no other kind of welfare from any other level of government.

District and ward leaders often operated from saloons or even from street corners and were therefore accessible to anyone who took the trouble to consult them. And at regular intervals they organized celebrations that gave them even more opportunities to build up personal followings.

When the reformers took office they tended to distance themselves from the poorer classes and even alienate them. As in the case of most progressives they were far more concerned with disorganization and waste than with social justice. They often cut back on public spending, stopped projects in order to investigate graft, and laid off workers. The middle classes welcomed these changes, but the working classes felt the impact of cutbacks, and not surprisingly, resented the fact that their interests were not being represented.

The reformers also tended to annoy people by taking the letter of the law more literally in enforcing kill-joy regulations. In 1897, for example, the New York reform administration that came in with the support of the Reverend Parkhurst tried to enforce a state law that shut down saloons on Sundays. The outrage over this was expressed in a popular song with particularly blunt lyrics called, 'I Want What I Want When I Want It!' For many New Yorkers the attempt to close the saloons was just one more irritation among many and the reformers lost the next election. Tammany Hall politicians came back in and immediately relaxed on enforcement. Until the 1930s New York government remained effectively Tammany government.[27]

As the twentieth century progressed, many more middle-class reformers committed themselves to the cause of police professionalization and centralization, partly as a means to end machine dominance. Police chiefs would be more secure in their jobs under the proposed new set-ups and vice control and other specialized functions would be transferred from ordinary patrolmen to special squads answerable to headquarters and not to the local politicians. In the process of centralization, according to Robert M. Fogelson's analysis in his book entitled *Big City Police*: 'The district leaders would lose access to policy makers, control over police practices, and most important of all, support in ethnic neighborhoods. Besides enhancing the quality of law enforcement, the centralization of the police forces would also undermine the local-ism of urban politics and, by implication, the foundation of machine government.'[28]

A professionalized police force and a reformed criminal justice sys-tem would, it was hoped, be efficient, honest, and independent of interests represented by local politicians, including most crucially prostitution, gambling, and liquor interests. The assumption was that such reformed police forces would enforce all existing laws strictly and vigorously. But as Fogelson also noted: 'In view of the record of the big-city police in the early twentieth century, the reformers' confidence was based on an extremely shaky foundation. The reformers refused to accept that large numbers of people did not share their objections to drinking, gambling, and other vices.'[29]

By the middle of the twentieth century, the hopes of reformers for an end to old-style political machine rule had been to a great extent real-ized. Civil service and other progressive reforms had reduced the number of jobs, contracts, and other favours that had once been at the disposal of the machines. Control over the police departments, district attorneys, municipal judges, and other public officials went from local politicians to city and state agencies. In New York, Philadelphia, San Francisco, Los Angeles, and most other cities, the machines were no longer able to count on the support of the more established groups of immigrants, and they had little to offer the millions of recent arrivals among African American, Mexican, and other groups.[30] As the per-sonal ties and neighbourhood loyalties once used by machine politi-cians to get elected declined, winning city elections became based much more on the use of the mass media and market research to con-struct an appeal to diverse electorates. While these reforms ensured the greater independence of city police forces from political interference, they also made them more bureaucratic and less accountable to local constituencies.

Reformers who had held up the removal of old-style machine poli-tics from policing as the key to more effective and honest policing and the end of organized crime were to be disappointed. Reforms and new administrations changed the systems of corruption without affecting its extent. As the sociologist V.O. Key noted in 1935, even honest reform administrations could only succeed in changing the beneficia-ries of corruption.[31]

Reform also implied changes in the organization of crimes created by the morality laws. Where once pimps, prostitutes, drug dealers, gamblers, and gangsters had needed to deal with local politicians as intermediaries between themselves and the law enforcement and criminal justice systems, now they simply dealt directly with specialist police squads or relied on lawyers for more discreet deals within the court system. Progressive reformers like Parkhurst and Pound had thus helped change the structure of some types of organized criminal activity without making a significant impact on its extent.

Corruption and Illegal Enterprise: Nullifying Alcohol Prohibition

National prohibition began on 16 January 1920 under the terms of the Volstead Act. John F. Kramer, the first Prohibition commissioner, claimed that from then on liquor would no longer be manufactured in the United States, 'nor sold, nor given away, nor hauled in anything on the surface of the earth or under the earth or in the air.' Two years later, his successor, Roy Haynes, made the assertion that enforcement of the law was 'rapidly approaching the highest point of its efficiency.' In April of the following year, Haynes claimed that 'bootleg patronage has fallen off more than fifty per cent' and that 'the redisstillation of denatured alcohol is now impossible.' In July he announced that 'moonshining in the cities was 'on the wane.' In August he declared that the business of bootlegging had reached a 'desparate plight'; 'the death rattle has begun.' By December he was reassuring the American people that the progress made by the Prohibition Bureau had been 'nothing short of marvellous ... There is but little open and above-board drinking anywhere.'[32] The quotes illustrate a truism: whenever governments attempt the impossible their officials are required to lie.

The nullification of the 18th Amendment began within hours of the Volstead Act's taking effect. Soon after midnight, there were liquor robberies and hijackings. On 19 February the first of many federal agents was arrested for liquor law corruption. By June it was estimated that doctors in Chicago alone had issued about 300,000 phony prescriptions for liquor. Courts were already congested with thousands of prohibition cases awaiting trial and city and state authorities had already shown no inclination to enforce the new law honestly.[33]

The scale of the United States alone made effective prohibition of any intoxicating substance an impossible dream. Smugglers had an immense advantage over Customs Service and the Border Patrol given the thousands of miles of borders with Canada and Mexico and the

12,000 miles of Atlantic, Pacific, and Gulf shoreline, abounding in inlets. With a land mass of around three million square miles and a population that exceeded 100 million after the First World War, the prospects for eliminating domestic manufacture and distribution of alcohol were also minimal.

Prohibition's main effect therefore was to transfer the once-legitimate income of brewers, distillers, and saloonkeepers to anyone willing to break the law. Rum-runners, bootleggers, gunmen, speakeasy operators, graft-seeking politicians, corrupt judges, bribe-taking cops, coast guards, plus a host of opportunists all shared in this immense new potential for easy money. In Chicago, New York, Cleveland, and a few other cities, large criminal gangs eventually came to the fore in alcohol production and distribution, but in the country as a whole, most alcohol production and distribution was on a smaller scale. There were stills and wine-making equipment set up in countless homes and buildings, and millions of journeys made across borders in cars, trucks, and boats.[34] Governor Al Smith did not exaggerate the scale of the problem of Prohibition enforcement much when he claimed that diligent state enforcement in New York would require 'one-third of the state's citizens to apprehend another third who were violators, while the remaining third would be tied up serving on juries.'[35]

Many Americans showed their defiance of the dry law by drinking more, and as Andrew Sinclair has detailed even the vocabulary of drinking was changed by the abolition of the saloon. Various terms disappeared; people no longer went on 'sprees, toots, tears, jags, brannigans, or benders.' During the 1920s people were so obsessed with drinking that these terms were replaced by at least 150 new words among which were: blind, blotto, bloated, buried, canned, cock-eyed, crocked, embalmed, fried, high, lit, loaded, lushed, oiled, organized, ossified, owled, paralyzed, pickled, piffed, pie-eyed, plastered, potted, polluted, scrooched, shicker, sloppy, soused, spifflicated, squiffy, stewed, stiff, stinko, wasped down, woozy, or zozzled. Drunkenness, once frowned upon, now became a perverse status symbol in some circles; it showed that one could afford to pay inflated prices.

During the thirteen-year life of Prohibition drinking alcohol actually became more fashionable in many middle-class communities. Stronger and more toxic spirits became more popular than beer among the middle classes; hip flasks and a new type of social gathering called the cocktail party became fashionable. Beer remained the drink of choice for the working classes. However, it was bulky and more difficult to manufacture and transport and therefore became less available during Prohibition. On arrival at retail outlets it was often watered down. With no consumer protection a pint of beer could become two with an extra pint of water. Spirits often became concoctions that were closer to poison. A barrel of neutral spirits, for example, could become Irish whiskey when a half-pint of creosote was dumped into it.[36]

Few people found it hard to find drink during Prohibition. In 1929 the *New York Telegram* asked where liquor could be bought in Manhattan and answered its own question:

> In open saloons, restaurants, night clubs, bars behind a peephole, dancing academies, drugstores, delicatessens, cigar stores, confectioneries, soda fountains, behind partitions of shoeshine parlors, backrooms of barbershops, from hotel bellhops, from hotel headwaiters, from hotel day clerks, night clerks, in express offices, in motorcycle delivery agencies, paint stores, malt shops, cider stubes, fruit stands, vegetable markets, taxi drivers, groceries, smoke shops, athletic clubs, grillrooms, taverns, chophouses, importing firms, tearooms, moving-van companies, spaghetti houses, boarding-houses, Republican clubs, Democratic clubs, laundries, social clubs, newspapermen's associations.[37]

Enterprising criminals found many ways to fill the demand for liquor. Not only doctors profited from the provision that permitted alcohol as medicine. George Remus, for example, bought up chains of drug stores in Ohio, Kentucky, Indiana, Illinois, and Missouri so that he could order truckloads of medicinal liquor and then arrange for them to be hijacked. By 1924 Remus had enough capital to buy fourteen distilleries and their warehouses, ostensibly for the production of industrial alcohol. From the bonded warehouses liquor was diverted in railcar lots. To continue his business Remus at one time employed around 3,000 truckers, salesmen and guards, and, in his estimation, had to pay around $20 million in bribes.[38]

Industry itself became one of the most prolific sources of home-produced alcohol. So much alcohol was needed in the legitimate manufacture of products ranging from shaving cream to rayon that large amounts could be siphoned off without arousing suspicion. The government required that industrial alcohol be 'denatured' – that is, poisoned – but it could easily be put through a process that, sometimes successfully, removed the poison. Governor Gifford Pinchot of Pennsylvania indicated the extent of diverted industrial alcohol in 1924 when he complained that 150 Pennsylvania firms authorized to buy denatured alcohol to manufacture perfumes and hair tonics had ordered enough to fulfil the needs of the population of the entire world.[39]

Direct distilling and home brewing also became organized on a large scale. Stills were installed in thousands of warehouses, garages, and tenements. People were supplied with the ingredients and operating instructions and paid generously to keep the fire burning and the alcohol running day and night. The product was collected every few days and sold to speakeasies or to nationwide distributors at a handsome profit. The Gennas, a gang of six brothers from Chicago's Little Italy section, were thought to make around $150,000 a month from this enterprise even after operating expenses had been paid.[40]

Paying off the police was the greatest expense. According to a patrolman assigned to the Italian quarter in 1922, the whole thing was so rampant, 'Nobody wanted to take Saturdays off because on Saturday you just drove up in front of a place, and someone came out with an envelope. They threw it in the car and you drove away.'[41]

Some pre-Volstead brewing and distilling interests formed alliances with criminals to organize successful robberies of existing stocks and then began to develop more long-term arrangements. One major Chicago brewer, Joseph Stenson, made an estimated $12 million out of such an arrangement. He escaped prosecution, even though his activities were well enough known for the *Chicago Tribune* to note:

> Mr Stenson has not been convicted of being a twin king of commercialized vice. He is the silk hat for the crowd. There are avenues into the federal buildings he knows well. He furnishes the money, buys the breweries, and makes the connections necessary to undisturbed brewing. Having financed a brewery, he installs as president, secretary, and board of directors a number of healthy, good-natured young men. These gentlemen operate at a high price and in return they take a fall when there is trouble.
>
> Taking the fall consists of being defendants when there is prosecution. Of course only the officials of a brewery are legally responsible. Which lets Stenson out.[42]

To distribute his illegal beer, Stenson needed the services of gangsters, most notably John Torrio, formerly of New York, who had been involved in various Chicago prostitution and gambling activities since

1909. With Prohibition, Torrio was at first successful, making arrangements with the likes of Stenson and buying sufficient official protection. His political protection, however, broke down when a new administration under Mayor William Dever took office in 1923. In May of the following year, police raids turned up enough evidence to indict Torrio, some of his associates, and several pre-Volstead brewers. The brewers had enough influence to avoid facing trial, while Torrio and two others were convicted and sentenced to short spells in jail. While on bail, Torrio was shot by rival gangsters and decided to leave the city and its increasingly violent rackets.[43] The Stenson-Torrio relationship had demonstrated the ease with which 'respectable' businessmen could profit from the new crime of Prohibition law evasion and, at the same time, the vulnerability of gangsters to a more active law and gun-happy rivals.

During Prohibition most middle- and upper-class Americans were unwilling to drink the poisonous distillations available to the poor, and instead they demanded that their spirits be properly distilled and blended. An international trade developed to supply this demand. Although the profits were high, organization was complex and costly. It required contracting for the liquor in many countries, getting it past the Coast Guard and Customs, landing it on the docks, carting it to warehouses, and delivering it to retail outlets. Hijacking was always a threat, as gangsters were liable to seize valuable cargo in transit to the warehouses and then sell it for the same price with none of the over-heads. Many operations hired gunmen for protection.

Within two years of Prohibition taking effect 'rum rows' began forming off the U.S. coasts. These were lines of ships that stayed outside U.S. territorial waters, until their cargoes were sold and unloaded onto smaller, faster boats for the ship-to-shore run. The smuggling business was wide open to begin with, but by the mid-1920s independents were joined by more powerful, better-organized syndicates.

The best known of the early rumrunners was Captain Bill McCoy, whose reputation for honest trading popularized the phrase 'the real McCoy.' Between 1921 and 1925 McCoy brought in some 175,000 cases of liquor and evaded the Coast Guard with some style before eventually being caught and sentenced to nine months in federal prison. On his release he commented that the rum-running 'game' had altered: 'Modern efficiency does away with individual enterprise and the spirit of adventure. Big business wants safety and results, and present-day rumrunning is big business.' McCoy left the business to lead a quieter life as a real estate investor based in Miami.[44]

McCoy's reputation for honesty was exceptional and consumers were more often fooled into thinking that 'rum row' liquor was likely to be genuine. Instead, good whiskey was often cut and sometimes completely fake. It was not uncommon for a bootleg gang to unload the good liquor from a ship and replace it with alternative concoctions. The vessel would then move to another point on the row and sell the cargo as if it were the original.[45]

William 'Big Bill' Dwyer from New York worked with gangsters in several cities to set up one of the nation's largest smuggling and distribution combinations. In his home town he recruited from the Gopher and Hudson Duster street gangs, and in Kansas City he was thought to do business with Solly Weissman, a thug whose business methods gave him the alternative names of 'Slicey' or 'Cutcher-Head-Off.' By the middle of the 1920s Dwyer's enterprises included racetracks hotels, restaurants, and real estate. He had offices in Manhattan, fleets of trucks, as well as ships and speedboats, a large number of 'drops' or storage warehouses, and teams of mechanics to keep the goods moving.

In 1926 he was convicted on a relatively minor bootlegging charge and spent a year in prison. After that 'Big Bill' bought himself a certain amount of respectability by acquiring a number of racetracks, and professional hockey and football teams. By 1936 the *New York Times'* society page now called him William Vincent Dwyer, managing director of the Gables Racing Association.[46] Dwyer, however, never escaped from Internal Revenue Service agents, who caught up with him in the 1940s with a demand for over $11 million dollars in taxes. They eventually agreed to settle the claim for $1 million dollars, which took away most of Dwyer's remaining fortune before he died in 1946.[47]

Bootlegging, the word used to describe the illegal trafficking in liquor, became one of America's leading industries during the 1920s and, as in other businesses, twentieth-century technology speeded things up in the bootleg business. Contacts and deals could be made on the telephone instantly, and cars and trucks made for easy and fast transportation. Local, regional, national, and international ties soon developed among bootlegging entrepreneurs. One reason for this, as the historian Mark Haller has pointed out, was that a large urban market could absorb not just vast quantities of liquor but also a large variety of types: beer, Scotch, bourbon, gin, wines, champagnes. No distributor of illegal beverages to speakeasies, roadhouses, and other outlets could possibly manufacture or import such a variety. Therefore some organizations specialized for good economic reasons, and any large organization necessarily had ties with other organizations.[48]

Competition in an unregulated market often became bitter and bloody. As in the early days of other U.S. industries, the struggle for markets and territory was fierce and expensive. New York and Chicago's gang wars were particularly savage, and thousands died because they were connected to the illicit liquor industry. As many journalists have detailed, rival gangsters were pistoled or machine-gunned, taken for rides on the front seat of sedans and their brains blown out from behind, lined up and shot by firing squads, packed in cement, tied up in sacks, or pinioned with wire and then dropped into rivers or lakes – killed in ways that were either convenient or served as a warning to others. The murder of a minor bootlegger became so ordinary that newspapers scarcely took notice. Police conducted cursory investigations and no one worried that they never got convictions. Being a gang boss was no protection, as the deaths of Jim Colisimo, Dion O'Banion, Hymie Weiss, Dutch Schultz, Salvatore Maranzano, and Joe Masseria demonstrated. When Masseria was shot in 1931, a press photographer arranged an Ace of Spades in the gangster's bloody hands to add significance to an otherwise routine killing.[49] Maxie Eisen, a Chicago racketeer, captured the essence of the situation when he was reported as saying, 'We're a bunch of saps killing each other and giving the cops a laugh.'[50]

To a great extent during Prohibition, bootleggers and other liquor law violators took the risks, while public officials took the money. In the country's two largest cities police and politicians were far more concerned with being paid off than with the accumulating numbers of dead gangsters. Violent and prolonged gang warfare was, moreover, limited to New York, Chicago, and a few other cities, and represented poorly organized crime. The public officials of San Francisco, Los Angeles, Philadelphia, Pittsburgh, and many other places ensured that fortunes could be made with the minimum of fatalities.

In every large city and many of the smaller ones it was common knowledge that the police and politicians colluded with bootleggers and speakeasy operators and that periods of genuine enforcement were exceptional and temporary. In January 1924, for example, an aggressive campaign by Philadelphia's police chief General Smedley

Butler closed 600 speakeasies and resulted in 2,000 arrests. The campaign was soon sabotaged, with high-level police officials warning speakeasies of impending raids, politicians and city officials interceding for violators, and magistrates dismissing most of the charges. 'Trying to enforce the law in Philadelphia,' General Butler said, 'was worse than any battle I was ever in.' Only 212 liquor law violators were convicted in his second year of office out of 6,000 arrested. 'Enforcement,' according to Butler, 'hasn't amounted to a row of pins after the arrests were made.' An additional problem was that liquor held as evidence tended to disappear. As the historian Herbert Asbury pointed out, immediately following these losses a number of policemen resigned from the force and opened up speakeasies. Others found it more profitable to stay put. In 1928 it was revealed that Philadelphia policemen, on salaries of less than $4,000 a year, had bank accounts ranging from $40,412 to $193,553.[51]

Pittsburgh's graft system was just as well organized. Among those implicated by a federal grand jury in 1928 were two police magistrates, two members of the state legislature, five Republican ward chairmen, the superintendent of police, fourteen police inspectors, five patrolmen, and a constable. Before 1926 the Pittsburgh system had provided for the sale and distribution of a moonshine whiskey, locally known as 'mooney,' and sold at countless restaurants, soft-drink bars, former saloons, and sandwich counters. In 1926 a new and inferior form of moonshine, called 'administration booze,' accompanied the new city government under Mayor Charles Kiln. Retailers had to pay $4 a gallon, twice the previous amount, an increase that they passed on to consumers. These proved unwilling to pay the price for a foul-smelling concoction that was often covered by a greenish scum. When retailers tried to reintroduce 'mooney' they were promptly raided by police and put out of business. The terms of the new system required that all retailers take a fixed weekly quantity of the new brand whether they could sell it or not. All that mattered was the continued profitability of the system.[52]

From the beginning enforcement agencies were integral parts of the organized distribution of alcohol. The Federal Prohibition Unit (renamed the Prohibition Bureau in 1927) was a small group of low-paid and inefficient agents, numbering only about 1,500 for the entire country. Dry agents were known to escort liquor trucks, protect smugglers, and even help them unload their cargoes, deal in withdrawal permits for alcohol, and give information about raids. It is said that once the chief of the New York office of the Prohibition Bureau asked his men to put their hands on the table and then fired anyone wearing a diamond ring. He lost half his staff.[53] Such clean-ups were unusual, and prohibition agents bought country homes, town houses, real estate, speedboats, expensive cars, and a host of other luxuries on salaries averaging less than $3,000 a year.

Hundreds of agents were accused of corruption, scores were arrested and indicted, and many of these were convicted and sent to prison. During the first four years of Prohibition, 141 agents were jailed. During the first ten years of Prohibition, the bureau employed 17,816 agents, of whom 11,926 were separated from the service without prejudice and 1,587 were 'dismissed for cause.' The latter were the ones against whom the evidence was lacking to justify court action. Proportionately, the turnover was about the same in the higher ranks of the enforcement service. There were four national commissioners during the first five years, and New York and Pennsylvania each had six different state directors in less than four years. In each of these states one director was indicted for conspiracy. The Pennsylvania case against State Director William McConnell involved a conspiracy to withdraw 700,000 gallons of alcohol and share a corruption fund of about $4 million. Charges against McConnell were subsequently dropped, when government attorneys announced that most of their documentary evidence against McConnell and his associates had disappeared.

The most extensive corruption found in the Customs Service was at Detroit. In 1929 a grand jury revealed that smugglers paid an average of $2 million a year to operate. About 100 agents were involved in the 'graft trust,' and their monthly take averaged $1,700 each. There were lump sums for 'free nights' on the border with Canada, when smugglers were permitted to run in as much liquor as they could handle. Some rum-runners were also bribed to give government agents information leading to the seizure of liquor shipments on which the graft toll had not been paid.[54]

Prohibition's potential for illegal enrichment was also exploited by the informal but venal collection of presidential associates and appointees that became known as the Ohio gang, after the home state of President Warren Harding. Although the best known of this group's many crimes were the multimillion dollar swindles involving the Teapot Dome oil reserve and Veteran's Bureau funds, Prohibition's potential for illegal enrichment was also exploited.

Extortion was especially profitable. A file from the Department of Justice, for example, listed convicted bootleggers who could be sold pardons. In 1924 one of the department's special agents, Gaston Means, told a Senate committee that he had collected around $7 million from bootleggers for his political bosses. He had rented two adjoining rooms at a New York hotel for these purposes, placing a large goldfish bowl in one and waiting for the bootleggers to keep their appointments. While Means watched from the other room, the bootleggers fille d the bowl with large amounts of $1,000 and $500 bills. At the same hearings, the aforementioned bootlegger George Remus also testified that he had paid more than $250,000 to Jesse Smith to stay in the liquor business. Enough evidence was uncovered to show that for a price the government gang would drop prosecutions, sell federal enforcement jobs, and permit the illegal withdrawal of bonded liquor.[55]

'Fixing' cases became even more of an American institution during Prohibition. There were thousands of arrests, but when protected bootleggers stepped in front of judges, district attorneys suddenly found that they had 'insufficient evidence,' or witnesses failed to turn up, or police officers admitted that they had overstepped themselves in the performance of their duties. The blatant fixing of cases caused Assistant Attorney General Mabel Willebrandt to complain that she spent more time prosecuting prosecutors than the people they should have prosecuted.[56] Judges were also more prone to the pressures of corruption and anyway were forced to dispense an assembly-line justice to relieve the congestion of the courts.

In 1929 the new president, Herbert Hoover, recognizing the widespread nullification of the 18th Amendment, announced the creation of the National Commission on Law Observance and Enforcement, to be headed by former Attorney General George Wickersham. After two years of investigation the Wickersham Commission's reports made it clear that Prohibition had failed to deliver the hard-working and moral population that was promised by its supporters. Instead of the controlled working class and healthy environment for business promised by the prohibitionists there had been a progressive breakdown of respect for law and order. In fact, so many people expressed opposition and resentment to the dry law that one consultant concluded: 'The prohibition laws, so far, have been detrimental and harmful to the workers and their families and that the situation as regards manufacturing, trafficking in, and drinking liquor is getting worse from day to day and has now grown to such proportions that real control of it or enforcement of the law against it ... is almost an impossibility.'[57]

The evidence was overwhelming that the dry law had a rotting effect on U.S. society in general and, in particular, on U.S. law enforcement, and criminal justice. The commission found, for example, that 'when conspiracies are discovered from time to time, they disclose combinations of illicit distributors, illicit producers, local politicians, corrupt police and other enforcement agencies, making lavish payments for protection and conducting an elaborate system of individual producers and distributors.'

'Organized distribution,' the report added, 'has outstripped organized enforcement,' and, 'as to corruption':

> it is sufficient to refer to the reported decisions of the courts during the past decade in all parts of the country, which reveal a succession of prosecutions for conspiracies, sometimes involving the police, prosecuting and administrative organizations of whole communities; to the flagrant corruption disclosed in connection with the diversion of industrial alcohol and unlawful production of beer; to the record of federal prohibition administration as to which cases of corruption have been continuous and corruption has appeared in services which in the past have been above suspicion; to the records of state police organizations; to the revelations as to police corruption in every type of municipality, large and small, throughout the decade; to the evidence of connection between corrupt local politics and gangs and the organized unlawful liquor traffic, and of the systematic collections of tribute from that traffic for corrupt political purposes.[58]

The commission's evidence suggested that economic realities would always undermine prohibitionist ideals. Its conclusions about alcohol could equally be applied to the more recent wars on drugs:

> The constant cheapening and simplification of production of alcohol and of alcoholic drinks, the improvement of quality of what may be made by illicit means, the diffusion of knowledge as to how to produce liquor and the perfection of organization of unlawful manufacture and distribution have developed faster than the means of enforcement. But of even more significance is the margin of profit in smuggling liquor, in diversion of alcohol, in illicit distilling and brewing, in bootlegging, and in the manu-

facture and sale of products of which the bulk goes into illicit or doubt-fully lawful making of liquor. This profit makes possible systematic and organized violation of the National Prohibition Act on a large scale and offers rewards on a par with the most important legitimate industries. It makes lavish expenditure in corruption possible. It puts heavy temptation in the way of everyone engaged in enforcement and administration of the law. It affords a financial basis for organized crime.[59]

Although the Wickersham commission did not recommend the repeal of the 18th Amendment, its findings made it very clear that Prohibition had created or worsened a situation of widespread and systematic lawlessness.

Prohibition was not, however, the overriding political issue of the 1920s. Prosperity and continued industrial expansion ensured Republican national government throughout the decade. Neither the rampant corruption in the administration of President Harding, nor the complacence of his successor Calvin Coolidge, could threaten the Republican ascendancy. Generally lax liquor law enforcement and the fact that growing numbers of people could afford to pay inflated bootleg prices meant that the demand for alcohol could be satisfied while the country remained officially dry.

The Fall of Al Capone and the Rise of the IRS

The most famous Prohibition gangster was, of course, Al Capone. He made most of his money bootlegging, but was also involved in various gambling, prostitution, and industrial rackets. But it was Capone's cultivation of crime reporters rather than his criminal success that made him into the world's most famous gangster. He ranked with Henry Ford, Will Rogers, Babe Ruth, and Charles Lindbergh as an American institution during the 1920s, and, as his biographer F.D. Pasley put it, 'The hoodlum of 1920 had become page one news, copy for the magazines, material for talkie plots and vaudeville gags.'[60] Capone encouraged the press, often feeding reporters with a quotable remark and justification for his operations. He would talk about anything including his weight and the need for women to stay at home, but only his remarks about crime are worth repeating here. Bootleg liquor was obviously in such great demand during the 1920s that few could argue when Capone said, 'Somebody had to throw some liquor on that thirst. Why not me?'[61]

Mayor William 'Big Bill' Thompson, convincingly demonstrated the limits of Capone's power in 1928. Briefly under the illusion that he might be in the running for the presidency, Thompson decided that harbouring the nation's best-known gangster might be an electoral liability. He therefore gave the word to his chief of police and a campaign of harassment commenced. Capone associates were arrested on tenuous charges, breweries, brothels, and gambling houses were repeatedly raided, and Capone himself was kept under continuous supervision. Capone left the city, grumbling to reporters about people's lack of gratitude. As soon as Thompson realized the hopelessness of his ambitions Capone felt safe to return home and resume operations.[62]

One of Capone's main achievements was, in fact, simply to survive in a city where gangsters were assassinated so routinely. On 10 November 1924, three men walked into the flowershop of the leading north side gangster, Dion O'Banion. While one of the three shook hands with O'Banion, and then held on, the others shot him. On 11 October 1926, O'Banion's successor Hymie Weiss was hit by at least ten bullets and killed instantly in front of the Holy Name Cathedral, which still shows signs of the shooting. A few weeks before Weiss's death Capone himself had been lucky enough to survive a spectacular attempt on his own life in Cicero, the Chicago suburb where his operations were based. As journalist Frederick Lewis Allen described it, the attack came in broad daylight from scores of men pouring machine-gun fire out of eight touring cars: 'The cars proceeded down the crowded street outside the Hawthorne Hotel in solemn line, the first one firing blank cartridges to disperse the innocent citizenry and to draw the Capone forces to the doors and windows, while from the succeeding cars, which followed a block behind, flowed a steady rattle of bullets, spraying the hotel and the adjoining buildings up and down. One gunman even got out of his car, knelt carefully upon the sidewalk at the door of the Hawthorne, and played one hundred bullets into the lobby back and forth, as one might play the hose upon one's garden.'[63] Capone survived, flat on the floor of the hotel's restaurant.

Not surprisingly Capone was a nervous man. He travelled around in an armoured sedan, appropriately described as a 'portable fort.' The body was of steel construction, the windows bulletproof, and the fenders toughened. It weighed seven tons, compared with the less than two tons of the average family sedan, and was always preceded and followed in a convoy of cars, all of which contained heavily armed bodyguards.[64]

Capone neither 'ran' Chicago nor the Chicago rackets. On the contrary, as Mark Haller has demonstrated, 'the group known to history as the Capone gang is best understood not as a hierarchy directed by Al Capone but as a complex set of partnerships.' Capone, his brother Ralph, Frank Nitti, and Jack Guzik formed partnerships with others to launch numerous bootlegging, gambling, and vice activities in the Chicago Loop, South Side, and several suburbs, including their base of operations, Cicero. These various enterprises, Haller continues, 'were not controlled bureaucratically. Each, instead, was a separate enterprise of small or relatively small scale. Most had managers who were also partners. Coordination was possible because the senior partners, with an interest in each of the enterprises, exerted influence across a range of activities.' Like other criminal entrepreneurs, Capone did not have the skills or the personality for the detailed bureaucratic oversight of a large organization. Criminal entrepreneurs are 'instead, hustlers and dealers, for whom partnership arrangements are ideally suited. They enjoy the give and take of personal negotiations, risk-taking, and moving from deal to deal.'[65] Haller's analysis helps to explain why Capone's removal as a criminal force in Chicago made no difference to the extent of illegal enterprise in the city.

All of Capone's luck, fire power, obsessive precautions, and entrepreneurial ability would not have ensured the continuing fortunes of his partnership. More important was the environment of corruption that in Chicago, as well as in most other places, ensured that illegal enterprises could operate. Capone, like most gangsters, paid off enough policemen and local politicians to buy himself immunity from arrests on serious charges. But local political protection proved to be insufficient for someone as notorious as Capone and this notoriety reached a peak on 14 February 1929, St Valentine's Day. At a garage at 2122 North Clark Street, headquarters of the North Side gang of George 'Bugs' Moran, seven of his associates were waiting for a shipment of liquor. A Cadillac drew up and five men, two dressed as policemen, got out and entered the garage. They disarmed the Moran men, who assumed it was the inconvenience of a routine raid and did not object. They were lined up against a wall, as if for a search, and then suddenly sprayed with machine-gun bullets. One man briefly survived to tell the police, 'Nobody shot me.' Many Chicago citizens apparently believed that it actually was the police that carried out the massacre and no one has ever disproved this thesis, but the newspapers and the police themselves had no doubts that Al Capone was responsible for the massacre.[66]

The St Valentine's Day massacre, more than any other single act, made it politically necessary to 'get Capone.' A deputation of Chicago business interests went to Washington to ask President Herbert Hoover to intervene, and once Hoover directed the law enforcement resources of the federal government against Capone, the gangster's days were numbered.[67]

A coordinated attack was launched. Eliot Ness of the Prohibition Bureau made sudden, unexpected wrecking expeditions on Capone operations and destroyed valuable equipment and merchandise. Ness was the first of a wave of crime-fighting personalities to achieve national prominence in the 1930s. He loved personal publicity, keeping the press informed of his battle plans, and often when he besieged a Capone brewery or warehouse, cameramen would be there to record the scene. The raids did not, as Ness claimed, dry up Chicago, with its 20,000 drinking places, nor did they do any lasting damage to the Chicago rackets. This did not matter to the press, who presented Ness as Capone's nemesis, the representative of Good in a triumph against Evil. Yet Ness did not exploit such a potential gold mine of political capital to the extent of those who followed in his crime-busting footsteps. Following Capone's downfall, Ness's career was undistinguished and he died in 1957; a few years later a television series called *The Untouchables* fictionalized his career.[68]

In the case of Al Capone, the federal government wanted Capone's conviction to show that the law could work. His ultimate arrest and imprisonment for tax evasion in October 1931 was the result of the persistence of the Intelligence Unit of Elmer Irey, chief of the United States Treasury Enforcement Branch. Treasury agents had planted spies, produced informants, and collected documentary evidence. At the trial, Capone's men had been unable to intimidate witnesses and jurors, and the government had refused to accept Capone's offer of $4 million for lenient treatment. The main defence his lawyers offered was that Capone had not known that money from illegal businesses was taxable. He was sentenced to eleven years in a federal penitentiary.[69]

As the historian James D. Calder has demonstrated, the story of Al Capone's rise and fall as a Chicago gangster has always depended on the selective dissemination of federal agency records, particularly records of the Internal Revenue Service (IRS). IRS records of the Capone case remain sealed from public access and only selective releases have been made to journalists, film producers, and historians. Sixty years on, 'there is no definitive history of Al Capone's involvement in organized crime.' What we are left remains, as Calder puts it, 'government-crafted history.'

The released documents, not surprisingly tend to reinforce the image of Capone as a supercriminal, but, more importantly, the releases also tend to reinforce the image of the IRS as an efficient tax-gathering government agency.[70] Government agencies have a lot to gain by exaggerating the importance of gangsters like Capone. The IRS in the 1920s was a young agency and Capone's brief and highly publicized success was a challenge. The conviction of Capone in 1931 made people aware of the U.S. federal taxing agency. Before the trial the agency was not taken seriously by most people; after the trial and Capone's eleven-year sentence more people began to take it much more seriously. A former IRS agent later wrote that once Capone was convicted, 'tax violators began to kick in, right and left ... Floods of amended and delinquent returns, with checks attached, showed up not only in Chicago but at other Internal Revenue offices all across the country from scared tax cheaters ... the estimate of the amount of income taxes collected through these returns was over $4,500,000.[71] Capone died in Miami on 25 January 1947. His body was taken to Chicago to be buried, and as his coffin was lowered into the ground, IRS agents stood close by, ready to seize any assets they thought should belong to the government.[72] In a sense, Capone's criminal activity had in these ways benefited the IRS more than any other party, as other government departments must have noted.

With the conviction of the world's most notorious criminal the federal authorities virtually withdrew from Chicago law enforcement. Capone was finished as a criminal power, but continuing official corruption and scores of other racketeers made sure that it did not make any difference. Law enforcement authorities and politicians had an abundance of 'public enemies' and 'Mr. Bigs' to replace Capone in newspaper columns across the nation.

Business and the Repeal of National Prohibition

Despite the growing awareness of the corruption and futility of Prohibition, not many people believed that repeal of the 18th Amendment was a realistic possibility. It was thought that a few dry states could block it indefinitely. Few would have disagreed with Senator Morris Sheppard of Texas when he said: 'There is as much chance of repealing the 18th Amendment as there is for a hummingbird to fly to the planet

Mars with the Washington monument tied to its tail.' Neither would they have disagreed with Clarence Darrow, the famous lawyer, when he said that talk about 'the repeal of the 18th Amendment is pure non-sense. One might as well talk about taking his summer vacation on Mars.'[73]

President Hoover himself made a more accurate prophecy in 1929 when he suggested that 'if the law is wrong its rigid enforcement is the surest guarantee of its repeal.' By the end of his administration more than 40,000 liquor law offenders overstretched federal prisons, and Hoover had been obliged to undertake the building of six new institu-tions. But more arrests, convictions, and incarcerations cost ever-increasing amounts of money. In 1931 Senator Robert Wagner of New York caught the mood of fellow legislators when he asked what pur-pose would the hiring of more men and the spending of more money serve, 'Why heap more sacrifice upon the altar of hopelessness?'[74]

By that time there had already been a surge of support for the move-ment to repeal the 18th Amendment. The crucial difference was the changed attitude of businessmen to Prohibition. Manufacturing and commercial interests had discovered that the promised beneficial effects of enforced abstinence were illusory. Instead of the controlled working class and healthy environment for business promised by the prohibitionists there had been a breakdown of respect for law. Busi-nessmen looked on in horror as non-WASP gangsters, made rich and powerful by bootlegging, were buying and muscling in on other indus-tries. The vast resources of publisher William Randolph Hearst and those of several dozen millionaires including T. Coleman and Pierre Du Pont, John J. Raskob, and Edward S. Harkness were used to further the repeal cause. Even John D. Rockefeller Jr, the son of the Anti-Saloon League's most famous backer, withdrew his support and began to fund research into more effective liquor control than Prohibition.[75]

The wets had only to report the news to win the propaganda battle. Publishers and writers made sure that the public knew that the main epidemic during Prohibition was hypocrisy. There were many exam-ples. Legislators who voted dry and had their own personal bootleg-gers; police and prosecutors who made selective arrests and convictions while their bank accounts expanded; innocent people who suffered injustice and even death through incompetence or worse. Moreover, the economic disaster of the Depression after 1929 gave even more force to their arguments. Prohibition deprived men of legit-imate jobs, deprived government of revenue, contributed to the continuing economic problems, and only succeeded in enriching a few murderous and corrupt individuals.

The possibility that the Depression would increase the threat of a wider breakdown in law and order also served to concentrate the minds of America's business and professional classes. Fifteen million men were out of work, thousands of 'panhandlers' or beggars walked the streets, and riots broke out in several cities. In some cities businessmen formed committees to take control 'should railroad and telephone lines be cut and surrounding highways blocked.' New York hotels found that 'wealthy guests who usually leased suites for the winter were holing up in their country homes.' Some had machine-guns mounted on their roofs.

The government also overreacted to manifestations of discontent, notably when General Douglas MacArthur led cavalry and infantry troops down Pennsylvania Avenue against some 22,000 disheartened First World War veterans on 28 July 1932. MacArthur then ordered the use of bayonets, tanks, and tear gas in a charge against ordinary, unarmed Americans who were just down on their luck. MacArthur justified this action by suggesting that they had faced a 'bad-looking mob animated by the essence of revolution' that severely threatened ... 'the institutions of our Government.'[76]

In this context of fear and insecurity repeal became a requirement rather than an option for the powerful in the United States, largely because they thought that legalizing alcohol might reduce discontent and lawlessness. Rockefeller Jr, for example, argued this point in a widely published letter on 7 June 1932: 'When the Eighteenth Amendment was passed I earnestly hoped ... that it would be generally supported by public opinion and thus the day be hastened when the value to society of men with minds and bodies free from the undermining effects of alcohol would be generally realized.' He had 'slowly and reluctantly' come to believe that 'this has not been the result, but rather that drinking has generally increased; that the speakeasy has replaced the saloon ... that the vast army of lawbreakers has been recruited and financed on a colossal scale; that many of our best citizens ... have openly and unabashedly disregarded the Eighteenth Amendment; that as an inevitable result respect for all law has been grossly lessened; that crime has increased to an unprecedented degree.'[77] By coming out so strongly in support of repeal at such a time, Rockefeller carried many wavering businessmen and politicians with him.[78]

In such an atmosphere of panic even the unthinkable could be contemplated – a hummingbird could fly to Mars. The repeal of the 18th Amendment was finally achieved on 5 December 1933. The legalization of alcohol provided legitimate employment for over a million people in brewing, distilling, and related jobs, from serving drinks to making barrels or pretzels. Federal, state, and local tax and licence receipts exceeded $1 billion yearly by 1940 and there was no noticeable increase in drunkenness and alcohol-related problems.[79] Most Americans soon came to regard Prohibition as a ridiculous and costly mistake, and an unacceptable intrusion into personal behaviour.

After repeal, bootlegging continued to be a flourishing but localized business in the few Southern states that preserved anti-liquor laws. In such states as Mississippi and Oklahoma, the temperance lobby could always rely on the covert support of bootleggers, whose business required that the attempt to impose abstinence continued.[80]

In most states, however, bootleggers could not successfully compete once the legal liquor trade was fully established, and they soon folded up or adapted to the new conditions. Some successfully legitimized smuggling operations to become importers, some of the more thuggish variety were employed by companies to 'persuade' retail outlets to sell particular brands of liquor, and some such as Abner 'Longy' Zwillman of New Jersey, continued as liquor distributors at the local level. After repeal Zwillman and his partners formed Browne Vintners to distribute liquor in the New York area. In 1940 they sold the company to the giant Seagram Corporation for $7.5 million.

Seagram, which became one of the world's leading alcohol conglomerates, itself had bootlegging origins. When prohibition began in the United States, a Canadian-Jewish entrepreneur, Sam Bronfman, set up cross-border smuggling rackets. He began by transporting liquor across the border in his own or hired vehicles, but soon adopted a more convenient system. He established a string of export stores in the towns most convenient to the border and invited his U.S. customers to cross over themselves and load up their own vehicles. He even guaranteed to replace any liquor seized by Canadian authorities. Within a few years Bronfman had exploited the combination of loopholes in Canadian liquor laws and massive demand from the United States to make millions of dollars. By the end of the 1920s, Bronfman and his brothers had stakes in the Atlantic, Pacific, and Gulf Coast trades. In 1928 they bought the distilling company of Joseph E. Seagram in Ontario and from then on operated under that name. After repeal Seagram moved to the Chrysler Building in New York, paid the U.S. government

$1.5 million to settle prohibition violations, and then became a major player in the national and international distribution of liquor. By 1980 Seagram sold around 600 brands in 175 countries at a total annual value of nearly $3 billion. Its famous brands included Chivas Regal, Mumms, and Martell.[81]

Prohibition of alcohol was dead, but the Anti-Saloon League had accomplished one of its primary objectives – the old type of saloon did not reappear in most U.S. cities. One of the reasons for this was that licence regulations in many states prohibited screens, upstairs rooms, and back rooms in the new type of drinking places. The inside of bars had to be visible to policemen from the street because, so the argument went, behind the blinds of pre-Volstead saloons 'degradation and vice were fostered.'[82] Although such restrictions proved irrelevant as far as vice in the United States was concerned, they could prove useful to any authorities wishing to curtail trade union or political activity within bars. Those, like Rockefeller, who supported Prohibition as a crude means of social control, did have this important victory. After repeal, few drinking places were saloons either in name or form. They were called bars, taverns, or something else, and their function was restricted as much as possible to the consumption of alcohol.

Prohibition was not a historical aberration or a 'great experiment' as many writers have suggested. American Protestants, including many wielding power and influence, still believed that governments were capable of imposing the same standards of moral behaviour on huge and diverse populations. Repeal was a setback but America's ambitious program of moral reform would continue. Although repeal immediately cut off an immense source of illegal income, corrupt networks, consisting of gangsters, businessmen, and public officials, continued to profit from the demand for such illegal activities as gambling, prostitution, and drug taking.

The Organization of 'Vice' and the Search for Scapegoats

Unlike alcohol and drug prohibition, the prohibitions of prostitution and gambling were not based on federal law. Instead, a myriad of state laws and local ordinances made wagering and commercialized sex subject to criminal sanctions in every state, until Nevada legalized gambling and prostitution in selected areas in 1931. The enforcement of these laws was left to the state and local governments with their limited, conflicting, and overlapping jurisdictions.

By the First World War anti-vice organizations like Parkhurst's Society for the Prevention of Crime had pushed local police forces into closing down red-light districts in most towns and cities. It soon became clear, however, that this merely dispersed prostitution rather than ended it. Many cities soon noticed an immediate increase in street walking and soliciting. Moreover, without recognized districts or brothels, prostitutes could no longer receive clients in a relatively protected environment, and the search for custom made them more vulnerable to both customer violence and police shakedowns. The situation also led to an increase in the number of pimps, as they moved in to fill the legal, physical, and emotional needs formerly met by madams and other prostitutes. Prostitutes paid a high price in financial terms for this protection and could be subject to indiscriminate beatings. Customers were also more prone to be beaten, robbed, or cheated as the prostitution business adapted to its new conditions.[83]

'Badger games' and 'creep houses' became increasingly common. In the first, the prostitute would take the client to her apartment or hotel. About the time they would begin intercourse, the woman's 'husband' would come in and threaten both. The prostitute would suggest to the client that money or jewelry was needed to cool the situation. Clients tended to pay off and rarely took their complaints to the police. At other times some prostitutes would take their clients to places where their 'creeper' associates could enter the room and go through the clients' pockets without being noticed. As one study of prostitution put it, 'A client approaching orgasm is usually so preoccupied that he is relatively uninterested in what is going on around him.' Understandably, the client would again be unlikely to complain once the theft was discovered![84]

The policing of prostitution also allowed for the development of innovative extortion techniques. This was most famously revealed in the early 1930s, when an investigation headed by Judge Samuel Seabury found that corruption in New York City's criminal justice system allowed numerous 'vice squad' rackets to flourish. Seabury reported that the city's vice squad had two types of arrest concerning prostitution – the direct and the indirect. In the direct, the police officer approached the victim and arrested her after she had accepted money for prostitution. In the indirect, the police informer or 'stool-pigeon' was the customer and at any given moment the officers broke in and made the arrest. The Seabury report detailed a number of ingenious traps for innocent and guilty alike, contrived to inflate arrest quotas and extort graft. One of these involved the informer renting a room in a small hotel, paying for it with marked money, and bringing in a woman purporting to be his wife. Almost immediately the police broke in and arrested the landlady for maintaining a house of prostitution. Landladies tended to pay off to avoid court costs and bad publicity. Another racket involved the informer, posing as a patient, entering a doctor's surgery while the doctor was away and demanding treatment. He then placed money in a conspicuous spot and began to undress, ignoring the protests of the nurse. At that point, police officers would charge in and arrest the nurse for prostitution. Numerous innocent working women or housewives were framed as prostitutes and, if they could not raise the cash to buy their freedom, served prison sentences. The Seabury report indicated that the police and their informers were just a part of a cabal that included court clerks, magistrates, bondsmen, defence lawyers, and prosecutors: 'The picture of the ring is complete. The stool-pigeon or the officer framed the woman, the officer arrested her, the unlicensed bondsmen bailed her out at an exorbitant charge and usually recommended a lawyer, the lawyer gouged her savings and either he himself, or through the bondsmen, "fixed" the arresting officer and the District Attorney.' Five vice squad detectives had accumulated bank accounts each exceeding $500,000 through these methods.[85]

The organization of prostitution differed from place to place, usually according to the official or unofficial policies of the local authorities. This is made clear by the accounts of madams such as Polly Adler and Carol Erwin. Gangster involvement tended to be as extortionists rather than as organizers. Erwin, for example, described how she and other madams ran their houses in Alaska independently during the Second World War and catered mainly to U.S. servicemen. The racketeers moved in and tried to force her to pay them $1,300 a month. Unlike the others, she refused, and the racketeers forced her to close down and leave town. As the sociologist Mary McKintosh concluded, 'In this sort of situation it is common to talk of the racketeers as 'running' or 'controlling' prostitution. It would really be more accurate to say that they have a racket that enables them to extract money from prostitutes, just as they may extract money from laundries, drinking clubs, or any other vulnerable tradespeople.'[86]

When racketeers did make an effort to expand operations out of state, they ran the risk of bringing themselves to the attention of the FBI. From the late 1930s and early 1940s, federal investigators uncovered several large-scale racketeering enterprises. These rings, according to David Langrum's study, 'supplied women to New England and Florida resorts and moved them in and out of Atlantic City, New Jersey.' FBI Director J. Edgar Hoover gained a great deal of favourable publicity as he orchestrated simultaneous raids on brothels to round up potential Mann Act violators, but, as Langrum suggests, these were just a side story of FBI enforcement of the Mann Act:

> An important by-product of vice investigations was the possibility that Hoover could obtain some information he could use to buttress his political position. In July 1949 he advised his agents that during a vice investigation they might come across address books containing data concerning prominent public officials, presumably with names, addresses, and sexual preferences. He ordered that 'unless the names, appearing therein are material to the investigation, this type of information should be placed in the administrative section.' It was in this manner that Hoover gained access to information that he could use to strengthen his political position, by leaking or threatening to leak it to the press.[87]

Langrum's claim that Hoover used of evidence of sexual peccadilloes as a form of blackmail to strengthen his political position can be supported by a number of documents released under the Freedom of Information Act. The more sensational claim by Anthony Summers in a 1993 biography of Hoover that the FBI director was a homosexual, cross-dresser, and thus himself vulnerable to blackmail by the Mafia to lay off their operations has no such solid support.

At the same time as the crusade against red-light prostitution, the system of open gambling came under sustained attack. In the cities, lavish and conspicuous gambling houses gave way to dark, smoky rooms reached through discreet entranceways, as law enforcement campaigns made their mark. Out-of-town horseracing also declined so that by the First World War only six states, New York, Maryland, Kentucky, Louisiana, Colorado, and Nevada still had tracks. Despite the greater need for caution, *Life* magazine reported that gambling remained a multimillion dollar business in the 1920s. The magazine noted: 'A stranger in almost any U.S. city can quickly find a horse-race bookmaker by making discreet inquiries of bell hops, elevator men, barbers, or bartenders or by hanging around the news stand where racing publications are sold.'[88]

Technology and mass communication joined corruption as important factors undermining efforts to cut down on the extent of gambling
as the career of Chicago gambling entrepreneur Mont Tennes demonstrated. Tennes helped to undermine gambling prohibition by establishing the General News Service and gaining a monopoly of racing
news information that lasted for three decades. Bookmakers required
prompt and accurate information to ensure that they were not cheated
by bettors getting to know the winners before them. By 1911 Tennes's
service supplied information to twenty cities across the nation. In the
process Tennes had forced his main competitors, including John Payne
of Cincinnati, out of the business, by methods described by his former
partner Timothy Murphy. Murphy charged that 'Tennes secured power
through a system of persecution; that the Payne race-track system and
others were put out of business by dynamite bombs and the torch;
race-tracks and even private residences bring fired or dynamited in the
war of extermination; and that pool-rooms in Chicago which failed to
subscribe to the service were closed down by the police.'

Tennes continued to run his operations until the late 1920s, as part of
a much larger political-police-criminal set-up. He left the business,
according to John Landesco, when a new generation of gangsters
began to demand protection money from his bookmaker operations.[89]

The 1920s also saw the innovation of suburban vice centres catering
for both local and city trade. Gangsters such as John Torrio realized
that it was far easier to collaborate with the authorities of small towns
and suburbs than with the more complex and changing city administrations. He helped set up operations in towns like Burnham, Stickney,
and Cicero to the west of Chicago where gambling and prostitution
were openly tolerated and which a large population could easily reach
by car. 'This symbiotic relationship,' according to Mark Haller, 'in
which surrounding blue-collar communities provided protected vice
and entertainment for the larger city, was not limited to Chicago. Covington, Kentucky, had a similar relationship to Cincinnati, while East
St Louis serviced St Louis.'[90]

Throughout the 1930s downtown areas of the cities supported dozens of illegal gambling houses running roulette, blackjack, and dice
games, and at the same time, illegal slot machines were operating in
thousands of bars, clubs, and stores.

Policy or numbers games rapidly became citywide and profitable
operations. Policy was the more complex original, but in both games
customers placed their bets on combinations of numbers that they

hoped would match a combination that was published daily and yield a return at a rate which was usually between 450 to 1 to 650 to 1. Both had originally been played and run mostly by black Americans, but white gangster syndicates with their better police and political connections did take over some operations. In New York's Harlem, for example, Dutch Schultz was able to consolidate the fragmented numbers business through force and financial manipulation. 'You worked for Schultz or you didn't work at all,' as one contemporary numbers runner put it. Schultz's domination was brief, however, and he was shot dead in 1935. By contrast, in Detroit and adjoining cities such as Ypsilanti, Dearborn, Ann Arbor, and River Rouge, African Americans fought off white gangster take-over bids and kept control of an industry that employed thousands of people and wielded substantial local political power.[91]

Many city authorities scarcely even pretended to enforce the vice laws. Ruling politicians tended to appoint judges, prosecutors, and police chiefs who posed no threat to the regular pay-offs. They knew the political realities of illegal enterprises in urban America. Handbook, policy, and numbers operators, for example, constituted the nucleus of a political bloc that included the votes of families, friends, employees, and customers. Vice operators made large contributions to campaign funds to ensure that whatever city administration was elected would be friendly. State politicians only took an interest when they decried these conditions at election times, and this interest rarely lasted long.

The organization of vice varied from city to city with their different forms of government, but personal greed was always the common denominator. In Jersey City, New Jersey, a top official of the dominant political machine of Mayor Frank Hague had a full-time job screening applicants for unofficial bookmaking licences. Those successful were given a 'location,' usually the house or store of a loyal precinct worker. They paid an inflated rent of which a high proportion was 'kicked back' into the machine treasury. In order to stay in business, no one worked harder for the Hague machine than the city's 1,000 or more bookies and their landlords. City policemen and officials supplemented their meagre official salaries and wages with the money collected from vice interests and had every reason to maintain the status quo.

Hague's control over the city was absolute for more than two decades, from the 1920s to the 1940s: in his own words, 'I am the Law.'

Politics for him was business. He never received more than $8,000 a year in salary, but at the end of the 1920s the IRS ordered him to pay more than $2 million in delinquent taxes and penalties. But Hague was also a major power in national Democratic Party politics and his support helped clinch the election of Franklin D. Roosevelt in 1932. Hague's problems with the IRS eased when the new administration took over.[92]

San Francisco experienced one of the most complete investigations of gambling and prostitution during the 1930s. Edward Atherton, a former FBI agent, was brought in by the city after the IRS had revealed that a police captain had amassed a fortune 'presumably, in part, from pay-offs from houses of vice.' Atherton soon found numerous brothels operating quite openly. There were so many in the North Beach area, for example, that tenants found it necessary to put signs on their front doors announcing the fact that they were private residences. He also found that bookmaking was the most important form of gambling in the city. In all, Atherton's report estimated 'very conservatively' that the annual graft toll from gambling and prostitution operations at around $1 million annually, and this figure can probably be multiplied. Atherton named sixty-seven police officers and twenty-four city, state, and federal officers in the running of what was known as 'the business.' In particular he noted the pivotal role played by the bailbond firm run by Pete McDonough and his nephew Harry Rice. 'No one,' the report stated, 'can conduct a prostitution or gambling enterprise in San Francisco without the direct or indirect approval' of this firm. 'Anyone engaged in these activities, who incurs the firm's disfavour, is sooner or later forced out of business.' A police officer that defied the graft system to enforce the law honestly was regarded as a 'snake in the grass' and his career sabotaged. Most policemen cooperated with the firm that the report described as 'the fountainhead of corruption' in San Francisco, 'willing to interest itself in almost any matter designed to deflect or circumvent the law.'

Atherton recognized that most San Franciscans were tolerant of prostitution and gambling activities and recommended that 'legal bars' against them should be removed. Such activities 'should be licensed and subject to close supervision and regulation by some agency separate and apart from the Police Department.' He likened those who thought that prostitution and gambling could be stopped by prohibitive legislation to 'the ostrich of popular repute.' These recommendations, however, were ignored. McDonough's power was broken as a result of the investigation but the conditions that allowed his firm to prosper remained in place and new systems of corruption evolved.[93]

Off-track bookmaking also had grown in significance during the 1930s. Many states had legalized wagering at horse and dog tracks as a means of raising revenue during the Depression. More races and better long-distance communications enabled bookmakers in virtually every city and state to turn a substantial profit in defiance of the laws against betting. Independents and syndicates, with their police and political protectors, capitalized on the duplicity of the state legislatures; these allowed those who had the money and leisure the privilege of gambling legally at the tracks, while the majority of the gambling public were officially denied the same privilege.[94]

Frank Erickson became New York's best known bookmaker, being involved in operations that grossed millions of dollars each year. Basing his operations in Bergen County, New Jersey, he employed a large staff to wait by the telephone and accept bets from bookmakers when they had too much money wagered on a particular horse or dog. He provided this facility to bookmakers from all forty-eight states of the Union. From this and from special bets from wealthy sports fans Erickson made deposits of more than $100,000 a day in the National Bank of New York, for example, and opened other accounts that showed deposits of more than $6 million in a four-year period.[95]

The laws against off-track bookmaking were treated with as much contempt as the laws that prohibited alcohol. For example, newspapers in cities thousands of miles from the tracks provided details of form, weight, and the state of the going, details that of course were only relevant to gamblers. In 1936 Moses Annenberg of Chicago, building on the businesses established by John Payne and Mont Tennes, established a service that provided bookmakers all over the United States with racing information, from almost every race track in the country as well as those in Canada, Mexico, and Cuba. This included the almost instant communication of highly technical items, such as the changing odds on the tote board and the *pari mutuel* prices paid at the track. Again, the information was only relevant to gamblers in a country where gambling was, for the most part, a crime. According to IRS agents investigating Annenberg for income tax evasion, the operation was 'one of the largest rackets ever developed in this country.' At Annenberg's trial, records were introduced to show that his operation was the American Telephone and Telegraph Company's fifth-largest customer. In 1940 Annenberg was sentenced to a three-year prison term and that left the lucrative racing information business literally up for grabs.

James Ragen and Arthur McBride, former managers of the old organization, soon filled the vacuum created by Annenberg's abdication. They pieced the organization together, renamed it Continental Press, and through subterfuge concealed their ownership of the distributors. The Ragen-McBride outfit was soon violently competing with a rival service, Trans-American, which was controlled by former Capone associates, Jack Guzik, Tony Accardo, and Murray Humphries. On 24 June 1946 Ragen, of Continental, was murdered in Chicago and warfare between the two organizations continued in different parts of the country for several months, during which time neither made any money. In May 1947 the two groups came to an understanding: McBride's son Eddie was left in charge of Continental, which, for a few years, became America's chief source of racing information, with the Guzik distributorship getting special rates.[96]

All efforts to enforce the anti-gambling laws either failed completely or only served to shift the location of gambling activity to other cities, counties, or states. Mayor La Guardia in New York, for example, did all he could to suppress gambling throughout the twelve years of his tenure, which began on 1 January 1934. The La Guardia administration's first crusade was against slot machines – a novelty that had become so popular that more than 25,000 stood in the city's stores, bars, and restaurants. The fear was that they might be a corrupting influence on the young who might become addicted to gambling and steal to finance their play. La Guardia ordered the police to seize, confiscate, and destroy these devices and, on some occasions, did the destroying himself with a fireman's axe having made sure that newspaper photographers were present. By the end of his administration's first year in office both slot machines and, in La Guardia's words, their 'big brother' pinball machines had been effectively barred in New York City.[97]

Frank Costello, Bill Dwyer's bootlegging partner, had been New York's biggest slot-machine operator, but he now had hundreds of machines either broken up or stacked up uselessly in New Jersey warehouses. As Costello later testified, this situation was remedied in the spring of 1935 when Governor Huey Long of Louisiana invited him to set them up again in the New Orleans area. Police protection was to be guaranteed for a substantial yearly fee.[98]

'Dandy' Phil Kastel, another of Costello's partners, went down to the South to supervise the installation and operation of 1,000–odd machines installed around the business district of New Orleans. The profits and protection continued even after Long's assassination in September 1935. In 1944 Costello declared earnings of $71,346.46 from the city's slots for the benefit of the IRS. There is no way of calculating how much local officials were paid off but, as Costello's biographer put it, when it came to accepting bribes, 'it was never a question of would they or wouldn't they. It was always a question of how much.'[99]

La Guardia, meanwhile, was frequently claiming victories in the 'war to end gang power' in New York: ' We have driven the so-called big punks out of the city ... they can't come back because we'll run them right out again.' In reality his crusade did no more than increase business in neighbouring New Jersey. Every night fleets of rented black limousines would leave New York for illegal casinos in New Jersey's Bergen, Hudson, and Passaic counties. High rollers were well cared for, often given caviar and champagne on the house in luxurious rooms, before they lost their money in places owned by such gangsters as Longy Zwillman, Joe Adonis, and Willie Moretti. These also operated dingier joints for poorer players, packed into places with sawdust on the floor, and green blankets to serve as the craps-table or card-games covers.[100]

Even in New York City itself, despite the efforts of its energetic mayor, gambling continued unabated. La Guardia finally admitted defeat in his final year of office when he told radio listeners that he had received 'tens of thousands of letters complaining about gambling with such accurate information that he could not help but wonder 'what the police are doing!' He called on the police to 'Go on and act now. Snap into it. Clean them out!'[101] It was an impotent gesture.

Like their New York equivalents, Cleveland gangsters were prepared to relocate to exploit America's hypocritical attitude towards gambling. The 'Cleveland Four' – a group of former bootleggers that included 'Moe' Dalitz, Samuel Tucker, Morris Kleinman, and Louis Rothkopf – invested in gambling clubs based in Newport and Covington, Kentucky, just across the Ohio River from the large and well-policed city of Cincinnati.

In Newport, the Clevelanders made alliances with several local gangsters, most notably Albert 'Red' Masterson, to drive out competitors, such as the owner of the Beverly Hills Club, Peter Schmidt.

Schmidt repeatedly refused offers by the out-of-towners to buy in and, probably as a result, suffered from a run of 'bad luck,' which began on 3 February 1936. A fire at the Beverly Hills Club took the life of the caretaker's five-year-old daughter as well as destroying the property.

Schmidt rebuilt the club, but six weeks after the reopening in April 1937, it was robbed by six armed men. Such bad luck only ceased after he had sold out to Dalitz and the others. On 18 November 1940 the renamed Beverly Hills Country Club again reopened, but this time successfully. Large profits were made as people from all over the Midwest and beyond came to gamble and be entertained by top Hollywood and Broadway stars.

It was later discovered that Red Masterson had bought the gasoline that set the original fire. For his efforts Masterson was given a small percentage of some casinos owned by the Cleveland gangsters, and he continued to represent their interests as an 'enforcer' for almost thirty years. Masterson's role was to keep undesirable street crime out of Newport. In particular, the syndicate wanted tourists to spend their money and come again, and not be fleeced by 'bar girls' or rigged games at small downtown operations, called 'bust out' joints. Although cutting out these smaller operations completely proved to be impossible, by 1960 Masterson had done his job well enough and become such a well-respected member of the community that he was made a Kentucky Colonel by Governor Bert T. Combs, ironically for his 'help in the fire-fighting field.'[102]

Benjamin 'Bugsy' Siegel was the most notable eastern gangster to go west in the 1930s. Siegel, a New York bootlegger and 'enforcer' during Prohibition, decided to move to Los Angeles in the mid-1930s. Siegel had arrived in the country's fastest growing metropolitan area in 1937, intending to batter his way into control of local bookmaking. His plans were, however, constantly frustrated by too many law enforcement agencies overlapping each other in Los Angeles City and County. The city police, the sheriff's deputies in the county, and various district attorneys' offices, all had to be taken care of. Over all these were the state's attorney-general officers who could move and demand tribute anywhere in the state of California. By the 1940s Siegel was reduced to borrowing large sums of money from his Hollywood filmstar friends, who were foolish enough to lend it to him, but not foolish enough to ask for it back.[103]

In 1938 Siegel faced another problem when a reform-minded mayor called Fletcher Bowron was elected. Bowron pursued an anti-vice crusade in the La Guardia tradition in the early year of his administration. Slot and pinball machines were banished from the city, and prostitutes and bookmakers were harassed more than usual. The mayor claimed to have 'broken the most powerful ring that ever had an American city in its grip,' but only actually succeeded in making gambling less accessible in Los Angeles. It became more secretive and dependent on regular custom built up over the years. Some gambling operators moved across city lines into more amenable county territory, and others, such as Guy McAfee, Tutor Scherer, and Siegel himself decided to go legitimate and buy casinos in Las Vegas, Nevada, an easy drive from Los Angeles.

In 1931 the mainly desert state of Nevada had decided to raise revenue by legalizing gambling and prostitution. Development was at first slow and Las Vegas remained for over a decade little more than it had been before legalization, a stopping-off place where travellers could drink, gamble, and visit prostitutes before setting off. However, because it was close to Los Angeles, Las Vegas took off during the 1940s to become the most successful of several Nevadan 'sin cities.'

Siegel was among the first to see the potential profitability of a haven of legalized gambling in an America coming out of the Great Depression. When he visited Las Vegas he had no intention of building a low-key gambling house. Instead, he helped transform the city into the 'entertainment capital of the world,' with the dazzle to attract not only the high rollers on card, dice, and roulette games but the millions of low-stake players on which U.S. casino gambling depends. Siegel put all the money he could raise into building the lavish Flamingo Hotel on Highway 91, which became known as The Strip. He succeeded in building the hotel during wartime by paying extortionate black-market prices. The Flamingo opened on 26 December 1946 with a guest list of Hollywood filmstars and an entertainment bill headed by Jimmy Durante. The following June, Siegel was dead, shot in the living-room of his girlfriend Virginia Hill, in the wealthy Los Angeles suburb of Beverly Hills. Siegel became another unsolved gang murder statistic. Newspapers all over the country competed in supplying gory details of the damage that resulted from four bullets fired at close range from a .30–calibre U.S. Army carbine.[104]

After an uncertain beginning the Flamingo turned a handsome profit. In the following decade professional criminals from Chicago, Minneapolis, New York, and the Dalitz syndicate from Cleveland poured money into a growing chain of luxury casinos. The new out-of-state operators had naturally come from the big city crime networks because these were the people who knew the business of gambling. Many of these soon learned the business of 'skimming' to avoid paying the full costs of taxation. Money was easily skimmed from the casino's take, because only those who count up the money can know how much has been taken in, and they can be persuaded or ordered to divert substantial amounts before the final total is arrived at. Only honest and diligent state regulation can minimize this practice, but this came slowly to Nevadan authorities. In the meantime couriers were kept busy carrying suitcases, briefcases, and envelopes full of banknotes around the country and away from the public treasury.[105]

After the lean years of the 1930s the Second World War provided an immense boost to illegal as well as legal businesses. More people were employed and earning good wages, rationing and war production cut back on available consumer goods, an increasing amount of money became available to spend on prohibited goods and services, and the profitability of vice increased.[106]

Gambling, in particular, enjoyed a wartime and post-war boom. Gallup polls indicated that 45 per cent of the population gambled in 1945 and this rose to 57 per cent in 1950, in spite of the fact that all of the states but Nevada had laws prohibiting gambling. Off-track bookmaking and slot-machine gambling flourished in most cities, bookmakers made arrangements to operate in factories, offices, building sites, and on the waterfront; slot-machine distributors ensured that thousands of private clubs and lodges gave their members the opportunity to play on what were known as 'devil machines' to moral crusaders and 'one-arm bandits' to everyone else. Illegal casinos operated in many areas throughout the country, notably northern Kentucky, Hot Springs (Arkansas), Saratoga (New York), northern New Jersey, East St Louis (Missouri), Nashville (Tennessee), and Greater New Orleans. Operations were sometimes but not always discreet. In southern Louisiana the law was held in such contempt that Celestin F. Rowley, sheriff of St Bernard Parish, adjoining New Orleans, complained bitterly that the press notoriety of Jefferson County and its sheriff Frank Clancy was drawing business away from his own wide-open parish. *Newsweek* magazine quoted the indignant Rowley as saying, 'I'm thinking about taking out some ads, Sheriff Clancy is getting too much publicity for the joints in Jefferson.'[107]

An 1950 article in *Life* surveyed the gambling situation across the whole country and found: 'In any city where gambling exists ... the police department knows the addresses and owners of every joint in town. The reason the joints stay open is always just one thing: graft, paid either to the police, the city officials or the political machines and in some cases all three. The United States is full of policemen, sheriffs, and prosecuting attorneys who have built mansions, bought yachts or loaded their safe deposit boxes to bursting.'[108]

In many ways gambling in postwar America resembled the liquor situation during Prohibition. Gambling was a popular and socially approved pastime and the fact that it was illegal only succeeded in enriching corrupt politicians, policemen, and criminal entrepreneurs. The fact that the gambling laws were plainly not being enforced produced some calls for regulating rather than trying to prohibit the activity, so that tax revenue would replace criminal gain. The legislatures of several states considered but soon rejected proposals to legalize various forms of gambling. These proposals failed partly because the state legislatures were still dominated by the Protestant culture of rural America, which regarded gambling as sinful, but more because the proponents of legalized gambling lacked the immense financial support that had pushed through the repeal of the Prohibition amendment. Business interests were either uninterested or accepted the anti-gambling arguments of Virgil Peterson of the Chicago Crime Commission. Gambling, according to Peterson's line, was bad for business because it 'withdraws money from the regular channels of trade vital to the well-being of a nation or a community.' The legalization of gambling could thus not be contemplated and the hopeless and corrupting task of gambling prohibition continued.[109]

Because of the strength of the opposition it took a brave politician publicly to favour legalizing gambling. In 1950, for example, Mayor William O'Dwyer of New York, well aware that gambling enforcement was a hopeless and corrupting task, urged the state legislature to legalize gambling on sporting events. He was immediately attacked from every side: newspaper editorials, religious and business organizations, and even Governor Thomas E. Dewey castigated the mayor for such an immoral idea. Given the torrent of abuse that greeted O'Dwyer's suggestion, it is not surprising that most city executives preferred a passive approach to the gambling laws; gambling arrest statistics were compiled with the minimum of disruption to protected gambling operations.[110]

New Orleans Mayor deLesseps S. Morrison was a far more expedient and, as it turned out, influential politician than O'Dwyer. He had been elected in 1946 after a campaign that was on two levels. The first was that of a holy crusade against the incumbent Mayor Robert Maestri and his corrupt political machine. 'This is a battle of the masses against the few in the corrupt political clique that holds our city in an iron grip,' Morrison declared in his opening statement, and continued, 'New Orleans now stands in the shadow of vicious gangster rule, a rule made possible by the consent and co-operation of the corrupt leaders of the present city machine.'[111]

Morrison's pledges to end vice and corruption secured him the support of the religious and women's organizations; the most publicized image of the campaign was a demonstration of women in support of Morrison, brandishing brooms as a symbol of the sweeping out of corruption. His dynamism, campaign organization, and promises to serve the interests of business helped win him the election.

The other side of Morrison's campaign was not revealed for several years but was just as essential for victory as the first. Morrison knew that his prospects of winning the election were remote if he threatened an important part of the city's economy – gambling and prostitution. To reassure the vice interests he held a special meeting in the early hours of election day, 22 January 1946, at a hall on Esplanade Avenue. At the meeting were representatives of the city's vice operations including prostitutes, gamblers, nightclub owners, and racketeers. Morrison was quoted as telling them: 'I know how you people make your living and I assure you I will do nothing to stop you from continuing if I am elected Mayor. I am not a silk-stocking candidate and I do not try to ever change things, so vote for me and here's to bigger and better things.'[112]

In the years that followed Morrison did everything he could to live up to this promise, but was thwarted for a while by the efforts of a zealous police chief called Adair Watters. Watters did everything he could to enforce the gambling and vice laws in New Orleans and to make life difficult for the policemen who organized graft collections. Morrison forced Watters to resign in February 1949, and replaced him with the more amenable Joseph Scheuering, who allowed the old graft system to return. By that time Morrison had acquired a crime-busting reputation in local and national newspapers, thanks ironically to the efforts of Watters. However, in the run-up to the 1950 elections, Morrison's crime-busting reputation began to look shaky as the normally compliant local press ran some critical articles about Morrison's police force. The *Item*, for example, charged that the police were once again being systematically paid off and that the operations of brothels, lotteries, and handbooks were wide open.[113]

Morrison's initial response was complete denial. He stressed that the police were doing a good job and that the city was free of vice, crime, and corruption. While sticking to this patently false position, Morrison began to use his presidency of the American Municipal Association (AMA) to divert attention away from the shortcomings of law enforcement in New Orleans. The AMA provided a national platform for Morrison's new ideas about organized crime. In a speech in Chicago, Morrison urged the federal government to investigate the political activities of Frank Costello of New York, 'the reputed leader of a nationwide gambling syndicate,' and continued: 'A national and international syndicate, which is reportedly headed by Costello, is attempting to seize power in key cities in the nation ... A few years ago they occupied behind-the-scenes positions of power in Chicago, Los Angeles, New Orleans, Miami, and other cities. Good government administration has kicked them over the municipal borders. Now they are trying to bring their operations, power and influence back into key cities.'[114]

Morrison was cynically capitalizing on Costello's notoriety and his own mythical reputation as being a foe of the New York gambling operator. As noted earlier, Costello's connection with New Orleans was that in 1934 he and his partner Phil Kastel had placed slot machines in New Orleans at the invitation, as Costello later testified, of Governor Huey Long. In 1947 Police Chief Watters began very publicly to destroy the machines by having them heaped up and then having police officers fire machine-guns at them. Although at the time Morrison had actively opposed the destruction, by 1949 he was loudly claiming that he had chased the Costello-Kastel syndicate out of the city.

Morrison continued the nationwide 'crusade' against organized crime after his re-election, and pressure from him, in particular, provoked a response from the federal government. Attorney General Howard McGrath agreed to hold a conference of mayors and law enforcement officials, which Morrison used as a platform for his organized crime ideas. In his speech Morrison again boasted about his administration's ousting of Costello's slot-machines, and stated that two groups, the Costello syndicate and the Chicago syndicate, ran the wire service and the slot machine racket across the whole country. These two groups were, according to Morrison, 'the root of the whole evil' of organized crime in America and he continued:

We do not have the whole picture – but each of us present – and hundreds of other mayors, public officials, and crime commissions in various States – have seen small segments of this national scene of organized interstate crime. These pieces fit together in a pattern of mounting evidence concerning several highly organized gambling and racketeering syndicates whose wealth, power, scope of operations, and influence have recently grown to gigantic and alarming proportions. It is an ugly, vicious, un-American picture of systematic law violation, huge profits, corruption of public officials who can be bought – and operations outside the jurisdiction of those who cannot be purchased ... Does all this not point up the very vital fact that the great need is not to get at the small fry, but the absentee syndicate bosses who direct the financing, supplying, strategy, and rapid movement of law breakers back and forth across the country? All States and cities are not yet infected, but no State or community is immune from invasion. At the very worst, these underworld czars, through entrenched special privileges in a community, can wield tremendous influence over its government. From profits and power in one locality they go on to another. That is a danger and threat to our democratic way of life hardly less real than the Communist menace.

Morrison presented these views along with a ten-point plan of action against organized crime. In addition to legislation dealing with slot machines and the wire service, the program called for a 'co-ordinated masterplan of action' against nationwide rackets by the attorney general's office. Most significantly, Morrison's program endorsed Senator Estes Kefauver's bill for a congressional investigation of interstate crime, which was then being referred to the Senate Judiciary Committee and in danger of being discarded.[115] The publicity generated by the attorney general's conference and by Morrison's speech in particular, helped rescue Kefauver's bill from oblivion.

A few months later Kefauver's congressional investigators preparing for Senate committee hearings found that Morrison himself was deeply involved in the local organization of gambling and prostitution, but a decision was taken not to reveal this involvement.[116] Morrison had hit on a way that local officials could use to absolve themselves from responsibility for vice-related crime and corruption.

Organized crime was 'un-American' and simply too big for local authorities to deal with. Morrison was therefore an early champion of the opinion that organized crime had become a national threat that therefore demanded federal involvement in matters usually reserved to the states. His was also an understanding of organized crime appropriate to a new generation of ambitious politicians and public officials wanting to be in the vanguard of a crusade that would parallel and eventually eclipse the Red Scare in its intensity. In the process, as we shall see in Chapter 5, the knowledge that some Italian-American gangsters had become rich and powerful in some cities and had contact with racketeers of different ethnic origins in other cities, became distorted into something far more mysterious, menacing, and ethnically exclusive. The new version would be far more effective in distracting from the failure of America's moral crusade.

Racketeering, Racism, and the First War on Drugs

The state and federal anti-drug laws passed at the beginning of the First World War immediately created a black market in the prohibited substances as criminals moved in to supply both addicts and users with the newly illegal drugs. In 1915 an editorial in *American Medicine* noted the immediate consequences of drug prohibition and foresaw much of the tragedy that would follow:

> Narcotic drug addiction is one of the gravest and most important questions confronting the medical profession today. Instead of improving conditions the laws recently passed have made the problem more complex. Honest medical men have found such handicaps and dangers to themselves and their reputations in these laws ... that they have simply decided to have as little to do as possible with drug addicts or their needs ... [The addict] is denied the medical care he urgently needs, open, aboveboard sources from which he formerly obtained his drug supply are closed to him, and he is driven to the underworld where he can get his drug, but of course, surreptitiously and in violation of the law ... Abuses in the sale of narcotic drugs are increasing ... a particular sinister sequence ... is the character of the places to which [addicts] are forced to go to get their drugs and the type of people with whom they are obliged to mix. The most depraved criminals are often the dispensers of these habit-forming drugs ... One has only to think of the stress under which the addict lives, and to recall his lack of funds, to realize the extent to which these afflicted individuals are under the control of the worst elements of society.[117]

The corruption of law enforcement added to these problems. Drug deals involve cash transactions between willing parties; the best evidence is lacking – no injured or robbed citizen complains to the police and serves as a witness. The police therefore had to learn to develop cases through informers and covert methods, before making arrests, seizing evidence, and undertaking interrogation. Until a case reached the courts, the police controlled the situation totally, since they alone decided whether an offence had been committed and whether they had a legal case against the suspect. This situation increased the possibility of corruption and decreased the possibility of controlling this corruption. In 1917 the first police officer was convicted for taking a large bribe to protect a drug-trafficking operation. Many more operations were successfully protected and completed, and at no time since has the anti-drug crusade been free of corruption.[118]

The most notable New York criminal entrepreneur to be involved in the 1920s drug trade was Arnold Rothstein. Rothstein ran illegal gambling games, provided gangster services during industrial disputes, and imported Scotch whisky during Prohibition. Drugs were just another simple way for him to make an illegal dollar. Two of his associates, Yasha Katzenburg and Dan Collins, bought quantities of drugs in Europe and Asia; these were then smuggled into the United States and sold to retailers in New York, Chicago, St Louis, and Kansas City by more Rothstein associates.[119]

Rothstein, like most other traffickers, did not set up any formal criminal organizational structures – which would have increased the chances of prosecution. 'The strength of all his many separate partnerships and deals,' according to Robert Lacey, 'lay in their separateness. The failure of one did not jeopardize the others.'[120] The success of Rothstein and others showed the way for many more to make deals or set up and run the many thousands of ventures and operations that provided Americans with illegal goods and services and effectively nullified all prohibitions.

The campaign against drugs during the 1920s was led by the man who had introduced alcohol prohibition to Congress, Richmond P. Hobson. Hobson founded a series of organizations with names that indicated a desire to globalize America's anti-drug crusade: The International Narcotic Education Association (1923), the World Conference on Narcotic Education (1926), and the World Narcotic Defense Association (1927). Backed by some of the top people in American society, he successfully transmitted his anti-drug message to millions of Americans through school textbooks, newspapers, and radio programs. Drugs, according to Hobson's new polemic, caused all kinds of crime and he likened heroin addicts to the 'Living Dead.' These, he told radio listeners in 1928, 'lie, cheat, steal, rob and, if necessary, commit murder' to get their supplies. Hobson continued:

> Heroin addiction can be likened to a contagion. Suppose it were announced that there were more than a million lepers among our people. Think what a shock the announcement would produce! Yet drug addiction is far more incurable than leprosy, far more tragic to its victims, and is spreading like a moral and physical scourge.
>
> There are symptoms breaking out all over our country and now breaking out in many parts of Europe which show that individual nations and the whole world is menaced by this appalling foe ... marching ... to the capture and destruction of the whole world ...
>
> Drug addiction is more communicable and less curable than leprosy. Drug addicts are the principal carriers of vice diseases, and with their lowered resistance are incubators and carriers of the streptococcus, pneumococcus, the germ of flu, of tuberculosis, and other diseases.
>
> Upon the issue hangs the perpetuation of civilization, the destiny of the world and the future of the human race![121]

Hobson's primary concern, of course, was still for the white elements of the human race and with this in mind he produced a book called *Drug Addiction: A Malignant Racial Cancer*.

Hobson's overheated claims about drugs were taken seriously. At one time he said that one ounce of heroin would cause 2,000 addicts and warned: 'In using any brand of face powder regularly, it is a wise precaution to have a sample analyzed for heroin.' In a 1929 radio broadcast he told listeners that drug addiction constituted 'the chief factor menacing the public health, the public morals, the public safety.' While an academic study of the extent of the drug problem in the United States put the number of drug addicts in the nation at 110,000, Hobson told his much larger audience that the number was more than a million.[122] He was thus an appropriate founding father of a crusade that continues to be fuelled by imaginative statements and exaggerated statistics.

In 1930 Hobson applied unsuccessfully to become the federal government's chief anti-drug enforcement officer as Commissioner of the Federal Bureau of Narcotics (FBN), but Harry J. Anslinger, the man who beat him, shared many of his opinions, racist assumptions, and ambitions for a toughened-up national and global response to drugs.

The FBN was created as a separate agency within the Treasury Department in 1930 in the wake of a scandal involving the Narcotics Division, which until then had had responsibility for federal drug law enforcement. A New York grand jury had found that there was 'gross dereliction and incompetence' within the division. Agents had not only been routinely falsifying their records by reporting city police cases as federal cases, but they had also been colluding with prominent drug traffickers. Small-time offenders were arrested while the higher-ups went free. The revelation that particularly embarrassed the head of the division, Levi Nutt, was that his son and son-in-law had both been employed by Arnold Rothstein, New York's 'Big Bankroll,' who was thought to be the organizer of the country's largest drug-smuggling organization. Nutt was soon replaced by Anslinger as head of the division which itself, in September 1930, was reorganized to become the FBN.[123]

Anslinger's background had given him the edge in the competition for the position as commissioner and at the same time would condition his response to the problem of drugs. According to his biographer, John C. McWilliams, Anslinger had dedicated his life to the U.S. federal bureaucracy. In 1926 he joined the U.S. Treasury Department and, as head of the Division of Foreign Control in the Prohibition Unit, he dealt with the control of smuggling through international agreements and the exchange of information with other countries. In 1928 he wrote a paper for a national competition that argued that Prohibition could work with efficient administration and effective enforcement. The plan included ways to prevent smuggling, eliminate illegal manufacture, and coordinate government agencies more effectively. The ways to prevent smuggling involved Congress giving 'power to the President to employ the Navy to co-operate with the Coast Guard in the suppression of the liquor smuggling.' Anslinger's plan also recommended that more prosecutors and judges should be appointed to catch more violators and that buying alcohol for non-medical consumption should be punished by heavy fines and prison sentences.[124] Repeal of alcohol prohibition in 1933 effectively scuppered these plans, but as commissioner of narcotics, Anslinger simply adapted them to the prohibition of drugs and thus helped establish the framework for present-day U.S. drug control policies.

Meanwhile more traffickers were exploiting the fact that drugs are less bulky than liquids and therefore much easier to smuggle, transport, and distribute. Importation was also aided by the worldwide network of business and political contacts established by bootleggers. Although the drug traffic remained much smaller than the traffic in alcohol, the profits were probably greater for those involved and the chances of disruption just as slim.

During the 1930s Anslinger joined a campaign that sought to prohibit another substance by making possession or sale of marijuana subject to draconian penalties. Until the 1930s marijuana had been known mainly in the United States by its medical name cannabis. It has been suggested that the anti-Mexican publications of William Randolph Hearst popularized the slang name of marijuana, giving the impression that a common American plant was an evil, foreign import.[125] Anlinger's campaign against marijuana had the familiar ingredients of moral crusades: hysteria and racism. For example, the following letter was sent to Anslinger from the editor of the Alamosa, Colorado, *Daily Courier*:

> Is there any assistance your Bureau can give us in handling this drug? Can you suggest campaigns? Can you enlarge your Department to deal with marijuana? Can you do anything to help us?
>
> I wish I could show you what a small marijuana cigarette can do to one of our degenerate Spanish-speaking residents. That's why our problem is so great: the greatest percentage of our population is composed of Spanish-speaking persons, most of whom are low mentally, because of racial and social conditions.
>
> While marijuana has figured in the greatest number of crimes in the past few years, officials fear it, not for what it has done, but for what it is capable of doing. They want to check it before an outbreak does occur.
>
> Through representatives of civic leaders and law officers of the San Luis Valley, I have been asked to write to you for help.[126]

Anslinger's own testimony before Congress showed that moralism still fed off racism, playing on and adding to the established racist associations mentioned previously. He claimed that marijuana made users promiscuous and violent and, to emphasize the dangers to whites, he tended to use descriptions of instances involving blacks and Hispanics. McWilliams quotes two examples from Anslinger's long list of 'horror' stories:

Colored students at the Univ. of Minn. partying with female students (white) smoking and getting their sympathy with stories of racial persecution. Result pregnancy.

West Va. – Negro raped a girl of eight years of age. Two Negroes took a girl fourteen years old and kept her for two days in a hut under the influence of marihuana. Upon recovery she was found to be 'suffering from' syphilis.[127]

Members of Congress responded to such tales by passing the Marijuana Tax Act of 1937 and thus added plants which, in Anslinger's words, grew 'like dandelions' to the illegal market. By the following year a quarter of the FBN's arrests were for marijuana. From then on Commissioner Anslinger's budget requests reflected this extra burden.[128]

On the question of racism Anslinger had almost lost his job in 1934 when he circulated the following description of the height and colour of an informer in a letter to district supervisors: 'Medium and might be termed a "ginger-colored nigger."' There were calls for his resignation, but a number of powerful Anslinger supporters ensured that these were ignored.

The pro-Anslinger lobby included moralist organizations like the General Federation of Women's Clubs and Hobson's World Narcotics Defense Association, the newspaper publisher Hearst, and most of the large manufacturers of pharmaceuticals in the United States. These companies included: Merck and Company in Rathway, New Jersey, Mallinckrodt Chemical Works in St. Louis, the New York Quinine and Chemical Works in Brooklyn, Hoffman-LaRoche in Nutley, New Jersey, Parke-Davis and Company in Detroit, Eli Lilly in Indianapolis, Sharpe and Dohme in Philadelphia, and E.R. Squibb and Sons in Brooklyn. Since one of Anslinger's duties was to monitor the internal control of manufactured drugs, these companies had an interest in his survival as head of the FBN. Anslinger authorized a limited number of pharmaceutical firms to import the raw opium that was used for the production of various medicines. The few favoured companies could exploit their exclusivity to make extra profits. 'The arrangement was mutually convenient for both Anslinger and the manufacturers,' as John McWilliams noted. 'The drug companies made money, and Anslinger was given control of a powerful lobby.'[129]

Some efforts, however, were made to challenge the punitive

approach to drugs favoured by Anslinger and his supporters, most notably by Representative John M. Coffee of Washington State. In 1938 Coffee introduced House Joint Resolution 642 'to provide for a survey of the narcotic-drug conditions in the United States by the United States Public Health Service.' Coffee felt that the Harrison Act had been misinterpreted and that the responsibility for drug enforcement should have been given to the U.S. Public Health Service rather than the FBN. He told fellow congressmen: 'In examining the Harrison Special Tax Act we are confronted with the anomaly that a law designed (as its name implies) to place a tax on certain drugs, and raise revenue thereby, resulting in reducing enormously the legitimate importation of the drugs in question, while developing a smuggling industry not before in existence. That, however, is only the beginning. Through operation of the law, as interpreted, there was developed also, as counterpart to the smuggling racket, the racket of dope peddling; in a word, the whole gigantic structure of the illicit-drug racket, with a direct annual turn-over of a billion dollars.'

Coffee noted that the problem of corruption was pervasive in the FBN, and he felt that corrupt cops and drug dealers would be put out of business if drug addicts were treated on the same basis as nicotine addicts and alcohol addicts. But, he said, that prompted a question: 'Why should persons in authority wish to keep the dope peddler in business and the illicit-drug racket in possession of its billion-dollar income?' This was, for Coffee, the significant question at issue: 'If we, the representatives of the people, are to continue to let our narcotic authorities conduct themselves in a manner tantamount to upholding and in effect supporting the billion-dollar drug racket, we should at least be able to explain to our constituents why we do so.' Coffee's resolution did not make it out of the House's committee stage and was not even considered by the Senate.[130]

Coffee's claims about the counter-productive effect of drug prohibition were supported, however, by a report from the Californian Crime Commission in 1950 which came to the following conclusion:

As long as there is abundant world supply of illegal narcotics it necessarily follows that vigorous and efficient enforcement of the narcotics laws will merely result in raising the price of narcotics locally thus increasing the possibility for fabulous profits to those who are able to engage in the traffic even for a brief time. The experience in California and in all other parts of the United States in recent years should suggest serious doubt as

to whether the narcotics traffic can ever be stopped by the mere prohibition of the possession and traffic of narcotics. Experience has indicated
that instead of limiting ourselves to a single line on the problem which
takes the form of attempting to prevent the evil by destroying the sources
of supply we would do well to consider the possibility of supplementing
our efforts with a second line of attack designed to destroy the demand.

The motivation of the narcotics traffic is strictly economic. It exists only
as long as the narcotics peddler is able to demand a high price from the
addict. If the addict could register, and as a matter of medical treatment
could receive at low cost his narcotics dosage from carefully supervised
dispensary the traffic in illegal narcotics would vanish overnight. It
would disappear because it would no longer be worthwhile financially to
bring illegal narcotics into the country which could not profitably be sold
in competition with a medical clinic.

The commission noted that England and other European countries
did not have narcotics problems to compare with those of the United
States despite 'the super abundance of the world supply.' It therefore
recommended further study of drug-control policies that could prevent 'the development of a narcotics traffic by undercutting the profits
of the peddlar.'[131] This approach, however, called into question the
very existence of the FBN, and Anslinger helped ensure that no such
study was undertaken.

Anslinger's political lobby was powerful enough to ensure that the
representatives of the American people never took the case against the
punitive approach to drug taking seriously. Instead, as we shall see in
Chapter 5, the approach got tougher, the profits got larger, and
Anslinger and his agents found ever more ingenious ways to distract
attention from failure. These included adding spurious substance to
the idea that the Mafia was a super-criminal organization that controlled both the worldwide drug traffic and the core of organized crime
in the United States.

Chapter 5

Organized Crime and the Dumbing of American Discourse, 1920 to the Present

Although, as we have seen, the phrase 'organized crime' had been used since the late nineteenth century, serious efforts to define and discuss it as a distinct problem only began in the 1920s and 1930s.

If there was a consensus among early commentators, it was that organized crime was an unfortunate and avoidable part of American life. Police, politicians, judges, lawyers, and ostensibly legitimate businessmen were all thought to be actively involved in organized crime. Commentators focused on different aspects of the problem and their recommendations for addressing it, taken in aggregate, would have involved a thorough restructuring of U.S. laws and institutions. Most of these early commentators were either independent of government or government officials prepared to voice independent opinions. From the 1930s, however, a line on organized crime began to emerge that was less critical of established laws and institutions, and by the 1950s the consensus of opinion on organized crime saw it in terms of Mafia conspiracy – an outside threat to otherwise sound U.S. laws and institutions. The Mafia conspiracy theory was updated in the 1980s to include other conspiratorial entities, but official U.S. thinking about organized crime keeps to the same simple formula. Forces outside of mainstream American culture threaten U.S. laws and institutions, and therefore these laws and institutions need to be strengthened. Structural reform of existing U.S. laws and institutions is not on the agenda of organized crime control. Chapter 5 traces the progress and implication of this reduced understanding of organized crime and suggests that police, politicians, judges, lawyers, and ostensibly legitimate businessmen are still as actively involved in organized crime as they were when commentators first addressed the problem.

Organized Crime as an American Problem: Early Perceptions

No serious commentator writing about the problem of organized crime before the 1940s suggested that conspirators among Italians, Jews, or any other group actually controlled or dominated urban crime. In the early 1920s, the motor manufacturer Henry Ford made an attempt to popularize notions about criminal and subversive Jews dominating world capitalism and corrupting American youth, but he was forced to make a complete retraction of these charges in 1927.[1] By the middle of the 1920s ethnic stereotyping and alien conspiracy theories had gone out of fashion as explanations for crime problems. There are two possible reasons for this. First, by the mid-1920s laws had been passed restricting immigration and there was no longer any political advantage in making wildly defamatory generalizations about foreigners based on the wrongdoing of a few. Second, bootlegging was considered by most people to be the main criminal enterprise until the 1930s, and not many thirsty and defiant Americans could consider bootleggers to be un-American. Al Capone, Dutch Schultz, Legs Diamond, and the rest were simply gangsters, never alien intruders or members of ethnically exclusive conspiracies.

To explain immigrant involvement in, as opposed to domination of, organized crime, some academics pointed to the process of assimilation. 'The overwhelming mass' of foreigners, according to James Thurlow Adams, were 'law-abiding in their own lands. If they become lawless here it must be largely the result of the American atmosphere and conditions.'[2] And, immigrants, like others of the 'socially inferior,' to use the words of sociologist Harry Barnes, 'tend to ape the socially superior.' Barnes testified before a Senate committee in 1933 that the businessmen and financiers of the previous generation had

> capitulated pretty thoroughly to the prevailing 'something-for-nothing psychology' of the era ... Freebooting in railroads, banks, utilities, receiverships – and other high-toned racketeering – becomes shockingly frequent.
>
> It was inevitable that, sooner or later, we would succeed in 'Americanizing' the 'small fry.' Their ancestors, if they lived in this country, had usually made an honest living conducting shoe-shining parlors, clothes-cleaning establishments, fruit stands, restaurants, and the like or at hard labor on roads, streets, and railroads. The younger generation looked with envy, not at the bowed backs and wrinkled brows of their parents,

but rather at the achievements of the American financial buccaneers who had made away with their millions, with little or no service to society. If our usurers of high estate could get theirs, why should anybody drown himself in perspiration? That was the question they asked themselves.[3]

Professor Raymond Moley of Columbia University was another who looked to the practices of late-nineteenth-century businessmen for antecedents of organized crime. 'Some of the aspects of business competition of a not too remote past,' he wrote, 'bore every mark of a racket.' He continued, 'The small competitor was subjected to a reign of terror from which he found the shortest route to deliverance to be to sell out or to come to terms with his more powerful rivals. Some of the cases prosecuted under the anti-trust laws of the Federal Government or the States provide graphic accounts of unfair methods of competition.[4]

Newspapers, biographies, and even the early gangster movies described the careers and methods of those who rose to positions of power in the 'underworlds' of the big cities in terms and images usually associated with industrialists or financiers. According to James C. Young, writing in the *New York Times* in April 1926, crime gangs were now organized as big business. He used terms such as 'technic' and 'vertical trust' to describe how gangs operated. They now had competent 'information systems' to learn of 'favorable opportunities to rob, elaborate arrangements with receivers, and, if the worst happened and they were arrested, equally elaborate systems of defense involving legal delays and intimidated witnesses.[5] Fred D. Pasley's 1930 book on Al Capone had the subtitle, *The Biography of a Self-Made Man* and claimed that the Chicago gangster was 'the John D. Rockefeller of some twenty thousand anti-Volstead filling stations.'[6]

The early gangster talkies also reflected the perception that gangsterism was a homegrown product. The main characters were American individuals first. Most of them could be recognized as the sons of immigrants from their names, but ethnicity was not emphasized. There was also something very American in the plot lines of early gangster movies. *Little Caesar* (1930), *Public Enemy* (1931), and *Scarface* (1932) starred dynamic actors playing criminals. Edward G. Robinson, James Cagney, and Paul Muni represented American outlaws in ways that reinforced some of the country's most deeply held myths about individual, entrepreneurial success. They were clearly shown as small guys on their way up in the world, going from rags to riches in the classic American way.

More serious commentators saw organized crime as much less static and hierarchical than the corporate analogies suggested. In a 1926 article, for example, Professor Raymond Moley stated that the conception of organized crime as a vast underworld organization, led by a 'master mind' with workers, lieutenants, and captains, was 'melodramatic nonsense.'[7] Frederic Thrasher in the first fully developed study of the problem made it clear that 'organized crime must not be visualized as a vast edifice of hard and fast structures.'[8] Frank Tannenbaum in his book *Crime and the Community* (1936) noted that 'while crime is organized, it is not unified.'[9] Edwin Sutherland in his study entitled *The Professional Thief* (1937) wrote that, organized crime was 'not organized in the journalistic sense, for no dictator or central office directs the work of the members of the profession.'[10]

Instead of a hierarchical organization, Moley submitted that organized crime should best be seen in terms of a division of labour involving 'shop-keepers who dispose of loot, lawyers who have more than a professional relationship to defendants, and others who grow rich on the proceeds of vice and bootlegging and who because of this wealth become masters of many criminals who actively perform the work of crime.' This 'semi-integrated underworld,' Moley continued, had its indirect relations with political organizations and could thus influence 'officials who dwell in the very citadels of "respectability."'[11] Thrasher noted the importance of 'certain specialized persons or groups, who perform certain indispensable functions' for professional criminals. These included doctors, political manipulators, professional or obligated bondsmen, criminal lawyers, and corrupt officials. Even when he was focusing on the community of career criminals itself, Thrasher emphasized its fluidity:

> While there is considerable definite organization, largely of the feudal type, there is no hard and fast structure of a permanent character. The ease of new alliances and alignments is surprising. Certain persons of certain groups may combine for some criminal exploit or business, but shortly they may be bitter enemies and killing each other. One gang may stick closely together for a long period under favorable conditions; yet if cause for real dissension arises, it may readily split into two or more bitter factions, each of which may eventually become a separate gang. Members may desert to the enemy on occasion. Leaders come and go easily; sometimes with more or less violence, but without much disturbance to the usual activities of the gangs. There is always a new crop coming on – of

younger fellows from whom emerge men to fill the shoes of the old 'barons' when they are slain or 'put away.'[12]

Moley, Thrasher, and other commentators also followed in the progressive urban reform tradition in emphasizing that certain political conditions were essential for successful organized crime. Moley's experience in undertaking the major Cleveland and Missouri crime surveys brought him to a conclusion similar to that of the Reverend Charles Parkhurst – machine politics was in effect a form of organized crime: 'The political machine is a group of men, usually without legal standing as a group, possessed of power to help or to injure others, and the possession of this power is the real reason it receives substantial support. This is a racket in every sense in which the word is commonly used.'[13]

Thrasher's study described in detail the use politicians made of gangsters at election times and argued that in these and other ways crime and politics in Chicago were joined in 'an intimate unity' that tied the hands of the police and secured virtual immunity for many types of illegal activity.[14] Another Chicago sociologist, John Landesco, came to a similar conclusion in his book entitled *Organized Crime in Chicago* (1929): 'Organized crime and organized political corruption have found a partnership to exploit for profit the enormous revenues to be derived from lawbreaking.'[15]

Other commentators joined Hostetter and Beesley (see chapter 3) in pointing to the active complicity of lawyers in the organization of crime. 'In every racket is a lawyer,' according to Henry Barret Chamberlin: 'This lawyer has studied in a law school; he is an associate of most of the lawyers of the community; he has a decent appearing home ... he is a member of his bar association; he is invariably a lawyer who is in politics; he is so strong in all sorts of activities that he can't be disbarred.'[16]

In one of the earliest definitional articles, Alfred Lindesmith of Indiana University stressed the fluidity and variety of organized crime activities and structures: 'The term 'organized crime' refers to crime that involves the cooperation of several different persons or groups for its successful execution ... The organization may be loose and general, or informal; or it may be definite and formal, involving a system of specifically defined relationships with mutual obligations and privileges. Crime organizations may involve small or large groups ... Organized crime ... requires the active and conscious co-operation of a number of elements of respectable society.'[17]

Towards the end of the 1920s more commentators began to see Prohibition and other aspects of America's moral reform program as exac-
erbating the problem of organized crime. According to E.W. Burgess,
in the Illinois Crime Survey of 1929, there was 'no blinking the fact that
liquor prohibition has introduced the most difficult problems of law
enforcement in the field of organized crime ... The enormous revenues
derived from bootlegging have purchased protection for all forms of
criminal activities and have demoralized law enforcing agencies.'[18] To
this Harry Barnes added: 'Prohibition promoted other rackets – the
hijacking racket among the wet outlaws, rackets in foods, milk, transportation, building construction, and the like.'[19]

Some extended the point to cover other prohibitions such as the anti-
gambling, anti-drugs, and anti-prostitution laws. Tannenbaum, for
example, argued: 'The number of unenforceable laws increased the
field of criminal activity and nurtured the criminals who profited by
these laws to the point of creating a system definitely outside of the
law and beyond the police power ... The profit-making aspect made
such organization possible, and played an important role in paralyzing
law-enforcing agencies through political manipulation and direct
corruption.'[20]

Providing illegal but popular goods and services, according to
Walter Lippmann in 1931, requires 'law-breaking, bribery, and coercion,' and enlists 'men and women who have little or no stake in the
social conventions, in honest government, or in the even-handed,
effective administration of the law.' Lippmann clearly stated the principal contradiction: 'The high level of lawlessness is maintained by the
fact that Americans desire to do so many things which they also desire
to prohibit.' The underworld, according to Lippmann, was a servant
that would continue to exist as long as it serviced the needs of consumers and business interests.[21]

Chamberlin made the connection between unworkable laws and
successful organized crime explicit. In 1931 he wrote: 'Organized crime
is today a great, unmanageable threatening fact in the lives of our communities. It is not enough to ask whether the machinery of law enforcement is good, we must go further, call in question the wisdom of the
laws themselves and discover whether or not some of our experiments
are not as menacing in their effect as criminal activities. It may be
found that some of the very best intentions of our idealists have supplied the pavement for the hell of organized crime.'[22]

August Vollmer was another among those who suggested that the problem of organized crime was in the laws and the system, and he was better informed than most about the problems of policing 'vice' of all kinds. As the foremost police reformer of the day, Vollmer had drastically improved the efficiency and organization of several police forces and then used this experience as the basis of a book called *The Police in Modern Society*, published in 1936. Vollmer argued that the policeman's duty was to protect society from criminals and not to try to control morality. Any other approach was dangerously counter-productive, distracting the police, and fostering crime and corruption. He considered that regular policing could not solve the problems of prostitution, gambling, and drug addiction. On the drug traffic, he wrote: 'Stringent laws, spectacular police drives, vigorous prosecution, and imprisonment of addicts and peddlers have proved not only useless and enormously expensive as a means of correcting this evil, but they are also unjustifiably and unbelievably cruel in their application to the unfortunate drug victims. Repression has driven this vice underground and produced the narcotics smugglers and supply agents, who have grown wealthy out of this evil practice and who by devious methods have stimulated traffic in drugs.'[23]

No expert suggested that prison was the answer to organized crime. 'Increased severity of punishment can accomplish very little,' according to Raymond Moley.[24] Others made it very clear that prison was part of the problem of organized crime. Frank Tannenbaum, for example, argued strongly that imprisonment ensures that the criminal continues his career 'by providing him with an intensified stimulus and heightened experience.' According to Tannenbaum:

> It would be difficult to invent a more effective method for conditioning the criminal in his career than imprisoning him with some hundreds of other prisoners, each of whom has a tale of adventure, of pride, of success and of failure, of ends and plans, all in terms of the past career as a criminal and in terms of a future career in the same field ... The way to confirm the criminal in his career is to throw him with other criminals for a long enough time for him to become thoroughly saturated with all their emotional and ethical insights into the ways of the world, and long enough for him to share, vicariously at least, in the criminal experiences of all his new found friends in prison.[25]

Or, as the sociologist Fred Haynes put it more succinctly, 'Our prisons probably train more criminals than they deter or reform.'[26]

The first federal government attempt to study organized crime was conducted under the auspices of the National Commission on Law Observance and Enforcement between 1929 and 1931. Although the commission's neglect of Southern systems of crime can be faulted, two of its consultants, Goldthwaite H. Dorr and Sidney Simpson, made a genuine effort to come to an objective understanding of the nature and extent of organized crime in the rest of the country.

In their report to the commission on the costs of crime, Dorr and Simpson found that organized crime consisted of two main types of activity. The first was criminal fraud, and they included insurance frauds, fraudulent bankruptcies, securities frauds, credit frauds, confidence games, forgery, counterfeiting, and the use of the mails to defraud. 'It must be emphasized,' they elaborated,

> that the criminal frauds which cause the largest losses are organized schemes, carried on as a regular business, and, in many of the most serious cases, masquerading as legitimate business enterprises. Such criminal schemes shade off by imperceptible degrees into enterprises which are so conducted as to avoid criminal liability although employing unethical or even illegal methods of doing business; and the line between criminal and noncriminal activity is thus frequently a rather arbitrary one. Commercialized fraud is more often business run amuck than an offshoot of ordinary crimes against property, and the typical criminal of this class is not the bandit or the recidivist, but the business man gone wrong.

The second type of organized crime activity for Dorr and Simpson was extortion or racketeering, or 'the forcing of persons to pay voluntary tribute to the perpetrators of the crime as a result of fear for life, liberty, bodily safety, reputation, or property.' In summary:

> Both of these forms of crime, in their more important manifestations, are examples of organized crime as a business. Both are modern in development and methods, and constitute, it is believed, by far the most serious with which criminal justice in present-day America must deal. It is strongly recommended that some responsible organization or organizations undertake detailed and comprehensive scientific studies, carried out by competent and properly directed staffs furnished with adequate financial resources, of (a) commercialized frauds, including methods employed, losses resulting, and all other important phases; and (b) the extent, character, causes and economic effects of racketeer-

ing. Such studies are urgently needed, and should be organized immediately.[27]

The commission accepted Dorr and Simpson's understanding of the
meaning of organized crime and the need for more study, as is clear
from the following taken from the conclusion of its letter of transmittal
to the president and Congress: 'The importance of dealing effectively
with organized crime, whether commercialized fraud or extortion, cannot be over-emphasized. Intelligent action requires knowledge – not,
as in too many cases, a mere redoubling of effort in the absence of adequate information and a definite plan. The carrying out of our recommendation for immediate, comprehensive, and scientific nation-wide
inquiry into organized crime should make possible the development of
an intelligent plan for its control.'

As Dwight Smith has shown in his analysis of the development of an
'official' definition for organized crime, the commission's consultants,
Dorr and Simpson, 'organized their data around categories based on
criminal law, not categories based on criminals. *What* was more important than *Who* ... Once Dorr and Simpson focused on events not people,
the logic by which the businessman was linked to the gangster was
simple. Given that business men and gangsters behaved like each
other what was the sense in having two categories that, by definition,
were not mutually exclusive?' Researchers, according to Smith, could
have used Dorr and Simpson's statements 'as the basis of testable
propositions by which a body of theory about organized crime could
have been assembled.'[28]

The Wickersham commission published a total of fourteen reports
on U.S. law enforcement, criminal justice, and penal systems, and these
exposed numerous patterns of brutality, corruption, and inefficiency.
The conclusion was inescapable that, as one report put it, something
was fundamentally wrong in 'the very heart of ... government and
social policy in America.'[29]

Dorr and Simpson would have agreed with every other serious commentator during the 1920s and 1930s that American organized crime
had developed from distinctively American conditions. They all
looked at different aspects of the problem, but they shared a sense that
organized crime was an unfortunate and avoidable part of the nation's
political, economic, social, and legal structures rather than a threat to
these structures. Politicians, public officials, professionals, and other
representatives of the 'respectable' classes were clearly part of the

problem of organized crime, not passive victims or tools of distinct gangster-dominated entities.

Unfortunately for Americans, the Wickersham commission's call for a comprehensive and scientific nationwide inquiry into organized crime was ignored, and no intelligent plan for the control of organized crime was formed. Most of the commission's other recommendations to address the many flaws in American crime control were similarly ignored. In the decades that followed the phrase 'organized crime' acquired a meaning that excluded or at least de-emphasized the part played by representatives of the 'respectable' classes in the problem. Reversing Dorr and Simpson's approach, evidence related to organized crime was grouped around categories of criminals rather than around categories of criminal law. *Who* would increasingly become more important than *What*. The body of professional theory about organized crime became locked in an analysis that whitewashed a flawed system and justified endless recommendations for more misdirected effort at local, national, and eventually international levels. As we shall see, the American approach to organized crime, based as it was on a limited understanding of the problem, has failed to address many problems associated with systematic criminal activity and it has actually succeeded in perpetuating many others.

Enforcement Exploits

The political use of the phrase 'organized crime' first increased dramatically in 1933 and 1934 when Roosevelt's Attorney General Homer S. Cummings declared and orchestrated a war against crime. The country, according to Cummings, was 'confronted with real warfare which an armed underground is waging upon organized society. It is a real war which confronts us all – a war that must be successfully fought if life and property are to be secure in our country ... Organized crime is an open challenge to our civilization, and the manner in which we meet it will be a test of our capacity for self-government.'[30]

Cummings's main intention was to inflate the powers and budget of the Bureau of Investigation, which until then had been a rather obscure agency in the Department of Justice. In 1934 as a result of his campaign, Congress gave the bureau – renamed the Federal Bureau of Investigation the following year – additional jurisdiction over a variety of interstate felonies, including kidnapping and auto-theft in 1934; soon after its budget was doubled to reflect its new responsibilities.

FBI Director J. Edgar Hoover immediately exploited the publicity value of his new powers by adding to the war of words and then directing his agents against bankrobbers who had been avoiding capture by crossing state lines. In a typical slice of rhetoric, Hoover warned of 'a horde of vandals larger than any of the barbarian hosts that overran Europe and Asia in ancient times ... roving bands of plunderers moving swiftly from city to city and state to state, their machine guns clattering death.'[31] In rapid succession a number of outlaws, aptly described as 'freelance products of the Depression,' were shot down by Mr Hoover's agents.[32]

Also in 1934 a new censorship code put an abrupt end to the *Little Caesar, Public Enemy, and Scarface* type of gangster film. These had outraged moral crusaders by 'glorifying' criminals. Instead, in 1935 there was a new Hollywood campaign to glorify G-men – the press's name for FBI agents. That year there were seven G-man movies sold by Hollywood as its contribution to the war on crime. 'See Uncle Sam draw his guns to halt the march of crime,' ran the ads for one of these films. In the original film production of *G-man* (1935) James Cagney played an FBI agent as forcefully as he had played gangster Tommy Powers in *The Public Enemy.* As film historian Andrew Bergman put it, 'exciting and benevolent law was in the hands of the U.S. Government and in fact *was* the U.S. government.'[33]

Hoover not only helped create a new pro-police mythology; he also became a prominent part of it. Before long his publicists had created an image for the FBI agent that lasted for decades. G-men were dedicated, clean-cut, familiar with the most up-to-date, scientific techniques of crime detection, and totally incorruptible. Books, magazines, even bubble-gum cards echoed the same theme as the G-men films: 'Crime does not pay' so long as the elite federal policemen and J. Edgar Hoover were around.

Hoover's news managers could even turn a tragic mistake into a triumph for law enforcement. The journalist Hank Messick has analysed the FBI shooting of Kate Barker, mother of the kidnapper and bankrobber Fred Barker, and suggested that the killing of an innocent, unarmed old woman was justified by an extraordinary story circulated by Hoover's publicists. Mother and son were shot on 16 January 1935. News stories at the time described this as another G-man success and suggested that 'Ma' Barker was the brains behind a gang of desperadoes. In 1938 Hoover made this claim himself, stating that she was 'the most vicious, dangerous and resourceful criminal brain of the last decade,' and that the criminal careers of her four sons were directly traceable to their mother. 'This woman,' he concluded, was 'a monument to the evils of parental indulgence.'

Messick argued that the idea of Kate Barker as a criminal mastermind is far-fetched. In fact, she had never been convicted of any crime and it is very unlikely that a female hillbilly from the Blue Ridge mountain area would be allowed to interfere with what was considered to be men's business in a male-dominated society. Hoover's interpretation was not, of course, questioned at the time; few people had any doubts about the integrity of his agents. The press liked the idea of a gun-crazy old woman, and the idea that she may have been an innocent victim was unthinkable.[34]

Hoover had given the producers of popular culture an idea that could be endlessly recycled. James Hadley Chase was first with a novel called *No Orchids for Miss Blandish* in 1939. In this 'Ma Grisson' was 'physically powerful and a hideous old woman; she was also the brains who determined the future of the gang ... Ma died in her office with a Thompson submachine gun in her hands, taking four cops with her.' Scriptwriters began adding 'Ma' Barker characters to the plots of films, most notably in *White Heat* (1949) and *Bloody Mama* (1970).

Hoover's chief mythmaker of the time was the writer Courtney Ryley Cooper. As Athan Theoharis and John Stuart Cox have noted, Cooper's book *Ten Thousand Public Enemies* was 'the first of many massproduced books about the Bureau, it drew on the careful mythologizing Cooper had already done on the Bureau's behalf in several popular magazine articles. The Cooper myth in essence was a melodrama involving villains preying on unoffending, ordinary Americans, fearless young G-Men using an army of ingenious weapons and arcane technologies, and their lieutenants reporting through a flawless command structure to the supercop at the top, "the most feared man the underworld has ever known" – J. Edgar Hoover.'[35]

Hoover was able to say just about anything he liked about crime without paying too much attention to accuracy or consistency. For example, the following Hoover claims were noted by a report submitted to the Government Operations Committee of the Senate:

The Director of the Bureau of Investigation referred in March 1936 to the 'armed forces of crime which number more than 3 million active participants.' Three months later he stated that 'the criminal standing army of America' numbered 500,000, 'a whole half million of armed thugs, murderers, thieves, firebugs, assassins, robbers, and hold-up men.' About six months afterward he gave the total criminal population as 3,500,000 and the number of crimes as 1,500,000. Five months later he stated that 4,300,000 persons were engaged by day and by night in the commission of felonies and estimated that 1,333,526 major felonies were committed in the United States during the year 1936.[36]

The mythical statistics and public relations were effective. Hoover's position as the nation's chief law enforcer was as secure as the ever-increasing appropriations from Congress. Every time Hoover appeared before the House Appropriations Committee, congressmen heaped uncritical praise and taxpayers' money on his agency. Other agency heads and local officials looked on enviously and doubtless learned from a man described as 'one of the greatest propagandists ever to grace the federal bureaucracy.'[37]

City police forces all over the country followed the FBI's lead and began to improve their images, if not their behaviour, during these years. Corruption was still endemic, but public relations units were set up to cultivate the goodwill of newspaper and magazine publishers as well as radio and movie producers. These gave out handouts to reporters and editors, supplied brochures and pamphlets to citizens' groups, sent speakers to meetings, and otherwise put out the police point of view.

It is not surprising, then, that the city policeman hero joined the G-man hero. In the movie *Bullets and Ballots* (1936) it was Edward G. Robinson's turn to join the side of law and order. He played Detective Johnnie Blake, who went undercover in order to join and then destroy the 'crime combine' that ran a city's numbers and public market rackets. Blake's answer to the problem was to restore respect for law: 'to kick the rats into line.' In the final scene the last gasp of the dying public official is: 'I'd like to think that when those mugs pass a policeman they'll keep on tipping their hats.' The message of this film and dozens of others that followed was that an aroused citizenry could smash the rackets by using their votes to install honest and effective public officials.

From the late 1930s Metro-Goldwyn-Mayer joined the war on crime by adding shorts from the *Crime Does Not Pay* series to many programs. In these, 'Your M-G-M Reporter,' Reed Hadley, introduced films on most types of crime from drug trafficking to faulty repairs on second-hand cars with one thing in common: police methods and intuition always inexorably tracked down the perpetrators. A well-ordered community was essential and this usually got precedence over basic human rights. Popular radio shows, such as *Gangbusters* and *Mr D.A.*, showed a similar sense of priorities.[38]

The 1930s also saw the beginnings of the glorification of the prosecutor. The career of New York Special Prosecutor Thomas E. Dewey provided a rich source for opinion-makers wanting to show the law triumphant. For a brief period Dewey had choreographed the downfall of a succession of gangsters and some of their political protectors. His greatest coup was the conviction of Charles 'Lucky' Luciano, who received a thirty- to fifty-year sentence on the charge of compulsory prostitution. The New York *Daily Mirror* greeted the verdict with absurd but typical claims, calling Luciano 'the czar of chain store vice,' and announcing: 'The 100% verdict was the most smashing blow ever dealt the organized underworld in New York. It was, moreover, hailed throughout the country as the definite beginning of the end of gangsterism, terrorism, and commercialized criminality throughout the United States.'[39]

In convicting Luciano, Dewey had pioneered tactics on the local level that much later became the model for organized crime control at the national level and, more recently, at the international level: close and prolonged surveillance and wire-tapping of suspects, inducements for criminals to become prosecution witnesses and convict their associates, and laws that make it easier to convict for conspiracy. These were presented to the nation as the answer to the problem of organized crime. Books, newspapers, and films such as *Marked Woman* (1937), *Racket Busters* (1938), and *Smashing the Rackets* (1938) sung the praises of thinly disguised personifications of Dewey and put over the message that the answer to organized crime lay exclusively in the prompt indictment and vigorous prosecution of law-breakers. Dewey had put dozens of illegal gambling operators, loan sharks, and industrial racketeers behind bars, but the popular accounts of his courtroom triumphs left out some uncomfortable details. He manipulated public hysteria, he coerced reluctant witnesses, he illegally used wiretaps against political opponents, and he failed to make more than a marginal impact on wholesale illegal profit making in New York. In 1940 Benjamin Strolberg in the magazine *American Mercury* commented that Dewey's conception of criminal justice had no place for constitutional rights and instead resembled that of 'a psychologist who builds a labyrinthian trap for rats, to learn whether or how soon they can get out of it.'[40] In

the following decades, as we shall see, the U.S. government constructed a labyrinthian trap of global dimensions.

The G-men and racket-busting films and radio shows established plot
patterns for thousands of crime films and television cop shows in the
following decades. The bad guys were very rarely at the centre of
the action and they always finished up dead or in prison, thanks to the
bravery, expertise, or superior intelligence of government agents or
prosecutors. Certain subjects were not encouraged. On one occasion, in
1963, a television writer called David Rintels was asked to write an episode of *The FBI* on a subject of his choosing. Rintels suggested police
brutality. The network said certainly, as long as the charge was
trumped up, the policeman vindicated, and the man who brought the
spurious charge prosecuted.[41]
    Given the pro-police mythology that prevailed in all forms of mass
media from the 1930s, it is not surprising that some police officers felt
confident enough to use semantics to define themselves out of the
problem of organized crime. In November 1947, Californian police
officers from all over the state met in one of the law enforcement community's earliest efforts to define organized crime. Their intention was
'to secure a consensus of opinion from the agencies and officers represented as to the principal fields in which organized crime is to be
found and their relative importance from the point of view of size,
degree of organization, and menace to the public welfare.' The definition they arrived at was as follows: 'The operations of two or more persons who combine to obtain financial advantages or special privileges
by such unlawful means as terrorism, fraud, corruption of public officers or by a combination of such methods.'
    The officers also agreed that 'the largest and most serious organiza-
tions of criminal character are to be found in connection with gambling
of a commercialized nature, prostitution, narcotics, and theft and fraud
schemes.'[42] Departing radically from earlier conceptualizations, this
was an understanding of organized crime that was appropriate to the
bureaucratic needs of new, more professional police departments.
Organized crime was now better seen as something that terrorized,
defrauded, or corrupted the police rather than something the police
were directly involved in, as before.[43]
    During the 1950s the new chiefs of massive and largely unaccount-
able police departments denied the very existence of systematic police
corruption. At the same time, pimps, prostitutes, drug dealers, gam-

blers, and gangsters simply dealt with specialist squads, without the need for local politicians to act as intermediaries. In the event of well-publicized scandals that, as we shall see, demonstrated that police officers were still actively involved in the organization of much criminal activity, 'the rotten apple in an otherwise healthy barrel' excuse was usually employed.

Throughout the 1930s, 1940s, and most of the 1950s, J. Edgar Hoover kept the FBI away from more complex and corrupting commercialized criminality such as fraud, extortion, and 'vice-related' crimes. He was supported in this not only by his superiors but also by the great majority of local and state officials anxious to preserve their jurisdictional turf. Hoover was forced to change in the 1960s, but until then, he consistently stuck to the position that since most of these crimes were local they were solely the responsibility of state and local governments. He did not deny that organized crime existed, as many writers have asserted, but his statements on the matter acknowledged the fact that neither the federal executive nor Congress were yet ready to contemplate the federalization of law enforcement. Citizens, according to Hoover in 1951, should demand that existing local and state laws should be enforced 'fairly and impartially, vigorously and relentlessly.'

Testifying before the Kefauver committee to investigate crime in interstate commerce, Hoover contradicted the Californian police definition quoted above by arguing in the Progressive tradition that local political and police corruption was the key to successful organized crime. To make his case, Hoover set out a test that could be applied by the citizens of any community to bring out the reasons why organized crime exists. People in every community, he said, should seek answers to the following questions:

What happened to the important cases which were in the newspaper headlines a few months ago? Were they vigorously prosecuted, or were the felons allowed to obtain delay after delay while witnesses disappeared and the final courtroom scene became a mere mockery of the law? Were juries tampered with, witnesses intimidated, perjury suborned? Did the criminal in a serious crime get off easier than some wayward youth who stole a car or burglarized a store while hungry? Are the operators of vice dens excused from prosecution by the paying of a mere fine which amounts to a license to traffic in human flesh? Are criminals allowed by the courts and prosecuting attorneys to plead guilty to a lesser offense than the one charged and thus receive a shorter sentence? Are convicted criminals afforded special opportunities and privileges in prison? Are pardons, paroles, and probations dealt with like common chattels? Do public officials live beyond their means? ... Are there alliances between the beneficiaries of crime and officialdom?[44]

There was logic to Hoover's position, since most organized crimes were locally organized, and local law enforcement and criminal justice officials were often actively involved in organized criminal activity. Hoover would, however, become increasing isolated in his stand against increased federal involvement in matters usually reserved to the cities and states. A consensus of opinion was emerging among politicians, law enforcement officials, and the press that changed the perception of organized crime from one that demanded honest and effective local law enforcement to one that demanded much more nationally coordinated action. Hoover was reflecting old wisdom about organized crime, while a new perception of organized crime was already emerging that would reduce discussion just as effectively as the 'sets of stereotypes' and the 'frozen images' used by moralists in the Progressive era.

Enter the Mafia

In 1946 Colonel Garland Williams of the Federal Bureau of Narcotics (FBN) gave Americans a new way to understand organized crime. After the arrest of six drug traffickers on 17 December, Colonel Williams dictated the following statement to *Herald-Tribune* reporter Joseph Driscoll:

> During the last several years the Mafia became a thing of great interest to the Federal Bureau of Narcotics, because throughout the United States the largest dealers in narcotic drugs are Italian speaking people. As a result of our investigations we found that these people were members of the Mafia ...
>
> From this we have made careful investigation of the Mafia and we have established that, contrary to a great many people's opinions, the Mafia is not dead; on the contrary, it is a very dangerous criminal organization that is being used to undermine the principles of American ideals of law enforcement.
>
> The organization is national in scope ... [Its] leaders meet annually, usu-

ally in Florida, and there agree upon policies for the control and correlation of their various criminal enterprises.[45]

Williams had introduced the public to his agency's interpretation of organized crime and an idea that gained momentum during the following decades, eventually dominating national and international perception of organized crime. It still provides the framework for the official U.S. interpretation of the problem. The idea was that a conspiracy with Sicilian origins was centrally organized and dominated organized crime nationally and internationally.

Williams provided no evidence for his assertions other than the arrest of six insignificant Italian drug traffickers. In the years that followed evidence supporting the idea of a centralized Mafia dominating organized crime nationally was in short supply and depended on intermittent statements by other FBN agents. In 1951, for example, Charles Siragusa testified before the Kefauver committee that Lucky Luciano 'ruled the narcotics traffic in the United States, operating from Sicily.'[46] The lack of evidence for these unsubstantiated assertions scarcely mattered, repetition of the idea was enough for it to take hold of the public's imagination.

According to Anslinger and his agents, the main peril faced by the United States during the 1940s and 1950s were two foreign conspiracies – communism and the Mafia – and both were misleadingly depicted as coherent and centralized international conspiracies of evil. Journalists were fed many stories about the FBN standing alone in brave defiance of the Mafia and the People's Republic of China. The stories suggested that the intention of both these foreign threats was to speed up the moral degeneration of the United States. Anslinger himself co-authored a book published in 1954 that claimed that most of the illegal drug supply was grown and processed in communist China, from where it was spread 'with cold deliberation' to free countries, notably the United States. He had previously provided a link between the two conspiracies by explaining that, although the Chinese communists were making the major profits, the Mafia was distributing the Chinese-manufactured heroin in the United States. Drug trafficking, it was said repeatedly, provided China with dollars for war, and weakened the health and moral fibre of its enemies.[47] Few chose to challenge these absurd ideas at the time, and newspapers repeated Anslinger's propaganda as fact despite all the evidence and logic that suggested that most drug-trafficking routes followed the established trading routes of friends and allies of the United States. His charges against the People's Republic of China were eventually repudiated by a series of statements issued by the U.S. State Department in 1971.[48]

The Kefauver committee, which highlighted organized crime in 1950 and 1951, gave undeserved substance and respectability to FBN's notions by supporting the idea of the Mafia dominating organized crime in America and thus also the idea that organized crime in America had foreign origins. The committee's *Third Interim Report* traced the history of the Sicilian Mafia and its 'implantation' into America:

> The various drives against the Mafia in Sicily which were made by Italian governments from the 1870s down to Mussolini's time, were ... largely ineffective in destroying the Mafia. However, these drives had the effect of causing large numbers of Mafia members to migrate to the New World and many of them came to this country ... The Mafia became established in New Orleans and other cities. Moreover, like many underworld organizations it became rich and powerful during Prohibition and since that time this organization has entered every racket promising easy money. Narcotics, pinball machines, slot machines, gambling in every form and description are some of its major activities at the present time.

The committee's report then made the following assertions:

> There is a nationwide crime syndicate known as the Mafia, whose tentacles are found in many large cities. It has international ramifications which appear most clearly in connection with the narcotics traffic.
>
> Its leaders are usually found in control of the most lucrative rackets of their cities.
>
> There are indications of a centralized direction and control of these rackets, but leadership appears to be in a group rather than in a single individual.
>
> The Mafia is the cement that helps bind the Costello-Adonis-Lansky syndicate of New York and the Accardo-Guzik-Fischetti syndicate of Chicago as well as smaller criminal gangs and individual criminals throughout the country. These groups have kept in touch with Luciano since his deportation from this country.
>
> The domination of the Mafia is based fundamentally on 'muscle' and 'murder.' The Mafia is a secret conspiracy against law and order which will ruthlessly eliminate anyone who betrays its secrets. It will use any means available – political influence, bribery, intimidation, etc. – to defeat

any attempts on the part of law enforcement to touch its top figures or to interfere with its operations.[49]

The Kefauver report did not attempt to substantiate the crudely inadequate historical and contemporary analysis contained in these two quoted excerpts. Jack Lait and Lee Mortimer, two journalists quoted in Chapter 2, had a point when they dismissed the report as 'practically a plagiarism of *Chicago Confidential* and *Washington Confidential*.'[50] Once the report had been issued, however, it, rather than Lait and Mortimer's cheap sensationalism, became a significant historical source adding the illusion of weight and coherence to the idea of organized crime as an alien implant.

The committee's funds had been limited and Senator Kefauver expressed his gratitude to the FBN after the hearings: 'Our greatest help in tracking down the trail of the Mafia came from the Federal Bureau of Narcotics ... Because of the Mafia's dominance in the dope trade, the Narcotics Bureau has become the leading authority on this sinister organization.'[51] Anslinger had ensured that the Kefauver committee came to conclusions that were acceptable by lending them one of his top agents, George White. In the early months of the investigation, White was particularly influential, briefing the committee's members and counsel. His help was frequently acknowledged during the hearings and he was referred to as 'one of the great experts on the Mafia.'[52]

Since none of the evidence the committee actually produced indicated centralized national control, it is probable that Halley took FBN advice and worked the Mafia conclusions into the committee's report partly in the interests of the agency. Logic and evidence certainly had no impact on the committee's Mafia conclusions, but the weight of a prestigious Senate investigative committee had been put behind an alien conspiracy interpretation of organized crime, an interpretation that featured, in Halley's words, 'the Mafia criminal super-government in America.'[53]

Despite a great deal of hopeful effort no evidence was produced at the hearings to support the view of a centralized Sicilian or Italian organization dominating organized crime in the United States. The committee expressed incredulity when Italian-American racketeers denied they were in an organization called the Mafia. These, if they testified at all, were constantly prodded, probed, and encouraged by committee members and counsel to admit that they were in the Mafia, but none did so. This effort became farcical when the committee's counsel Rudolph Halley asked New Jersey racketeer Willie Moretti whether he was a member of the Mafia. Moretti answered with another question: 'What do you mean by a member, carry a card with Mafia on it?'[54]

The only evidence the report offered for its Mafia conclusions were a number of drug-trafficking stories supplied by the FBN involving Italian-American gangsters. Neither these stories nor any testimony at the hearings were at all convincing about the idea of a centralized organization dominating or controlling organized crime. In fact, virtually all of the hard evidence produced by the committee contradicted its Mafia conclusions. The committee found men with different ethnic origins at the head of criminal syndicates around the nation and there was frequent contact and cooperation between different ethnic groups. All significant gangsters had been born or at least nurtured in the United States. The networks of illegal activities that the committee described cut across ethnic designations and always depended on the compliance of local officials. The evidence the committee uncovered showed that gambling operators in different parts of the country had sometimes combined in joint ventures, in the same way as businessmen everywhere, and had made a lot of money for themselves and for public officials.[55]

Apart from getting organized crime accepted as a national problem, the Kefauver committee's other accomplishments were very limited. The committee made twenty-two recommendations to combat crime in interstate commerce. These included a number of acts tightening up existing anti-gambling legislation, the establishment of a Federal Crime Commission, imposition of heavier penalties for narcotics violations, and proposals related to the regulation of immigration and deportation. Most of the proposals for new legislation generated little enthusiasm in Congress and were dropped.

The Kefauver committee had concluded that, while federal agencies could not be a substitute for state and local enforcement in dealing with organized crime, the federal government must provide leadership and guidance, establish additional techniques for maximum coordination of law enforcement agencies, take a positive approach in using its power to fight organized crime, and seek legislation when its powers were insufficient. Given that organized crime was by then mainly associated with gambling operators and drug traffickers, the committee was effectively arguing the case for increased federal involvement in the enforcement of the gambling and drug laws. Although the committee's own proposals were shelved, Kefauver and his colleagues had set an important process in motion. The federal government was more and more committed to the policing of illegal markets.

The committee's lack of evidence for its Mafia conspiracy theory did not matter, since its conclusions had been decided on before the hearings began. In effect, the committee's goal was to reduce the complexities of organized crime to a simple 'Good versus Evil' equation. The committee had accepted the arguments against gambling and drugs, and no serious consideration was given to the possibility of government regulation and control of these activities. The public had to be convinced that that prohibitions were the only options and prohibitions had to be made effective. Enforcement had to be seen as the only answer. The committee thus chose to put the weight of its opinion behind a bizarre and unsubstantiated interpretation of America's organized crime problems.

Organized crime was, according to this interpretation, a centralized conspiracy. Alternative ways of regulating and controlling gambling and drugs were out of the question; that would be a capitulation to powerful and alien criminal interests. The only solution, according to the committee and a growing consensus of opinion in the law enforcement community and among opinion makers, was increased federal commitment. This involved the enactment of more laws and the establishment of a federal law enforcement capacity that was capable of succeeding where local authorities had failed. By some means, according to the new line, people had to be prevented from indulging in activities that filled the coffers of the Mafia.

Anslinger's motives for using his agents to help propagate the idea that the Mafia supercriminal organization controlled both the worldwide drug traffic and the core of organized crime activity in the United States are unknown and are likely to remain so. It might simply be a case of using scare stories in the same way as Hoover did to keep his agency's budgetary appropriations up to the required levels.

Whatever his motives Anslinger had given the nation's media managers an easy way to edit a multitude of disparate events into a digestible package that was consistent with American thinking during the Cold War era.[56] Hundreds of books and articles repeated variations on his themes in the style of the journalists featured in the Chapter 2, Jack Lait, Lee Mortimer, and Ed Reid. These had produced a formula that lazy and ill-informed journalists would regularly turn to when writing about U.S. organized crime. The trick was to describe briefly how a secret criminal brotherhood developed in feudal Sicily, was transplanted to urban America at the end of the nineteenth century, and then took over organized crime operations in the entire country. As 'proof' of the supercriminal Mafia crime combine all editors required were unrelated anecdotes about Italian-American gangsters, mainly from New York, with the narrative livened up with words like 'godfather,' 'tentacles,' and most essentially 'omerta,' the 'secret and unwritten' code of silence of the Mafia. These were mythical interpretations, magically stringing together disconnected fears, prejudices, and hatreds about crime, drugs, communism, and foreigners. Anslinger, aided and abetted by a committee of easily manipulated senators and a host of crime writers, had found a way to absolve the United States from any responsibility for its drug and organized crime problems.

Lait and Mortimer can be truly described as the founding fathers of Mafia journalism. They cashed in on the interest aroused by the Kefauver committee by bringing out a book called *USA Confidential* in 1952. In this as in all their other books they featured the two main preoccupations of postwar America – communism and organized crime – in an amalgam of racial and political bigotry.

The Mafia was in Lait and Mortimer's fantasies 'the nucleus on which all organized vice, crime and corruption, not only in the United States but all over the world, had been built.' They named 'Lucky' Luciano and Frank Costello, as the 'Mr Bigs' of the Mafia. Luciano was 'the key figure in the executive set-up' and 'the president of the International Crime Cartel.' He was 'the richest man in Italy' who 'pays off half the government and most of the cops.'[57] Costello was the 'president of the American Crime Corporation' and 'in addition to the Eastern Seaboard, Costello also runs Louisiana and controls the entire slot-machine industry in the United States.'[58] Under Luciano and Costello in Lait and Mortimer's underworld hierarchy came Joe Adonis, again from New York, 'the deputy chief in the East for Costello,' and Charles Fischetti from Chicago, who, as national vice president shares with Costello the conduct of all underworld affairs in the United States and has his fingers in the pie in every city.' These mobsters, they concluded, 'become more brazen and more open every day. Their money has purchased immunity from the law. Time and again honest Federal agents find evidence against them, but regardless of who is sitting in the main offices, no prosecution gets past the barriers of dough and drag.'[59]

The authors acknowledged their debt to Anslinger in other ways by repeating variations of many of the FBN's favourite themes. They wrote that there were '300,000 school age dope addicts,' and that the great growth of the 'plague' of narcotics addiction had been 'parallel to the spread of Communism in our country.'[60] 'Organized gangsters' combined with 'Communists and pinks' were working 'to turn Americans into addicts ... The major source of opium is behind the Curtain, where Italian mafistas buy it with good American money.'[61]

The implication of Lait and Mortimer's work was that agencies of the federal government should be given more powers to combat conspiratorial threats to American society. The FBN, the FBI, and the 'honest, fearless and hardworking intelligence unit of the Treasury' were all doing great jobs but were 'handcuffed' by elected officials. The claims in the Confidential books may now see m ridiculous, but they were simply elaborated variations on the propaganda messages of federal agencies and played an important part in the development of an understanding of American organized crime fit for an age of short attention spans.

From the 1950s writers dependent on FBN information or recycled unsubstantiated claims by other writers continued to misinform Americans about Luciano's importance. Fred Cook's book *Mafia!* (1973) for example, claimed that on 10 September 1931:

> Lucky Luciano was determined to bring a new orderliness to the American underworld, and he did it in just twenty-four hours, eliminating the old 'Moustache Petes' in a cross-continent carnival of murder.
>
> ... Across the nation, in precisely timed executions, some forty of the old 'Moustache Pete' contingent were murdered. It was a purge made possible only by the executive genius of Lucky Luciano, and it was carried out with an efficiency and ruthlessness that would have done credit to a Stalin or a Hitler.
>
> The face of the American underworld had been changed, literally overnight. The Mafia had been Americanized.

Cook called this nationwide purge of old-style 'Moustache Pete' Italian gangsters 'a sweeping and historic and bloody changing of the guard.'[62] Alan Block in his book *East Side–West Side* (1981) exposed this story as virtual invention, pointing out that for the purge story to have any credibility at the very least more than one or two of the victims should have been named.[63]

Almost as essential to the Luciano legend is the claim that he helped the United States win the Second World War while still serving out the sentence for the 1935 compulsory prostitution conviction. Martin Short, for example, in the book *Crime Inc.* (1984) claimed: 'Only Luciano could have drafted the entire American Mafia into the war against Mussolini.'[64] In fact, Luciano had played a minor part in Naval Intelligence's effort to prevent sabotage on the New York waterfront during the war. Crediting him with more influence than that enters writers into the realms of fantasy.[65]

The claims about Luciano's career after the war are equally outrageous, but equally essential for writers seeking some historical foundation for their conspiracy theories. Frederic Sondern in the book *Brotherhood of Evil* (1959) stated that after the Second World War, Luciano 'began an internationally organized narcotics attack against the United States which dwarfed everything that had gone before.'[66] In 1975 Martin Gosch, who produced a book of doubtful authenticity called *The Last Testament of Lucky Luciano*, made the absurd but not unusual suggestion that 'no important decision that might affect the future of organized crime in the United States ... was made without his consultation and advice.'[67] In 1995, Brian Freemantle in his book *The Octopus: Europe in the Grip of Organised Crime*, adapted the Luciano legend for the European market. Freemantle introduced Luciano by stating that he 'created the ruling Commission – that forged all the American-based Families into the syndicate that operates organised crime throughout every state of the United States.' Luciano then, according to Fremantle, became the 'boss of bosses' started 'nothing less than a Mafia joint venture bringing together in common organised crime enterprise the continents of Asia, Europe and America.'[68] U.S. government studies, far from correcting such fantastic notions, have also continued to put Luciano's alleged 'national' reorganization of the underworld at the heart of their historical analysis of organized crime.[69]

It is true that Luciano was an important Manhattan racketeer who knew other gangsters from further afield. There is, however, no evidence of his possessing genuine national and international power. The endlessly repeated claim that Luciano was some kind of criminal organizational mastermind, who had managed to restructure organized crime operations, locally, nationally, and internationally, was simply the invention of a very convenient past.

Lucky Luciano remained in exile in Italy until 1962, where he died after a heart attack in the Naples airport. His only period of prolonged criminal success lasted from the late 1920s to the mid-1930s. He spent the next decade in prison before being deported in 1946. He may have been involved in drug smuggling after the war, but there is nothing in his recently declassified State Department file to substantiate this.[70] The frequent suggestions by FBN agents that he controlled the international drug trade were not based on any substance. Luciano had been transformed into a criminal mastermind by a U.S. government agency feeding a journalistic construction of an absurd conspiracy theory that proved to be a distraction from the reality of organized crime in America.

On 27 January 1953, Governor Dewey received the following desperate and poorly spelled plea in a letter from the exiled Luciano:

Salvatore Lucania

Via Tasso 464
Napoli Italy
Jan. 20, 1953

Dear Sir.

I hope you dont mind the way this letter is written, and also that I am writing to you, it is the best I can do, and also my only hopes for some relief.

Till this last election I thought they wanted to knock you out of politics, but after election I see that they dont want to let up, the agents that Anslinger has here are stooping to everything to get me.

I wish you would take some interest in this matter, because I never gave it a thought in going into the dope business, direct or indirect, and if it wasn't so I wouldn't be writing to you.

If you dont believe me I make a sujestion, and that is to have the Attorney General appoint one investigator to investigate the Narcotic Division there and all the European Interpol, including me. I have another sujestion if you want to. I could send direct to you my side of the story, of what I know, which I would like it much better.

Governor, since I left the U.S.A. I haven't had a day in peace, and there isn't any let up in sight.

If you dont want to do it for me, please do it for yourself, that you didn't let out of jail an international dope smugler.

That great power that the Narcotic Division has, is in the wrong hands.

Sincerely

Salvatore Lucania[71]

Luciano was reacting to the attention being heaped on him by the Federal Bureau of Narcotics. FBN agents were following him around Naples and claiming that he was responsible for the global trade in drugs. Dewey as Governor of New York State did not have the power to help, even if he had been so inclined. The letter suggests only that Luciano did not know how power really worked in the United States.

Producers of fiction were not slow to enliven their narratives with references to the omnipotent Mafia. In the detective novel *Kiss Me Deadly* (1952) Mickey Spillane described the Mafia as a 'slimy, foreign secret army' that 'stretched out its tentacles all over the world with the tips reaching into the highest places possible.'[72]

The first film to suggest that organized crime was controlled by a nationwide criminal organization was *The Enforcer* (1951). This was based on the real-life investigations of 'Murder Inc.'[73]Although the reality was a loose association of New York gangsters prepared to kill for a fee, the film created the impression of an invisible criminal empire that specialized in wholesale killing.

After *The Enforcer* gangster films repeatedly portrayed the underworld as consisting of groups of racketeers working together in businesslike organizations behind respectable 'fronts.' 'The Syndicate' or 'the Organization' was still usually confined to citywide operations, such as the one featured in the film called *The Big Heat* (1953), but the idea of a national organization resurfaced in *The Brothers Rico* (1957). In this a retired mobster played by Richard Conte sets out to expose the syndicate after it had killed his brother – and finds a criminal dragnet out to kill him, one that is more efficient and geographically more wide-ranging than anything the police can offer. The implied solution is public support for a stronger federal law enforcement response.

In 1960 the film *Underworld USA* represented organized crime as one big conspiracy. A vast syndicate, masquerading under the corporate name of 'National Projects,' controls organized crime throughout the country. The leaders of the syndicate head separate departments: drug traffic, labour racketeering, gambling, and prostitution. The syndicate keeps power by murder, intimidation, and bribery and 'by maintaining a legitimate business facade from basement to penthouse.' But, according to the film's publicity handouts, the syndicate's strongest weapon is 'public indifference': '*Underworld USA* provides a scathing portrait of the American public who have allowed the 'punks' to take office. The totalitarian threat to the democratic way of life comes not from communism but from organized crime.'

The first film to put a strong Italian ethnic identity to organized crime on a national scale was *Inside the Mafia* (1959), which was about 'the world's number one secret society of crime,' according to the posters. However, the film was poorly made and failed both commercially and critically.[74] The 1970 film of Mario Puzo's book *The Godfather* was much more successful, as we shall see.

Crime films of the period continued to justify intrusive and coercive police tactics. The informant is glorified in Elia Kazan's classic film about union racketeering, *On the Waterfront* (1954), probably because Kazan and Budd Schulberg, the scriptwriter, had recently named people they knew as former communists before the House Committee on Un-American Activities. Wiretaps and bugging devices provide the crucial evidence to destroy gangster dominance in the film *Hoodlum Empire* (1952). Undercover and entrapment operations enable a single individual, in the film *Damn Citizen* (1957), to shatter vice and crime in Louisiana. Of course, violent police activity, such as kicking doors down, roughing-up, and shooting suspects, would always be the correct response in any crime film.

Plot patterns for thousands of crime films and television cop shows were established in the 1950s. The bad guys were very rarely at the centre of the action, and they always finished up dead or in prison thanks to the bravery, expertise, or superior intelligence of government agents or prosecutors.

Frank Pearce makes another important observation about crime films of the period. After the film *Force of Evil* (1948), which depicted the rationalization of the numbers racket in a way that paralleled the rise of capitalist big business, films about organized crime generally looked away from its connection with capitalism.[75] It was a sign of the times that the director Abraham Polonsky and star John Garfield of the film *Force of Evil* were blacklisted from the movie industry because of their 'un-American' sentiments.

During the 1950s a mythological and fundamentally faultless America was created. Problems such as organized crime and corruption were either minimized or externalized as the result of foreign influences. The all-powerful Mafia interpretation was simply an aspect of the Cold War mythologizing of U.S. history. Myths, of course, need to contain some truth to be at all convincing, and we shall return to this later. But the fact that some powerful Italian-American gangsters existed in some U.S. cities and sometimes cooperated did not amount to a nationally coordinated and centralized structure.

The idea of an all-powerful Mafia idea was rarely challenged during the period of Cold War paranoia, which David Caute described in his book aptly called *The Great Fear*. J. Edgar Hoover's FBI organized legions of informers to report on the movements and activities of communists or alleged communists. The House Committee on Un-American Activities forced thousands of journalists, diplomats, authors, unionists, and scientists to testify against themselves. If they exercised their 5th Amendment rights and refused to answer questions this was interpreted as admitting guilt, and many lost their jobs as a result. Individual states and cities emulated the federal government and instituted loyalty programs and demanded loyalty oaths from their employees. Local interrogation bodies and private vigilante groups also hounded suspected communists.

The famous Hollywood blacklist was only one of many. Hundreds of academics and journalists lost their jobs for 'un-American' thinking. Mostly, however, American intellectuals, journalists, and filmmakers wanted to keep their jobs. Journalists and filmmakers stayed with safe subjects and patriotic themes, within strictly circumscribed limits. It was a time when most repeated variations of accepted orthodox thinking or kept their heads down, fearful of producing anything that could be considered out of line.[76]

Academics were generally muted about organized crime during these years; frequently caution and qualification obscured critical analysis. The only notable dissent from Mafia mythology during the 1950s and early 1960s came from a liberal perspective that was almost as uncritical about American development as the conspiracy theorists. This liberal dissent was best represented by the sociologist Daniel Bell, whose article entitled 'Crime as an American Way of Life,' first appeared in the *Antioch Review* in 1953.

Bell had little time for conspiracy theories. According to him, the high proportion of Italian Americans known to be racketeers could be explained without invoking the notion of an omnipotent Mafia. Bell pointed out that, like other immigrant groups, Italians had little political influence and were initially excluded from most legitimate economic opportunities. 'Finding few open routes to wealth,' he continued, 'some turned to illicit ways' and made good use of the new opportunities created by Prohibition for organizing crime. After Prohibition, according to Bell, Italian-American gangsters attempted to gain respectability and move into legitimate business, but since opportunities were still limited, many turned to gambling enterprises. Organized crime was thus 'one of the queer ladders of social mobility in American life.' Italian Americans used criminal opportunities to advance economically just as white Anglo-Saxon Protestants, Irishmen, and Jews had before them in a kind of ethnic succession.[77]

The 'ethnic succession' thesis was a reminder that organized crime was a multiethnic phenomenon at a time when professional and media opinion was moving towards a perception that significant organized crime was ethnically exclusive to Italian Americans. However, Bell also reflected the reluctance of 1950s American liberals to be as critical of the American political and economic systems as their 1920s forerunners had been. Corruption was considered in the article, but not emphasized or treated as a serious problem. Organized business crime was also glossed over, as Bell located the source of America's organized crime problems among the least powerful groups in society on their way up to middle-class respectability. In effect, the only perception Bell was adding to the Mafia conspiracy theory was that Italians were preceded by, and would be succeeded by, different ethnic and racial groups. Bell's thesis proved inadequate to challenge the developing consensus about Mafia supremacy during the 1950s and 1960s, but a version of it would later be adapted by government officials to help form the current federal perspective on organized crime.

The FBN's indispensability was firmly established during the 1950s. FBN agents were featured in countless books and articles as tough, dedicated, and efficient professionals guarding against Mafia or communist plots to poison America. The agency's wisdom about organized crime was rarely challenged. The rest of the law enforcement community, with the temporary exception of the Federal Bureau of Investigation (FBI), came to accept and elaborate on its all-powerful Mafia interpretation.

Ironically, the agency responsible for giving credence to a theory that diverted attention away from corruption had to be abolished in 1968, when it was found to be riddled with corruption. Almost every agent in the New York office of the FBN was fired, forced to resign, transferred, or convicted, and this constituted about one-third of the agency's total manpower. The chief investigator of the affair, Andrew Tartaglino, testified that FBN agents had taken bribes 'from all levels of traffickers,' had sold 'confiscated drugs and firearms,' had looted 'searched apartments,' had provided tip-offs 'to suspects and defendants,' and had threatened 'the lives of fellow agents who dared to expose them.'[78] Effectively, federal drug enforcement in New York during these years was a form of organized crime.

After the investigation, a new agency with a new name, the Bureau of Narcotics and Dangerous Drugs, had to be created in the Department of Justice to fill the role of the FBN. In 1973, after another bureaucratic shake-up, the Drug Enforcement Administration was created and it remains the federal government's chief anti-drug agency.

The 1968 investigation attracted minimal press attention, and full details will not be released until the year 2020.[79] This keeps the reputation of the FBN as the first federal agency to challenge the Mafia intact. Recent books about the Mafia still rely on much of the propaganda put out by Anslinger and his agents from the 1940s onwards, and refer to the commissioner with glowing tributes. Anslinger is usually hailed as the first man to see the 'evil of organized crime in the United States' or various versions of the same idea.[80]

The existence of the American Mafia as a centralized organization dominating organized crime nationally could never be proved, but incidents and revelations involving Italian-American gangsters continued to give some credibility to the concept.

In November 1957 Mafia mythology was given a boost when New York State police disrupted a gathering of about sixty suspected Italian-American racketeers at Appalachia, New York. No useful information resulted from this action, but the fact that a few of the sixty-odd conventioneers came from as far afield as Florida and California gave a boost to the alien conspiracy theory at a time when interest was dwindling. Most of the guests had legitimate 'fronts' in a variety of businesses ranging from taxicabs, trucks, and coin-operated machines to olive oil and cheese. The most credible account of the Appalachian gathering was by Serrell Hillman of *Time* magazine. The guests were not part of a tightly knit syndicate, but instead a loose 'trade association' of criminals in various cities and areas, who ran their own shows in their own fields but had matters of mutual interest to take up.[81]

Meanwhile, earlier in the year, Robert Kennedy had been appointed chief counsel of Senator John McClellan's Select Committee on Improper Activities in the Labor and Management Field and from then on made a crusade against what was understood to be organized crime his chief priority. Kennedy added his support to those who saw the Appalachian meeting as proving the dominance of the Mafia. He wrote that the guests, 'control political figures and threaten whole communities. They have stretched their tentacles of corruption and fear into industries both large and small. They grow stronger every day.'[82]

In 1961 John F. Kennedy became president and appointed his brother attorney general. In this position Robert helped accelerate the federalization of law enforcement by further strengthening the consensus in law enforcement circles about the Mafia.

In 1962 Robert Kennedy reiterated the Kefauver line by describing the Mafia as 'a private government ... in charge of "organized lawlessness" in the United States ... with an annual income of billions, resting on a base of human suffering and moral corruption.' The Mafia, according to Kennedy, lurked behind every neighbourhood bookie and drug pusher and thus weakened 'the vitality and strength of the nation.'[83] The same year in *Look* magazine Kennedy also placed himself squarely in America's moral reform tradition and emphasized the administration's commitment against gambling. Kennedy is quoted as saying:

'What's wrong with the $2 bet?' That frequently raised question might just as well read: 'What's wrong with a multimillion-dollar narcotics ring, or widespread prostitution, or a corrupt mayor?' The $2 bet is the key to all these evils, for it bankrolls the underworld. The $2 bet doesn't stop in the hands of the small-time bookie at the corner cigar store. Ultimately, it is fed to big-time 'lay-off' gamblers who use their huge gambling profits to finance racketeering ventures – and, worst of all, to corrupt local officials. Vigorous law enforcement is only a partial solution. The only lasting solution will come when people everywhere realize their own responsibilities to abide by the law.[84]

Kennedy then organized a concerted federal drive against gambling and continued to oppose any moves to legalize this 'baleful influence.' A number of anti-gambling statutes were pushed through Congress including the prohibition of the interstate transportation of wagering information or paraphernalia, and interstate travel with intent to engage in certain unlawful activities, one of which was gambling. The Department of Justice and the Internal Revenue Service also went on the offensive, arresting hundreds of gamblers in a series of raids. However, Kennedy and other influential members of the law enforcement community felt that more laws and more police manpower were required to combat organized crime and therefore they needed to add some credibility to Mafia mythology. The Valachi show was put on to mobilize support.

With Robert Kennedy's support, another congressional committee chaired by Senator McClellan held televised hearings before which a small-time New York criminal, named Joseph Valachi, revealed what he knew about organized crime. In his testimony, Valachi did not use the word 'Mafia,' but instead talked about being part of 'Cosa Nostra' or 'Our Thing.' Although some of his testimony does ring true in the light of later events and revelations it was certainly not enough to justify the assertions about the structure of U.S. organized crime that were based on it. The McClellan subcommittee claimed that the Cosa Nostra was a national criminal structure that had emerged from a New York gang power struggle in 1930–1. This structure was based on military levels of authority and organized into entities called 'families.' There were five such families in New York City, and equivalents all over the country, linked into a national crime syndicate by a commission of approximately twelve members 'who decide policy, settle disputes, and regulate territorial operations.' The main sources of income for the Cosa Nostra were specified as illegal gambling and trafficking in narcotics. Murder was the main instrument of organizational control and the conspiracy had a code of absolute obedience and authority, reinforced by an initiation ceremony based on blood, fire, gun, and knife.[85]

A new rush of books and articles came out, embellishing Valachi's words. But Valachi's qualifications for such a comprehensive analysis of organized crime in the United States were in reality minimal. He had been a getaway driver for a burglary ring in the 1920s, a mercenary in the New York gang war involving Joe Masseria and Salvatore Maranzano in 1930–1, and from then on until his conviction for drug smuggling in 1960 no more than a criminal odd-jobs man around New York with connections to the gangster Vito Genovese. Valachi's own criminal career was not in the least well organized and his 'singing' produced no convictions. Although Valachi had never claimed any expertise on the national scene, his limited knowledge of crime in the

New York area was used to explain the structure of organized crime throughout the entire United States.

At least one of Valachi's contemporaries in New York had a far less exalted opinion of the racketeer than the federal government. According to former New York police officer, Robert Leuci: 'I was fascinated with Valachi. I remember talking to my cousin about him. I said, "This guy must have something, eh?" And he said, "Valachi was a moron that walked around with a baseball bat and beat people over the head. That's all he did." He said that the guy didn't know which way was up. He didn't know what he was talking about. He exemplified a group of people. Borderline morons. You read books and you hear people talking about the Mafia running the country, taking over the United States, running Las Vegas. You know, I've never met a Mafia guy who could run a candy store without a baseball bat, and that's the truth.'[86]

As several commentators have shown, Valachi's testimony actually contradicted many of the conclusions that the subcommittee drew from it. For example, membership of Cosa Nostra was said to confer benefits, such as a share in its illicit gains and protection in times of trouble. But Valachi's testimony made it clear that he got nothing from crime other than what he took for himself and that he got no protection when he needed it. Cosa Nostra was also said to require the total obedience of its members, yet Valachi testified that he was just one of many who took part in the drugs business even after being told not to by the bosses – 'Because,' as he explained, 'of moneymaking, the profit of it.' But these inconsistencies and contradictions did not matter, Valachi's testimony was successfully distorted to fit political and bureaucratic needs.[87]

Robert Kennedy described Valachi's testimony as 'the biggest single intelligence breakthrough yet in combating organized crime and racketeering in the United States.' And the hearings helped justify Kennedy's strategy to expand the federal government's capacity to fight racketeering. When Kennedy became attorney general in 1961 the government had twenty-six investigative units at work on the domestic crime scene. The Organized Crime and Racketeering Section of the Department of Justice had been set up in 1954 to coordinate the efforts of these units, but it was poorly staffed and got minimal cooperation, especially from the FBI. Robert Kennedy quadrupled the Organized Crime Section in size to over forty attorneys and encouraged these to target suspected racketeers. Convictions of racketeers by the federal government steadily increased from nineteen in 1960, to ninety-six in 1961, 101 in 1962, 373 in 1963, and 677 in 1964. Gambling, being the 'principal source' of organized crime revenue, was a specific target. Information services such as Delaware Sports and Athletic Productions Inc. were closed down. The Biloxi, Missouri, and Newport/Covington, Kentucky, lay-off centres were put out of operation. Slot machines were destroyed in Kentucky, and pressure was put on the Arkansas state government to end the wide-open but illegal casino gambling in Hot Springs.[88]

Valachi had originally been arrested by the FBN, but FBI agent James Flynn spent eight months with him in 1962 helping him develop his final story. The agency switch has symbolic significance, because from that time onwards the FBI led professional and public perception of organized crime.

Valachi's use of Cosa Nostra instead of Mafia to describe his associations gave J. Edgar Hoover, who had consistently refused to credit Mafia conspiracy theories, a chance of a volte face without too many people noticing. Before this, Hoover had successfully kept the FBI busy looking for evidence of the communist menace or pursuing freelance bankrobbers or kidnappers and away from dealing with most problems associated with gambling, drugs, fraud, extortion, and corruption. From 1963, however, Hoover chose to go along with the consensus of law enforcement opinion and reduce organized crime to a single unified entity.

The FBI became the leading standard-bearer against what it called 'La Cosa Nostra.' No one has offered a satisfactory explanation for the addition of the Italian definite article to 'Cosa Nostra.' Valachi did not use it. J. Edgar Hoover claimed that the Valachi testimony merely corroborated what the FBI already knew and began to repeat the new conventional wisdom about organized crime. In 1966, for example, Hoover told a House Appropriations subcommittee: 'La Cosa Nostra is the largest organization of the criminal underworld in this country, very closely organized and strictly disciplined. They have committed every crime under the sun ... La Cosa Nostra is a criminal fraternity whose membership is Italian either by birth or national origin, and it has been found to control major racket activities in many of our larger metropolitan areas.'

Hoover's words were quoted by the 1967 report of President Lyndon Johnson's Commission on Law Enforcement and the Administration of Justice to substantiate the report's own assertion that 'the core of organized crime in the United States consists of 24 groups operating criminal cartels in large cities across the nation. Their membership is exclusively Italian, they are in frequent communication with each other, and their smooth functioning is insured by a national body of overseers.'

The commission's report emphasized that gambling was the greatest source of revenue for organized crime, followed by loan sharking, narcotics, 'and other forms of vice.' But, the report added, 'organized crime is also extensively and deeply involved in legitimate business and in labour unions' and continued: 'Here it employs illegitimate methods – monopolization, terrorism, extortion, tax evasion – to drive out or control lawful ownership and leadership and to exact illegal profits from the public. And to carry on its many activities secure from governmental interference, organized crime corrupts public officials.'

The commission definition still serves as a template for more recent attempts and reads as follows: 'Organized crime is a society that seeks to operate outside the control of the American people and their governments. It involves thousands of criminals, working within structures as complex as those of any large corporation, subject to laws more rigidly enforced than those of legitimate governments. Its actions are not impulsive but rather the result of intricate conspiracies, carried on over many years and aimed at gaining control over whole fields of activity in order to amass huge profits.'

The commission recommended a complete package of laws to combat the Cosa Nostra's subversion of 'the very decency and integrity that are the most cherished attributes of a free society.'[89] These included more powers for investigative grand juries, a general witness immunity statute that would 'assure compulsion of testimony,' wiretapping and bugging laws, witness protection programs, and extended prison terms for offenders occupying 'a supervisory or other management position.' As John Dombrink and James Meeker concluded: 'These recommendations formed the blueprint for the developments of the next 25 years, and indeed, laid out a course of action and change in emphasis, strategy and criminal law reform that would begin to affect organized crime investigation and prosecution soon after the enactment of the Organized Crime Control Act of 1970.'[90]

The phrase 'organized crime' had thus become a common noun by the 1960s, signifying a hierarchically organized criminal conspiracy with a meaning far removed from its early use. It now threatened the integrity of local government. It corrupted police officers and lawyers.

It infiltrated legitimate business. It subverted the decency and integrity of a free society. Organized crime was now seen as a criminal army; this was far away from earlier perspectives that emphasized the involvement and responsibility of 'respectable' society for the pervasive problem of organized crime activity in the United States.

A definition had finally been found that most important groups in American society could accept. Local politicians and officials found the new understanding of organized crime a convenient way of explaining their failure to check vice-related or industry-related racketeering in their cities. Nationally ambitious politicians found organized crime a useful vehicle to raise their profiles. National agency officials, including J. Edgar Hoover from the 1960s, found it a useful vehicle to raise their budgets and increase their powers. Legal experts and bar association reports used references to organized crime to help explain away the 'few unworthy members' of the bar who were 'of the criminal type.'[91] Moreover, U.S. business could assert its basic integrity by claiming that it was threatened by organized crime. However, despite this wholesale evasion of responsibility, 'respectable' society and institutions remained part of the problem of organized crime, and laws such as those that tried to prohibit gambling, narcotics, and 'other forms of vice' remained as easily exploitable as when they were first enacted.

Back in the late 1940s when the FBN had begun to talk up their discovery, very few people would have associated organized crime exclusively with Italian ethnicity. By the late 1960s the problem had been reduced to 'The Mafia v America' on the cover of *Time* magazine.[92] Government officials were more than happy to supply journalists with the 'facts' to support this explanation for the country's organized crime problem. The knowledge that some Italian American gangsters had become rich and powerful in their own cities, and had contact with other gangsters in other cities, had been distorted into a meaning that seemed far more mysterious and menacing.

There is no doubt that Italian-American gangsters have been among the most prominent gangsters since the Prohibition years. The dispute is over the identification of organized crime almost exclusively with Italian Americans and the suggestion that organized crime is some sort of alien transplant onto an otherwise pure political and economic system. Many people, in every part of the world, not just in America, now believe that something called the Mafia runs organized crime in the

United States. A single work of fiction that put the law enforcement perspective into its most digestible form, on top of decades of misinformation, helps to account for this mass misperception.

The writer of *The Godfather*, Mario Puzo, was an Italian American and to many this somehow confirmed that he knew what he was talking about. In fact, on his own admission and like the vast majority of Italian Americans, Puzo had never met 'a real honest-to-god gangster,' and wrote the book entirely from research.[93] The research was obviously much influenced by journalistic Mafia histories, and clearly reflected the law enforcement perspective on organized crime. *The Godfather* depicts an Italian-American crime family bending American industrial and governmental institutions to its will. Corporate bosses, judges, police officers, and other gangsters either obey the Godfather or they are 'made offers they can't refuse.' Don Corleone and his family are put squarely at the centre of America's organized crime problems.

Puzo's publishers hyped the book as an inside look at 'the violence-infested society of the Mafia,' and it enjoyed immediate critical and popular success. Most reviewers thought it was real. Fred Cook, for example, who was a well-known popular crime writer, wrote that Puzo had brought home the reality of Mafia power 'more vividly than the drier stuff of fact ever can.'[94] Not surprisingly law enforcement officials approved of the book, even in some cases by placing it on recommended reading lists in organized crime control training manuals.

The novel was on the *New York Times* best-seller list for sixty-seven weeks and sold just as impressively in overseas markets. The film of the book was even more successful, breaking numerous box-office records and enriching its producers, but in the process fixing misleading images about American organized crime for years to come.

A kind of Godfather industry has since developed with innumerable cheaper versions of the same themes turned out in every form of media communication – even Superman and Batman waged war on the Mafia in the August 1970 issue of *World's Finest Comics* and with by-products ranging from Godfather sweatshirts and car stickers to pizza franchises.[95] Mafia mythology had taken a firm grip on people's imagination; the fictional creation of the likes of Jack Lait and Lee Mortimer had finally been given almost universal credibility by constant repetition of an image.

The federal government's conception of organized crime as an alien and united entity was vital. It could then plausibly be presented as many-faced, calculating, and relentlessly probing for weak spots in the armour of American morality. Morality had to be protected from this alien threat. As Robert Kennedy had put it in a book called *The Enemy Within*, 'If we do not on a national scale attack organized criminals with weapons and techniques as effective as their own, they will destroy us.'[96] A foreign conspiracy was corrupting the police; therefore the police had to be given more power. Compromise such as reconsideration of the laws governing gambling and drug taking was out of the question – the only answer was increased law enforcement capacity and more laws to ensure the swift capture of gambling operators and drug traffickers behind whom the Mafia or Cosa Nostra was always supposed to be lurking. The process that involved federalizing American law enforcement would accelerate.

By constantly highlighting the 'Mafia supercriminal organization,' U.S. opinion makers had ensured that people's perception of organized crime was as limited as their own. The constant speculation, hyperbole, preaching, and mythmaking served to confuse and distract attention away from failed policies, institutional corruption and much systematic criminal activity that was more damaging and destructive than 'Mafia' crimes.

Richard Nixon and the Setting of Organized Crime Control Priorities

By the 1960s, Mafia mythology had provided U.S. bureaucrats and politicians with an easy-to-communicate threat to the nation; concentration on the Mafia diverted attention away from corruption in government and business. This not only saved much embarrassment, but it also helped to limit people's awareness of the flaws in an approach to crime based exclusively on giving the government more power to combat threats to America's business-dominated system. These flaws would be abundantly illuminated during the administration of Richard Nixon.

The two main contestants in the 1968 presidential race were Vice-President Hubert Humphrey for the Democrats and Richard Nixon for the Republicans. Nixon's presidential campaign was aimed squarely at the 'average American' or the 'silent majority' – the millions of Americans concerned and confused by the disruptive social changes of the preceding years. Nixon's campaign managers banked on a backlash against rising crime rates, anti-war protest, campus disorders, black power militancy, and moral permissiveness. The Republicans concentrated on achieving the support of middle- and working-class Americans and ignored liberals, blacks, Hispanics, and the poor in general. The South, the suburbs, and the white ethnic working class were targeted with the intention of securing a majority coalition that would replace the old Democratic coalition of big cities, unions, and minorities forged by Franklin D. Roosevelt in the 1930s and maintained by both Kennedy and Johnson during the 1960s.

Nixon's strategists had recognized that 'law-and-order' rhetoric was an essential ingredient to the campaign, and at every opportunity the candidate repeated his solemn pledge to 'restore order and respect for law in this country' and commitment to establish a new tough agenda on crime.

Television commercials got the Nixon message across to a mass audience. One showed a nervous middle-aged woman walking down the street on a dark, wet night with the following commentary: 'Crimes of violence in the United States have almost doubled in recent years ... today a violent crime is committed every sixty seconds ... a robbery every two and a half minutes ... a mugging every six minutes ... a murder every 43 minutes ... and it will get worse unless we take the offensive.'[97]

Nixon narrowly won the election of November 1968 and needed to maintain his 'law-and-order' constituency to win re-election in 1972. Headlines had to be made, results had to be achieved, otherwise the tough talk and promises to restore law and order might backfire. Nixon's first step was to appoint John Mitchell as attorney general. As Nixon's former law partner and chief campaign adviser, Mitchell could be counted on to continue promoting the new president's interests. The Nixon administration's problem was that it had limited jurisdiction over crime. Constitutionally and historically the cities and states were chiefly responsible for crime control. Therefore, the Nixonites decided to increase federal jurisdiction to an unprecedented level. Nixon articulated the rationale for this in a series of letters and 'special talks' to Congress on crime and drugs.

First, he gave an immense boost to Mafia mythology and added the weight of the presidential office to the notion of an alien conspiracy. On 23 April 1969, Nixon described the Mafia's influence as 'more secure than ever before' and warned that its operations had 'deeply penetrated broad segments of American life.' Three lines of headlines in the *New York Times*, for example, spelled out the message,

Nixon Requests Wide U.S. Powers to Combat Mafia

Gambling Target

President Seeks Halt in 'Subversion' of Society by Crime

Nixon spoke of government successes against racketeers but warned: 'It is vitally important that Americans see this alien organization for what it really is – a totalitarian and closed society, operating within an open and democratic one. It has succeeded so far because an apathetic public is unaware of the threat it poses to American life ... It will not be eliminated by loud voices and good intentions. It will be eliminated by carefully conceived, well-funded and well-executed action plans.' Among these action plans he announced that the focus of the government's effort would be in New York City: 'I have authorized the Attorney General to establish a unique Federal-state racket squad in New York City. I have asked all Federal agencies to cooperate with the Department of Justice in this effort and to give priority to the organized crime drive.' The fight against New York City's gangsters was to become the government's showcase in the fight against organized crime.

'Furthermore,' Nixon continued, 'our action plans against organized crime must be established on a long-term basis in order to relentlessly pursue the criminal syndicate.'

Success depended on the support of the public, state, and local governments and Congress. Nixon asked Congress to increase the fiscal year 1970 budget for dealing with organized crime to 'the unprecedented total of $61 million' and for 'new weapons and tools ... to enable the Federal Government to strike both at the Cosa Nostra hierarchy and the sources of revenue that feed the coffers of organized crime.' Among these new laws he specified 'a new broad general witness immunity law to cover all cases involving violation of a Federal Statute,' amended wagering tax laws, and improved procedural laws.

Under the witness immunity law, 'a witness could not be prosecuted on the basis of anything he said while testifying, but he would not be immune from prosecution based on other evidence of his offense. Furthermore, once the Government has granted the witness such immunity, a refusal to testify would bring a prison sentence for contempt. With this new law, Government should be better able to gather evidence to strike at the leadership of organized crime and not just the rank and file.' Nixon then stated the administration's support for wagering tax amendments and new laws against illegal gambling businesses:

> This Administration has concluded that the major thrust of its concerted anti-organized crime effort should be directed against gambling activities ...
>
> While gambling may seem to most Americans to be the least reprehensible of all the activities of organized crime, it is gambling which provides the bulk of the revenues that eventually go into usurious loans, bribes of police and local officials, 'campaign contributions' to politicians, the wholesale narcotics traffic, the infiltration of legitimate business and to pay for the large stables of lawyers and accountants and assorted professional men who are in the hire of organized crime ... Gambling income is the lifeline of organized crime. If we can cut it or constrict it we will be striking close to its heart.'

Finally, Nixon introduced a new approach to organized crime that, as we shall see in Chapter 7, had especially far reaching implications: asset forfeiture. He argued: 'The arrest, conviction and imprisonment of a Mafia lieutenant can curtail operations but does not put the syndicate out of business. As long as the property of organized crime remains, new leaders will step forward to take the place of those we jail. However, if we can levy fines on their real estate corporations, if we can seek treble damages against their trucking firms and banks, if we can seize the liquor in their warehouses I think we can strike a critical blow at the organized crime conspiracy.'

His administration could, he argued, only strike this critical blow, if 'Congress will supply the funds and the requested legislation, the states and the communities across the country will take advantage of the federal capability and desire to assist and participate with them and the Federal personnel responsible for programs and actions will vigorously carry out their mission.'[98]

Nixon had thus placed himself squarely among a long line of Mafia conspiracy theorists, from Mayor Shakspeare, Harry Anslinger, and crime journalists of the Jack Lait and Lee Mortimer school, to the recently converted J. Edgar Hoover. His speech was in a style of Amer-

ican politics described by the historian Richard Hofstadter as 'paranoid.' To use Hofstadter's terms, Nixon had explained the enemy as a
'perfect model of malice ... sinister, ubiquitous, powerful, cruel.' But
unlike other 'paranoid' spokesmen, Richard Nixon had the power to
boost the resistance to his conspiracy.

The speech was also in the tradition established since the Progressive era of 'sets of stereotypes' and 'frozen images, specifically
intended to exclude discussion.' There were no significant challenges
to Nixon's analysis in the news media. Congress was already considering a bill introduced by Senator McClellan and, after Nixon's support,
few senators and representatives resisted passage of the Organized
Crime Control Act in 1970, which supplemented legislation passed in
1968 and gave federal law enforcement and intelligence agencies an
unprecedented array of powers. Organized crime control provisions
now included asset forfeiture, special grand juries, wider witness
immunity provisions for compelling or persuading reluctant witnesses, extended sentences for persons convicted in organized crime
cases, and the use of wiretapping and eavesdropping evidence in federal cases. Such a major alteration in constitutional guarantees was justified by the belief that the problem was a massive, well-integrated,
international conspiracy. The measures extended the headhunting
powers that Thomas E. Dewey had used in the 1930s on a local level to
federal police and prosecutors. They tipped the balance away from
such civil liberties as the right to privacy and protection from unreasonable search and seizure and towards a far stronger and, as we shall
see, far richer, policing presence in America. However, the potential of
these laws for genuine and effective control of systematic criminal
activity was minimal because the conditions that fostered endemic
crime and corruption in the United States did not change. Instead, as
constitutional scholar Leonard Levy put it, the new control measures
were 'a salvo of fragmentation grenades that missed their targets and
exploded against the Bill of Rights.'[99]

The 1968 and 1970 organized crime control laws and concurrent anti-
drug legislation had a great potential for politically as well as financially motivated abuse that was soon realized. Federal policemen were
given more scope to spy on and suppress political dissent. Nixon's administration used its new powers more actively against anti-
Vietnam war protestors than against Italian-American or any other
gangsters. Between 1970 and 1974, in particular, grand juries, along
with increased wiretapping and eavesdropping powers, became part

of the government's armoury against dissent. A list of abuses during these years includes harassing political activists, discrediting 'non-mainstream' groups, assisting management during strikes, punishing witnesses for exercising their 5th Amendment rights, covering up official crimes, enticing perjury, and gathering domestic intelligence.[100]

By the early 1970s the Nixon administration had substituted drugs for gambling as the 'lifeline' of organized crime, after a cynically devised escalation of the country's drug control efforts. The intention was first to inflate the drug problem, second to blame crime on drugs, and finally, to give the impression of firm executive action by waging 'war' on drugs. According to Edward J. Epstein's account, based on interviews with top Nixon administration officials, the strategy that justified a massive expansion of drug law enforcement was to persuade Americans that their lives and the lives of their children were threatened by a rampant 'epidemic' of drug addiction. Americans would then support draconian measures to produce results. As Nixon's chief domestic adviser John Ehrlichman later testified, parents worry, and 'narcotics suppression is a very sexy political issue. It usually has high media visibility.'[101]

Attorney General Mitchell introduced the first phase of the war on drugs soon after taking office:

> The battle against narcotics is an integral part of the Administration's anti-street crime program. A narcotics addict may need $70 or $80 a day to satisfy his habit. Thus, he turns to robbery, mugging, and burglary in order to obtain money. It was recently estimated that in New York City alone $2 billion a year is stolen by narcotics addicts and that a substantial proportion of violent crimes are committed by narcotics addicts.
>
> ... Persons who live in ghetto areas, which have substantial numbers of narcotics addicts, literally bar the doors of the apartments at night. They are attacked in broad daylight on the streets. They are terrorized by the knowledge that the heroin addict who needs a fix will commit the most vicious crime in order to obtain a TV set for resale for a few dollars. Even our high school children are beginning to use hard narcotics.[102]

Mitchell and other government spokesmen based their arguments on dishonest statistics. When a reputable economist, Max Singer, examined them, he found that the figures implied that addicts stole almost ten times as much as was actually stolen annually in New York City.[103]

But, as with the overblown Cosa Nostra rhetoric, accuracy was not necessary for Nixon, Mitchell, and the rest; creating a climate of fear was.

Such misinformation went unchallenged by the news media. As Epstein has demonstrated, White House press releases on drugs were abridged and printed by the newspapers almost verbatim. If any journalists had pressed government officials about the method they used for estimating the number of addicts, or the cost of their daily habit, they would have quickly found that the officials' certainty and assurance was a bluff. They had no way of knowing the number of addicts, made no distinction between addicts and occasional users, and in effect, made up the numbers to support drastic measures. Journalists failed to challenge the figures because multimillion numbers provided dramatic news, while the lack of credible data did not. Thus, when the number of heroin addicts escalated from 69,000 in 1969 to 322,000 in 1970 and to 560,000 in 1971, few were sceptical. More spoke of the sensational heroin 'epidemic,' without realizing that the same 1969 data were used for all three estimates. The higher numbers were arrived at by using different statistical formulas rather than by discovering new addicts.[104]

In a letter to Congress on 14 July 1969, the president restated the themes of the crusade and then outlined a ten-point program of action. He first warned that 'within the last decade, the abuse of drugs has grown from essentially a local police problem into a serious national threat to the personal health and safety of millions of Americans. A national awareness of the gravity of the situation is needed; a new urgency and concerted national policy are needed at the federal level to begin to cope with this growing menace to the general welfare of the United States.'

The number of addicts, Nixon said, had grown to where it had to be estimated 'in the hundreds of thousands,' that 'several million college students had at least experimented with marijuana, hashish, LSD, amphetamines, or barbiturates. Nixon then continued: 'It is doubtful that an American parent can send a son or daughter to college today without exposing the young man or woman to drug abuse. Parents must be concerned about the availability and use of such drugs in our high schools and junior high schools. The habit of the narcotic addict is not only a threat to himself, but a threat to the community where he lives. Narcotics have been cited as a primary cause of the enormous increase in street crimes over the last decade.'

272 Organized Crime and American Power

The president then stated that an 'addict will reduce himself to any offense, any degradation' to acquire drugs and mentioned 'street robberies, prostitution, even the enticing of others into addiction to drugs.' 'Society,' he concluded, has few judgements too severe, few penalties too harsh for the men who make their livelihood in the narcotic traffic.'[105]

This campaign to inflate the fear of drugs succeeded. Even in parts of the country that did not have a problem with illegal drugs, people now felt threatened by the spreading epidemic. Drugs, in the words of Ehlrichman, had 'high media visibility.' The measures Nixon proposed for congressional support were more international cooperation, a 'major new effort' by the Bureau of Customs, comprehensive new federal and state laws, suppression of domestic trafficking with 'action task forces,' 'no-knock' warrants, and heavier penalties, more education, research, rehabilitation, and better liaison with local enforcers.[106]

The first sign of the administration's international effort came in September 1969, when an attempt was made by Customs and Immigration officers to curb the importation of illegal drugs from Mexico by stopping and searching over two million people crossing the United States–Mexico border. After three weeks the operation was called off after the seizure of a negligible amount of drug contraband and the creation of immense traffic jams. A new approach was begun and the administration gave the Mexican government $1 million to 'eradicate' poppy and marijuana fields.[107]

More expensive international intervention began in 1971. Turkey was thought to be the major source of heroin and was vulnerable to diplomatic pressure because of its dependence on massive U.S. economic and military aid. The Turkish government therefore agreed to ban all opium-growing for a three-year period in return for a payment of $35 million – intended to assist the development of alternative crops to replace opium. Little of the money reached the tens of thousands of farmers who lost income because of the ban, and by 1974 the Turks had found the policy to be unworkable and lifted the ban. Any vacuum in the U.S. heroin market during the years of the Turkish ban was filled by Mexican and southeast Asian heroin.[108]

During the Nixon era, as Professor Ethan A Nadelmann has demonstrated, a small overseas complement of U.S. narcotics agents grew into the 'first global law enforcement agency with operational capabilities':

In 1967, the last full year of the FBN's existence, the budget of the Treasury department's drug agency was approximately $3 million. Roughly a dozen of its 300 agents were stationed in eight locations outside of the United States. Six years and two bureaucratic reorganizations later, in the last full year of BNDD operations, the drug agency boasted a budget of $74 million and 1,446 total agents, of whom 124 were abroad in 47 offices in 33 countries. By 1976, just before a minor contraction in its size, the DEA's budget was just short of $200 million. Some 228 of its 2,117 agents were stationed overseas, in 68 offices in 43 countries.[109]

U.S. drug control agents were, as Nadlemann explained, expected to do much more than make cases against drug traffickers. They also had to act as drug enforcement diplomats and advocates 'to push for structural changes in drug enforcement wherever they were stationed, to lobby for tougher laws, to train local police in drug enforcement techniques, to sensitize local officials to U.S. concerns in this area, and so on.'[110]

Nixon's administration more than doubled the corps of drug control officers assigned to U.S. embassies and missions abroad and their numbers have since continued to expand. Other countries were bullied or persuaded to make futile, often cynical, drug-control gestures on America's behalf. U.S. consumers continued to pay the top prices, and the effort only revealed that processable plants grow everywhere and that foreign drug enforcers accept bribes just as enthusiastically as their counterparts in the United States. Drug control, as we shall see in the final chapter of this book, would simultaneously remain the primary justification for U.S. intervention into the affairs of other countries and an important reason behind a dumbing of global discourse about organized crime.

Domestically, the Nixon administration's main legislative innovation was to secure the passing of the Comprehensive Drug Abuse Control Act of 1970 – a statute that brought together everything Congress had done in the drug field since curbs on opium-smoking in 1887. The law gave the Department of Justice an array of powers over licit and illicit drugs, covering possession, sale, and trafficking. Drug offenders faced severe sanctions including life imprisonment for those engaged in 'continuing criminal enterprise' or who qualify as 'a dangerous special drug offender.' Treasury funds were to be made available to enforcement agents to hire informants, pay for incriminating information, and make purchases of contraband substances. Agents were given the power to seize on sight any property they thought was contraband or forfeitable and to execute search warrants at any time of the day or night, with a new 'no-knock' procedure if a judge had authorized it.[111]

The act was passed without difficulty. As would be the case from then on, few legislators dared to appear 'soft' on drugs and point out the dangers inherent in the new law's policing provisions. The hysteria about drugs had reached a new peak, and in such circumstances most politicians are even more likely to follow the paths of least resistance. It was thought that action had to be taken because, as Senator Thomas Dodd put it: 'People are watching us. The hoodlums are watching us. The dope peddlers are watching us. They all want to know if we mean business.'[112]

Nixon had stated that his intention was to 'tighten the noose around the necks of drug peddlers, and thereby loosen the noose around the necks of drug users.' For this the BNDD was given more men and even larger budget appropriations. At its formation in 1968 the agency had 615 agents and a $14 million budget. The number of agents then increased from 760 in 1969 to 900 in 1970 and 1,150 in 1971. By 1973 the BNDD had 1,586 agents operating within the United States alone and a budget of $74 million.[113]

The White House, however, wanted to go further and created a new agency under its direct control – the Office of Drug Abuse Law Enforcement (ODALE), to be headed by Customs Chief Myles Ambrose. ODALE was intended to dramatize Nixon's war on drugs by concentrating on lower levels of heroin distribution networks and piling up arrest statistics. Its strike forces were generously funded with 'buy money' to purchase drugs and pay informants and for numerous undercover operations. A 'Heroin Hotline' was set up in April 1972 to encourage informers. With the authority of 'no-knock' warrants ODALE agents could strike any time against virtually anyone selected as a target. Targets tended to be street addicts who traded in drugs to pay for their own habits.

The ODALE and other Nixon initiatives still held promise before the 1972 elections. As intended, the public had been given the impression of firm executive action against drug trafficking and other crime, and few opportunities were missed to remind them of this action. In October, for example, the new Attorney General Richard Kleindienst claimed that 'the crime wave which shocked us in the 1960s is now under control and America once again is becoming a safe and lawful society.'[114]

Nixon's rival in the election, Senator George McGovern was successfully identified with a 'soft' attitude to drugs and crime, and in
November 1972 the president was re-elected by an overwhelming mar-
gin. His commitment to fight the 'totalitarian' Mafia and the 'menace'
of drugs had achieved its primary purpose and Nixon's tough law-
and-order image was maintained. The tawdry realities behind the
image remained, for a while, concealed.

Nixon's creation, ODALE, along with state and local drug squads, pursued a campaign against drugs of unprecedented hostility and intensity. One immediate effect was that scores of innocent Americans were
subjected to mistaken, violent, and often illegal raids and harassment.
Two examples follow:

> On 24 April 1972 local and federal police moved in on the mountain
> retreat of 24–year-old Dirk Dickenson near Eureka, California, to seize
> what their informants had told them was a 'giant lab' producing drugs.
> Arriving on foot with dogs, the agents, who were not in uniform and
> did not identify themselves, assaulted the cabin with rifles and hand-
> guns. Mr Dickenson ran towards the woods, apparently baffled and
> frightened. He was shot in the back as he fled and died later. No 'giant
> lab' was found.

> On the night of 23 April 1973 there were ODALE raids on the homes of
> Herbert Giglotto and Donald Askew in Collinsville, Illinois. Mr Giglotto
> and his wife were asleep when more than 15 roughly dressed men broke
> down two doors, handcuffed and then held the couple at gun-point. They
> then emptied drawers and closets, shattered pottery, threw a television set
> on the floor and shouted obscenities at the couple. A half-hour later a sim-
> ilar event occurred across town at the home of Mr Donald Askew. In both
> cases the raiders were at the wrong address, they had no search or arrest
> warrants and did not identify themselves until well into the raids.

There were many more cases of mistaken entry and frequently tragic
consequences.[115]

There is no doubt that there was considerable federal, state, and
local persecution of politically active Americans during the Nixon
years based on the drug laws. Two cases attracted some attention in
the early 1970s. John Sinclair, a poet and leader of the insignificant
White Panther Party in Michigan, received a ten-year prison sentence
for lighting a marijuana cigarette while two undercover police intelli-

gence officers had him under surveillance for his political activities. Lee Otis Johnson, a black militant and anti-war organizer at Texas Southern University, got thirty years for giving a marijuana cigarette to an undercover officer who had posed as his friend.[116]

Partly as a result of the kind of negative publicity noted above, ODALE ceased to exist in July 1973, when it was swallowed up in another reorganization. The Heroin Hotline had already been wound up. Agents deemed 28,079 out of the 33,313 calls received in the first three months useless – obscene calls, pranks, or simply heavy breathing. Most of the remainder were thought to be sincere but of no immediate use. Only 113 calls provided any leads at all, and even these produced only one seizure and four arrests. The first four months of Hotline's operation cost $260,000 and resulted in the total seizure of two grams of adulterated heroin which, even using the magnified street values of drug enforcement agencies, only amounted to $2 worth.[117]

In July 1973 the Drug Enforcement Administration (DEA) was created by the presidential fiat of Richard Nixon to take over the functions of the BNDD, ODALE, and the narcotics intelligence programs of other agencies. This move was described by a top BNDD official as 'the old reorganization shell game' – the cannibalizing of enforcement agencies and the creation of new bureaucratic titles. By 1975 the new agency had a staff of more than 4,000, about half of whom were investigators, and it possessed, in Rufus King's words, 'every armament and prerogative that could conceivably be conferred on a peacetime domestic agency.'[118]

As Nixon's chief domestic Adviser John Ehrlichman later told a Senate committee, the expansion of drug enforcement capacity and anti-drug rhetoric was mainly a show for the voters: 'We can consolidate, we can reorganize, we can budget and you can put up a lot of money. You can hire a lot more agents and put them out there. It is going to be marginal ... I think there is a genuine question of hypocrisy in all of this, as to whether the Federal Government, the people in the Federal Government aren't just kidding themselves and kidding the people when they say we have mounted a massive war on narcotics when they know darned well that the massive war that they have mounted on narcotics is only going to be effective at the margins.'[119]

In 1973 an official report on drug use in the United States warned about the 'rapid institutionalization' of the 'drug abuse problem.' The National Commission on Marijuana and Drug Abuse, appointed by Nixon in 1971, described how:

The high degree of public concern has generated a shifting of large quantities of money, manpower, and other resources at the federal, state, and local levels to meet the problem and lessen the public concern. The response has created, in the short span of four years, a 'drug abuse industrial complex.'

With spending at the federal level alone of upwards of one billion dollars annually, with a rapid growth of bureaucracy, with an almost compulsive spending on drug projects without benefit of evaluation or goal setting, the drug abuse industrial complex has firmly established itself as a fixture of government and society.

The Commission is concerned that the underlying assumptions about the problem and the organizational response of the 'complex' may, rather than resolve or de-emotionalize the issue, tend to perpetuate it as an ongoing part of the American way of life. There is a real need to evaluate the present system to ensure that the government directs its efforts towards the achievement of success rather than the perpetuation of government activity.[120]

Later in the report, in a section entitled 'Perpetuating the Problem,' the commission elaborated on this theme:

Because of the intensity of the public concern and the emotionalism surrounding the topic of drugs, all levels of government have been pressured into action with little time for planning. The political pressures involved in this governmental effort have resulted in a concentration of public energy on the most immediate aspects of drug use and a reaction along the paths of least political resistance. The recent result has been the creation of ever larger bureaucracies, ever increasing expenditures of monies, and an outpouring of publicity so that the public will know that 'something' is being done.

Perhaps the greatest consequence of this ad hoc policy planning has been the creation at the federal, state, and community levels, of a vested interest in the perpetuation of the problem among those dispensing and receiving funds. Infrastructures are created, job descriptions are standardized, 'experts' are created and ways of doing business routinized and

278 Organized Crime and American Power

established along bureaucratic channels ... In the course of well-meaning efforts to do something about drug use, this society may have inadvertently institutionalized it as a never-ending project.[121]

The commission called for a new approach to drug use before it was too late: one that was coherent and flexible, emphasized treatment rather than punishment for addiction, and stigmatized only those habits that threatened society.

The Nixon administration's reaction to the report was described as 'frosty.' No photographs were permitted when the commission's chairman Raymond Shafer formally presented the report to the president. Its major recommendations were ignored.[122]

Succeeding administrations also failed to heed the commission's warnings. U.S. drug control policy has been one of emotionalizing the issue, reacting to pressure, increasing expenditures, following the paths of least political resistance, and giving the appearance that 'something' is being done. Drug policy remains incoherent and inflexible, punishment of offenders not treatment for addicts is emphasized, and drug habits which do not threaten society are stigmatized. More bureaucratic empires were created and electoral advantage usually went to the hardliners. As we shall see in Chapter 7, criminals and corrupt public and private professionals continued to prosper as the law of the land continues to accommodate to the law of supply and demand.

From the beginning of 1973 Americans gradually came to realize that they had bestowed an armoury of repressive crime control powers on people who were themselves criminally inclined. Almost as soon as President Nixon had been inaugurated for his second term there began an avalanche of revelations and disclosures of criminal activity by top officials indicating endemic corruption. The most systematic corruption involved a form of organized crime that had not been covered in Nixon's series of messages to Congress – corporate crime.

Nixon had long been aware that the more money there was available to fight election campaigns the better – the presentation of issues is important, but the better financed candidate tends to win. In 1957 he had advised another politician to 'get to know the big finance men, that's the key.'[123] He also knew that corporate interests expect something back for their generosity.

The dairy industry's desire to get on the right side of the Nixon administration provided the most clear-cut evidence of abuse. Federal

policy directly affects the prices of dairy products and corporate farming interests wanted an increase in the price support of dairy products.
Associated Milk Producers, Inc. (AMPI), the nation's largest dairy
cooperative, made substantial contributions to Nixon's 1972 re-election
campaign that were directly tied to the 1971 price support increase
authorized by Nixon. Other major cooperatives renewed a pledge for a
total of $2 million to the campaign the day before the administration
announced a large increase in diary price supports. These supports
were worth tens of millions of dollars to dairy farmers and cost the
American consumer equivalent amounts.[124]

Other revelations concerned the undue influence that large corporations such as International Telephone and Telegraph (ITT) and Gulf Oil
had over the administration. In 1971 ITT offered a large contribution to
Nixon's campaign effort at the same time as it was engaged in negotiations over whether the corporation had violated the anti-trust laws. On
19 April Nixon made the following point to John Ehrlichman, recorded
by the White House taping system: 'I don't know whether ITT is
bad, good or indifferent ... But there is not going to be any more anti-
trust actions as long as I am in this chair ... goddam it, we are going to
stop it.'[125]

The Gulf Corporation was revealed as having a systematic, endur-
ing, and illegal system of political 'slush' funds, of which a $100,000
contribution to Nixon's 1972 campaign was just one of many. A Gulf
subsidiary vice-president was known to deliver envelopes stuffed with
cash to useful politicians.[126]

As part of its promises to look after the interests of the 'silent majority' or 'forgotten Americans,' the Nixon administration oversaw the
enactment of the Occupational Health and Safety Administration Act
of 1970, which on the surface looked to be against the profit at-all-costs
interests of corporations. The law promised federal intervention to
require employers to provide a workplace 'free from recognized hazards that are causing or are likely to cause death or serious physical harm to employees' and to meet the specific standards set by the
Labor Department's Occupational Safety and Health Administration
(OSHA). Although the creation of the new agency seemed to be a triumph for the many years of campaigning for safer working conditions
by trade unions and other groups, the promise of OHSA was immediately undermined by those appointed to administer it. These tended to
be either weak administrators or more responsive to the interests of
business than workers.[127]

Nixon's own attitude to corporate violations of the health and safety laws was encapsulated in the following taped conversation he had in the Oval Office with motor manufacturers Henry Ford II and Lee Iacocca on 27 April 1971:

> My views in this field ... my personal views – Henry, you will not be surprised at this but, uh, we, uh, uh, the, uh, uh, whether its the environment or pollution or Naderism or consumerism, my views are extremely pro-business. Uh, we are fighting, frankly a delaying action. There is pollution and maybe there are safety problems. I think they are grossly exaggerated, but we can't have a completely safe society or safe highways or safe cars and be pollution-free or we would have to go back and live like a bunch of damned animals. And these environmentalists aren't one really damn bit interested in safety or clean air. What they're interested in is destroying the system! They're the enemies of the system.[128]

It was a statement that helps explain why legal markets are so inadequately policed.

Nixon's most immediate enemies, however, were not 'enemies of the system' but mainstream opposition politicians, and it was a short step to use covert intelligence mechanisms against Democratic politicians – either to discredit them or to find out their campaign strategy. The bungled attempt to install wiretaps at the Watergate Hotel in June 1972 was merely the extension of existing practices and just the tip of an iceberg of abuse. 'The subsequent concealment,' according to John Conyer's comments to the House Committee on the Judiciary, 'was intended not merely to protect the White House from its complicity in the Watergate incident itself, but to avoid disclosure of the entire train of illegal and abusive conduct that characterized the Nixon presidency,' which Conyers proceeded to summarize:

> obstruction of justice, perjury and the subornation of perjury, offers of executive clemency, attempts to influence a federal judge, destruction of evidence, disclosure of secret grand jury proceedings, withholding information of criminal activity, impounding of Congressional appropriations, willful tax evasion, possible bribery in connection with the ITT antitrust and milk support decisions, and interference with the lawful activities of the CIA, FBI, IRS, Special Prosecutor, House Banking and Cur-

rency Committee, Senate Select Committee on Presidential Campaign Activities, and finally, the House Judiciary Committee. In these ways, the President sought to avert disclosure of a seamless web of illegality and impropriety.[129]

In August 1974 Nixon resigned, faced with the certainty of an impeachment vote in the Senate, and relinquished his office to Vice-President Gerald Ford. Ford had replaced Spiro T. Agnew a few months before, after Agnew had resigned over tax evasion and kickback revelations. Subsequently, several key Nixon officials were tried and convicted of Watergate-related offences, notably Chief Domestic Affairs Adviser John Ehrlichman, who served eighteen months in prison for perjury and conspiracy. White House Chief of Staff Bob Haldeman served the same sentence for perjury and obstruction of justice, and former Attorney General John Mitchell served nineteen months for his role in the cover-up. Nixon himself was pardoned by his successor.[130]

In order to be elected in November 1968, Richard Nixon had repeatedly told the American people that he was going to restore order and respect for the law. By November 1973 he was trying to reassure them that he was 'not a crook,' but by then fewer people believed him. He was forced to resign when he could no longer cover up the fact that an administration pledged to fight crime had directed massive burglary, sabotage, spying, and campaign fund illegalities.

Watergate, however, discredited only Nixon and his administration, and by the time of his death in 1994, the former president had managed to regain his credibility in the opinion of many. His 'hard line' against drugs and whatever the government chose to define as 'organized crime' remained politically useful. In the aftermath of Watergate there was only moderate reform of the organized crime-control laws and minimal re-examination of U.S. drug-control policy, which, in essence, remains today the one established by the Watergate conspirators. The fight against both corruption and corporate crime also remained low on the nation's list of crime-control priorities.

In his message to Congress about organized crime, Nixon had associated corruption entirely with gambling and the Mafia. However, he would later appoint a commission to study corruption that ironically gave the most appropriate epitaph for his crime-control policies. As long as official corruption flourished, the commission concluded, 'the war against crime will be perceived by many as a war of the powerful against the powerless, 'law and order' will be a hypocritical rallying cry, and 'equal justice under law' will be an empty phrase.'[131]

Despite the investigative efforts of Bob Woodward and Carl Bernstein of the *Washington Post*, and others, Watergate did not signal the beginnings of serious news media attention to the crimes of the powerful. In fact, as Danny Schechter's account of the development of television news coverage shows, the years since Watergate have seen an increasing media obsession with celebrities and frivolous issues at the expense of serious subjects. Schechter considers this to be the result of a even greater degree of concentration of media power in the hands of the few and a growing partnership between public relations specialists, political leaders, and corporate interests which 'routinely screens out unwanted perspectives.' 'The White House,' writes Schechter, 'attempts to control the news agenda every day. And corporate America sets its agenda by buying it – through advertising campaigns, sponsorship of TV shows, political action committees that finance campaigns, lobbyists, paid advertising, and behind-the-scenes wheeling and dealing. Programs like *20/20* ultimately serve their agenda even if from time to time they expose a product defect here or a corporate scam there. The business of the mass media is first and foremost business.'[132]

In this context, organized crime became even more associated with the easy-to-digest Mafia package, as attention was focused on gangsters of Italian-American ancestry, mainly from New York.

The Mafia since 1970

Despite the assurances of President Richard Nixon, the existence of the Mafia as a centralized organization dominating organized crime could never be proved, but incidents and revelations involving Italian-American gangsters continued to be distorted by the press and television, thus keeping the idea alive. The most notable Italian-American racketeer of the early 1970s was Joseph Colombo Sr. He was notable not for his criminal success or power, but because he orchestrated probably the most counter-productive anti-defamation campaign in the history of the United States.

Colombo was under increasing legal pressure, particularly from the federal authorities, and faced tax evasion, perjury, and gambling charges. When his son was also arrested on charges of conspiracy to melt silver coins into more valuable ingots, Colombo's reaction was to organize a picket of FBI headquarters and help to form a militant pressure group called the Italian-American Civil Rights League in order to protest against what he thought was unreasonable and selective harassment of Italian Americans. The league soon attracted over 40,000 paid-up supporters and belatedly tried to do what the Jewish Anti-Defamation League had been doing for Jews for decades, that is, protect them from ethnic slurs and stereotyping. However, Colombo's complaints about persecution and the claims of some of his supporters that the Mafia did not exist appeared ridiculous to those who knew or suspected his criminal activities and connections. The FBI made its opinions clear by publicizing stories about Colombo's 200 strong 'Mafia family' and its various rackets in Brooklyn.

Colombo's crusade came to an abrupt end on 28 June 1971, when a black gunman shot him in the head less than an hour before a league rally was due to begin at Columbus Circle in New York. Colombo's bodyguards immediately killed the assailant. Colombo himself survived, but was paralyzed and unable to organize either crime or ethnic pride any longer. The circumstances of the shooting confirmed people's suspicions and discredited any progress the league had made. Colombo's self-interested use of the league backfired, but the crudity of the effort does not support exaggerated notions of Mafia power.[133]

A succession of Italian-American gangsters have been slain in New York since the near-fatal shooting of Joseph Colombo, often in spectacular 'gangland' style. All the shootings were followed by examples of what Jack Newfield called 'the myth of Godfather journalism,' ill-informed speculation about who ordered the hits and who benefited by rising up the Mafia hierarchy.

Newfield was writing in July 1979 after the shooting of Carmine Galante; a drug trafficker promoted to *capo di tutti capi* ('boss of all bosses') by the newspapers. Newfield described most Mafia reporting as 'consumer fraud' with the need to 'name new godfathers with the frequency of new Miss Subways' and an overreliance on clipping files and leaks from law enforcement agencies. The agencies' motive to exaggerate was 'bigger budgets derived from greater publicity,' but their knowledge of organized crime was in fact very limited, as reflected in their inability to control any of the criminal activities. An FBI agent admitted that in truth, 'It's all bullshit. We don't really know what's going on. It's all tribal warfare with shifting alliances.' Newfield concluded: 'There is no one Mafia godfather. There is no *capo di tutti capi*. There are just law enforcement agencies trying to arrest gangs of career criminals. And newspaper publishers trying to improve circulation. The rest is hype, the rest is myth.'[134]

Jimmy Fratiano, the most famous gangster informant of the late 1970s, made a similar point. Fratiano had been a successful hit man but an unsuccessful criminal entrepreneur, earning the less than impressive nickname 'the Weasel.' He was associated with the small and weak Los Angeles 'Mafia' family. He did, however, help produce a number of significant convictions, testifying against three New York gangsters, one Los Angeles gangster, and Rudy Tham, an important San Francisco Teamster official.

Fratiano thought that most Mafia journalism was a joke and poured scorn on the presentation of the Mafia as a tightly knit national organization controlling organized crime. In an interview with crime writer Ovid Demaris, Fratiano revealed what he thought of a May 1977 article in *Time* magazine. The article was entitled 'The Mafia – Big, Bad and Booming,' and it began with a brief description of the organization and its chain of command: 'The Mafia is overseen nationally by the commission, a dozen or so dons who, usually, but not always, defer to the dominant boss in New York because he controls the most men and rackets.' The story contended that the Mafia was in a state of unrest since the death of 'Don Carlo Gambino,' the 'boss-of-all-bosses' who had brought a measure of peace to the nation's Mafia families 'through guile, diplomacy, and strong-arm discipline.' Fratiano's reaction to this was, 'How they liked this boss-of-all-bosses bullshit.'

The article, in the usual way, then 'supported' its assertions with a list of Italian-American gangsters including Tony Spilotro, one of Fratiano's associates. Spilotro, according to *Time*, controlled loan-sharking, prostitution, and narcotics along the Las Vegas Strip, and the assertion was supported with a quote from an unnamed Justice Department official. Fratiano's first-hand knowledge of Spilotro and Las Vegas was different: 'Spilotro was nothing but a strong-arm errand boy. The thought that he could control loansharking, prostitution and narcotics along the Strip was mind-boggling. It would be like trying to control three tidal waves with a machine gun.'[135] In 1986 Spilotro was found beaten to death in an Indiana cornfield. Since then writers and law enforcement officials continued to make highly speculative claims about his importance without offering much by way of substantiation.[136]

Since the 1980s the FBI's concentration on the twenty-plus Italian-

American crime families that undoubtedly existed and at times cooperated has continued to give superficial substance to Mafia mythology. In 1986 a series of trials in New York began and were used by the government to claim victories against the Mafia. The government's efforts were coordinated by Rudolph Giuliani, the U.S. attorney in Manhattan, who brought Anthony 'Fat Tony' Salerno and Anthony 'Tony Ducks' Corallo to trial on racketeering charges in September. These crime bosses, both in their seventies, could not contest evidence that they were part of a 'commission' of New York Mafia families and that they had lucrative stakes in garbage disposal and building trades rackets and that Salerno, in particular, was shown to be a significant influence on the Teamsters Union.

The evidence also showed the limits of 'commission' power. Old men meeting in dingy social clubs could approve new Mafia members and could resolve some of the conflicts among their associates, but they could not direct or control criminal activity in New York, let alone nationally. All five of the commission members were from New York, and it was clear that New York's gangster set-up was very different from the set-up in other parts of the country. They were certainly gangsters, but definitely not part of a tightly knit, all-powerful, national syndicate.

Judging from their recorded conversations, the New Yorkers feared and mistrusted gangsters from other cities. 'I think,' as Salerno told some of his associates in one intercepted telephone conversation in 1984, 'these fuckin' Chicago guys are going to knock my brains in.'[137]

Another conversation this time between Salerno and Corallo, recorded in the Palma Boy Social Club on 12 December 1984, again indicates more insecurity than strength. Salerno is complaining about the lack of respect shown him by a younger gangster:

SALERNO: No, I'll retire, I don't need that.
CORALLO: I know you'll retire, I know you'll retire.
SALERNO: Fuck that shit ... I won't take orders from the guy.
CORALLO: ... the rest of the guys you got around here that you, you, like, that you made.
SALERNO: They'll always be here. Listen, Tony, if it wasn't for me, there wouldn't be no mob left. I made all the guys. And everybody's a good guy. This guy don't realize that? I worked myself. Jeez, how could a man be like that, huh? ... I go over and talk to him ... like, like the first time, the argument I had with him in the barbershop ... that day. So he says, 'Fat Tony ...'

CORALLO: No, I know the way he talks, I've been in meeting with him.

SALERNO: Oh [moans].

CORALLO: ... I seen the way he talks, 'Fuck him, shoot him.'

SALERNO: I can't talk to no one. I used to do anything I wanted with the guy. All of a sudden, since this fuckin' shit with this kid there, when this kid did this fuckin' job there, see.

CORALLO: Tony, he's, he's, he's ... One thing, get rid of them, shoot them, kill them, but then, you know, you can't go on. It's disgusting. Well, here's to your health, and fuck everything ...[138]

In November 1986 both were given 100-year-long prison sentences.

The most recent gangster in the hyped-up tradition of Capone, Luciano, and Costello is John Gotti. From the time of the Salerno/Corallo trials in 1986 Gotti's name kept appearing in the newspapers as the government's most wanted 'Godfather.' Variously called 'Dapper Don,' because of his expensive dress sense, or 'Teflon' Don because of the inability of government charges to stick, Gotti 'strutted through the pages of the New York tabloid,' even to make it to the cover of *Time*.

Gotti's rise and fall undoubtedly had drama. He was born in the South Bronx, the fifth of thirteen children, dropped out of high school at sixteen, and soon began to get arrested. Before 1969, he faced charges of street fighting, drunkenness, car theft, gun possession, and burglary, and served short sentences in county prisons. In 1969 Gotti was sentenced to three years in federal prison for a bungled truck hijacking at Kennedy Airport. In 1973 he took part in the barroom killing of an Irish gangster called James McBratney. The case went to court in Staten Island, where the district attorney generously offered Gotti the chance to plead guilty to the charge of attempted manslaughter. In 1976 he was back on the streets. Towards the end of 1985, Gotti suddenly became boss of the Gambino family after the shooting of 'Big Paul' Castellano. From then the federal authorities pursued him relentlessly, bringing him to trial unsuccessfully twice and recording enough on tape to provide much of the substance for his eventual conviction in 1992.[139]

On the tapes Gotti frequently incriminated himself in murder and racketeering activities. On 17 January 1990 he was also recorded in an apartment above the Ravenite Social Club in Little Italy, Manhattan, at a ceremony in which new members of Cosa Nostra are 'made.' Gotti rebukes some of the others for laughing and then gives a speech about the seriousness of the occasion:

And this is gonna be a Cosa Nostra till I die. Be it an hour from now or be it tonight or a hundred years from now when I'm in jail. It's gonna be a Cosa Nostra. This ain't gonna be a bunch of your friends are gonna be 'friends of ours,' a bunch of Sam's friends are gonna be 'friends of ours.' It's gonna be the way it's gonna be, and a Cosa Nostra. A Cosa Nostra! ... I wanna see an effort. I gotta see an effort for, starting now, a Cosa Nostra. I don't need a guy who come, tell, tell me, 'I feel sorry you got trouble. And I don't mean the cops. I mean the people who can make this a joke. You know what I mean? That's not a fucking joke. And I (inaudible) some guys. See even, even, even some guy, some of the people downstairs now. You know I know whose fucking stomach is rotten. And I know whose stomach ain't rotten. You think I, could smell it. The way a dog senses when a guy has got fear in him, you know what I mean.[140]

On other occasions Gotti made it clear that, for all the oaths of unquestioning loyalty and eternal silence, there was no unity in the world he lived in. His words scarcely reveal a criminal mastermind leading a coherent organization.

Gotti also turned out to be not such a good judge of character as he imagined he was with all the talk of rotten stomachs. One of the men he was addressing was Salvatore 'Sammy Bull' Gravano, whose testimony in 1992 probably did more than the tapes to sway the jury towards convicting him. Gravano admitted to nineteen murders himself and told of Gotti's sponsorship of the killing of Castellano. Castellano had been caught in a brief and expert burst of semi-automatic gunfire from three gunmen outside a Manhattan steakhouse. According to Gravano, he and Gotti drove by shortly after the shooting, ready to finish the job if necessary.

The jury found Gravano's testimony and Gotti's recorded words convincing enough to find Gotti guilty on forty-three federal charges of racketeering, multiple murders, loan-sharking, gambling, and jury tampering. He was guilty, in effect, of being a racketeer in a city full of racketeers.

Gangsters recognize their relative impotence to their lawyers as the following exchange between John Gotti, 'Sammy the Bull' Gravano, and Frank Locascio indicates. The transcript was taken from a conversation they had on 4 January 1990 in an apartment above the Ravenite Social Club in Little Italy, Manhattan. They are talking about their defence lawyers: John Pollok, Gerald Shargel, and Bruce Cutler,

GRAVANO: I hate them -

GOTTI: You know they are 'rats,' er, Sam. And I gotta say, they all want the money up front. And then you get four guys that want sixty-five, seventy-five thousand a piece, up front. You're talking about three hundred thousand in one month, you cocksucker. Take it easy, you mothef ... I don't give a fuck, Frankie ...

LOCASCIO: (Inaudible)

GOTTI: Where you guys going? Once you get hit with a fuckin' (inaudible) – who's on trial? Where we going here? You think I'm going to break my 'Family' for them. There! I go see J. B. I'll go in there, and I'll moon the fuckin' judge, you know what I mean? (Snickers) Kiss my fuckin' ass! ... They go, they get a, a 848, one hundred fifty years. They're in there. A lawyer's living in Greenwich, Connecticut, and their family's at the mercy of [the] welfare department. Hey! You got motherfucker if you want. But that's where it ends, you cocksucker.

GRAVANO: (Inaudible)

GOTTI: ... I paid a hundred thirty-five thousands for their appeal ... That was not for me ... I paid seventeen thousand five hundred for printing. I just got hit with another twelve thousand eight hundred for pri – That's one hundred seventy (inaudible) printing these fuckin' minutes and [to] prepare briefs, whatever you fucking call 'em.

LOCASCIO: You can throw 'em in the fucking toilet.

GOTTI: (Coughs) Yeah.

LOCASCIO: That's how much good they done.

GOTTI: Yeah, right, that's right ... Where the fuck are we going down here? You give these motherfuckers, and what I'm trying to say, that's what I told him last night, 'I gave youse three hundred three hundred thousand in one year. Youse didn't defend me ... What the fuck is your "beef"? "Beef," ya, ya, ya, youse, youse gonna defend me here? Before youse made a court appearance, youse got forty thousand, thirty thousand, and twenty-five thousand. That's without counting John Pollok. He's brand-new on the scene.' They each need backup fuckin' lawyers ... But where are we going here? Youse wanna laugh at us? You know what it felt like? You standing there in the hallway with me last night, and you're plucking me. How are you? Tony Lee's lawyer, but you're plucking me. I'm paying for it. You got Sammy, you got one hand in his pocket. You got both hands in

'Joe Butch's' pocket. Where does it end? Gambino Crime Family? This is the Sharlgel, Cutler, and whattaya call Crime Family. You wanna go steal? You and your fuckin' mother.

GRAVANO: They wind up with the money.

GOTTI: The fuckin' you kidding'? You know what I mean?

LOCASCIO: They're overpriced, overpaid, and, and underperformed.

GOTTI: The only thing I could say is, er, Frankie, is that I get my shit off them.

GRAVANO: I don't even know, I don't even know about underperformed. They just can't win, Frank. They just ain't got the ...

GOTTI: Yeah, but you know why, too, they can't -

GRAVANO: They can't win.

GOTTI: – you know why they can't win, Sammy? They got no fuckin' cohesion. They got no unity. It's like us ...

Later in the conversation, Gotti sums up his likely feelings in the event of his lawyers losing the case: 'Man, you, you just got me a hundred and fifty years. You want me to leave my son destitute and my family destitute. What the fuck is this all about? Was it you that put me on this earth to rob and make you rich and me poor? Go fuck yourself!'[141]

The taped conversations should have ended the idea of an organization with almost unlimited global power. Gotti was 'a cheap thug, and not a particularly bright one,' according to Ronald Goldstock, director of New York's Organized Crime Task Force.[142] But other comments heaped praise on the government for its success and the 'Teflon Don' predictably became 'Velcro Don' as all the federal charges stuck.

For his help to the government, Gravano was rewarded with a greatly reduced prison sentence and a place on the FBI's Witness Protection Program. Gravano's subsequent career, however, took a turn that illuminated some of the problems involved in using bad guys to get bad guys. In February 2000, Gravano was arrested on drug trafficking charges. He had resigned from the Witness Protection Program in 1998, having been relocated close to Phoenix, Arizona. He later told an *Arizona Republic* reporter that life was boring in the state except for the pleasure he got from giving advice to youngsters and from 'wheeling and dealing.' When they arrested Gravano, Arizona authorities charged that the advice he gave to youngsters was not of the 'crime does not pay' kind and that the wheeling and dealing' was in Ecstasy and other drugs. Officers claimed that Gravano served as a mentor to a local white gang known as the 'Devil Dogs' and that the Dogs provided the muscle for a network that trafficked in Ecstasy, marijuana, steroids, and amphetamines.[143]

Evidence from the Mafia trials and from the popular genre of books about Mafia members turned FBI informers suggests a treacherous and often not very well-organized Italian-American underworld. Although some mafiosi found themselves lucrative niches in the legal and illegal economies of these cities, studies in recent decades have made it clear that no one organization or cartel could possibly control illegal markets, notably the illegal markets that concerned Americans most: gambling and drugs.

Italian-American career criminals will continue either to operate separately, compete, or cooperate on occasion. They will also continue to be collectively called the Mafia and be much overrated in films and newspaper articles wishing to applaud government successes. After the Salerno trial of 1986, for example, an editorial in the *New York Times* reflected the government's view with the claim that, 'Society, at last is organized. With convictions like these, it's the mob that's coming apart.'[144] It is as well to remember that similar claims had been made fifty years earlier when Manhattan prosecutor Thomas E. Dewey had convicted Luciano and other New York gangsters. Gangsterism in the meantime has become much more pervasive and destructive, despite the government's many notable successes against the Italian-American variety.

During the trials of Salerno, Gotti, and others, the Department of Justice and the FBI made notable use of the Racketeering Influenced and Corrupt Organizations Act (RICO), as a courtroom tool to develop cases against syndicate leaders. This act, passed as part of the Organized Crime Control Act of 1970, made it illegal to acquire, operate, or receive income from an 'enterprise' through a 'pattern' of racketeering activity. Therefore, any individual or group who commits two or more indictable offences characteristic of organized crime within a ten-year period, as part of a continuing criminal enterprise, can receive extended prison sentences, fines, and be subject to asset forfeitures. RICO was largely thought out by G. Robert Blakey, who claimed that the convictions of Salerno, Corallo, and the like were the equivalent of the Cold War: 'It was sort of like George Kennan's containment policy of the Soviet Union. We tried it and by God it worked.'[145]

No neat and tidy hierarchy of capos, consiglieres, and soldiers can explain the tidal wave of crime and violence associated with gangster-ism and other forms of systematic illegal activity. Had Mafiosi con-trolled organized crime in the United States then Blakey's conceit may have been justified. However, since they only participated in a much larger and more complex criminal environment encompassing both legal and illegal markets, there is no reason to believe that locking up scores of aging patriarchs or Gotti-type upstarts has made even a mar-ginal impact on the extent of organized crime activity in America.

Organized crime was flourishing in the United States before the late nineteenth century waves of Italian immigrants entered the country, and it continues now that generations of the descendents of Italian immigrants have assimilated into the mainstream of American society. Organized crime in the United States is not the result of an alien intru-sion. In reality, as Hank Messick has pointed out, it is 'so interwoven with the political and economic life of the United States that to simplify it is to be dishonest.'[146] The idea of an all-powerful Mafia was and is a dishonest concept.

Corruption as Organized Crime

While politicians and law enforcement officials were clamouring for action against the monolithic Italian conspiracy that was thought to control organized crime, some of the many thousands of corrupt con-spiracies on which successful systematic criminal activity depends were unraveling at local and national levels.

A large part of the organization of gambling in New York City began to be revealed in the late 1960s. In 1966 a police officer named Frank Serpico was invited to join a gambling 'pad': a group of officers in a plain-clothes gambling squad who were paid off by gamblers. Serpico refused to join, as he had refused similar offers in the past. When he reported the existence of the pad to his superior officer, he was told that 'by the time it's all over, they'll find you face down in the East River.' When other superior officers showed a similar lack of interest Serpico took his information to the *New York Times*, which began pub-lishing a series of articles in April 1970.

The newspaper's stories, written by David Burnham, found other officers to support Serpico's allegations and concluded that bookmak-ing and policy play were the main sources of highly systematic corrup-tion in the police department: 'New York gamblers maintain an intimate and financially rewarding relationship with many policemen that at times perverts law enforcement into a system of "licensing" the city's vast gambling industry.'

Each plain-clothes unit had a regular monthly meeting to decide which gamblers to take on and which to drop; those who had become 'too hot' were dropped. Charges to gamblers were based on their take. The policemen interviewed reported that while the basic graft collectors were plain-clothes detectives, the payments circulated up through the department to inspectors and lieutenants. The basic payment to corrupt detectives from gamblers was about $800 to $1,000 a month, with lieutenants sometimes getting double. Some got much more. 'You really are limited only by your own initiative,' one detective said, 'Like you go out and make your own scores. I heard one guy openly boasting that he made $60,000 in the past two years.' The police were still organizing crime in New York City. As one numbers operator later testified: 'You can't work numbers in Harlem unless you pay. If you don't pay, you go to jail ... You go to jail on a frame if you don't pay.'

In October 1971 a commission chaired by former Assistant District Attorney William Knapp held public hearings and revealed the extent of police corruption in New York. Testimony and tape-recorded evidence provided conclusive documentation of highly organized corruption in almost every area of the police department.[147] In the following years, revelations about police corruption in such cities as Chicago, Indianapolis, Albany, Philadelphia, and Washington, DC, indicated that conditions were similar to New York throughout the country.

Frank Serpico, the idealistic young officer who refused to go along with a well-established system, was shot on 3 February 1971 on a drug raid, in what appeared to be a set-up. Serpico survived but thought it advisable to leave the force and the country.[148]

Although high-level officials and politicians are much less likely to be prosecuted for corruption than detectives and patrol officers, studies by John Gardiner and William J. Chambliss highlighted their role. Gardiner in his book entitled *The Politics of Corruption* (1970) focused on the small city of Reading, Pennsylvania. Gardiner describes the relationship between political influence and gambling corruption there. The non-enforcement of the gambling laws was achieved through campaign contributions to help ensure the elections of tolerant officials and regular pay-offs to those elected as well as to the police department. During one prolonged period the mayor had appointed a police chief who shared the graft with him, while a city councilman kept the books for the rackets boss. In Johnstown, also in Pennsylvania, a similar situation existed between the mayor and his police department. Any gamblers who refused to pay off were harassed by raids, while those who cooperated were warned in advance of a 'crackdown.'[149]

William Chambliss researched conditions in the city of Seattle, Washington in depth. He found that the people who ran the organizations that supplied gambling, drugs, prostitution, and pornography were members of the business, political, and law enforcement communi-   ties – not simply members of a criminal society. Seattle's crime network included police officers, politicians, and racketeering businessmen, and relied on coercion or co-option to continue the profitability of the system. Usually intimidation was enough to keep people in line, but Chambliss noted fifteen deaths between 1955 and 1969 that were suspiciously convenient for the network. Eric Tandlin, for example, had developed extensive knowledge of the network's operations in his job as county auditor for the city. Unexpectedly he lost his job to the brother-in-law of the chief of police. Soon after he began drinking heavily and talking. One evening he met a reporter who promised to put him in touch with someone from the attorney general's office. On the following night he was found drowned in the bay. The coroner, who was the brother-in-law of one of the leading network members, could be relied on to diagnose all such deaths as 'accidental.'

The network was disrupted in 1971 when fifty-four public officials were indicted on charges of bribery, corruption, and misuse of office. They included the former county prosecutor, the former chief of police, the president of the city council, the county sheriff, the undersheriff, the head of the county jail, and a former sheriff. Most of those indicted were exonerated or the charges dropped. In the end only two former high-ranking police officials were convicted on charges of conspiracy to promote and allow gambling, bribery, extortion, blackmail, and liquor law violations through a system of police pay-offs. Since most of Seattle's illegal operations continued after the case, Chambliss concluded that a new, even more discreet network shared the profits of illegal enterprises. The faces changed but the system went on.[150]

The national government's efforts against gambling were as futile if not as corrupt as those at local levels. Among the 1970 measures were a series of bills that extended federal jurisdiction over gambling offences further than ever before. Federal prosecutors could now bring cases against gambling operations involving more than five persons and involving either thirty continuous days of operation or $2,000 per day in wagering. The FBI and the Department of Justice were then began an aggressive anti-gambling campaign in many cities with the intention of attacking organized crime where it was supposed to hurt most – in the pocket. Organized crime strike forces, recruited from different agencies, were set up in seventeen cities and initially put most of their resources into investigations of illegal gambling – around 60 per cent of strike force time was taken up with this effort.[151]

However, the FBI and the Department of Justice did not distinguish themselves against gambling – the 'lifeline of organized crime,' to use Richard Nixon's description. By the mid-1970s the strike forces' effort against gambling had subsided with little accomplished despite the enormous expense involved in surveillance. Relatively few prison sentences resulted and those that did were short. In 1982 a former strike force chief told the *Wall Street Journal* that gambling cases had become something to keep the statistics up: 'We would investigate a couple of low grade bookmakers, call them organized crime figures and go after them.'[152]

The most celebrated gambling case involving the FBI began sensationally on 6 May 1971. More than 400 federal agents and local police took part in a Michigan operation, which resulted in 151 people being arrested, including sixteen Detroit police officers. They were charged with being involved in a $15 million-a-year gambling operation. The dragnet had been carried out in thirty-seven Michigan cities. Attorney General John Mitchell announced that this police action was the largest in the nation's history involving gambling. J. Edgar Hoover also crowed about this 'massive blow' against 'the underworld.' The case, however, fell apart in court. In 1974 charges against all 151 defendants were dropped when a federal court ruled that the government had obtained information through illegal wiretaps.[153] With corruption at the local level and ineptitude at the federal level the debacle is representative of the country's crusade against gambling.

By the middle of the 1970s the trend towards decriminalization and legalization of gambling was well established. Pompous lectures about the evils of gambling, delusions about alien conspiracies, and deceptive claims for the potential of anti-gambling measures could no longer halt a re-examination of policy by many state and local authorities looking for ways to increase revenue.

Casino and other forms of gambling in the United States still have racketeering problems. The process of legalization was too slow to prevent gangsters and corrupt public officials from continuing to exploit the ineffectual laws and too late to allow for a smooth transition to a policy of effective regulation and control. Most gangster owners of Las Vegas casinos had sold out to corporate interests by the 1970s. In 1967, for example, Meyer Lansky was thought to have collected $1 million as his share of the sale of the Sands Hotel. This might seem a lot of money, but as Robert Lacey has pointed out, 'the new purchasers had picked themselves a bargain ... 'In the course of the next decade, Las Vegas casinos multiplied many times in value and came to change hands for hundreds of millions of dollars. It was like the legal state lotteries that proliferated in the 1970s and 1980s, instantly dwarfing the numbers games they mimicked. The corporate inheritors of Las Vegas have proved that the legitimate world can run a racket better than any crook.'[154]

A tightening up of accounting regulations and internal control mechanisms did not end the skimming of casino profits by operators and hidden owners. In 1985 a presidential commission listened to tapes of casino executive Carl Thomas, teaching Kansas City gangsters Nick and Carl Civiella and Carl DeLuna how to skim. Before the 1970s, however, the practice was probably much more rife.

In 1976 the state of New Jersey legalized casino gambling in Atlantic City and gangsters were immediately drawn to a potential honey-pot. However, the links between gangsters, the management, and ownership of the resort's giant casinos were to be remote. Gangsters, instead competed to exploit the city's service industries and labour unions. Competition for the city's lucrative peripheral businesses was the likely motive for an upsurge in gangster slayings in nearby areas during the early 1980s. Angelo Bruno, reputedly the top Italian-American racketeer in Philadelphia, was shot dead in March 1980; his successor Philip Testa and several others met similar fates. In December 1980, prominent Atlantic City labour leader John McCullogh was murdered at a time when he was attempting to organize casino security guards. Nicodemo Scarfo, a former associate of Bruno, was thought to be behind many of the slayings. His operations were finished in 1988, when he was convicted of federal racketeering and conspiracy charges and sentenced to sixty-nine years in jail at the age of sixty. Five of Scarfo's associates, including his nephew Philip Leonetti testified against him.[155] In the meantime, state officials did not use the revenues from gambling to improve the quality of life for the residents of Atlantic City. The city used to be 'a slum by the sea,' according to an expert in gambling law speaking in 1994, 'Now it's a slum by the sea with casinos.'[156]

Drug deals, as noted in Chapter 4 involve cash transactions between willing parties and the best evidence is lacking – no injured or robbed citizen complains to the police and serves as a witness. The police therefore develop cases through informers and covert methods, then make arrests, seize evidence, and interrogate. The police control the situation totally until a case reaches the courts, since they alone decide whether an offence has been committed and whether they have a legal case against the suspect. This situation increases the possibility of corruption and de-creases the possibility of controlling this corruption.

Despite the federal government's increasing involvement in drug control from the 1970s, the main responsibility for drug law enforcement remained with the cities. Responding to political demands for action, most city drug squads also expanded in size, most notably in New York, the nation's largest city and the one with the largest drug problem.

The Narcotics Division of the New York Police Department more than doubled during the 1960s so that by the end of the decade more than 500 detectives directed enforcement activity. At the beginning of 1970 Police Commissioner Howard Leary reflected the change of emphasis in the nation's moral crusade by announcing a shift of 200 men from gambling law enforcement to anti-narcotics work and requested 2,000 more to add to his 32,000–man force because, as he said, 'You have to protect people against narcotics in spite of what they think or what they want to do or their feelings toward it. It's something very much like a contagious disease.' All the department's 'energy and effort' should be directed at control of the drug problem, but, Commissioner Leary added, he needed more manpower to do this effectively by making 'arrests, arrests, arrests.'[157]

The early results of Leary's new offensive seemed impressive – drug arrests rose from 27,000 in 1968 to 72,000 in 1970 – but the reality behind these statistics was less impressive. The Knapp commission, already mentioned in connection with the Serpico case, scrutinized police drug-enforcement methods in unprecedented detail. Their investigators found that arrest quotas were largely made up of the same addicts, users, and low-level pushers brought in time and again. Ploys to counter constitutional safeguards and secure convictions were routine.[158] In the course of its investigations the commission became familiar with many corrupt police practices including:

Keeping money and/or narcotics confiscated at the time of arrest or raid.
Selling narcotics to addict-informants in exchange for stolen goods.
Passing on confiscated drugs to police informants for sale to addicts.
'Flaking,' or planting narcotics on an arrested person in order to have evidence of a law violation.
'Padding,' or adding to the quantity of narcotics found on an arrested person in order to upgrade an arrest.
Storing narcotics, needles and other drug paraphernalia in police lockers.
Illegally tapping suspects' telephones to obtain incriminating evidence to be used either in making cases against the suspects, or to blackmail them.
Purporting to guarantee freedom from police wiretaps for a monthly service charge.
Accepting money or narcotics from suspected narcotics law violators as payment for the disclosure of official information.
Accepting money for registering as police informants persons who were in fact giving no information and falsely attributing leads and arrests to them, so that their 'cooperation' with the police may win them amnesty for prior misconduct.
Financing heroin transactions.[159]

These were typical patterns. The commission also learned of individual instances of corrupt conduct, for example:

Determining the purity and strength of unfamiliar drugs they had seized by giving small quantities to addict-informants to test on themselves.
Introducing potential customers to narcotics pushers.
Revealing the identity of a government informant to narcotics criminals.
Kidnapping critical witnesses at the time of trial to prevent them from testifying.

Providing armed protection for narcotics dealers.
Offering to obtain 'hit men' to kill potential witnesses.[160]

Soon after the Knapp commission had completed its report more scandals revealed that the most successful drug squad in the NYPD was also the most corrupt. The Special Investigating Unit (SIU) was an elite squad of detectives that could trace its origins from a much-publicized drugs case known as 'the French Connection,' on which a bestselling book by Robin Moore and two award-winning films were based.

In October 1961 two detectives Eddie Egan and Sonny Grosso stumbled on a ring that imported heroin processed in France. Egan and Grosso were backed up by a small group of the best detectives available, and this group essentially became the SIU. Eventually these detectives arrested several important drug traffickers and seized ninety-seven pounds of heroin – the largest street seizure up to that time. It was thought that a major source of supply had been seriously curtailed and that this end justified some unorthodox police procedures including illegal wiretapping and brutality. Robin Moore represented the case as 'the most crucial single victory to date in the ceaseless, frustrating war against the import of vicious narcotics into our country' and claimed that the case was leading to 'the progressive breakdown of Mafia investment and proprietorship in the United States narcotics market,' despite the fact that it was a sophisticated French smuggling ring that had been disrupted![161]

Although people flocked to see the exciting, filmed account in 1971, the case itself was to be rendered a worthless exercise. In December 1972 the new Police Commissioner Patrick Murphy disclosed that fifty-seven pounds, of the French Connection heroin had been stolen from the property clerk's office. Two-thirds of the largest drug seizure therefore ended up in the New York market anyway. The following February, Murphy concluded from further investigation that about one-fifth of all the heroin and cocaine seized by the New York police between January 1961 and December 1972 had also been stolen – 398 pounds, to which he gave a 'street value' of $73 million. The thieves were never found, but it was thought that they were a relatively small group of policemen who were aware of the drug cases involving large seizures. Also not in the book or the two films relating to the case was the fact that Eddie Egan was fired from the NYPD for failing to deliver narcotics evidence to the property clerk upon completion of court hearings.[162]

The integrity and effectiveness of the SIU had not been in doubt at the end of the 1960s. It was a small group of about seventy detectives who, according to former New York police officer David Durk seized more heroin and other drugs in 1970 than were seized by all customs, border patrol, and federal narcotics agents working throughout the country. SIU detectives had citywide jurisdiction, chose their own targets, and made their own decisions as to whether or not to enforce the law.

Many of the detectives had a lavish lifestyle and an income far exceeding their official income. Some even carried self-addressed, stamped envelopes with them for making 'night deposits' in mailboxes soon after seizing large sums of money. In this book *The Pleasant Avenue Connection*, Durk detailed how money, jewelry, and drugs were stolen from drug dealers and then shared out between lieutenants, sergeants, and detectives, how cases were fixed for a price, and how the unit had become a kind of 'heroin brokerage' in which cases were made to regulate competition by taking out unprotected dealers.[163]

In February 1971 this lucrative world began to come apart. In that month Detective Robert Leuci began a series of meetings with Nicholas Scoppetta, a lawyer with the Knapp commission, and disclosed that he had direct and hearsay evidence of widespread corruption at every stage of the criminal justice system – from assistant district attorneys who routinely told detectives how to perjure themselves and lawyers who offered as much as $15,000 to detectives to fix cases to the judges at the very top. Leuci was persuaded to go undercover in the pursuit of evidence that would stand up in court and to wear a recording device attached to his body while talking to lawyers, prosecutors, private investigators, bail bondsmen, drug traffickers, and his detective colleagues. Leuci had wanted to prove that to focus only on corrupt cops, as the Knapp commission was doing, was to see only a small part of the picture. He was prepared to help convict corrupt police officers, but he intended to work primarily against higher level and better paid criminals within the criminal justice system. He had not intended to work against his friends and partners in the SIU.[164]

Inevitably, the cases against policemen proved to be the easiest to make. Fifty-two of the seventy-odd SIU detectives were convicted of various corrupt practices, and two committed suicide, while Leuci and most of the rest served as the pardoned witnesses. For years top police officials had been explaining away instances of corruption as 'rotten apples' in otherwise sound barrels; after the New York police scandals fewer people believed them.

Robert Leuci stayed with the police force for a few years after the final trial of his SIU partners but, shunned by fellow officers, he took early retirement in July 1981.[165] As we shall see, the convictions obtained with his testimony did not end systematic corruption in the NYPD.

The cities of Detroit, Chicago, Miami, Portland, New Orleans, and New York experienced major scandals during the 1980s and countless individual transgressions have been uncovered in every type of community. The offences involved have a familiar ring: 'skimming' cash and drugs from seizures, pocketing money earmarked for informants, lying to obtain search warrants, committing perjury in court to obtain convictions, selling drugs and guns, accepting bribes, and protecting drug syndicates. In 1982, for example, ten Chicago policemen were convicted on various drug-related charges including aiding and abetting a continuing criminal enterprise and extortion. The violations related to the defendants' three-year symbiotic relationship with two large drug distributorships in which the police officers received substantial sums of money, weapons, and goods in exchange for warning the distributors of impending police raids, delivering drugs seized from other dealers to the favoured syndicates, and threatening competitors.[166]

In March 1991 seven former Los Angeles County sheriff's deputies who were part of an elite narcotics unit were sentenced to up to five years in prison for offences ranging from money laundering to conspiring to skim $1.4 million in seized drug money.[167] Miami police had acquired a reputation for 'pervasive drug trafficking' by the 1980s. According to the city's Chief of Police Clarence Dickson, one out of every ten officers in his force had been involved in drug-related corruption. In one case, policemen were found to have murdered some of their partners as well as drug dealers, and the prosecution concluded that those involved were 'full-time dope dealers who moonlight as police officers.'[168]

In recent years higher level officials have also been prosecuted for drug-related corruption. In 1982 the sheriff, chief of police, a judge, and others from Henry County, Georgia, were convicted of aiding and abetting smugglers when landing at an airstrip and 'providing an escort service' into Atlanta. Southern sheriffs, in particular, have been revealed to be as involved in drug trafficking as their predecessors were in bootlegging. Most notable is Sheriff Howard Leroy Hobbs of

Harrison County, Mississippi, who was sentenced to twenty years in prison in May 1984 following a guilty plea to a variety of drug-related offences. Hobbs had been elected on a promise to crack down on drugs and corruption. Also in 1984, Frank Robin of the U.S. Attorney's office in Houston, Texas, was sentenced to ten years for seeking $200,000 in exchange for leaking information to suspects in a major drug case.[169]

'Reverse stings,' in which undercover officers sell drugs to buyers, have become popular with police departments in recent years, opening up new potential for abuse and legal confusion. In February 1992 Sheriff Richard Dee Thompson of Presidion County, Texas, pleaded guilty to conspiracy to import cocaine into the United States from Mexico. Thompson claimed that he intended to use the 2,400 pounds of cocaine in a 'reverse' sting to catch drug dealers.[170] In 1989 Sheriff Nick Navarro of Broward County, Florida, began a program that involved manufacturing crack cocaine by boiling water and baking soda with cocaine powder. Undercover deputies then took the crack to school zones and lured buyers inside, where they could arrest people on a charge carrying a mandatory minimum three-year prison term. Sheriff's department chemist Randy Hilliard admitted to cooking 13,000 crack rocks over a three-year period and estimated that a thousand people were arrested in these sting operations. On some nights the crack was so popular that the undercover deputies selling the drugs herded buyers to jail in paddy wagons. An assistant public defender said that 'It was like cattle going to slaughter.' In early 1992 an appellate court decided that the stings were illegal and that all those convicted using the sheriff's homemade rocks should be released.[171]

The DEA itself has not had the problem of wholesale corruption on the scale of its predecessor, the FBN, but in August 1982 Jeffrey Scharlatt, an agent attached to the Miami office, became the first DEA agent to be indicted on charges of smuggling and distribution. Scharlatt was a top agent who a year earlier had helped direct an undercover DEA operation code-named 'Grouper' that led to 155 indictments and 127 convictions. At the same time, however, it was charged that Scharlatt was smuggling marijuana, obstructing justice, and accepting bribes. In 1984 another DEA man, Harold Lawrence, was convicted of selling drugs and received a five-year sentence. Lawrence decided to supply the DEA's Internal Security Department with the names of three agents, who, he said, had sold up to $1 million of marijuana to smugglers in 1973. Subsequently all three, one a DEA agent, the others U.S. Customs Service agents, resigned, but none could be prosecuted because the statute of limitations had expired. According to a Justice Department official, this affair was 'not a one-time incident, and many agents are concerned it has gone on and on and on.' In April 1991 there was evidence that their concern was justified when Darnell Garcia, a DEA agent for ten years, was convicted on one count each of conspiracy, theft of heroin, distribution of heroin, and two counts of money laundering. Garcia was described by an associate as a karate expert who could 'throw his gun away and rip your head off.'[172]

Michael Levine, one of the DEA's most effective undercover agents, confirmed this impression of increasing corruption after he left the agency in disgust in 1989. He wrote that he personally had known many of his 'colleagues, who had gone bad and every one of them was the last guy in the world you would have suspected. The past decade has brought with it the worst epidemic of corruption in the history of law enforcement – and almost all of it related to our war on drugs.'[173]

The temptation of easy money has consistently proved too strong to resist. After the scandals of the 1960s and 1970s, the New York Police Department assigned over 350 officers full-time to anti-corruption duties, but the problem of endemic corruption in drug enforcement persisted despite this effort to police the police. A scandal in the early 1990s led Mayor David Dinkins to appoint a commission headed by Deputy Mayor Milton Mollen to find out how serious and widespread the police corruption problem was. The commission found that there were significant pockets of officers serving in poor neighbourhoods around the city who 'seek out sources of money, drugs and guns, and often employ sophisticated and organized methods to carry out their criminal activities.' A police officer called Michael Dowd testified that it was his practice to race to radio calls outside his area because he knew that if he got there first he could simply confiscate whatever drugs or guns he found in the house of a drug dealer for himself. Dowd and a crew of other police officers would systematically steal money and drugs from cocaine dealers in Brooklyn and then resell the drugs in Long Island. At the same time his crew had a deal with a local drug dealer to protect him and harass his competitors in exchange for $8,000 a week. As a result of his activities Dowd was able to buy a $35,000 Corvette and three homes in Long Island.

The commission also found that citizens could and would make complaints about police behaviour, but in New York the practice was to harass anyone who did so and crumple up and bin anything written down. As another officer testified, 'Who's going to catch us? We're the police. We're in charge.'[174] The commission concluded that a culture of corruption existed in the New York City Police Department:

> The problem of police corruption extends far beyond the corrupt cop. It is a multi-faceted problem that has flourished in parts of our City not only because of opportunity and greed, but because of a police culture that exalts loyalty over integrity; because of the silence of honest officers who fear the consequences of 'ratting' on another cop no matter how grave the crime; because of willfully blind supervisors who fear the consequences of a corruption scandal more than corruption itself; because of the demise of the principle of accountability that makes all commanders responsible for fighting corruption in their commands; because of a hostility and alienation between the police and community in certain precincts which breeds an 'Us versus Them' mentality; and because for years the New York City Police Department abandoned its responsibility to insure the integrity of its members.[175]

These findings could have been applied to police forces across the country.

As Mike Davis has detailed in his book *City of Quartz* (1990), the Los Angeles Police Department has acquired a reputation for brutality and institutionalized racism since the 1960s. From 1978 Daryl Gates, who shaped his 8,300–strong force into a paramilitary-style organization, modelled on the U.S. marines, headed the LAPD. In his first year on the job, a thirty-nine-year-old African-American woman was shot twelve times by LAPD police officers. She had been in default of her gas bill. Gates explained it away, as he did all other such incidents. His most famous excuse came in 1982 when he suggested that young African Americans died more easily from chokehold in custody than 'normal people.'

Gates was police chief when a derivative of cocaine called 'crack' hit the headlines. When early efforts failed to stem gang violence, Gates escalated the police response and launched Operation Hammer, in which police squads up to 1,000–strong swarmed through south-central Los Angeles. On 5 April 1988 they shot down an unarmed African-American teenager who was allegedly reaching into his trouser pockets. A few weeks later they poured rounds of ammunition into an alleged 'rock house' for selling crack and killed an eighty-one-year-old retired construction worker. There was a strong suspicion that they had the wrong address, but no disciplinary action was taken after the LAPD offered the explanation that the gangs were now paying off old people to use their homes as sales points.

In August 1988 Southwest Los Angeles police raided a group of apartments where drug trafficking was suspected. The *Los Angeles Times* reported: 'Residents were punched and kicked while police officers spray painted walls with slogans such as "LAPD Rules." Residents also accused officers of throwing washing machines into bathtubs, pouring bleach over clothes, and smashing walls and furniture with sledgehammers and axes. Damage was so extensive that the Red Cross offered disaster assistance – a service they usually offer in the wake of major fires, floods and earthquakes. Thirty-two residents were taken to the police station, forced to whistle the cops' favourite TV tune, and then beaten up. As a result of all this a small quantity of marijuana was found on two non-resident teenagers.'[176]

Operation Hammer continued, but mainly to bring in drunks, delinquent motorists, and teenage curfew violators. By 1990, 50,000 suspects had been picked up; most of these were released without charges.[177]

Another of Gates's innovations was the 'School Buy' program intended to combat drug selling in schools. In 1988 young undercover cops, often chosen for their sexuality and attractiveness, infiltrated high schools and enticed students to sell them drugs. They were particularly effective in entrapping backward students who were being approached for possibly the first time in their lives.[178]

Despite all these and many more instances of unethical or brutal police activity, Gates kept the support of the city's white power structure and therefore his job. He did this at least partly with the support of a little-known unit in the LAPD called the Organized Crime Intelligence Unit (OCIU) which used an elaborate spy network and illegal surveillance devices to collect information on southern Californian politicians, union leaders, Hollywood stars, professional athletes, and journalists. The idea according to former OCIU agent Mike Rothmiller was to collect this information, which was often no more than gossip, because it might prove useful to Gates or other top policemen. Rothmiller's explanation for Gates's survival as head of the LAPD despite a great deal of negative publicity during his years in office is as follows: 'He seemed to possess some mysterious key to personal survival. But the key was no mystery to anyone in OCID ... its agents spent countless man-hours in preparation for just such an emergency. Because of OCID, the LAPD had secret files on the gay council member hiding in the closet and on the council member who was sleeping with an aide. The department had intelligence files on questionable deals and campaign funding and a mountain of other embarrassing, sticky business. As soon as someone declared candidacy, a full-scale investigation began. OCID had files on everything and everybody that counted.'[179]

The squad was instructed not to make arrests, since that would attract attention and its commanders had minimal interest in or understanding of organized criminal activity of any kind. On one occasion an OCID detective reported about an Italian named Albino Luciani, with worldwide connections, who had just assumed a position of even greater power in an organization that conducted immense money transfers, maintained a chain of wineries and other investments, and apparently paid little or no taxes on its immense holdings. The detective was told to, 'Stay on this,' and build up a file on the man. He did not let on that it was all a joke based on *Godfather*-mythology. The man's new name was Pope John Paul I![180]

Gates eventually left the job in June 1992, claiming that he had done 'an outstanding job.' Others thought he had made a significant contribution to a breakdown in non-white community support in an increasingly violent and racially divided city.

The most recent LAPD scandal began in 1998, when large amounts of cocaine went missing from the property office of the Rampart station. Officer Rafael Perez was arrested and later convicted of stealing the cocaine. Perez's testimony detailed many of the corrupt practices of the department's elite anti-gang Community Resources Against Street Hoodlums (CRASH) units. CRASH units in some ways acted like the gangs they were supposed to be policing, terrorizing black and hispanic neighbourhoods. Officers routinely stole drugs from dealers and then used prostitutes as their own dealers. As a result of the revelations nearly 100 convictions of gang members have been overturned. Critics have claimed that the cost of legal actions from victims could bankrupt the city.[181]

In 1972 a special prosecutor, Maurice Nadjari, was appointed to find out how high the corruption went in the New York criminal justice system – a difficult task since bribes, deals, and favours take place behind closed doors and between allies and willing partners. Therefore, to test the integrity of the system, Nadjari's agents worked undercover, used wiretaps and recording devices, and even staged a mock robbery. Judges and prosecutors were thus subjected to the same methods routinely used to arrest and convict less well-connected people. By the end of the first eighteen months of his investigation Nadjari had indicted a number of high-ranking public officials and won a string of major courtroom victories, including the conviction of a district attorney. But by the end of 1975 many of his most impressive investigations had begun to disintegrate under the harsh legal tests imposed by the appeals courts. Convictions were reversed, indictments were dismissed. Nadjari charged that the closer he got to the hard core of corruption – 'the small band of franchised corrupters who manipulate all of us' – the more he was abused and pressured to resign. In the end no judges, district attorneys, or prominent people finished up behind bars, although the prosecutor had used the 'same tools and means of law enforcement' as in 'investigations and prosecutions of killers, robbers, rapists and drug pushers.' The only difference was that Nadjari's targets had power. Nadjari was removed as special prosecutor on 29 June 1976.[182]

During the 1980s there was a more successful investigation of criminal justice by the Department of Justice, code-named Operation Greylord. This was an undercover operation to detect corruption in the Cook County, Illinois, court system, the largest court system in the nation. It produced indictments against eighty-eight judges, lawyers, police officers, and court personnel on charges including racketeering, bribery, and tax and mail fraud. One of the judges eventually convicted had accepted bribes totaling $400,000 and eight cars. Going undercover was necessary, because despite years of corruption, no lawyers had ever come forward to report the malfeasance. According to John Jiganti, president of the Chicago Bar Association, even honest lawyers decided not to use the internal mechanisms for reporting fraud, because they knew they did not work.[183]

Legislative corruption at the national level was dramatically illustrated in 1979 when Federal Bureau of Investigation agents used videotaping and eavesdropping techniques to show some of the ways political power could be used for illegal financial gain. In Abscam – short for Arab Scam – agents disguised themselves as the financial representatives of oil rich Arabs and offered politicians money for their help in criminal activity. The politicians were then videotaped stuffing wads of cash into their suit pockets; one of them asking, 'Does it show?'

Robert W. Greene wrote an account of Abscam in his book called *The Sting Man* (1981) based on the part played by an FBI informant Mel

Weinberg. According to Weinberg, Mayor Angelo J. Errichetti of Camden, New Jersey, was one of the first to become enthusiastically involved in Abscam. His schemes for securing Arab money included offers of hot diamonds, guns and munitions, forged certificates of deposit, counterfeit money, stolen paintings, leasing contracts, municipal garbage contracts, unregistered boats for drug running, use of Port Camden to unload drugs, Atlantic City zoning changes, and a list of thirteen bribe-taking state and city officials, as well as five U.S. congressmen and a senator.[184] The senator was later convicted of accepting a hidden interest in a Virginia titanium mine in exchange for promises to obtain government contracts for the venture and to introduce a private immigration bill for an Arab sheik who was actually an FBI undercover agent. He did not, however, lose his $45,000 a year pension.[185]

Many attempts have been made to curb institutionalized corruption in the United States, but the corrupt have always managed to circumvent earlier reforms. The list of American corruption scandals can go on indefinitely, and in recent years there has been far greater exposure of corrupt activities in the executive and legislative branches of local, state, and federal government. Every corruption scandal reveals that 'respectable' members of society are as involved in organized criminal activity as they were when organized crime was first conceptualized. This helps to explain a continued need for the powerful in American society to keep corruption peripheral to people's understanding of organized crime.

The Reagan Era and the Pluralist Revision of Organized Crime

On 14 October 1982 President Ronald Reagan announced a plan intended to 'end the drug menace and cripple organized crime.' As he announced this plan the president claimed that 'no weapon against organized crime had proved more effective or more important to law enforcement than the investigations carried on by the Kefauver Committee and the McClellan Committee in the 1950s.' On the basis of this Reagan announced the creation of a panel of 'distinguished Americans from diverse backgrounds and professions with practical experience in criminal justice and combating organized crime.' This nationwide investigation was to last for three years, 'analyze and debate the data it gathers,' and 'hold public hearings on the findings.' Apart from legislative recommendations, the intention was 'to heighten public awareness and knowledge about the threat of organized crime and mobilize citizen support for its eradication.'[186] On 28 July 1983, Reagan signed Executive Order 12435 and thus formally established the President's Commission on Organized Crime to be chaired by Judge Irving R. Kaufman and composed of eighteen other men and women, mainly from the law enforcement community.

The commission's stated intention was to investigate the power and activities of 'traditional organized crime' and 'emerging organized crime groups.' By then it was clear that gangsters from every racial and ethnic origin were involved in systematic criminal activity and that making organized crime synonymous with Mafia was no longer viable. There was a need to adapt Mafia mythology to a new age.

At the first hearing in November 1983 the nation's top law enforcement officers articulated a new federal perspective. The Kaufman commission's lack of independence from the Reagan administration was illustrated from this first hearing. The main speakers were Attorney General William French Smith, FBI Director William Webster, and DEA Administrator Francis Mullen, and each identified 'traditional organized crime' exclusively with Italian Americans or 'the La Cosa Nostra.' They all made it clear, however, that organized crime was not synonymous with any one group and stressed the importance of 'emerging groups,' mentioning motor-cycle gangs, prison gangs, and 'foreign-based' organizations.

At the hearing no doubts were expressed about the essential correctness of the law enforcement approach to organized crime control based on long-term investigation, undercover operations, informants, wiretaps, and asset forfeiture. Successes against 'traditional organized crime' and the need to 'stay in front' of the emerging 'cartels' were emphasized throughout. Drug trafficking was identified as the most profitable organized crime activity, and speakers stressed that this was the problem that most needed addressing.[187]

After three years of selective investigation of its identified problem areas of drugs, labour racketeering, money laundering, and gambling, the commission added very little to the government line outlined at the first hearing. It did, however, help in the effort to adapt Mafia mythology to a new age by adding its weight to an idea already circulating in the media. The Mafia, according to the new conventional wisdom, had once been the dominant force in U.S. organized crime, but it was now being challenged by several crime 'cartels,' 'emerging' among Asian, Latin American, and other groups. As Gary W. Potter argues in his book *Criminal Organizations* (1994), this was an adaptation of the alien conspiracy interpretation rather than an overhaul in official thinking about organized crime. The argument remained the same: forces outside of mainstream American culture threaten otherwise morally sound American institutions. Potter described the new official consensus as the 'pluralist' revision of the alien conspiracy interpretation.[188]

Although the conduct of the commission's hearings and the tone of its recommendations were generally uncritical of the government's organized crime control policies, half of the commission's eighteen members did admit the inadequacy of the three-year effort. They co-authored a statement that concluded:

> The true history of the President's Commission on Organized Crime is a saga of missed opportunity. Poor management of time, money and staff has resulted in the Commission's leaving important issues unexamined, most notably the questions of the effectiveness of federal and state anti-organized crime efforts ...
>
> We have failed to make a complete national and region-by-region analysis of organized crime. Further we have not done an adequate job in assessing the effectiveness of the Federal Government's response to organized crime. Neither have we assessed the nature and quality of state and local responses to the problem. These failures point up the desperate need for the systematic collection and analysis of organized crime intelligence from all corners of the nation.[189]

Despite these admissions, the federal and state governments took up most of the commission's recommendations. On 3 March 1986 the report on narcotics trafficking was issued. 'The ultimate goal of the nation's drug policy,' the commission stated, ' is the effective suppression of drug abuse in the United States.' To this end were the following recommendations:

> The Attorney General should direct 'the formulation of a long range national offensive against drug supply and demand, including long term funding proposals.'
>
> The cost of this nation's anti-drug efforts can be subsidized to a great extent by the seizure and forfeiture of drug traffickers' assets. That portion of the Federal Government's asset forfeiture fund derived from drug cases should be devoted exclusively to anti-drug programs ...

Domestic drug law enforcement efforts directed at high-level trafficking groups should be supplemented by and integrated with enforcement efforts directed at lower-level trafficking groups and street-level drug activity ...

To respond effectively to the drug problem, state and local jurisdictions will have to increase expenditures for such critical resources as prison facilities, increased manpower, and sophisticated equipment.

... The President should direct the heads of all Federal agencies to formulate immediately clear policy guidelines, including suitable drug testing programs, expressing the utter unacceptability of drug abuse by federal employees. State and local governments and leaders in the private sector should support unequivocally a similar policy that any and all use of drugs is unacceptable. Government contracts should not be awarded to companies that fail to implement drug programs, including suitable drug testing. No Federal, state, or local government funds should go directly or indirectly to programs that counsel 'responsible' drug use or condone illicit drug use in any way. Laws in certain states which 'decriminalized' the possession of marijuana constitute a form of such condonation, and should be reconsidered.[190]

In sum, the commission concluded that the government's basic approach to the problem was sound but needed a harder line on all fronts: more wiretaps, more informants, and more undercover agents in order to get more convictions, which would require more prisons. The commission's only real function was to maintain public support for existing government policies. Witnesses who might have pointed out the deficiencies of this approach were not consulted. The American people, by then, had been conditioned to see organized crime as groups of separate and distinct gangsters rather than organized crime as the more fluid, varied, and integrated phenomenon portrayed by the earlier commentators. The commission therefore did not consider corruption within the system as part of the problem of organized crime, and by the 1980s they did not have to – people had been conditioned to ask the wrong questions.

The Kaufman commission's understanding of organized crime was representative of a pervasive dumbing down since the early conceptualizations discussed at the beginning of this chapter. These had focused on defects in U.S. laws and institutions and found them responsible for America's organized crime problems. Kaufman's group focused on different groups of criminals and found them responsible for America's organized crime problems. The logic of early conceptualizations suggested the repeal of unworkable laws and the honest and effective enforcement of the rest. The Kaufman group's restricted understanding of organized crime allowed them to avoid confronting faults in U.S. laws and institutions, leaving only recommendations of tougher and more intrusive policing of unworkable laws.

Chapter 6

Industrial and Corporate Racketeering, 1950 to the Present

Chapter 6 surveys organized criminal activity in the labour and corporate sectors of the U.S. economy during the latter half of the twentieth century. After the Second World War, the United States entered one of its longest periods of growth and prosperity, based on increasing industrial output and increasing consumer demand. For twenty-five years the U.S. economy grew at an average rate of 3.5 per cent and the gross national product rose from just under $210 billion in 1946 to $285 billion in 1950, $504 billion in 1960, and close to $1 trillion in 1970.[1]

The trend towards economic concentration that began in the late nineteenth century continued. By the end of the 1980s the 100 largest U.S. corporations controlled a larger proportion of all manufacturing assets than was controlled by the 200 largest firms in 1950 or the 1,000 largest in 1940. Less than one per cent of U.S. manufacturers held about 88 per cent of all industrial assets and earned about 90 per cent of all profits, and the 100 largest manufacturing firms received a much larger share of all profits than all 370,000 other manufacturing firms put together.[2]

Most of the wealth generated by this enormously productive corporate system went to a relatively small elite, and as the tax and welfare spending cuts of the 1980s took effect, this elite got even richer as the American poor became poorer. During the decade, while the top fifth of American families earned 27 per cent more and the top 1 per cent saw their incomes double, the incomes of the bottom fifth fell by 13 per cent. By 1989 the top 1 per cent (834,000 households with $5.7 trillion in net worth) was worth more than the bottom 90 per cent (84 million households with $4.8 trillion in net worth).[3]

Despite this concentration of wealth at the top and deepening pool of poverty among the excluded, more Americans were employed and were paid more than ever before. Thus, they had more money to spend. In the 1950s, per capital real income rose by 15 per cent; in the 1960s by 32 per cent.[4] Middle-class Americans once again became confident consumers as memories of the Great Depression began to fade. They bought goods and services on a scale never imagined before.

Economic growth and industrial production had environmental and occupational costs that were scarcely acknowledged during the 1950s and 1960s. Until federal and state governments began to enact environmental and occupational protection legislation during the 1970s, few corporations were concerned about the health and safety of workers, consumers, and local communities. Since then, there have been improvements, but governmental controls are evaded. Corporations still produce goods that can be dangerous to consumers, in conditions that can be dangerous to workers, and they still pollute air, water, and soil on a wide scale.[5]

The second half of the twentieth century also saw trade union power eroded. New Deal reforms and wartime labour scarcity had seemed to put labour in a strong position in American society, but the movement was soon put in its place by the Taft-Hartley Act of 1947. Taft-Hartley outlawed the closed shop, gave employers the privilege of suing unions for broken contracts and for damages brought about by strikes, forbade union donations to political campaigns, and empowered the president to seek an injunction to put an eighty-day moratorium on any strike that would, in his opinion, 'if permitted to continue, imperil the nation's health or safety.'[6]

AFL and CIO leaders blustered at the new law, but as Tom Kemp notes in his book *The Climax of Capitalism* they had 'no taste for confrontation with the state.' The postwar unions, he continued, were ruled by a conservative bureaucracy that 'settled for bargaining within each industry to win wage increases and other concessions which would keep their members happy ... Management expected union officials to police their own members so that industrial discipline could be maintained ... The big unions, including those of the CIO, had become bargaining agents for a largely passive membership looking to the unions to win periodic wage rises and better fringe benefits. Mainstream unionism, though now including the big mass production industries, in other respects was back where it had been before the great CIO organizing drive had begun.'[7] The labour movement as a whole remained mainly content with its subordinate role in a corporate-dominated society, while individual unions remained vulnerable to racketeering.

Labour Gone Wrong

In Hostetter and Beesley's 1933 analysis, industrial racketeering consisted of five distinct but interdependent elements: business, labour unionism, politics, lawyers, and criminals. All five of these elements were still involved in the problem after the Second World War, although in less direct and visible ways than before. In addition, more accountants, brokers, and public officials added their skills to the organization of labour-management corruption. As the problem became more complex, however, attempts to analyse it became less sophisticated. From the 1950s, attention was focused on just two elements of the problem: labour union racketeers and labour leaders such as Jimmy Hoffa of the Teamsters who dealt with them. Businessmen, politicians, public officials, accountants, brokers, and lawyers were from time to time excoriated, but essentially they were let off the hook. This chapter focuses on aspects of the postwar history of two unions already discussed in Chapter 3, the International Longshoreman's Association (ILA) and the Teamsters, and governmental responses to the problem of labour-management racketeering.

Conditions on the New York waterfront did not improve after the Second World War. However, continued revelations about violence and corruption and frequent industrial action by the discontented rank and file brought a belated response from Governor Thomas Dewey in November 1951. He issued an order to his State Crime Commission to investigate the waterfront. More than 700 witnesses were questioned in private sessions and 188 were selected for public hearings. Although the commission steered the hearings away from political explanations for the continued existence of waterfront gangsterism and corruption, it did expose the venality of Joe Ryan and the ILA and could not disguise the fact that the employers were the chief beneficiaries of gangster control of the union.[8]

James C. Kennedy, president of a trucking and stevedoring firm called Daniels and Kennedy, testified that he had paid $1,500 a year in bribes to Ryan. When Kennedy's testimony was pointed out to the union boss, Ryan explained that he used such gifts 'to fight Communism.' Ryan was also found to be taking money from union funds apparently for the same cause but, in fact, the money was also used to subsidize an extravagant lifestyle.

Ryan was indicted on various charges but managed to stay out of prison. The only union official convicted was Ed Florio, who got an eighteen and a half month sentence for falsely denying that he was paid thousands of dollars in bribes by stevedoring company executives for overlooking irregular working conditions.

Frank W. Nolan, president of Jarka Corporation, the largest stevedoring firm in the country, testified that he had given W.W. Wells, president of the Isthmian Steamship Company, two $10,000 U.S. Treasury bonds. Nolan also admitted directly bribing other steamship company officials to gain their contracts. A much lower level of payments went to gangsters. N.J. Palihnich, a Jarka vice-president, admitted that he paid Anthony (Joe the Gent) Giantomasi, an ILA thug, $100 a month because 'he was always available' to sort out labour problems. The John J. McGrath Company made secret payments to a racketeer called Harold Bowers. The Pittston Stevedoring Company paid a total of $1,250 in 1951 to Vincent 'Barney Cockeye' Brown and Anthony 'Tony Cheese' Marchitto, ILA business agents, for supplying labour gangs at $50 per ship.[9]

William J. McCormack, Ryan's closest ally among the employers and a leading waterfront political and economic power, owned four firms that failed to account for nearly $1 million paid out in 'petty cash' between 1947 and 1951. The hearings suggested that most of this cash was for the purposes of bribery in a business world that had no place for democracy, union or political, but made room for a host of rackets.[10]

In the summer of 1953, acting on recommendations of the State Crime Commission, Governor Dewey and Governor Alfred Driscol of New Jersey obtained state and federal legislation enabling establishment of the Bi-State Waterfront Commission with dictatorial powers to regulate longshore hiring. The bill provided for state-controlled hiring halls and permanent registration of all dockworkers. This became the basis for a blacklist of union militants and any suspected communists; in other words, it did legally what gangsters had been doing illegally for years.

The Bi-State Commission did not end gangsterism and corruption on the waterfront, but merely confused the issue. The longshoremen

needed an honest union but the ILA emerged victorious from a jurisdictional battle with an American Federation of Labor (AFL) rival, the
International Brotherhood of Longshoremen (IBL). The election to
decide between the two unions in December 1953 was marked by knifings and beatings and by gangster foremen herding workers to the
polls to vote for the 'right' side. On the eve of the election, an independently minded foreman, Michael Brogan, who had expressed a prefer-
ence for the IBL, was murdered. The police asked for information from
longshoremen on the dockside itself in full view of gangster foremen,
ensuring that the investigation was bungled from the start. The
reforms failed to change the situation on the waterfront; labour was
still controlled by gangsters. The ILA, however, now had the Bi-State
Commission as a ready-made opponent and could appear militant
while remaining in cohoots with the employers.

Waterfront racketeering became so stable that gangsters could
bequeath power to the next generation. Anthony 'Tough Tony' Anastasio, for example, headed the powerful Brooklyn ILA Local 1814
throughout the 1950s, appointing his son-in-law Anthony Scotto to a
series of union jobs. In March 1963 Anastasio died and Scotto took over
the local and was soon made a vice-president of the ILA. Scotto
became active in politics, and for a while had the image of an honest,
committed representative of port employees. However, on 15 November 1979 Scotto was convicted of taking $200,000 in a pattern of illegal
pay-offs. A representative of the McGrath Company had approached
Scotto in an attempt to reduce the costs of longshoremen's compensation claims, which were 'exploding.' Claimants were apparently feign-
ing or exaggerating injuries, going to lawyers who would process the
claims with the Labor Department and doctors who fraudulently certified to the accuracy of the false claims. The gangsters who had allegedly set the racket up in the first place were costing the company more
than $1 million a year and bringing it close to bankruptcy. However,
once Scotto began receiving his money the figure began a downward
trend, from $1.4 million in 1974 to $302,000 in 1976. In 1980 Scotto was
given a five-year prison sentence for the offence. The McGrath Company survived, but another firm with a long-established reputation for
paying off, Pittston Stevedoring Company, went out of business
because it could not get the insurance to cover injuries to its workmen.[11]

From the 1960s the ILA began to practice its extortionist methods
further south. The union sent down George Barone, Douglas Rago,

James Vanderwyde, William Boyle, and Fred J. Field, Jr, to Florida in the mid-1960s as organizers. All of these, however, were either criminals or had close criminal contacts and proved to be more interested in organizing corrupt schemes with Gulf Coast maritime executives than organizing to represent their members.

In 1975 the FBI began an investigation into the patterns of racketeering throughout the maritime industry on the Gulf Coast. They found that corruption was not limited to union leaders, but involved a system of kickbacks among businessmen and 'illegal payoffs to union officials by businessmen who found it more advantageous to cooperate with corrupt union officials than with law enforcement.' In particular, the FBI's investigated bids on a container service contract with the Zim American Israeli Shipping Company of New York and Haifa, Israel. Zim was to ship Ford cars for the Ford Export Corporation of Newark, New Jersey, from the east Coast to Japan. A government report would later describe the Zim contract – 'and the complex plotting that surrounded it' – as a 'microcosm of the shipping industry and a perfect example of the far-reaching effects of waterfront corruption.' The FBI's investigation revealed:

A substantial kickback being paid to a union official who promised to obtain business for a shipping company at a certain port; Fraudulent billings and inflated costs to absorb the kickback; The manner in which labour racketeers paid off company officials who responded by giving the racketeers special treatment; Shipping companies' practice of absorbing the cost of illicit payments by inflating bills and passing the added expense on to the consumer; The fact that shipping companies not wishing to make kickbacks were precluded from competition in a free marketplace; ... The failure by company officials and other participants in the scheme to keep accurate records and pay taxes on their incomes. Shipping companies are perfectly willing to accept union payoffs as a cost of doing business and only the exposure of their own employees (in the) scheme generated any reaction. This clearly demonstrates ... the acceptance and pervasiveness of payoff and kickback schemes on the waterfront.

The FBI investigation resulted in an impressive series of convictions of ILA officers, including the New Yorkers, but, according to the judgment of George R. Havens, chief investigator in the state's attorney's office in Miami, 'a genuine clean-up of corruption on the waterfront had not occurred.' Most of the federal agents were dispersed throughout the country and a different set of gangsters, union leaders, and company officials made new arrangements.[12]

In 1957 the Senate established a Select Committee on Improper Activities in the Labor or Management Field, appointing John McClellan of Arkansas its chairman and Robert Kennedy its chief counsel. The committee had little difficulty showing that corruption and racketeering permeated U.S. industry and business. The first hearings examined the extent and organization of corruption in Portland, Oregon, and featured the testimony of the city's most prominent racketeer James Elkins. Elkins had been involved in various illegal enterprises for decades and had a reputation for brutality. He decided to talk to the committee after it had become clear to him that his local power was threatened after Portland's district attorney, who happened also to be his father-in-law and protector, Murray Gamrath, had moved on to become chief of detectives for Seattle's sheriff's office. Elkins testified that he had originally been approached in 1954 by two Seattle gangsters, Tom Maloney and Joseph McLaughlin, and invited to join a new combination which, with Teamster Union support, would control 'vice' in Portland. It was intended that Elkins would use his muscle and connections and, in return, get a percentage of the profits.

The key to any successful illegal enterprise was official protection, and with this in mind the Seattle gangsters decided to encourage support for William Langley, a candidate to succeed District Attorney Gamrath, in the 1955 election. The Portland Teamsters, led by Clyde Crosby, duly supported Langley's subsequent campaign and victory. After he took office, Langley was referred to jokingly as 'Honest Abe.'

Maloney and McLaughlin then began to take over the city's pinball operations, setting up a distribution company and using Teamster pickets to stop deliveries of bread, milk, beer, and other commodities to cafeteria and bar owners who failed to cooperate. Having accomplished this, the two gangsters also began to distribute punchboards, which had been illegal until Crosby succeeded in persuading the city council to pass an ordinance making it legal to have punchboards on the premises of stores and bars.[13]

Elkins testified that he was happy to go along with these developments until attempts were made to move into the field of prostitution. He then came into conflict with Frank Brewster, head of the Western Conference of Teamsters. Brewster had told him: 'I make chiefs of police and I break chiefs of police. I have been in jail and I have been out of jail. There is nothing that scares me.' Referring to the two Seattle emissaries, he said, 'If you bother my two boys, if you embarrass my two boys, you will find yourself wading across Lake Washington with a pair of concrete boots.'[14] Brewster denied he had said this, but he was unable to refute evidence produced by the committee that showed that Maloney and McLaughlin's expenses had been paid by his union.

After the talk with Brewster, Elkins decided to record subsequent conversations with Maloney, Crosby, and others on tape as protection from the alliance of gangsters, Teamsters, and public officials. He felt that the tapes would add credibility to what would otherwise be an unlikely story. Seventy hours of tape were eventually turned over to Wallace Turner and William Lambert, reporters for the Portland *Oregonian*, and these produced a series of articles on the whole affair.[15]

No one went to prison as a result of all this. Frank Brewster was exposed as a labour leader who helped himself to much of the union's funds. Crosby, Maloney, McLaughlin, and Elkins faced a variety of charges, all of which were later dropped. Some time after that Elkins died as a result of the type of car accidents that arouse suspicions. District Attorney Langley, Portland's Chief of Police Jim Purcell, and eleven other policemen were indicted, but none of them lost more than their jobs.

Back in 1957 Elkins's testimony, plus the playing of some of the tapes, had given the McClellan committee the dramatic start it wanted to capture the attention of the news media. Subsequent hearings found gangsters to be prominent in such industries as steel, laundry and dry cleaning, garbage disposal, frozen foods, and numerous others. Attention was usually focused on union leaders and gangsters, but businessmen and lawyers were still just as involved in racketeering as they always had been.

On businessmen, Robert Kennedy, the committee's counsel, wrote: 'The improprieties and illegalities were occasioned solely by a desire for monetary gain ... We found there is often a thin line between bribery and extortion, shakedown and pay off. Labour-management corruption is a crooked two-way street. That is why company officials who conspire with union officials won't talk. They have bought something, just as the labour leader has sold something. And those management officials who aren't involved themselves are usually satisfied to let things go along with everybody happy. They don't want anyone to rock the boat.'[16]

Kennedy's verdict on lawyers was equally critical. He noted that large corporations had taken to employing attorneys, 'who played the role of "middlemen" or, as we came to think of them, "legal fixers" or "legal prostitutes."'[17] This, Kennedy continued, was to ensure that if corporations had to deal with unions at all they would be 'friendly' unions. A Chicago labour relations consultant, Nathan W. Shefferman, for example, used illegal tactics in the interests of a clientele that included Sears, Roebuck and Company, and 400 other organizations or individuals. Shefferman specialized in developing devices to abort union organizing drives. In the case of already unionized industries, he helped develop pay-off systems to union officials, which insured that they would not press their members interests too hard.[18]

The committee's report noted Shefferman's immunity from punishment: 'Despite the fact that firms he represented had been involved in scores of unfair labour practices, Shefferman has never received even a slight reprimand, and the companies that he represents merely make a written statement that they will not do again what they have done. Shefferman moved from town to town, from State to State, with impunity, and the law as presently written is apparently powerless to deal with his activities.'[19]

Lawyers were rarely banished from the profession even after they had been found to be corrupt. For example, although William Langley's connections with Portland and Seattle gangsters were well known, he simply returned to private practice after he had left the district attorney's office. The committee exposed much more corruption and chicanery in the legal profession without prompting a response from the bar associations.

Although the McClellan committee questioned scores of gangsters, businessmen, and lawyers, the undoubted highlight of the proceedings was the clash between Robert Kennedy and the Teamster president already discussed in Chapter 3, Jimmy Hoffa. Many of Hoffa's gangster connections and some of the consequences of these connections were revealed at the McClellan hearings. For example, Hoffa had hired Herman Kierdorf and his nephew Frank as business agents for the Flint, Michigan, area directly from prison. The Kierdorfs were protection racketeers and continued to extort money from small businesses until 1958 when the younger man accidently set himself alight and died while trying to 'torch' the Latrielle Cleaners near Flint.[20]

Senator McClellan queried Hoffa about the Kierdorfs' shakedowns. Hoffa replied that he had asked Herman Kierdorf about the charges and Kierdorf had denied them.[21] A pattern was established: the committee would pile up evidence indicating gangster activity in the union, ask Hoffa what he had done about it, and Hoffa would usually indicate that he had done nothing about it.

Those who dissented from gangster control in some cities faced rough treatment, as the testimony of Arthur L. Morgan showed. Morgan, a former Teamster official from Minneapolis, had reacted to corruption in the union by forming an independent local. Since then, as he described, 'my life has been a living hell. Every night practically the telephone would ring all night long, and my wife would get calls that asked if the children were home from school, and she would say that they are, and they would tell her, "Maybe you are lucky tonight, and maybe you won't be so lucky tomorrow night."'[22] When he was questioned about the situation in Minneapolis, Hoffa acknowledged only that he had done nothing about the Teamster officials who had been convicted of extortion.

At these hearings Hoffa first came into conflict with Robert Kennedy, the committee's counsel. The result of their many bitter exchanges was a lasting enmity. Kennedy presented Hoffa as an arch conspirator and worked night and day to discredit a man he later wrote ran the Teamsters not 'as a bona fide union' but as a 'conspiracy of evil.' The Teamsters Union under Hoffa, according to Kennedy, was

> the most powerful institution in this country – aside from the United States Government itself. In many major metropolitan areas the Teamsters control all transportation. It is a Teamster who drives the mother to the hospital at birth. It is the Teamster who drives the hearse at death. And between birth and burial, the Teamsters drive the trucks that clothe and feed us and provide the vital necessaries of life. They control the pickup and deliveries of milk, frozen meat, fresh fruit, department store merchandise, newspapers, railroad express, air freight, and of cargo to and from the sea docks.
>
> Quite literally your life – the life of every person in the United States – is in the hands of Hoffa and his Teamsters.[23]

As in his Mafia mythmaking, Robert Kennedy was wildly exaggerating the Teamsters' importance and cohesion. By doing so he was providing the rationale for the relentless pursuit of Hoffa through the criminal justice system. In 1961, as part of his anti-organized crime drive as attorney general, one of his first acts was to organize a special team of twenty lawyers and investigators which soon became known as the 'Get Hoffa' squad.

The underlying motivation behind Kennedy's exaggerated version of Teamster power and the formation of the squad was probably more than just personal animosity. During the McClellan hearings, Senator Karl Mundt had spoken of the Teamster corruption and gangster connections as constituting a national security threat by opening the door to communist control over the American transportation system:

> If we permit a situation to prevail whereby an unscrupulous cell of powerful hoodlums can tie up our transportation systems and close down our factories we will be making a mockery of our entire program of civilian defense ...
>
> Foreign agents or Communist saboteurs by gaining control of this unchecked power to paralyze America could go far toward destroying our war potential and our capacity for self-defense ...
>
> I would ask that our fellow citizens envision with me as these hearings proceed, what a quick transfer from the hands of a few hoodlums into the hands of a few Communists for thirty dirty pieces of silver could mean to the entire country and our capacity to defend ourselves.

It was revealed during the hearings that Hoffa favoured an alliance of transport unions to allow for coordinated industrial action and that this would involve cooperation between the Teamsters, the ILA, railroad unions, and the West Coast Longshoremen's union led by the communist Harry Bridges. It was an immensely fanciful leap of imagination on Mundt's part to suggest that this proposed alliance between Bridges and several other unionists who were anti-communist, such as Hoffa, would constitute a national security threat by allowing communists to take over, but such leaps were commonplace during this period.

In March 1964 the 'Get Hoffa' squad achieved its purpose when Hoffa was found guilty on a charge of jury tampering, and received an eight-year sentence. To achieve this Kennedy's squad had freed a convicted felon from jail to plant him inside Hoffa's defence team. This informant then learned of Hoffa's plan to bribe the jurors. The conviction stood after an appeal to the Supreme Court. Chief Justice Warren dissented calling the case 'an affront to the quality and fairness of federal law enforcement': 'Here the government reaches into the jailhouse to employ a man who was himself facing indictments far more serious [and later including one for perjury] than the one confronting the man against whom he offered to inform. It employed him not for the purpose of testifying to something that had already happened, but rather, for the purpose of infiltration, to see if crimes would in the future be committed. The government in its zeal even assisted him in gaining a position for which he could be witness to the confidential relationship of attorney and client.'[24] The case was, however, a clear indication that the U.S. government was prepared to go to any lengths, including working with known criminals, to get anyone that threatened national security even as tenuously as Jimmy Hoffa did.

The pursuit and conviction of Hoffa set a dangerous precedent for civil rights and made no impact on Teamster corruption. Hoffa was replaced as head of the union by successors who all had similar criminal associations: Frank Fitzsimmons, Roy Williams, and Jackie Presser. Presser was exceptional only because he was a long-term FBI informer at the same time as he was a crook. After serving his sentence Hoffa attempted to regain control of the union during the early 1970s. On 30 July 1975 he went missing and has since been presumed dead, although his body was never found.[25]

The government eventually reacted to the Teamsters failure to reform itself by filing a massive anti-racketeering lawsuit in 1988 charging virtually the entire top leadership of the union with forming 'a devil's pact' with gangsters. The union accepted a consent decree that called for the first direct election of top officers by the rank and file and for continuing federal supervision. In 1991 Ron Carey was elected president and narrowly reelected in 1996. The result of the 1996 election, however, was overturned because of campaign finance irregularities and Carey's opponent James Hoffa, son of Jimmy, became president. The younger Hoffa's union still has over a million members, but like the rest of the labour movement, the Teamsters have lost power and influence in the United States.

After the McClellan hearings, and despite laws intended to combat abuses in the handling of union funds, pension funds remained virtually unprotected by the government and easy to plunder in ways explained by the gangster turned government informer Jimmy Fratiano:

There are billions of dollars sitting around in trust funds set up by employers and unions. All you do is find out who controls the money. Then you go and see them and see if you can work out a deal. You do something for them and they do something for you. It works this way.

One, you can pay a union officer or a trustee some money up front. Two, you can pay him a kickback when you get the favour. Three, you can do him a favour. You can do a favour for a friend of his. Four, If that doesn't work, you can find out who his superior is and put pressure on the man to come through. Five, if this doesn't work, you might try threats of physical violence. Six, if all else fails, you might break the guy's leg or worse.[26]

During the 1980s only ninety-four Labor Department agents and 172 auditors policed pension funds amounting to $70 billion. This kind of odds allied to a historic lack of protection for union pensions funds help explain why gangsters have plagued the union movement in the United States for so long. 'It's a license to steal,' according to Raymond Maria, a former Labor department official.[27]

The McClellan and other exposures help justify a body of U.S. labour law that was more anti-union than in other industrialized countries. American unions now face an uphill task in organizing new workers. To begin with, 55 per cent of a group of workers has to sign cards saying that they want to be represented by a union. Then, the National Labor Relations Board (NLRB) sets a date for the certification election, and in the interim the employer is allowed to say and do anything to discourage workers from voting for the union. As Peter Siskind explained in an article in *Lies of Our Times*: 'Legal restraints hardly matter. Although firing workers for union activity is illegal, one in five workers who support an organizing drive lose their jobs. An employee who seeks retribution by filing an unfair labour practice claim with the NLRB has to wait months and frequently years for a ruling on the case. Even if the employee wins, penalties against the employer usually amount to no more than back pay and a minor fine. In the meantime, no certification elections can be held while there are outstanding unfair labour practices claims. Firing workers is therefore a sensible, cost-effective measure for intimidating the work force and avoiding unionization.'[28]

In the wake of President Reagan's sacking of striking air traffic controllers in the early 1980s, U.S. industry waged a campaign to break or tame unions, illegally firing thousands of workers for exercising their rights to organize. Partly as a result, union strength, which has always been fragile, diminished. In 1996 union membership levels were 14.5 per cent of the total workforce, down from between 30 and 40 per cent during the 1950s and 20.1 per cent in 1983.[29] Gangsters are therefore now rarely needed as union busters in the United States.

Business Gone Wrong

As we have seen, public awareness and academic study of organized business crime or corporate crime declined after the muckraking era. There was, however, a revival of interest from the 1960s and the beginning of a steady stream of exposures of the frauds and the unsafe, often criminally negligent, practices of corporations by people such as Ralph Nader, Gilbert Geis, Marshall Clinard, and others.

An early indication that the majority of Americans who believed that corporations were now 'socially responsible' were wrong came in 1961, when a criminal conspiracy in the electrical industry of at least seven years' duration was revealed. During the 1950s many local authorities and public bodies used a sealed bid procedure to get the best prices when buying equipment from manufacturers. In mid-1959, however, officials from the Tennessee Valley Authority (TVA) noticed they were getting lists of identical prices. For example, an order for four power transformers got this response from five out of seven corporations: General Electric (Rome, Georgia) $62,872; Allis-Chalmers (Pittsburgh, Pennsylvania) $62,872; Pennsylvania Electric (Cannonsburg, Pennsylvania) $62,872; Westinghouse (Sharon, Pennsylvania) $62,872; and Wagner (St Louis, Missouri) $62,875.[30]

These and other bidders were too careless to avoid suspicion, and eventually four grand juries were convened to probe price-fixing in the electrical industry. Twenty indictments were handed down, involving forty-five individual defendants and twenty-nine corporations. Most thought it best to plead guilty. Seven defendants were jailed for terms of thirty-days and fines amounting to $1,787,000 were set against the corporations.[31]

Evidence produced at the trials revealed that executives from supposedly competing corporations would regularly get together to fix prices and would go to some length to avoid suspicion. One offender testified: 'It was considered discreet to not be too obvious and to minimize telephone calls, to use plain envelopes if mailing material to each other, not to be seen together on travelling and so forth ... not leave wastepaper, of which there was a lot strewn around a room when leaving.' The officials spoke in code, calling their meeting 'choir practice' and taking a 'Christmas card list' of those attending. Gilbert Geis has explained how the meetings then worked:

> Negotiations centred about the establishment of a 'reasonable' division of the market for the various products. Generally, participating companies were allocated essentially that part of the market which they had previously garnered. If Company A, for instance, had under competitive conditions secured 20 per cent of the available business, then agreement might be reached that it would be given the opportunity to submit the lowest bid on 20 per cent of the new contracts. A low price would be established, and the remainder of the companies would bid at approximately equivalent, though higher, levels ... Sometimes, depending upon the contract, the conspirators would draw lots to determine who would submit the lowest bid; at other times, the appropriate arrangement would be determined under a rotating system conspiratorially referred to as the 'phase of the moon.'

A senate investigating committee later asked one of the officials whether he knew that these meetings were illegal and got this response: 'Illegal? Yes, but not criminal. I didn't find that out until I read the indictment ... I assumed that criminal action meant damaging someone, and we did not do that ... I thought that we were more or less working on a survival basis in order to try to make enough to keep our plant and our employees.'[32] In fact, this price-fixing conspiracy cost U.S. consumers millions of dollars – it 'involved theft from the American people of more money than was stolen in all of the country's robberies, burglaries, and larcenies during the years in which the price-fixing occurred.'[33]

The two corporations with the heaviest fines were General Electric's $437,500 and Westinghouse's $372,500, but as Geis pointed out, 'a half-million dollar loss was no more unsettling than a $3 parking fine would be to a man with an income of $175,000 a year.'[34] This conspiracy against the anti-trust laws and the public was exceptional only in that it was revealed and some perpetrators punished.

Another scandal that puts the profits from even big time gangsterism into perspective involved the Equity Funding Corporation. From 1960 to 1972 Equity was a Wall Street success story that brought together dozens of companies such as savings and loan institutions, insurance trusts, and oil, gas, and land development ventures; it claimed to be on its way to becoming 'the largest, fastest growing, most successful financial institution in the world.'[35] An investigation, however, showed that Equity had written 56,000 bogus insurance policies, created $120 million in phony assets, and even 'killed' some of its phony insurees to collect on their policies. When the scheme collapsed, more than 7,000 stockholders lost more than $100 million.[36]

In 1982, the same year President Reagan launched his wars on crime and drugs, he signed the Garn–St Germain Depository Institutions Decontrol Act and, with his gift for the one-liner, said, 'I think we've hit the jackpot.'[37] This act was the culmination of a series of administrative and legislative changes intended to 'deregulate' America's savings and loan (S&L) institutions and allow them to compete for more business. Garn–St Germain allowed S&Ls to go beyond their traditional role of offering affordable mortgages to ordinary people and invest up to 40 per cent of their assets in almost any ventures they liked the look of, with deposits that were insured by a government agency, the Federal Savings and Loan Insurance Corporation (FSLIC). In various other ways 'the yoke of excessive regulation' was released from the S&Ls and the race was on to attract new business and, at the same time, freely loot outrageous sums of money.

S&L operators took their government-insured deposits and went on a wild spending and embezzlement spree. They spent vast amounts of other people's money to cultivate legislators and keep them away from effective regulatory measures. Don Dixon of Vernon Savings, for example, made his Potomac River yacht and fleet of six aircraft available to members of Congress. According to Paul Z. Pilzer and Robert Deitz in the book *Other People's Money: The Inside Story of the S&L Mess*:

> Not only did he live rent free for eighteen months at a $2 million mansion purchased by Vernon Savings in Del Mar, California ... he also billed Vernon for more than $500,000 in personal living expenses, including $36,780 for flowers, $37,339 for telephone calls, $13,446 for catering services, and $44,095 for 'out of pocket' incidentals. When Dixon and his wife, Dana, filed for personal bankruptcy in California in April, 1989, an action that prevented the FSLIC from seizing their personal assets, the Dixon's possessions included an art collection valued at almost $1 million; twenty-four cases of wine valued at $1300 each; six Fabbri shotguns and other expensive firearms valued at almost $170,000; a Victorian-era Steinway

piano worth at least $15,000; hundreds of thousands of dollars' worth of jewelry; and several luxury cars including a Rolls Royce and a Ferrari. The list of possessions filed with the bankruptcy court was as long as it was opulent. Between 1983 and 1986, Dixon allegedly withdrew more than $8 million from Vernon in salary bonuses and dividends, not counting the bills paid by Vernon for living and entertainment expenses. In all, according to the FSLIC lawsuit Dixon and six other former executives looted Vernon of $40 million in inflated compensation and dividends while they squandered some $350 million of the institution's assets.[38]

Vernon Savings' financial difficulties were disguised for some time through the use of some creative practices including 'participation loans.' This involved selling off loans that were likely to go into default. When examiners were expected, Vernon executives tended to farm out bad loans to other troubled S&Ls until the heat was off, making the company look more solvent than it actually was. In one case, nineteen of the largest thrifts in Texas sent representatives to a secret meeting in Houston in 1985 to exchange bad assets, 'dead horses for dead cows' as they put it, for the purpose of keeping regulators in the dark. Vernon's insolvency would cost taxpayers an estimated $1.3 billion.[39]

Many S&L officials used their new freedoms to embezzle staggering sums of money. One type of deal involved 'land flips,' which were transfers of land between related parties, which in the process artificially inflated its value. One condominium project in Lake Tahoe, Nevada, was bought for less than $4 million and sold back and forth until it cost $40 million. The transactions often took place in the same room.[40] Loan broker J. William Oldenburg bought some property in California in 1979 for $874,000, 'flipped' it back and forth, then, in 1981, had the land appraised at $83.5 million. He then bought State Saving and Loan in Salt Lake City, Utah, for $10.5 million and sold his property to his newly acquired thrift for $26.5 million. The S&L soon went bankrupt, leaving $416 million in outstanding debts, insured by FSLIC.[41]

Charles Keating of Lincoln Savings and Loans in Irvine, California, once gave his salespeople the following advice: remember that 'the weak, the meek and the ignorant are always good targets.' He was talking mainly about the elderly, many of whom were led to believe that the bonds they bought in Lincoln were government insured. But, as several commentators have pointed out, Keating could also have been describing the American taxpayer. The collapse of his thrift would cost taxpayers much more than any other, thanks partly to the so-called Keating Five – Senators Dennis Deconcini and John McCain of Arizona, John Glenn of Ohio, Alan Cranston of California, and Donald Riegle of Michigan. All these senators had received large campaign contributions from Keating and then acted as Keating's representatives in a meeting with federal regulators, based in San Francisco. The senators attempted to persuade the regulators of the financial health of Lincoln and the absence of any 'smoking gun' to demonstrate misconduct.[42] The investigation was taken out of the hands of the 'hostile' San Francisco regulators and moved to Washington, DC. The delay cost the government an estimated $2 billion. Lincoln was eventually declared insolvent and closed down in 1989. In 1991 Keating and several associates were convicted of fraud and conspiracy to divert funds from federally insured thrifts to their own use. Five years later Keating was cleared of all charges involving the failure of Lincoln, on the grounds that several members of the federal jury had improperly discussed his earlier conviction on state fraud charges. Keating, however, lost an appeal against rulings that he had to repay $36.4 million to his collapsed former company.[43]

Estimates of the total costs of the S&L debacle suggested that it would cost $200 billion to bail out insolvent thrifts and up to $500 billion by the year 2021. The average prison terms for convicted S&L fraudsters are around two years, to be served in minimum security federal prisons. The five senators who acted on Keating's behalf were simply admonished by the Senate Ethics Committee because they 'gave the appearance of being improper.' In fact, these and other politicians had been instrumental in allowing the development of 'the largest and costliest venture in public misfeasance and larceny of all time,' according to John Kenneth Galbraith.[44]

Following the publication of Ralph Nader's book *Unsafe at Any Speed* (1965), there was also increasing awareness that organized business crime not only robbed, but killed and maimed as well, as the cases in the following sections demonstrate. Nader's book alleged that the General Motors corporation had placed a car called the Corvair on the market with a rear suspension system that caused the back wheels to change camber by as much as eleven degrees on curves, 'a horrifying shift causing violent skidding, rear-end breakaway or vehicle roll-over. The change occurs without warning and in an instant.' Nader argued that GM's desire for profits had allowed for the marketing of a car that it knew to be unsafe.[45]

The most notable charge against GM's leading competitor involved the unsafe gas tank in the 1971 through 1976 model Ford Pintos. The National Highway Traffic Safety Administration's verdict was: 'Low to moderate speed rear-end collisions of Pintos produce massive full tank leaks due to puncture or tearing of the fuel tank and separation of the filler pipe from the tank.' According to one estimate, 'five hundred men, women and children burned to death in Pinto crashes' between 1971 and 1977.[46]

The Pinto was pushed from the drawing board into production in record time. This process usually took forty-three weeks; in the Pinto's case it was twenty-five weeks. Evidence from memos and other sources suggests that Ford knew about safety defects before the Pinto was put on the market. In 1977 a report in the modern muckraking magazine *Mother Jones* revealed that Ford had placed a $200,000 value on its customers' lives and decided against spending $11 per car to protect Pintos from exploding.

Russell Mokhiber in the book *Corporate Crime and Violence* (1988) described some of the results of these defects: 'The Pinto stalled suddenly and was struck from behind by a van that was travelling, according to witnesses, anywhere from 30 to 50 mph. The Pinto's gas tank crumpled, fuel leaked out, and the car caught fire. Moments later, the Pinto was engulfed in a ball of smoke. Lily Gray was burned to death. Richard Grimshaw suffered burns over 80 per cent of his body. He also lost his nose, his left ear, and much of his left hand in the fire. His face was burned beyond recognition, but he survived after undergoing 60 operations. The Pinto accident left him scarred for life.'

In February 1978 a California jury awarded punitive damages of $125 million against Ford, after hearing evidence that indicated that Ford was aware of producing a hazardous product before it marketed that product. The judge in the case overruled the jury and cut this figure down to $3.5 million. Ford decided to recall the faulty Pintos, but this was too late to save the lives of three teenage girls in a 1973 Pinto on their way to a volleyball game near Elkhard, Indiana. After rear-end collision, the car exploded and all three burned to death.[47]

The Dalkon Shield was a popular intrauterine birth control device in the late 1960s and early 1970s. It was marketed as 'modern,' 'safe' – the 'Mother Superior' of these kind of devices – and 4.5 million were sold in the United States and seventy-nine other countries.[48] Doctors implanted the shield into around 2.2 million American women, but more than 200,000 of these would report injuries. In 1974 it was withdrawn from the market, but not before it had caused an immense amount of damage. The problem, according to Marshall Clinard, was:

> The Dalkon shield tended to cause life-threatening forms of infection known as pelvic inflammatory disease. The tail string of the shield, made up of tiny strands encased in nylon, hangs out of the uterus in such a way that a woman could check to verify that it is in place. The wicking properties of the string facilitated the movement of bacteria from the outside of the uterus, resulting in infection. In case of a pregnancy, which sometimes did occur, the infection was much worse, possibly impairing or destroying the women's ability to bear children. Even after the removal of this device, former shield wearers suffered chronic pain and illnesses that sometimes required hospitalization and surgery. Thousands of women throughout the world who had conceived while the shield was still implanted miscarried, developed infections, or gave birth to children with grave congenital defects, including blindness, cerebral palsy, and mental retardation.[49]

Apart from the thousands injured, at least eighteen women in the United States alone died from pelvic inflammatory disease caused by the shield. The shield's manufacturer, A.H. Robins, had not properly tested it for safety, either in animals or humans, and when reports first came in from doctors about the device's disastrous consequences, the company still refused to withdraw the device. A quality control supervisor for Robins told his boss about his reservations about the product and was rebuked for 'insubordination.' A former Robins attorney admitted in 1984 that boxes of memos relating to the shield case had been burned to keep them out of the hands of the victims' attorneys. Morton Mintz's account of the affair, in his book *At Any Cost*, reveals how Robins's executives 'stonewalled, deceived, covered up, and covered up the cover-ups. And in so doing they inflicted on women a worldwide epidemic of pelvic infections.'[50]

Russell Mokhiber detailed the experience of one young woman called Carie Palmer. Despite the shield, Palmer had become pregnant and until 18 November 1973 the pregnancy was uncomplicated. Then she began to experience extreme pain and her doctor ordered her rushed to the hospital:

Palmer was admitted to the hospital, and as daytime turned to night her condition worsened. At 2.00 a.m. the next day, Palmer lost her baby, and then went into septic shock. She rapidly became critically ill. Her doctors were giving her massive blood transfusions and drugs designed to stimulate her blood pressure, but she failed to respond. Her blood pressure dropped dramatically, first to 60/20 then to 50/40. Eventually the doctors stabilized her condition, then attempted to find out what was wrong.

A needle was inserted into the abdominal cavity and came back full of blood. After getting consent from Palmer's husband, the doctors decided to do exploratory abdominal surgery. They opened her up and found a quart of free blood originating from no obvious source. This indicated to the doctors that Palmer's blood clotting abilities had been totally exhausted. She was oozing blood internally through her organs. Again, the doctors went to Mr Palmer to get his consent. This time they wanted to remove her tubes and ovaries – an emergency hysterectomy. Again, Mr Palmer agreed. The operation was done in order to save her life.[51]

On 29 February 1984, U.S. District Judge Miles W. Lord for Minnesota approved a $4.6 million dollar products-liability settlement of seven cases against Robins and said the following to E. Claiborne Robins Jr, the president of the company and two other top executives:

'I did not know.' 'It was not me.' 'Look elsewhere.' Time and again, each of you has used this kind of argument in refusing to acknowledge your responsibility and in pretending to the world that the chief officers and the directors of your gigantic multinational corporation have no responsibility for the company's acts and omissions. Gentlemen, the results of these activities and attitudes on your part have been catastrophic. Today, as you sit here attempting once more to extricate yourselves from the legal consequences of your acts, none of you has faced up to the fact that more than 9,000 women have made claims that they gave up part of their womanhood so that your company might prosper. It is alleged that others gave their lives so you might prosper. And there stand behind them legions more who have been injured but who have not sought relief in the courts of this land. if one poor young man were, by some act of his – without authority or consent – to inflict such damage upon one woman, he would be jailed for a good portion of the rest of his life. And yet your company, without warning to women, invaded their bodies by the millions and caused them injuries by the thousands. And when the time came for these women to make their claims against you company, you attacked their characters. You inquired into their sexual practices and into the identity of their sexual partners. You ruined families and reputations and careers – in order to intimidate those who would raise their voices against you. You introduced issues that had no relationship whatsoever to the fact that you planted in the bodies of these women instruments of death, of mutilation, of disease. Mr Robins ... you have taken the bottom line as your guiding beacon and the low road as your route. This is corporate irresponsibility at its meanest ... Please, in the name of humanity, lift your eyes above the bottom line. You, the men in charge, must surely have hearts and souls and consciences.

Please, gentlemen, give consideration to tracking down the victims, sparing them the agony that will surely be theirs.

The company responded by filing a complaint with the Eighth Circuit Court of Appeals, charging the judge 'with a gross abuse of judicial discretion and power' and seeking to have him sanctioned and his remarks stricken from the record. The judge was not disciplined, but his remarks were expunged from the record because, as the court argued, Lord had censured the Robins officers 'without giving them due notice' he was intending to do so.[52]

In 1918 a U.S. government report pointed out that many asbestos workers were dying prematurely. In 1928 the *Journal of the American Medical Association* reported the case of a young woman who died of asbestosis, a crippling disease of the lung. By 1935 asbestos had also been linked to lung cancer, and by 1955 the causal link between asbestos and lung cancer was conclusively established.[53]

Long after the dangers of asbestos were known, working conditions in the factories maximized profitability and minimized safety. As one worker later testified there was so much dust that 'you couldn't see from one end of the machine to the other ... you were covered with dust and the fibres ... It would be in your ears, it would be in your nose, even through the mask. It would be under your pant legs, it would be inside your socks. You'd be just covered with it. You'd be blue.'[54] The industry responded to all the evidence of the hazards of asbestos by suppressing and distorting as much as it could. Both workers and consumers have suffered as a result.

Until the late 1960s, for example, Johns-Manville, the leading asbestos manufacturer, refused to tell workers of early evidence of asbestos diagnosed by their medical staff. When illness forced workers to leave their jobs, the company offered them nothing but the advice to get another job.[55] In 1977 a congressional committee asked the corporation's medical director if he had ever advised officials to put warning labels on asbestos-containing insulation products. The director replied: 'The reasons why the caution labels were not implemented immediately – it was a business decision as far as I could understand. Here was a recommendation, the corporation is in business to make – to provide jobs for people and make money for the stockholders and they had to take into consideration the effects of everything they did, and if the applications of a caution label identifying a product as hazardous would cut sales, there would be serious financial implications. And the powers that be had to make some effort to judge the necessity of the label vs. the consequences of placing the label on the product.'[56] Dr Irving Selikoff, a leading authority on the relationship between cancer and asbestos, has estimated that 240,000 of the one million workers who were exposed to or are working with asbestos will die within thirty years because of asbestos-related cancer and that is not taking account of the consumers or members of the public exposed to the product.[57]

In the early 1980s U.S. juries began to agree with the verdict of South Carolina attorney Ronald Motley who described Johns-Manville as 'the greatest mass murderer in history.'[58] The company decided to file for bankruptcy as millions of dollars were awarded to former workers and consumers. In 1986 present and former asbestos manufacturers settled a class action suit, brought by 751 former workers or workers' survivors, for more than $100 million.[59] Despite the financial and personal costs of their fraudulent behaviour no asbestos executives were prosecuted on significant charges. In 1986 two top Manville executives who had to leave the corporation when it filed for bankruptcy were awarded more than $1.8 million in 'golden parachute' payments.[60]

The corporate criminal activity that will possibly cause most damage in the twenty-first century is the disposal of dangerous waste products from the chemical, oil, and other industries. Until the 1970s most corporations treated their waste products as they would ordinary garbage and simply dumped tons of toxic materials wherever it was most convenient – often in coastal waters or landfills. In 1942, for example, the city of Niagara Falls, New York, decided to lease an unused excavation called the Love Canal as a garbage dump. In particular, they allowed a chemical company to dispose of its industrial waste there.

Hooker Chemical and Plastics later bought the Love Canal and used it to dump over 43 million pounds of chemical wastes there between 1947 and 1952. The waste products were covered with clay and dirt and, eventually, after grass and weeds had grown over the former hole, there was no visible sign of their existence.[61]

In 1953 Hooker sold the land back to the city for $1 for the building of a school, with a proviso that the school absolve the company from any future liability for injuries or property damage caused by the dump's contents.[62] In June 1958, three schoolchildren were burned near the Love Canal, and internal memos indicated that Hooker officials attributed the problem to the toxic chemicals left there. This information was kept from the city and the public for twenty years. From the late 1960s, however, the extent of pollution could no longer be kept secret. Massive leaks of brown-black liquid oozed from the canal into nearby homes, particularly after heavy rain. Investigations revealed that neighbourhood children suffered high rates of asthma, nephritis, and hepatitis, and the population as a whole was more prone to suffer miscarriages, stillbirths, birth defects, and, most significantly, cancer. By the end of the 1970s the state was forced to evacuate several hundred families and the total legal claims for damages were in excess of $2 billion.[63]

The Love Canal scandal prompted federal legislation in 1981 providing for a billion-dollar 'superfund' to clean up old dumps and outlawing disposal that endangered the water supply and public health. Penalties of five-year prison terms and fines for knowingly putting people at risk could now be imposed. However, much of the damage had already been done. Hooker alone had also dumped about 350 million pounds of toxic waste at three other sites near Niagara Falls.

In 1983 most of the residents of Times Beach, Montana, fled from the town when it was revealed that a highly toxic substance known as dioxin had been sprayed on horse arenas, streets, parking lots, and farms throughout the state by a local waste hauler. It cost the taxpayer $36.7 million to buy out virtually the entire town. In 1991 a University of Tennessee study, estimated that the number of sites in need of cleaning up will exceed 3,000 and the total cost will be between $106 billion and $302 billion – and open pits, ponds, and lagoons across the country are also full of industrial poison.[64]

The damage continued after the new laws had been passed. Private waste disposal companies, sometimes run by gangsters but more often by unethical businessmen, made themselves available to dispose of a corporation's toxic waste cheaply and often illegally. As James Coleman has reported:

> New Jersey, with America's largest chemical industry (and, not coincidentally, its highest rate of cancer mortality), is experiencing especially severe problems with such illegal dumping. Legal testimony indicates that some waste disposal companies send out tanker trucks in the dead of the night to find empty streets, vacant lots, or quiet streams, and simply open the valves and let their dangerous cargo pour out. Not only do such crimes contribute to New Jersey's alarming incidence of cancer, but many of the chemicals are flammable and thus pose the additional threat of fire and explosion. One illegal dumping site was discovered when an empty lot suddenly burst into flames. Another was discovered by a fire inspector who found that his shoes were being eaten away by the chemicals dumped in a lot he happened to walk across.[65]

Donald J. Rebovich, who completed a study of hazardous waste crime in four states, found that criminals involved in the disposal of hazardous waste had become increasingly able to corrupt or evade regulatory efforts. He uncovered a criminal world very different from that of popular perceptions. The world of the hazardous waste offender was one in which the intensity, duration, and methods of the criminal act were more likely to be determined by the criminal opportunities available in the legitimate marketplace than by the orders of a controlling criminal syndicate. The criminal dumper, he concluded, was 'an ordinary, profit-motivated businessman who operates in a business where syndicate crime activity may be present but is by no means pervasive.'[66]

Major corporations have also continued to flout the new laws in more direct ways. In 1984, for example, the government charged General Motors with failure to comply with water pollution regulations at ten plants. Water contaminants such as cyanide, copper, chromium, and zinc were being discharged as by-products in making bumpers and other car parts. Waste Management Incorporated, 'known for its leaky landfills, its convictions for price-fixing, and its violations of environmental regulations,' was penalized with fines of more than $30 million from 1982 and 1987. The list can go on indefinitely, and the leading corporations seem to be as likely to be involved in violations as the dumpers themselves.[67]

These cases of corporate fraud and violence represent just a part of a much larger problem. The cost of business crime far outweighs that of any other type of crime, both in dollar terms and in terms of lives lost or damaged.[68] U.S. government estimates of the yearly losses from street crime put the figure at about $4 billion – less than 5 per cent of the estimated losses from business crime. More significantly, an estimated 14,000 deaths per year are caused by industrial accidents, many of which result from violations of safety codes; 30,000 deaths result from unsafe and usually illegal consumer products; and hundreds of thousands of cancer deaths are caused by legal and illegal environmental pollution. This proportion of corporate killing is, of course, far higher than the proportions of people murdered by acts that are listed as criminal homicide.[69]

As many commentators have pointed out, corporate crime is organized crime. Russell Mokhiber in his book *Corporate Crime and Violence* (1988) profiled thirty-six cases of corporate criminality and concluded that corporate crime is 'more than just isolated instances of errant corporate behaviour. Patterns emerge, including destruction of documents, suppression of dissent within corporate bureaucracy, and intricate cover-ups and stonewalls.'[70] James Coleman surveyed many examples of corporate crimes and concluded that 'in many ways the organizations themselves, and not individual employees, are the real perpetrators of organizational crime.' He elaborated: 'In many cases, criminal activities are rooted in an organizational subculture and a set of attitudes that have developed over many years, and they cannot be traced to any single individual or group of individuals. Of course, individual actors must carry out the criminal deeds, but there is ample evidence to show that the attitudes and characteristics of those individuals are of little importance. Those who refuse to carry out the illegal activities demanded by their organizations are simply replaced by others that will.'[71] In sum, as Frank Pearce noted in 1976, 'The corporations provide the most efficient and largest examples of organized crime in America.'[72]

Despite an increasing awareness of the costs of corporate crime the U.S. government's response has been and continues to be slow and inadequate. Between the passage of the Occupational Safety and Health Act in 1970 and 1992, 200,000 Americans have died while working, and large numbers of these deaths were not the results of accidents. The Labor Department referred just eighty-eight criminal cases to the Department of Justice, and federal prosecutors agreed to bring criminal charges in twenty-five of these. Only one businessman went to prison and then just for forty-five days. According to David Burnham, 'This record speaks for itself: 200,000 deaths, twenty-five Justice Department prosecutions, one forty-five-day jail sentence. Without giving any credence to the possibility of knowing conspiracies, it is clear that hundreds of responsible federal officials under five separate political administrations – beginning with Nixon and ending with Clinton – have somehow carried out an unstated, perhaps even unconscious, government policy of great consequence: In direct violation of the 1970 law, corporate executives who knowingly exposed their workers to conditions that caused their deaths have almost always been protected from the unpleasant mess of criminal charges.'[73]

Corporate power lies behind the lack of an adequate government response to corporate crime in the United States. As we saw in Chapter 3 corporate power bent regulatory law to its interests from the beginning of the Republic and it continues to do so today. Most importantly, as Marshall Clinard points out, 'Corporate power has seen to it that in the event of a law violation, legislatures have provided besides or in lieu of the criminal law a wide range of administrative and civil penalties. These include warnings, injunctions, consent orders, and non-criminal monetary payments. Even where the criminal penalty is available, it is infrequently invoked ... Since corporate offenders are rarely seen or treated by the government as criminals, the public has developed the perception that most corporate violations are basically "non-criminal" and thus not serious in nature.'[74]

Laureen Snider has noted another reason for regulatory inadequacy related to corporate power, 'present modes of control focus on the corporate actors who do the least damage – the largest and most powerful organizations are the least sanctioned.' After documenting this, Snider noted the following advantages held by large organizations in managing regulatory agencies: 'Political (large organizations are powerful, control more jobs and influence more politicians more efficiently); ideological (regulators tend to believe that only "fly-by-night" business stoop to crime); and practical (cases involving large concerns are usually more complex, harder to document and prove, and most costly and time-consuming for agency staff).'[75]

Many corporate strategies for avoiding prosecution are completely legal, but, as David Burnham points out, others are not, such as bribery or more subtle arrangements involving the 'revolving door' between public and private service. In the case of the latter, a Justice Department lawyer may be promised a lucrative job in a private law firm representing a target company on the usually unstated assumption that he or she help achieve the law firm's goal of maximum leniency for the client.[76]

For these and other reasons, the main deterrents to corporate crime are fines that are generally so small as to amount to less than a fraction of the profits made by large corporations in one hour of operation – the same 'flea-bite' deterrent that Edward Ross noted at the beginning of the twentieth century.

There has been and continues to be resistance to the corporate dominance of American life and many battles over specific issues have been won by trade unionists, environmental protestors, and other groups. Largely as a result of these activities, there is now at least a formal commitment by the federal government to enforce laws designed to protect ordinary people from unsafe consumer products and illegal environmental pollution. The problem remains, however, as Snider has pointed out: 'States will do as little as possible to enforce health and safety laws. They will pass them only when forced to do so by public crises or union agitation, strengthen them reluctantly, weaken them whenever possible, and enforce them in a manner calculated not to seriously impede profitability.'[77]

Despite the fact that tens of thousands of Americans die annually as a result of occupationally caused diseases and many more are left disabled, one of the first actions of the Reagan administration was to weaken the Occupational Safety and Health Administration. OSHA's budget was cut, and thus there were fewer inspectors, inspections, and follow-up inspections than required for adequate enforcement.[78] At the same time, showing the same sense of political priorities as Nixon's team, the Reagan administration was talking up the dangers of drugs to justify a massive increase in drug law enforcement efforts. The result of this political decision to de-emphasize one problem while emphasizing another was to more than double the percentage of all federal criminal cases involving drugs while cutting in half those involving regulatory matters such as health and safety violations, occupational health violations, and the illegal discharge of toxic waste.[79]

The fight against drugs to which we now turn consumes far more U.S. enforcement resources than those allocated to the fight against organized business crime in general and environmental and safety crimes in particular.

Chapter 7

Drugs: Private Enterprise and Government Bounty

Chapter 7 surveys the American war on drugs in recent decades. While the war has failed to make a serious impact on illegal drug use, it has significantly added to the fortunes of drug traffickers and corrupt officials at home and abroad. Despite continuing evidence of failure, there seems to be little prospect of a change in this situation. The war on drugs has now been institutionalized as an ongoing concern that benefits both corporate and government interests.

There is no doubt that more Americans took more illegal substances from the 1960s on. More than ten million Americans had used such illegal drugs as marijuana, heroin, and cocaine and a wide range of stimulants, depressants, and hallucinogens by the 1980s.[1]

Most statistics are unreliable, but the number of words now used to describe the state of drug intoxication does give an indication as to how obsessed Americans have become with drugs. While some 150 new words came into the American vocabulary during Prohibition to describe the state of alcohol intoxication, there are at least 357 new ways of describing the state of drug intoxication. These include: all geezed up, all lit up, amped, around the bend, backed up, baked, basted, beaming, beaned up, belted, bending and bowing, bennied up, bent, bent out, bent out of shape, besotted, blasted, blind, blissed out, blitzed, blixed, blocked, blowed, blowed away, blown away, blown out, boggy, bombed, bombed out, boxed, boxed up, bricked, brightened, buzzed ... warped, wasted, way out, weirded out, whacked, whacked out, wide, wigged, wigged out, wiggy, winged, wiped, wiped out, wiped over, wired, wired on whites, wired up ... wrecked, zapped, zerked, zerked out, zig-zag, zipped, zoned, zonk, zonked,

zonked out, zounk, zunked.[2] As in Prohibition, many have lined up to supply a market that was clearly expanding.

As the market increased, so did the efforts of federal, state, and local governments to suppress it. Since the Nixon era the federal government has massively increased its commitment. During the 1980s it spent around $20 billion, and in 1995 alone the commitment by the administration of President Bill Clinton amounted to nearly $15 billion. After adjusting for inflation, federal drug enforcement now costs more than ten times as much as Prohibition enforcement did during the 1920s. States, cities, and local governments also spent massive amounts to supplement the federal efforts.

The result of this effort has been a massive increase in arrests for drug violations. In 1989 alone, according to FBI statistics, there were 1,361,700 drug arrests, nearly 10 per cent of all arrests. Most of these arrests were for simple possession offences rather than sale or manufacture.[3]

More than any other single factor, the succession of Nixon-style wars on drugs declared by Presidents Reagan and Bush fuelled the largest and most rapid expansion of the U.S.'s prison population in its history. Between 1980 and 1994, the prison population tripled from 500,000 to 1.5 million. Add to that the number of people on probation or parole and the figure surpassed five million people at the end of 1994, or 2.7 per cent of the adult population.[4]

The United States has few positive and many negative results to show for the massively expanded enforcement effort and the policy that amounts to one of mass imprisonment. Since the 1970s, hundreds of billions of dollars has been spent prosecuting the war on drugs without significantly affecting the levels of illegal drug use or even the levels of potency of drugs available on the streets.[5] At the same time the war on drugs has helped keep drug prices inflated and profits high for smugglers, manufacturers, distributors, and all the many thousands of officials and professionals who facilitate the success of their ventures.

While enforcement capacity has been wasted trying to achieve the unachievable drug-free society, organized criminal activity continues to involve all ethnic and social complexions and to pervade American private and public life from the highest to the lowest in society.

Trafficking

Supplying marijuana and heroin remained lucrative operations, but from the 1970s, cocaine trafficking emerged on a larger scale than ever before to meet an increasing demand from all classes of Americans. Its use was first most noticeable among athletes, entertainers, and 'young upwardly mobiles' in well-paid professions. Much of the drug's glamour and mystique was related to its outlaw status.

The coca plant is relatively easy to grow – hardy, disease-resistant, and long-lived. The major known growing areas are in sparsely populated, inaccessible areas of South America. According to 1979 estimates, a peasant farmer could hope to realize $250 from the sale of 500 kilograms of coca leaves in regions where the average monthly wage was around $50. This same amount – not taking account of the costs of refining, smuggling, and distribution – might realize $80,000 in the United States.[6] The opportunities for entrepreneurs to buy cheap and sell dear were obvious.

Airplanes provided the fastest and safest means of smuggling cocaine. Pilots were paid enormous sums of money to take loads in small private aircraft. One pilot testified in November 1984 that he and his associates had flown more than 250 planeloads from South America without being caught. They found that the hardest part was what to do with the money.[7]

Larger quantities of cocaine and marijuana went by sea, most often by freighter to Caribbean and Bahamian islands close to the coast of Florida, and then transferred to smaller, faster boats for the shorter journey, although such transfers can also be made anywhere along the Atlantic and Pacific coastlines. When chased by inferior customs or coastguard boats, the smugglers tended to emulate their rum-running forefathers and win.[8]

Even small amounts of drug contraband have great value; thousands of dollars worth of heroin or cocaine can be smuggled into the country in containers the size of cigarette packets. There are countless devices: false petrol tanks in cars, false-bottomed suitcases, shipments of canned foods or any manufactured goods, even pregnancy cages worn by women who are not pregnant, or the hollowed-out heels of shoes. There is the so-called body-packing syndrome where the courier swallows condoms or balloons full of cocaine or heroin. In March 1985 customs agents in Miami discovered a dead baby which had been cut open, stuffed with cocaine, and sewn shut.[9]

Smuggling operations tend to restrict themselves to importation, leaving distribution within the United States to indigenous groups. No ethnically based monopoly in the drug business has ever existed.

WASP, Irish, Jewish, Italian, and other European Americans compete or cooperate with African, Hispanic, and Asian Americans to supply the world's richest market. There are many thousands of drug distribution and smuggling networks – decentralization characterizes the industry with a high turnover of personnel. Many sources of raw materials exist. Many organizations, large and small, buy and process the raw materials, import the product into the country, where it is sold to and processed and distributed at retail by a host of outlets. Although some operations have lasted for decades, organization in the drug business is largely spontaneous, with anyone free to enter it at any level if he or she has the money, the supplier, and the ability to escape arrest or robbery. Since the 1980s successful enforcement efforts against large trafficking operations have done no more than create more openings for other large trafficking operations and the ever-present small-scale entrepreneurs.

The heroin and cocaine distribution structure tends to be pyramidal, similar to food distribution. All deal in consumer goods bought on a frequent basis, typically in small amounts for immediate consumption, and have no need for special technology or equipment. There are relatively few suppliers at the top and thousands of retailers at the bottom. Drug distributors either sell the product to local wholesalers or transport large quantities to other cities for sale to regional wholesalers. Wholesalers divide the produce into pounds for sale to pound dealers, who further divide it into ounces for sale to ounce dealers and so on down the chain of distribution to the consumer. Adulteration with anything from powdered milk to talcum powder occurs at every stage. Lower-level heroin dealers are often addicted themselves and make minimal profits. The cocaine retail trade level tends to be an informal network of friends and acquaintances. Entrepreneurs need to insert themselves towards the top of the pyramid, buying cheap and selling dear, while minimizing such overheads as processing, transport, and bribery.[10]

The career of Frank Matthews illuminates the entrepreneurial potential of the drug trade. Matthews was an African American whose move as a young man from rural North Carolina to the big city signalled the beginning of a short but successful career. He found a base in the Bedford-Stuyvesant area of New York and, after employment in various numbers operations, decided that drugs offered great potential. Around 1967 he made a direct contact with French heroin refiners and smugglers for his supplies. For distribution he used an existing network of numbers sellers and collectors, after the raw materials had been 'cut' and 'bagged' in a number of fortified locations by employees working regular eight-hour shifts. Local police were probably paid off, since there is no record of them disturbing Matthews's operations. By 1970 he had expanded, and his organization distributed much of the heroin in the larger east coast cities, with outlets in Cleveland, Detroit, Cincinnati, Chicago, Kansas City, Las Vegas, and Los Angeles.

Matthews made no effort to hide his rapidly increasing wealth – buying expensive property and cars, turning up at championship boxing matches in floor-length sable or mink coats, and losing heavily and ostentatiously at Las Vegas roulette tables. He was arrested there by federal police on 1 January 1973 and indicted on numerous drug-related charges. While released on bail, he reportedly converted an estimated $20 million of his assets into cash and then disappeared with a bodyguard, a mistress, and the money.

A national and international manhunt followed with the DEA offering $20,000 in reward money for information about Matthews's whereabouts. One tip, as journalist Donald Goddard described it, mobilized a small army of police, state troopers, and federal agents in Syracuse, New York: 'After sealing off the area, an assault group armed with riot guns and automatic weapons filtered into a downtown rooming house and burst in suddenly on an 80-year-old man watching television,' whose name also happened to be Frank Matthews.[11] The real Frank Matthews, apparently, remained a fugitive.

Matthews was the most notable of a new generation of major African-American drug dealers. In New York he was followed by Leroy 'Nicky' Barnes, who was labelled 'Mr Untouchable' by the *New York Times*, until January 1978, when he was found guilty of operating 'continuing criminal enterprises' and sentenced to life imprisonment.

Violence in the drug trade far exceeds anything experienced during the bootleg wars of the 1920s and is not, as then, mainly confined to the big northern cities. The motives are, however, generally the same – protecting territory or goods from rivals, discouraging, or retaliating for, betrayal to the authorities, or stealing drugs or money or both from other traffickers. Police estimated that over a hundred of Detroit's 690 homicides in 1971 were related to the heroin trade. In New York in 1981 there were 393 drug-related slayings, including 160 in which drug dealers were killed during robberies. From the mid-1970s the homicide rate in south Florida jumped more than 400 per cent in a few years, mainly because of violence associated with the drug traffic. In 1981 the Dade County medical examiner had to rent a refrigerated hamburger van to cope with the increase in corpses, and by then Miami had become one of the world's most dangerous cities.[12]

Violence is most visible in the inner cities, where gangs proliferate and compete for territory and drug distribution networks. According to a nationwide survey, in 1961, there were twenty-three cities with known street gangs. By 1971, there were fifty, and this increased to seventy-eight in 1980. By the early 1990s, nearly 200 U.S. cities had street gangs, mostly composed of African American, Hispanic, and Asian ghetto dwellers.[13]

Gangs in the city and county of Los Angeles have to be counted in the hundreds. Among African Americans, most of these gangs have tended to claim an affiliation to either the Crips or the Bloods. These names should not suggest consolidation or centralization, just identification. Crip sets are as likely to fight each other as Bloods. Police officers are well aware of gang disunity and the easily manipulated egos of individual gang members and use this knowledge to make numerous cases. According to Roland Garcia of the Los Angeles Police Department: 'Probably what triggers their willingness to talk is the fact that they think they are business people. Since they consider themselves entrepreneurs in cocaine dealing, they will want to give up information about their competition. Most of their competitors are other Crips and Bloods working for different dope dealers. Crips and Bloods are very greedy, self-centered people. By ending their competition, they stand to make a larger profit. They do not care that their competition happens to be other Crips and Bloods.'[14]

Their lives are tedious for the most part but occasionally dangerous, as indicated by the deaths of hundreds of gang members each year during the 1990s.[15] Accounts of gang life such as in Leon Bing's book *Do or Die*, (1991), Luis J. Rodriguez's book *Always Running* (1991), and Sanyika Shakur's book *Monster* (1993) reveal how gang rivalry frequently results in the killing and wounding of innocents who happen to be in the wrong place at the wrong time.[16]

The motorcycle gang phenomenon shows that not all gangsters come from the racial and ethnic ghettoes and housing projects of the cities. Motorcycle gangs, notably the Hells Angels, are mainly composed of white Anglo-Saxon Protestants from rural or suburban America. The Hells Angels were the first nationally and internationally organized biker group and can date their origins from 1945. Rather like the origins of the Ku Klux Klan in Pulaski, Tennessee, a group of bored ex-servicemen got together in Berdoo, a small town in California, to form a club called the Pissed Off Bastards. In 1948 a breakaway group formed the first Hells Angels chapter. Other chapters were formed and the Hells Angels grew rapidly during the 1950s, declined almost to extinction by the mid-1960s, then revived, and are now well established. The Hells Angels, operating primarily on the west and east coasts, have been joined by three rival organizations: the Bandidos, operating largely in the South with some membership in the northwest; the Outlaws, mainly on the eastern side of the United States, as are the Pagans. Under these umbrella organizations there are now over 800 individual gangs.

From the 1960s, some 'outlaw' biker leaders developed criminal operations separate from the umbrella organizations. They have built up legal businesses with money gained through systematic criminal activity, often buying property to establish motorcycle shops and taverns, and then using these outlets to fence stolen parts and other merchandise and distribute drugs. Some operations require major crimes, such as rape or murder, as conditions of involvement. Informants are rare because of the threat of retaliation and surveillance is difficult because of the installation of sophisticated counter-surveillance and security.

Drug trafficking, mainly in domestically manufactured methamphetamine and the hallucinogen PCP, has become the major source of income for many outlaw bikers. During the 1980s a group of Hells Angels, for example, were found to be producing 'speed' from twelve clandestine methamphetamine laboratories in California; and in central Ohio, one illicit laboratory was said to be producing enough illegal drugs to distribute throughout Ohio into California, West Virginia, New York, and New Jersey. Individual members can supplement income derived from drugs by pimping, selling pornography, contract murders, and robbery.[17]

Many members of street gangs and outlaw biker gangs eventually get caught, convicted, and sentenced to time in prison. There they join more than three million other U.S. prisoners and their keepers in a booming prison industrial complex that now accounts for about 4 per cent of the nation's male labour force and thus keeps the U.S. unemployment rate impressively low.[18]

However, as many earlier commentators would have predicted, mass imprisonment has already proved to be part of the problem of organized crime rather than its solution. Many prisons in the United

States are grotesque parodies of the worst parts of the cities – gangs struggle to gain and retain control over prostitution, protection, and drug-trafficking rackets in systems based on brutality, informants, and staff corruption. Inmates craving cigarettes, drugs, or even such hard-to-get things as soap provide a literally captive market.

Most of the gangs are organized along racial and ethnic lines. During the 1970s and 1980s, some like the Aryan Brotherhood, the Black Guerillas, the Mexican Mafia, the Texas Syndicate, and La Nuestra Familia achieved statewide and even interstate influence, trading in drugs and often eliminating competition on the outside as well as the on the inside. Of these the Aryan Brotherhood have spawned other white supremacist gangs such as the Nazi Low Riders, which is said to be the fastest-growing white gang in California and is heavily involved in the production and trade of methamphetamine. Unlike other earlier loosely affiliated racist gangs, the Nazi Low Riders are said to be organized and motivated by profit.[19]

The 1990s in general saw a proliferation of prison gangs in most state prison systems and as the journalist Eric Schlosser puts it, 'America's prisons now serve as networking and recruiting centers for gang members.'[20] Nationally, violence in the prison system has increased dramatically. During the 1980s about 100 inmates and several staff members were killed each year, and there were thousands more beatings or non-fatal knifings. In the early months of 1997 there were 150 'slicings' a month in the New York state prison system alone. These assaults were part of the initiation rites of the United Blood Nation gang that required would-be members to 'blood in' or 'slice' another inmate. The number of 'slicings' declined to about twenty-five or thirty a month by the end of the year, perhaps because the Bloods had established their dominance over the scores of other prison gangs.[21]

Politicians from both major parties have been reluctant to address a problem that is directly related to the great expansion of drug arrests and convictions that have stretched penal institutions to breaking point. Although the full consequences of putting hundreds of thousands of young men in with career criminals will not be known until well into the twenty-first century, the American prison gang phenomenon has already added spectacular substance to the observation that prison serves best to train more efficient and determined criminals.

Corruption has also accompanied the policy of mass imprisonment. Between 1989 and 1994, for example, fifty correctional staff in the District of Columbia's prison system alone were convicted of serious crime, eighteen of them for smuggling drugs for inmates. Politicians, state officials, and rural landowners have also colluded in the sale of land for new prison developments. In one case highlighted by the *Los Angeles Times*, a 5,000–acre farm was bought in 1990 for $374 an acre. Two weeks later the state of California paid $3,500 an acre for the farm for a new prison. This happened after the intervention of a local legislator who also happened to be the recipient of large campaign donations and the co-author of the 'three strikes' legislation that increased the prison sentence for a second offence and required life in custody without parole for a third offence.[22]

The case noted above is just one example of the way business is done in the U.S. prison-industrial complex. Eric Schlosser has described this as 'a set of bureaucratic, political, and economic interests that encourage increased spending on imprisonment, regardless of the actual need':

It is a confluence of special interests [that] has given prison construction in the United States a seemingly unstoppable momentum. It is composed of politicians, both liberal and conservative, who have used the fear of crime to gain votes; impoverished rural areas where prisons have become a cornerstone of economic development; private companies that regard the roughly $35 billion spent each year on corrections not as a burden on American taxpayers but as a lucrative market; and government officials whose fiefdoms have expanded along with the inmate population.[23]

Meanwhile, no study has been able to show that mandatory minimum sentencing or the policy of mass imprisonment has made a noticeable impact on the extent of drug use or drug-related crimes.

Although drug enforcement continues to concentrate on low-level dealers from minority or marginal groups, it has become apparent that 'respectable' middle-class professional and businesspeople have added to their incomes by trading in high-status drugs, notably cocaine. In 1982, for example, local and federal officials announced a series of seizures and arrests of middle-class and upper-income Americans who had no previous arrest records:

In September federal officials announced that businessmen, physicians, lawyers, and bank officials were among the leaders of a ring that smuggled into the country 3,748 pound of cocaine confiscated in March in Florida – the largest seizure up to that date. In another case, officials in Georgia accused a once prominent local businessman and a former mayor of Clarkesville of smuggling 300 pounds of cocaine into the state.

In August two employees of the Environmental Protection Agency were arrested for operating a thriving cocaine business in the Kluczynski Building in Chicago's Loop.

In July a federal grand jury in Phoenix, Arizona, indicted 106 people, including businessmen and housewives, in nine states on charges of participating in an inter-state ring that netted some of the principals almost $400,000 a year.

Finally, in June, a lawyer, a restaurant owner and three other businessmen were arrested in Islip, Long Island with around 600 pounds of cocaine, the potential retail value of which was around $200 million.

These people were attracted by a large, fat untaxed profit. As a DEA agent told *New York Times* reporter Robert Lindsey, 2.2 pounds of cocaine sold for $50,000 to $60,000 on the black market and by the time it was sold at retail level it brought in $300,000 to $400,000 a pound. Ronald Cunningham, a young Iowan involved in the Phoenix case, testified that he had gone into the drug business with an investment of $500 and before long was earning more than $300,000 a year.[24]

In New York, many of the new breed of upper-level drug traffickers were, according to Patricia Adler in her book *Wheeling and Dealing* (1993), attorneys, accountants, bankers, and money brokers who met a booming demand from the 'fast-track mergers-and-acquisitions crowd on Wall Street and Madison Avenue.' They were 'part-time drug entrepreneurs, American businessmen employed in legitimate occupations who dabbled in importation and upper-level distribution or ancillary white-collar services for the drug crowd.'[25]

On full-time drug dealers, Adler's research concurred with that of Peter Reuter and John Haaga in their book entitled *The Organization of High-Level Drug Markets* (1989). The groups of convicted drug dealers Reuter and Haaga interviewed were loosely structured and resembled networks rather than formal organizations. Large crews were only required for the more specialized task of smuggling, otherwise individual dealers could operate alone. The dealers portrayed a fluid national market, where entrepreneurial dealers could travel to different regions and do business. They were not restricted by any monopolistic-style control over various territories.[26]

In recent years more has been revealed about what happens to drug money after it has been collected. Not only corrupt officials and ruthless gangsters benefit financially from the drug trade; ostensibly legitimate financial advisers and institutions have also prospered. Banks, most noticeably in Florida, have boomed by laundering vast amounts of cash generated by the drug prohibition laws. Since 1970 Miami has become an international banking centre rivalling London and New York, and no one seriously disputes that dollars generated by the trade in marijuana and cocaine helps account for this rapid rise to prominence.[27]

As the drug trade expanded dealers amassed mountains of cash, primarily in small-denomination bills. This cash – often stuffed into carrier bags or cardboard boxes – was then brought to the banks and pushed through to the tellers. Bales of it were then fed into high-speed money counters or simply weighed. The totals were usually just under $10,000, since each bank by law had to report cash deposits of more than this amount and this might have attracted the attention of regulators. Teams of cash couriers working for professional money launderers deposited hundreds of thousands of dollars in a day. And couriers have turned out to be the least likely people; one group of grandmothers on the west coast laundered more than $25 million before being noticed.[28]

The $10,000 currency transaction law itself has been regularly subverted. Some bank officials take bribes and neglect to file the report forms. Some launderers create accounts in the names of 'off-shore' shell corporations, so the forms can contain no useful information. Launderers with the assurance to pretend they are a legitimate retail outfit with large cash-flows can also obtain a legal exemption from the form.

Once the money is deposited in the bank, launderers can transfer it into the accounts of more 'off-shore' shell corporations in such places as Switzerland, Hong Kong, Panama, and Grand Cayman Island. Once the money is off-shore, local bank-secrecy laws will usually defy attempts to trace it. Little will then prevent it supporting the most lavish lifestyles and being invested in legitimate businesses, always with the option to reinvest in the drug trade.

From the 1970s it became clear that banks are willing accomplices to all this, since they have much to gain and little to lose. Some have been found to launder money knowingly on a regular basis, earning up to 3 per cent in commissions on it and lending it out profitably at the same time. Also, drug money tends to go into non-interest-bearing accounts or is changed into cashiers' checks, which usually remain uncollected for months, providing banks with yet more incentive to turn a blind eye. And, despite many instances of active or passive bank complicity revealed in recent years, few, if any, bankers have received jail sentences.

Since the late 1970s financial investigative task forces have been formed and have had a certain amount of success. Operation Greenback, a joint IRS, Customs Service, and DEA effort, for example, targeted entire laundering networks of attorneys, accountants, money brokers, money couriers, and bankers, and documented $2.6 billion laundered for sixteen drug-trafficking operations. By 1984, 164 had been arrested. The most notable money-launderer Greenback turned up was a Colombian, Isaac Kattan. He did business with four Miami, banks: the Bank of Miami, the Great American Bank, the Northside Bank of Miami and the Popular Bank and Trust Company, depositing as much as $1 million every day. Raids on the banks revealed a number of irregularities: employees had been switching funds from one of the Kattan accounts to another, pages of cash-deposit logs and some cashiers' checks were missing, and employees assigned to count the rushes of cash sometimes complained that the bills were wet or smelly – as if they had been buried. An agent testified that on one occasion he heard Kattan apologize to a bank official for a suspicious-looking transaction. The bank official reassured him: 'Don't worry – the main thing now is to count the money.'[29] The root of the problem, as Senator William Proxmire put it, was that 'many banks are addicted to drug money, just as millions of Americans are addicted to drugs.'[30]

During the 1990s the U.S. government had several high profile victories in a stepped-up drive on money laundering. In 1991 the Bank of Commerce and Credit International (BCCI) was found guilty of effectively defrauding depositors of several billion dollars as well as operating as a kind of laundering service for Colombian drug traffickers.[31] In August 1994, two bankers for American Express Bank International received prison terms on charges of conspiracy and money laundering. Later the same year, American Express settled for $32 million in exchange for the dropping of criminal charges.[32]

Despite numerous U.S. domestic and international initiatives against money laundering, meeting the demand for drugs still produces billions of dollars, and most of this still ends up in the U.S. economy. Criminals are ingenious, whether they work for banks or not, and as Margaret Beare puts it, 'New routes, partnerships, and smuggling techniques all attest to the criminals ingenuity.' The American and international action has closed doors, 'but others are quickly opened as new laundering schemes emerge.'[33]

Another problem has been pointed out in Jeffrey Robinson's book *The Laundrymen (1998)*. The U.S. government's strategy of following the money trail and concentrating on money laundering has simply driven up the traffickers' cost of doing business. An average trafficker is 'now paying anywhere between 6 and 25 per cent to get his money collected, washed, and into his pocket. The downside is that the added expenses are reflected in the street price, and there is a direct correlation between increased street prices and increased street crime.'[34]

Testing

The only recommendation made by the Kaufman Commission on Organized Crime to attract much attention was a call for a widespread national program to test most working Americans for drug use, in effect, to force most working Americans to submit to regular, observed urine tests. The tests required supervision because people might be tempted to bring in someone else's clean urine.

Soon after the report on drug trafficking was issued, several members of the commission revealed that they had not been informed about the urine-testing recommendation although the report had been issued under their names. Thomas McBride, for example, said that he first learned of the addition to the report from news accounts. Similarly, another commission member, Eugene Methvin, revealed that when he read in the newspapers the parts that caused all the furore he thought, 'Gee, did we recommend that?'[35]

At a news conference Judge Kaufman explained the recommendation. The investigation had convinced him that 'law enforcement has been tested to its utmost ... but let's face it, it hasn't succeeded. So let's try something else. Let's try testing.'[36] By suggesting that the immense problem of drug-related gangsterism and corruption was to be tackled by examining the urine of innocent people, the recommendation reached a new low.

A small number of liberals objected to the invasion of privacy involved, but a poll taken after the commission's report was issued showed that nearly 80 per cent of Americans did not oppose drug testing. The law enforcement community had announced that testing people's urine would reduce the demand and therefore hit organized crime in the pocketbook, so millions of Americans were prepared to line up and give their samples. One of the first was President Reagan himself who signed an executive order permitting the testing of more than a million civilian federal employees, gave his own sample as an encouragement, and 'persuaded' seventy-eight top aides to do the same.[37]

Although the results of these tests have often been shown to be wrong, and people's lives and careers have suffered as a result, the business of urine-testing laboratories and equipment manufacturers is booming. Like most wars, America's war on drugs has its profiteers. The Kaufman commission had given a major boost to an industry that has since just kept on expanding. By the beginning of the 1990s urine testing was big business and on its way to becoming bigger. Five companies took in an estimated $173 million in 1989 and more than $300 million in 1990. These companies include multinational corporations like Beechams and Hoffmann-La Roche.[38]

The United States now has a growing industry in urine and more and more people have a stake in perpetuating it. According to Milt Freudenheim writing in the *New York Times*, 'A policy has to be written for the corporations. That's money for lawyers. A minimum of one hour's training for supervisors is required – that's money for the trainers. Urine is collected forensically: money for collectors. Samples are taken in a hurry to a certified laboratory: money for Federal Express. And tests are reviewed by a licensed physician and then reported to the company. That's money for the doctors.'[39]

Like the military and other industrial complexes, the 'drug abuse industrial complex' has its revolving door between government and corporate or private employment. DEA, National Institute on Drug Abuse (NIDA), and other government officials leave their government agencies and go into private practice as drug consultants. One of their main tasks as consultants has been to encourage governments and corporations to institute more drug-testing programs.

Recent passers through the revolving door have been Bob Strang, Ann Hayes, and Robert Stutman, formerly of the New York DEA field office. In August 1989 Stang and Hayes told reporters that they would help private sector employers set up workplace drug programs as part of their roles as federal agents. Four months later they resigned to go into business as consultants. According to Stang, 'I'll make more money and I will be able to make a difference.' When asked what did ex-DEA agents know about treatment, Strang said, 'We know how to force people into treatment.'[40]

Again, like other industrial complexes, the drug abuse industrial complex has its own conferences where corporate and government officials can get together to discuss state-of-the-art equipment and program development.[41] But the business in American urine is so great that corporations and professionals cannot monopolize it. In 1986 a young Texan called Jeff Nightbyrd showed the way for less orthodox entrepreneurs. He began selling '100 per cent pure urine,' collected from a Bible study group, to people facing job-related drug tests. However, he soon had to turn to other sources, when he discovered that the churchgoers were using too many prescription drugs to ensure negative results. Nightbyrd gave his company the slogan, 'Pee for Pleasure, not Employment,' and helped organize a 'urine ball' to raise money for a legal defence fund against drug testing. The party featured a 1930s-style dance production called 'Urine the Money!' Nightbyrd and others have since been busy meeting a massive demand for clean urine, usually freeze-dried, and sent by mail.[42] Thus, this tragically ludicrous situation leaves plenty of scope for freelancers and small businesses.

There is, of course, no evidence that the bizarre and intrusive practice of wholesale drug testing has made any impact on the problem Judge Kaufman and his colleagues were supposed to be investigating – organized crime. But that such a recommendation could be taken seriously at all is comment enough on the progress the United States has made towards understanding the problem of organized crime.

Asset Seizures

Although drug control and organized crime control has clearly not worked in the United States, ways have been found to make it pay for itself. Measures passed in 1970 and 1978 made the seizure of assets from criminals or suspected criminals easier.

The Nixon administration's law-and-order package in 1970 included RICO – the Racketeering Influenced and Corrupt Organizations Act. The senator who introduced this act claimed that it would be a 'a major new tool in extirpating the baleful influence of organized crime in our economic life.' The RICO legislative tool provided for extended prison sentences for people found to be involved in 'continuing criminal enterprises.' A conviction on each RICO count carried a ten-year prison sentence. With penalties the government could exact triple damages, recover legal fees from attorneys defending racketeers, and seize any property connected with the convicted, no matter how remotely. The government did not have to wait until after the trial to seize these assets. The assumption was that organized crime people might run away with the money before trial. The government, however, has proved too willing to take from innocent and guilty alike.

The U.S. government has been seizing the assets of criminals since 1789 and the birth of the nation, but RICO made asset forfeiture a much more important part of the crime-control armoury. Since the Nixon era the tendency in general has been to make the seizure of assets easier, particularly the assets of alleged drug dealers. In 1978 a civil forfeiture law was enacted, declaring 'all moneys used in, and all assets acquired from, the illicit drug trade belong to the United States government and are subject to civil seizure under the forfeiture power.' The importance of this law is that the burden of proof is much less for civil law than for criminal law.

Previously the government had to prove guilt before depriving people of their property, now it was up to the individual to demonstrate that the seized property was 'innocent' of facilitating a drug crime – or that it was not obtained through criminal activity. If the claimant failed to satisfy a judge or jury that the property was 'innocent' of the alleged drug crime, then the goods were forfeited to the government. Usually, the seized property remained unclaimed because the legal fees involved were prohibitive and people were unlikely to risk criminal charges being brought against them. U.S. authorities now had the means to get much richer without the need to ask for extra taxes.

With this new tool the DEA was able to seize drug assets totaling $268 million in just three years between 1979 and 1982. These figures have continued to increase boosted by the passage of the Comprehensive Crime Control Act of 1984. This act strengthened and streamlined all federal forfeiture laws and created a new amendment that provides for the equitable transfer of property forfeited federally, to either state or local law enforcement agencies, or both, which participate in investigations. Between 1985 and 1992 the total value of federal asset seizures increased over 1,500 per cent to over $2.4 billion. In 1993 alone the Department of Justice's Asset Forfeiture Fund, took in $556 million.[43] Police officers from every level of government – local, state and national – now had the power and the incentive to seize assets.

The changes in the law since the Nixon era have dramatically reversed the concept of 'due process.' Under forfeiture laws the government could seize property based solely on probable cause to believe that the property was used unlawfully. Probable cause can be as little as hearsay or innuendo. The government therefore did not have to prove criminal guilt to obtain a forfeiture judgment over someone's property.[44]

Asset forfeiture laws, according to George Bush, 'allow us to take the ill-gotten gains of drug kingpins and use them to put more cops on the street and more prosecutors in court.'[45] But others have seen asset forfeiture as a means by which the state can take the bulk of the proceeds of criminal activity and a good deal of the proceeds of honest activity.

Police agencies across the country have certainly got richer through asset forfeiture. Federal, state, and local authorities soon began to see the proceeds from forfeiture cases to help fund everything from extra prosecutors and police officers to new supplies of vehicles and other law enforcement equipment, including high-tech surveillance devices such as night-vision goggles, infrared heat-detection devices, helicopters, and more sophisticated weaponry. If a ranking officer likes a seized car then he or she can claim it for personal use. Forfeitures have included a Chevrolet dealership, a recording studio, a 1,000-acre plantation, and many homes, cars, boats, and planes. In the early 1990s, for example, the seven-man police department of Little Compton, Rhode Island, managed to seize $3 million. Police Chief Edgar Hawes obtained a 1991 Pontiac Firebird, and his lieutenant a 1992 Formula Firebird. The force also took two new high-tech cruisers, a four-wheel drive Jeep, a van for animal control, a new pick-up truck to pull the new trailer carrying the new 23–foot boat, new weapons, bulletproof vests, a semi-enclosed firing range, a new tower for the new radio system, police radios for school buses, an extra $7,000 a year for his men for overtime, college for three officers, $500,000 set aside for salary and benefits, and a $725,000 police station. All that still left $1.5 million.[46] Today most state and local forces have their own asset seizure units and join in what amounts to a gold rush for law enforcement agencies.

As the amount seized in forfeiture cases has risen in recent years, a cycle emerged by which narcotics operations made seizures that could be used to finance other operations from which yet more assets might be seized. Two academics from Tennessee, Mitch Miller and Lance H. Selva, conducted a twelve-month study of asset forfeiture based on covert participant observation involving one of the authors assuming the role of confidential informant inside undercover operations in a southern state. They found that, 'narcotics enforcement is becoming a business in which officers and equipment are allocated so as to maximize profits rather than control or eradicate drugs. Efficiency is measured by the amount of money seized rather than impact on drug trafficking.' Their participant observations 'of clandestine reverse sting operations' pointed out the 'dangers and inherent contradictions of such an approach.' The participant informer, for example, asked one officer, why a search warrant would not be served on a suspect known to have resale quantities of marijuana in his apartment. He replied, 'Because that would just give us a bunch of dope and the hassle of having to book him (the suspect). We've got all the dope we need in the property room, just stick to rounding up cases with big money and stay away from warrants.'

The strategy of reverse stings where the officers become sellers was also found to be deficient because 'large-scale dealers could not have achieved their status without adequate connections and suppliers. Their ties and discretion make them largely inaccessible to seizure operation because they are not very 'reversible.' Many value safety more than profit and operate on a credit basis known as 'fronting.' Fronting occurs when drugs are purchased on credit. Clever drug dealers recognize the legal advantage of keeping cash separate from illegal drugs. The big dealers simply do not make natural suspects for seizure strategies, nor are they easy prey. Consequently, agents take who they can get, lower-level dealers and users who fall victim to enterprising informants.'[47]

Asset forfeiture has created a new form of commercial enterprise – informing for profit. Informants can now receive a salary and bonuses for information whether or not it leads to convictions, and up to 25 per cent of forfeiture profits. Federal, state, and local agencies now pay out over $300 million to informants each year and some informants have been active enough to make over $1 million out of an activity that used to be as stigmatized in the United States as in other countries.

Edward Vaughn of suburban San Francisco is one among many drug trafficking informants who have taken advantage of the government's new largesse. He ran a multimillion dollar, international drug-smuggling ring during the 1980s and served two terms in prison before arranging an early parole and paid informant deal with the government. From then he earned $40,000 in salary and expenses between August 1989 and October 1990 working for the DEA, and was promised a 25 per cent cut of any seizures. This information came out at a trial in Pittsburgh in 1990 in which Vaughn's testimony resulted in one man being found guilty of distributing marijuana. The other defendant in the case was acquitted because the jury felt Vaughn had entrapped him by pushing him too hard to make a drug deal.[48]

Many informants cheat in ways explained by Professor Steven B. Duke and attorney Albert C. Gross in their book *America's Lost War: Rethinking Our Tragic Crusade against Drugs* (1993): 'The contingent-fee crook can plant marijuana in the far corners of a field, or place some leaf under the seat of a car, in the hold of a ship, or on the floor of a million-dollar Learjet, "drop a dime" and become rich overnight. He probably won't even have to testify, because even if the forfeiture is contested, the forfeiture stands unless the owners can prove that they had no knowledge of the drugs. Their mere protestations of ignorance, even if uncontradicted, need not be – and usually are not – believed.'[49]

Although major racketeers were the original targets, the new forfeiture powers are now far more often directed against people who have never been accused of a crime. Informants are unlikely to risk their lives by informing on gangsters when they can turn in non-violent innocents. Already hundreds of cases have shown that this situation leads to injustice and even tragedy.

In 1991 the *Pittsburgh Press* analysed more than 500 cases nationally and found that 80 per cent of those who lost homes, cars, boats, or money to the authorities were never charged with a crime. One case involved James Burton, a Vietnam War veteran, who grew and smoked marijuana to relieve pressure in his eyes because of glaucoma. In 1988, after he was convicted on three counts of simple possession, the government simply took his house and 90-acre farm in Bowling Green, Kentucky.

The articles showed that people are often targeted because of their appearance or actions. Some can be stopped and searched in an airport because they paid cash for a plane ticket or simply because they are black or Hispanic. On one occasion, a ticket agent informed on Willie Jones, an African American, who operates a nursery in Nashville, Tennessee, because he paid cash for a plane ticket. As a small grower he preferred to deal in cash and he was carrying just under $10,000. Federal agents simply seized the money. Jones failed to get his money back and was nearly driven out of business.[50]

Other newspapers have added to a growing body of evidence that indicates that while important drug dealers have learned how to protect themselves from forfeiture, the innocent take no such precautions. In September 1993, for example, the *San Jose Mercury News* reported the case of Karri Welch. Sacramento County deputies had arrested her and seized $1,013 from her after discovering eight one-hundredths of a gram of methamphetamine – about the size of a grain of salt – in her purse. After being released from jail, she was given five days to file her claim for the money. Welch returned the form but signed it in only one place instead of the required two. The government waited until after the time had expired to tell her of her mistake and she lost the money.[51] Of course, Americans can turn to attorneys to help them take back their money or property from the government, but those with the necessary qualifications can charge around $10,000. For many it simply is not worth it.[52]

The case of Assistant U.S. Attorney Leslie Ohta shows that power can bring immunity from these kind of abuses. She was head of her office's asset forfeiture unit and gained a reputation as a hard-line expert in the area, making millions of dollars with her unit, often by making cases against parents and grandparents of children involved in small-scale trafficking possession. Her argument was that 'people should know what goes on in their own homes.' When, however, Ms Ohta's own son was found to be selling LSD to undercover agents, her property was not seized by the government. The U.S. Attorney's Office decided that seizing her property would be 'inappropriate' and she was simply transferred to another unit.[53]

The most publicized tragedy related to asset forfeiture to date involved a reclusive millionaire called Donald Scott, owner of a 250–acre estate in the Santa Monica Mountains. On the morning of 2 October 1992 Scott and his wife woke up to the sound of someone pounding on their door. As his wife was attempting to answer the door, a team of Los Angeles County Sheriff's Department officers burst in. She cried out, 'Don't shoot me, don't kill me!' Her husband ran to her assistance, waving a revolver above his head. A deputy sheriff reacted by shooting and killing him. The raid had been justified by an alleged sighting from a police helicopter of marijuana plants growing on Scott's estate but a search of Scott's estate found no drugs of any kind.[54]

Despite widespread criticism of the abuses of the forfeiture laws, the seizure of the profits and assets from illicit drugs by federal, state, and local agencies during the 1990s was, according to David Burnham, 'one of the fastest growing businesses in America.'[55]

In the nineteenth century vigilante groups punished their victims by taking their money, property, and lives of their victims. In the 1970s corrupt New York police officers justified the theft of cash from traffickers as 'taking the devil's money to do the Lord's work.'[56] During the 1990s U.S. government agencies were themselves the vigilantes, and they also genuinely believed that they were the 'good guys.' In a sense, corruption was legitimized, and the extra money helped perpetuate a drug crusade, which, as we have seen, involved racism and corruption from the beginning.

After years of campaigning by the Forfeiture Endangers American Rights Foundation (FEAR) and other civil rights activists, President Clinton signed the Civil Asset Forfeiture Act into law on 25 April 2000. The act stipulates that there will be court-appointed counsel for indigents, strengthens the innocent-owner defence, and in general, according to FEAR goes 'a long way to level the playing field for poor and middle class forfeiture victims – particularly innocent owners' and forces the U.S. Attorney's Office 'to take a look at the merits of the case, instead of having the seizing agency win most cases by default when the claimant fails to file a claim and cost bond on time.' The law shifted the burden of proof in asset forfeiture cases to the government. This reform should reduce some of the abuses of asset forfeiture in the United States.[57] In the meantime, however, the United States has been exporting its forfeiture techniques worldwide as part of the 'Americanization' of international law enforcement, discussed in Chapter 8.

Despite, and in many ways because of, the stepped-up enforcement, the war on drugs has continued to produce a world of institutionalized greed, chaos, corruption, betrayal, and terror that is far beyond that experienced during alcohol prohibition. The main victims in this war are African and Hispanic Americans, who are disproportionately more likely to be arrested, convicted, and sentenced for drug offences than whites.[58] Given the racist and manipulative origins of drug prohibition, these damaging consequences are sadly appropriate.

The only major federal legislative reversal suffered by America's moral crusaders remains the repeal of the 18th Amendment in 1933. In the case of drugs, the historical record has shown that representatives of the American people including every president since Nixon would rather tolerate corruption and racketeering on a massive scale than take part in a reasoned, well-informed debate that seriously considers alternatives to prohibition. Billions of dollars have been spent on enforcement but evidence of the corrupt and destructive consequences of drug prohibition continues to mount up. It seems, therefore, that the questions posed by congressmen Wagner and Coffee before the Second World War still need to be addressed: 'Why heap more sacrifice upon the altar of hopelessness?' and 'Why should persons in authority wish to keep the dope peddler in business and the illicit-drug racket in possession of its billion-dollar income?'

Racism and sensationalism influenced early U.S. drug control policy more than reason and realism. Today, the needs of the drug abuse and prison industrial complexes look set to perpetuate the American war on drugs. Until Americans acknowledge that its drug control efforts are based on prejudice, and the manipulation of evidence, they are unlikely to find or accept ways that might reduce the damage. In the meantime, the United States will continue to invest in failed efforts at repression and, as we shall see in Chapter 8, persuade other countries to do the same.

Chapter 8

American Power and the Dumbing of Global Discourse, 1945 to the Present

At the end of the Second World War only the United States of all the powers had a functioning physical plant capable of the mass production of goods, and excess capital. Only the United States had become richer rather than poorer because of the war. It possessed gold reserves of $20 billion, almost two-thirds of the world's total of $33 billion. The United States had a monopoly on the atomic bomb, and the U.S. Navy dominated the Pacific and the Mediterranean. American troops occupied Japan, the only important industrial power in the Pacific, and Americans dominated France, Britain, Western Germany, and Italy. The war had accelerated the process of French and British imperial collapse. The Soviet Union alone represented a serious threat to U.S. interests and ambitions.

'The Pax Americana had come of age,' as Paul Kennedy has argued, and new overseas markets had to be opened up to absorb the flood of U.S. products. Americans had to stay in control of strategically critical materials such as oil, rubber, and metal ores, or have unrestricted access to these materials. Such considerations combined to make the United States committed to the creation of a new world order beneficial to the needs of western capitalism in general and to the needs of the United States in particular. The International Monetary Fund, the International Bank for Reconstruction and Development, and later the General Agreement on Tariffs and Trade were the international arrangements to secure the compliance of most countries to this new world order. Countries wishing to secure some of the funds available for reconstruction and development under these arrangements were obliged to conform to U.S. requirements on free convertibility of currencies and open competition. The system eventually worked to the advantage of corporations in a reconstructed Western Europe as well as in the United States itself. Open competition conditions tend to favour strong, technically advanced countries. But countries less well equipped to compete – in particular developing countries in Asia, Africa, and South America – were tied into a system that has often proved to be against their long-term interests.[1]

The only significant rival faced by the United States stayed out of these monetary and trading arrangements. U.S.–Soviet antagonism long preceded the Second World War, but intensified as it became clear that the war had torn apart the old international order. The United States built up an arsenal of weapons of mass destruction to ensure the construction of a new order. The United States also kept a powerful conventional military presence in Western Europe and still had ample resources left over to intervene forcibly in peripheral areas of the world to prevent or impede the establishment of regimes thought to be incompatible with its interests. The Soviet Union concentrated its resources on building its own weapons of mass destruction, maintaining Eastern European satellite states, and supporting and influencing national liberation movements.

Whatever stability in international relations existed during the Cold War superpower impasse no longer existed with the collapse of the Soviet Union at the end of the 1980s. The world at the end of the twentieth century included within it zones of political and economic instability frequently characterized by devastating regional wars.

American influence ensured that this unstable world was largely open to trade. However, as legal markets increased and expanded, so did the potential for illegal activity within these markets. At the same time, U.S. influence ensured that it was a world officially committed to eradicating the illicit trade in drugs at a time when demand for drugs has soared. Opportunities for successful international organized criminal activity have proliferated in this new world order.

Chapter 8 begins by surveying evidence of U.S. government and corporate complicity in international organized crime. It then sketches the 'Americanization' of international drug control policy and the counterproductive impact of this process. Finally, it assesses the failure of international anti-drug efforts, and an American-inspired dumbing of global discourse on the problem.

International Organized Crime and American Foreign Policy

In 1946 George Kennan, the State Department's expert on Soviet affairs, was the first to articulate the rationale behind America's postwar foreign policy. According to Kennan, the Soviet Union was an imperial empire, expansionist and hostile; but an all-out clash for the United States could be avoided through 'containment.' Containment required 'the adroit and vigilant application of counterforce at a series of constantly shifting geographical and political points.' Hard-liners in the Truman administration interpreted containment as a justification for a wide variety of clandestine warfare tactics, ranging from radio propaganda to sabotage, murder, and collaboration with criminals, chosen to 'contain' left-wing initiatives virtually anywhere in the world.[2]

The Central Intelligence Agency emerged as the organization that directed the covert side of containment. It was established in 1947, first as a fact-finding agency, but soon afterwards as one authorized to carry out secret operations abroad. These operations were to be kept from Congress and the public. The process had begun earlier, but after 1947 it expanded and accelerated. The idea was to learn and then practice effective espionage and counterespionage techniques to keep the world safe for U.S. interests. As John Ranelagh put it in his history of the CIA, 'With the world up for grabs and with the Soviet Union taking what it could get, the CIA was charged with laying the U.S. claim ... The realization was clear that if it failed, the whole world might be lost.'[3]

American intelligence covert activity had already involved collaboration with gangsters. During the Second World War gangsters on the New York waterfront were enlisted by Naval Intelligence to prevent sabotage.[4] After this goal had been achieved these gangsters were left free to perform their more traditional role, which was to run rackets and help keep the workforce cheap and docile. In the early postwar era the CIA allowed a similar arrangement to become established in France. The agency feared that socialist waterfront unionists would come to an alliance with communists and increase the political chances of the communists nationally. Therefore, according to Alfred W. McCoy's study of the episode: 'The CIA ... sent agents and a psychological warfare team to Marseilles, where they dealt directly with Corsican syndicate leaders through the Guerini brothers. The CIA's operatives supplied arms and money to Corsican gangs for assault on Communist picket lines and harassment of important union officials. During the month long-strike the CIA's gangsters and the purged CRS police units murdered a number of striking workers and mauled the picket lines.'[5]

Marseilles' docks were, like New York's, left open to gangster and smuggling operations. One unanticipated consequence of this was that during the 1950s Marseilles became an important processing, packaging, and transshipment point for heroin to be exported to the United States. In what became popularly known as 'The French Connection,' opium grown in Turkey, Iran, and southeast Asia, was converted into a gooey paste known as 'morphine base,' brokered by Turkish businessmen and Lebanese warlords, and transported to Marseilles and then on to New York, hub of the richest drug market in the world. In New York it would be taken on by bulk buyers before being repackaged and adulterated for final sale. By the 1950s Sicilian Mafiosi had also began to form alliances with Italian-American gangsters to exploit the U.S. market.[6]

The U.S. government's toleration and even protection of the drug traffic in the cause of anti-communism can be traced back at least to the early 1950s when Chiang Kai-shek's Kuomintang government was evicted from mainland China by Mao Zedong's communists. Part of Chiang's army ended up in an opium-growing area of neighbouring Burma, where they used U.S.-supplied weapons to organize and extort from the trade. McCoy also cites Burmese intelligence reports that revealed that the CIA planes transporting military supplies for the Kuomintang loaded up with opium for the flights back to Taiwan or Thailand.

CIA involvement in the drugs business in southeast Asia intensified when the Americans invaded Vietnam in the 1960s. The former French rulers had collaborated with corrupt local elites in the export of opium through the South Vietnamese city of Saigon. American involvement opened up a much larger market as GI demand for heroin supplemented the growing demand among addicts and users at home. The area now known as the 'Golden Triangle' that stretches across 150,000 square miles of northeast Burma, northern Thailand, and northern Laos rapidly became the world's main source of supply for heroin.

Among America's few committed allies in southeast Asia were the opium-growing Meo tribesmen. Their territory was opened up when landing strips were built for CIA planes to bring supplies and advisers. According to the first-hand accounts of pilots, the CIA's Air America planes followed the precedent set in Burma and often flew back loaded with opium.[7]

Jonathan Kwitny's research has revealed that restrictions on drug enforcement made sure that this traffic could continue unhindered and profitable to U.S. allies and particularly to cooperative U.S. officials throughout the Vietnam War. One gruesome smuggling practice was to cut open, gut, and fill GI corpses with heroin before flying them back to the United States: 'Witnesses were prepared to testify that the heroin-stuffed soldiers bore coded body numbers, allowing conspiring officers on the other end, at Norton Air Base in California, to remove the booty – up to fifty pounds of heroin per dead G.I.' The army covered up this discovery and sent the investigators who revealed the racket to combat duty.[8]

The North Vietnamese victory in 1975 was accompanied by a wave of South Vietnamese immigration to the United States, and this dislocation produced by the war had the unintended consequence of transferring ancient conflicts with the Chinese to the United States. In July 1990 an incident dramatically illustrated this in New Jersey. Mayhem broke out during a funeral of a man killed in a drive-by shooting. According to police accounts, two or possibly three men, posing as mourners, threw aside the flowers they were carrying and opened fire on the crowd of 125 people with a shotgun and a 9-millimetre automatic handgun. Some of the genuine mourners shot back. Others scattered, some jumping into open graves. In the end five people died. The funeral was for a member of the Born to Kill gang, which operated in New York's Chinatown. The name is taken from a phrase U.S. soldiers scribbled on their helmets during the Vietnam War and was used by a group of young Vietnamese immigrants involved in robbery and extortion. Police officials reported that most of these grew up in the wartime chaos and this was likely to make them excessively prone to violence. A Chinese gang, the Chinatown Ghost Shadows, were suspected of being the instigators of the original drive-by shooting.[9]

U.S. involvement in Central and South America followed a similar course to that followed in Asia. Anti-communism justified alliances with corrupt rulers, or deposed rulers wanting to return to power, or any variety of expedient entrepreneurs wishing to cash in on chaos. This involvement was thus again accompanied by significant international organized crime activity with negative consequences for people in every country involved, including the United States.

One major difference is that U.S. consumer demand for South American cocaine far exceeds that for southeast Asian heroin. In the 1970s and 1980s this fed the growth of violence, chaos, and corruption in countries such as Peru, Bolivia, and Colombia. Private armies in these countries waged war against each other or against state officials on a scale far beyond that of the Chicago bootleg wars of the 1920s but basically for the same reasons: protection or expansion of businesses whose massively inflated profits derive from U.S. prohibition laws.

The story of Klaus Barbie and other intelligence entrepreneurs connects the cocaine trade with postwar U.S. recruitment and protection of Nazis and with U.S.-supported military regimes in South and Central America.[10] As chief of the Gestapo in Lyons, France, Barbie's war crimes included torturing and murdering captured resistance fighters and deporting Jews to death camps. In 1945 he was put on the U.S. Army intelligence payroll to mould clandestine Nazi cells in Eastern Europe into anti-communist spy rings. In 1951 he took on a new identity and joined the anti-communist crusade in Latin America.

Barbie settled in Bolivia, where he advised the country's rulers on torture, the setting-up and running of concentration camps, and the organization of squads whose main purpose was killing and intimidation. In 1978 Barbie became security consultant for Roberto Suarez, Bolivia's most notable drug trafficker of the day. For Suarez he helped organize a paramilitary squad to protect operations. This squad became known as the Fiancés of Death and played an active part in the campaign of terror initiated by the leaders of a 1980 military coup, one of whom was Colonel Luis Arce Gomez, a cousin of Suarez. The new regime immediately murdered many of the trade union leaders who had led the opposition to their takeover. With the help of the Fiancés they also came to dominate the cocaine trade, driving the smaller operators out of business and 'taxing' the shipments of Suarez and other major traffickers.[11]

The rise of the cocaine trade since the early 1970s has been accompanied by a confusing mixture of violence, corruption, and diplomatic expediency, and there is now no denying CIA knowledge of the large-scale trafficking operations of many of its friends and collaborators in South and Central America. In 1989 a Senate subcommittee confirmed that the U.S.-supported Contra rebels used drug money to support their fight against the Nicaraguan government: 'it is clear that individuals who provided support for the Contras were involved in drug trafficking, the supply network of the Contras was used by drug trafficking organizations, and elements of the Contras themselves knowingly received financial and material assistance from drug traffickers. In each case, one or another agency of the U.S. government had information regarding the involvement either while it was occurring, or immediately thereafter.'[12] All this was known to U.S. government agencies while the country was officially engaged in the war against drugs.

On 18 March 1986 President Reagan brought his administration's main domestic and foreign concerns together when he announced: 'Every American parent will be outraged to learn that top Nicaraguan government officials are deeply involved in drug trafficking. There is no crime to which the Sandinistas will not stoop. This is an outlaw regime.' Reagan made this statement to support his request to Congress for $100 million more in aid to the Contras. The priority was to bring down the Nicaraguan government. He spoke on prime-time television and his words were reported uncritically by most of the media. Much less exposure was given to both the State and Justice departments' rebuttals of Reagan's assertion.[13] The Sandinista drug-connection story was in fact largely fiction, which makes it representative of the misinformation that has characterized U.S. government announcements on international crime since the Second World War.[14]

On 29 January 1998 the CIA issued a report by its Inspector General Frederick Hitz into allegations of connections between CIA, the Contras, and drug trafficking made by journalist Gary Webb in the *San Jose Mercury News* just over a year earlier. The articles made the case that cocaine was 'virtually unobtainable in black neighbourhoods before members of the CIA's army' – the Nicaraguan Contras – started bringing it into South Central Los Angeles in the 1980s.' The report found fault with specific details in the newspaper series, and it is clear that Webb's overall thesis was overstated. However, in testimony to Congress, Inspector General Hitz admitted for the first time that his agency knew that 'dozens of people and a number of companies connected in some fashion to the Contra program' were involved in the drug trade' and added: 'Let me be frank. There are instances where the CIA did not in an expeditious or consistent fashion cut off relationships with individuals supporting the Contra program who were alleged to have engaged in drug trafficking or take action to resolve the allegations.'[15] Hitz's admission was, however, an example of an art that the CIA has perfected during its fifty-year existence. Alexader Cockburn and Jeffrey St Clair have called this art the 'uncover-up' and explained that 'this is a process whereby, with all due delay, the Agency first denies with passion, then concedes in profoundly muffled tones, charges leveled against it. Such charges have included the Agency's recruitment of Nazi scientists and SS officers; experiments on unwitting American citizens; efforts to assassinate Fidel Castro; alliances with opium lords in Burma, Thailand and Laos; an assassination program in Vietnam; complicity in the toppling of Salvatore Allende in Chile; the arming of opium traffickers and religious fanatics in Afghanistan; the training of murderous police in Guatemala and El Salvador; and involvement in drugs-and-arms shuttles between Latin America and the U.S.'[16]

Since the Second World War the U.S. intelligence community has operated in ways that either included criminal activity or protected criminal activity and has disguised this involvement. All the rhetoric and Mafia mythmaking by U.S. officials and politicians obscured the fact that historically the United States has been very selective about which forms of organized crime activity it opposes.

Although rhetorical commitments to human rights and democracy are frequently made, the overriding aim of American foreign policy since the Second World War has been to keep the world safe for capitalism, especially American capitalism. CIA, State Department, and armed service activity has been consistently directed towards an aim that was never openly admitted but can be found in unreleased documents. George Kennan, already mentioned as the author of the containment policy, for example, wrote confidentially in 1948: 'We have about 50 per cent of the world's wealth, but only 6.3 per cent of its population ... In this situation, we cannot fail to be the object of envy and resentment. Our real task in the coming period is to devise a pattern of relation-ships which will permit us to maintain this position of disparity ... We need not deceive ourselves that we can afford the luxury of altruism and world-benefaction ... We should cease to talk about vague and ... unreal objectives such as human rights, the raising of living standards, and democratization.'[17]

From the Eisenhower administration onwards, the covert side of American foreign policy consistently favoured the interests of Western corporations over 'vague and ... unreal objectives such as human rights, the raising of living standards, and democratization' as the fol-lowing accounts of CIA operations demonstrate.

In 1953 Operation Ajax, run jointly with British intelligence, facili-tated the removal of Iranian Prime Minister Mohammed Mossadeq and the return to power of the monarchy in the figure of Shah Moham-med Reza Pahlavi. Two years earlier Mossadeq had pushed through the nationalization of his country's oil industry. Mossadeq's action was a blow not only to the British-owned Anglo-Iranian Company (later to become British Petroleum) but also to U.S. oil companies with ambi-tions to exploit the vast reserves of Middle Eastern oil. The British and

Americans then cooperated in organizing a boycott of Iranian oil and, according to William Blum's account, plunged 'the already impoverished country into near destitution.'[18] Mossadeq's response involved looking to the Soviet Union for support and this provided the rationale for CIA involvement. The agency provided financial and logistical aid for Mossadeq's opponents to affect a coup d'état and restore the Shah to power. In the words of one of Operation Ajax's planners it created 'a situation and an atmosphere in Tehran that forced the people to choose between an established institution, the monarchy, and the unknown future offered by Mossadeq.'[19] After the operation, Iran remained firmly in the West's orbit for the next two and a half decades, while Shah Mohammed Reza Pahlavi's regime was maintained with torture and police terror. Much of the revenue for the country's oil went to a consortium dominated by British Petroleum, Royal Dutch Shell, and a number of U.S. corporations, including Gulf, Mobil, Standard Oil of New Jersey, and Standard Oil of California.[20]

In 1954 Operation Success in Guatemala benefited just one corporation – the United Fruit Company. United Fruit owned much of the small Central American country, including large landholdings and its railroad, its major port, and its telephone and telegraph service. Guatemalan leaders, notably President Jacobo Arbenz, threatened this dominance in the early 1950s by attempting to implement a program of land reform and building alternative communications services to those owned by the company. United Fruit responded by hiring a corps of publicists and influential lobbyists to convince the U.S. government that Arbenz was a threat to freedom and therefore had to be deposed. President Eisenhower's Secretary of State John Foster Dulles, as a former United Fruit legal representative, needed little convincing that the company's interests needed protection. His brother Allen Dulles, director of the CIA, was given the task of toppling Arbenz, and Operation Success was launched at the beginning of 1954. At an estimated cost of around $20 million, an invasion force of mercenaries, trained by the CIA at military bases in Honduras and Nicaragua, was organized under the leadership of Colonel Carlos Castillo Armas. With U.S. air support, the invasion was successful, and Armas became the first of a series of Guatemalan military dictators acceptable to and even trained by the United States. In the decades that followed Arbenz's downfall, the country remained impoverished, while tens of thousands of dissidents were murdered by official or semi-official death squads.[21]

Although there is not the space here to elaborate, CIA planning, finance, and organization also contributed to successful coups in the Dominican Republic, Vietnam, and other countries, and many efforts to assassinate foreign leaders, such as Cuba's Fidel Castro. The best documented example of corporate involvement in these efforts involved the International Telephone and Telegraph Company and the removal of Chilean president Salvatore Allende in 1973. ITT and other U.S. multinationals had become increasingly worried about their Chilean interests from the late 1960s, when it became apparent that Allende and his Socialist party were capable of winning electoral power. In 1970 John McClone, a member of the ITT board of directors and former CIA head, contacted the agency to offer $1 million for anti-Allende efforts. Without directly accepting the money, the CIA advised the company on 'secure' funding channels to opponents of Allende.

Despite these efforts, Allende narrowly won the 1970 elections. From then on, as James Coleman summarizes, ITT 'repeatedly urged the CIA to take tough action against Allende, traded information with the agency, and tried to persuade other U.S. corporations to bring economic pressure to bear against Chile.'[22] A government-corporate assault on the Chilean economy began involving such tactics as asking banks to delay credits and companies to drag their feet in shipping supplies necessary for Chile's industry. In the words of President Nixon, the intention was to 'make the economy scream.' The assault succeeded in destabilizing the Chilean economy and preparing the way for the coup of 11 September 1973 and the murder of President Allende. Another brutal and repressive military regime was set up in South America, under the leadership of one of the coup's plotters, General Augusto Pinochet.[23]

The murders, assassinations, and terrorist acts that accompanied the aforementioned coups and many others were criminal acts in law, both in the United States and in the country in which they took place and, as such, were examples of what William Chambliss has termed 'state-organized crime.' Chambliss has provided a link between state-organized crime in the modern world and that of the early stages of capitalist development:

> The impetus for the criminality of European states that engaged in piracy was the need to accumulate capital in the early stages of capitalist formation. State-organized crime did not disappear, however, with the emergence of capitalism as the dominant economic system of the world. Rather, contemporary state-organized crime also has its roots in the ongo-

ing need for capital accumulation of modern-nation states, whether the states be socialist, capitalist, or mixed economies.

... At the most general level, the contradictions that are the force behind state-organized crime today are the same as those that were the impetus for piracy in sixteenth-century Europe. The accumulation of capital determines a nation's power, wealth, and survival today, as it did 300 years ago. The state must provide a climate and a set of international relations that facilitate this accumulation if it is to succeed. State officials will be judged in accordance with their ability to create these conditions.[24]

David Kauzlarisch and Ronald Kramer in their book *Crimes of the American Nuclear State* (1998) acknowledged Chambliss's pioneering study as a major influence and showed how forms of state-organized crime have harmed Americans themselves. They document that the building of weapons of mass destruction by corporations contracted by the government led to massive pollution of the environment. Radioactive and other hazardous wastes 'contaminated the air, soil, and water at most of the nuclear weapons production facilities around the country, often in violation of federal environmental law.'[25] After detailing a long and continuing record of abuse and neglect concerning the environment, they conclude that the organization of the nuclear weapons production has normalized deviance: 'As a result of placing primacy on production goals through the most expedient and effective means, the [weapons] complex has engaged in, and continues to engage in, the illegal disposal and storage of toxic waste. These illegal practices, then, can be seen as a logical result of the organization's patterned method of operation. Since virtually every weapons production facility is or has operated in violation of one or more environmental laws, the organization as a whole could be viewed as a "culture" of non-compliance.'[26]

The authors also detail the background to the thousands of radiation experiments on unwitting U.S. citizens conducted under official U.S. auspices in the decades after the end of the Second World War and until recently kept secret. The vast majority of these experiments were illegal under international law, because they violated the Nuremberg code, which outlaws non-consensual, reckless, and coercive experiments.[27] 'Today,' the authors sum up, 'we face landscapes poisoned by the effluent of a long history of nuclear weapons production' and there are also 'people who suffer the effects of illegal or ethically questionable radiation tests' and 'those who mourn the untimely death of loved ones who were victims of such tests.'[28]

As far as conventional weaponry is concerned, R.T. Naylor has done most to explain the complexities involved in the interplay between legitimate arms manufacturers, regulators, and the illicit trade during the Cold War and post–Cold War era. According to Naylor, the arms business is 'inherently dirty.' Even when 'weapons are produced within major industrialized countries for sale strictly to their own military forces, business-as-usual means commercial espionage, bid-rigging, phony invoicing, and a revolving door relationship between producer, purchaser, and public overseer that, a century earlier, would have made an American railroad baron blush.'[29]

In the 1970s U.S. arms manufacturers began to face major competition from European firms and 'the application of criminal methods to grease otherwise legitimate deals in major weapons systems became a common occurrence.'[30] The giant Lockheed Corporation, for example, bribed officials in at least ten countries and, in Japan, paid $7.1 million to former war criminal Yoshio Kodama to act as a company sales agent.[31]

The actual black market in arms remained quite contained during most of the Cold War years, but in the 1980s, according to Naylor, demand 'literally exploded' in response to prolonged regional conflicts in the Persian Gulf, Afghanistan, Central America, Southern Africa, the Andes, the Horn of Africa, and the Middle East. War and the potential for war encouraged regional arms races.

In theory most major arms-producing countries attempt to regulate the sale of weapons, but in practice smuggling and evasion are easy.[32] Arms are part of a massive global black market economy that is not organized by a monolithic criminal conspiracy but consists of a series of arm's-length commercial relationships. Naylor shows that a modern covert arms deal is likely to take place within a matrix of black market transactions:

> Weapons might be sold for cash, exchanged for hostages, bartered for heroin or religious artifacts, or counter-traded for grain or oil.
>
> The transactions can be handled by middlemen equally at home in smuggling rubies from Burma, sneaking counterfeit computer chips into the U.S. or dumping toxic waste in Lebanon.
>
> The transportation can be entrusted to a company whose headquarters is designated by one of several dozen brass-plates on the door of a small Cayman Islands' office staffed by one employee who sits watching American soaps for the whole working day.

Such companies in turn will hire to haul the arms, ships registered in one of the many flag-of-convenience centers that are so much the bane of seafarers' unions ...

The payments can move through a series of coded bank accounts in the name of a network of shell companies – protected by the banking and corporate secrecy laws of one or several of those financial havens that are proliferating faster than accountants specializing in tax evasion can keep track of them.

And behind it all might well be a complex of (often merely tacit) alliances between groups as varied as career smugglers, legal arms manufacturers, political party bagmen, 'organized crime' families, insurgent armies, and intelligence service agents.[33]

Naylor's description captures the nebulous nature of much international organized crime activity perfectly.

International Organized Crime and Corporate Policy

U.S. and other Western corporations have extended their activities globally since the Second World War. Some of these activities would have been illegal if practised in the United States, others were illegal in their host countries but unlikely to be punished or monitored for a variety of reasons, including corruption and lack of enforcement resources.

While occupational safety and environmental laws were being passed or tightened up in the United States, corporations, seeking to maintain high profit levels, looked to countries where regulations concerning safety, health, and pollution were less severe or less likely to be vigorously enforced.[34] The inadequacy of consumer protection in many developing countries has meant, for example, that pharmaceuticals found to be too dangerous for the U.S. consumer were widely sold in other countries, particularly in poorer parts of the world where facilities for testing or monitoring drugs are at best rudimentary. According to Marshall B. Clinard, where regulations are loose, as in most Third World countries, 'there is a great temptation to make greater profits by remaining silent or by misleading patients and physicians, and possible lethal side effects of important and widely-used drugs are often either ignored or minimalized.'[35]

A similar situation existed with pesticides. In 1982 Oxfam estimated that each year in the Third World there were 375,000 pesticide poisonings with a resulting 10,000 deaths. The U.S. government banned many of the most lethal pesticides such as DDT, paraquat, dioxin, and parathion, yet U.S. corporations continued to export them, often without warnings about their possible dangers or recommendations as to their safe use. Crop-dusting airplanes sprayed pesticides indiscriminately on fields, field hands, and homes, poisoning the soil and therefore the food chain, as well as more direct victims.[36]

As for environmental protection, the U.S. Environmental Protection Agency alone had an inspection staff of more than 4,000 in the 1980s, while Mexico had only 230 safety inspectors for a workforce of more than 20 million, and India had a federal environment protection staff of only about 150.[37] Such discrepancies in safety standards and enforcement did not go unnoticed by corporations, with disastrous consequences for many workers and local communities. According to Clinard:

> A Liberian iron ore mine under the partial management of U.S. Steel ... was the site of a 1982 disaster in which a rain-swollen tailings dam burst and swamped the mining camp directly below it, killing 200 persons. In 1981, tests showed that one-third of the plant workers in Pennwalt's Nicaraguan plant were suffering from mercury poisoning. Under the Somoza regime, which was highly favourable to U.S. corporate interests, it had been able to dump between two and four tons of mercury into the lake for 12 years, killing fish and polluting the adjacent area. One report indicated that toxic mercury in the air of the plant was 12 times higher than the safety level recommended by the U.S. National Institute of Occupational Safety and Health. In an Indonesian battery manufacturing plant of Union Carbide Corporation, tests showed that more than half the work force was suffering from kidney diseases attributable to mercury poisoning and contamination, according to the company physician.[38]

The prospect of looser enforcement of environmental regulations also partly explains the explosive growth of *maquiladoras* or assembly plants in the free-trade zone on the Mexican side of the U.S.–Mexico border since 1980. That year there were 620 maquiladora plants employing 119,550 workers. Twelve years later there were 2,200 factories employing more than 500,000 Mexican workers as many giant U.S. companies including General Electric, Ford, General Motors, and Westinghouse located there. Studies have shown evidence of massive toxic dumpings in the maquiladora zones, polluting rivers, groundwater, and soils and causing severe health problems among workers and deformities among babies born to young women working in the zone.[39]

The industrial disaster that to date dwarfs all others, with the possible exception of Chernobyl, was caused by a leak at a U.S. transnational plant making pesticides in the Indian city of Bhopal. This plant operated by Union Carbide of India Limited, a subsidiary of Union Carbide Corporation, used highly toxic chemicals including methyl isocynanate (MIC) in its production processes. On the night of 2 December 1984, as a result of a leak from the plant, a white cloud of toxic fumes killed, maimed, or injured around half the city's population. As many as 10,000 people may have died as an immediate result of the tragedy.[40]

Study of the causes of the tragedy has revealed corporate responsibility. Warnings made prior to the leakage were not heeded. In 1982, for example, reports pointed out safety deficiencies at the plant in instrumentation and safety valves, lax maintenance procedures, and a high turnover of both operational and managerial staffs. Although the plant stored a large quantity of MIC in tanks that should have been refrigerated, the refrigeration unit had been turned off in order to save $50 per week.[41] Frank Pearce and Steve Tombs in their book *Toxic Capitalism* (1998), have also pointed out problems in the plant design itself: 'Plant instrumentation was inadequate to monitor normal plant processes ... The refrigeration plant at Bhopal, even when working, was not powerful enough to cool all of the MIC stored there, and the vent gas scrubber and flare tower were only designed to deal with single phase ... emissions.' They conclude that far fewer people would have died if 'the plant had not been sited near shanty towns; there had been adequate risk assessment, modelling and monitoring of discharges and emergency planing and management; the plant personnel, local medical services and the state and national government had known more about the nature and effects of the deadly gaseous emissions.'[42]

Five years after the disaster Union Carbide and the Indian government reached a settlement of $470 million to compensate the 20,000 people seriously injured by the toxic fumes and the families of those who died. Once divided up individual payments were paltry and not even enough to cover medical expenses.[43] The settlement would have probably been far greater had the case been tried in the United States. The legal representatives of the Bhopal victims and the Indian government had argued that the case should be tried in the the United States partly because the relevant documents and personnel were to be found there and partly because discovery procedures were inadequate in India. Their arguments were ignored and the case was settled in India.[44]

Using Bhopal as a case study but citing many more cases, Pearce and Tombs reach the general conclusion that 'corporations, as organisations, can, do, and will commit health, safety, and environmental crimes – workers and local communities regularly suffer death, injury and ill-health due to the actions or inactions of corporations.'

There is also evidence that the interests of some U.S. corporations are still served by violence and intimidation; just as they were in the United States from the nineteenth century onwards, although rather less directly. In 1987, for example, during a strike in Mexico, the Ford Motor Company tore up its union contract, fired 3,400 workers, and cut wages by 45 per cent. The workers responded by supporting dissident labour leaders. However, resistance collapsed after gunmen hired by the official government-dominated union shot workers at random in the factory.[45]

More recently, the human rights organization Amnesty International has documented the harassment, arbitrary arrest, and ill-treatment of Indians protesting the construction of a power plant by the Dabhol Power Company (DPC) in the Ranagiri district of Maharashtra. The DPC was a joint venture between three U.S.-based multinational corporations, led by Enron with an 80 per cent share. Opposition to the project was based partly on allegations of corruption surrounding the setting up of the project and concerns about the procedures used for the granting of official clearance for the project, including the lack of consultation of affected people and the inadequate environmental impact assessment. After affected villagers and environmental activists took part in protests against the project, DPC employed private security guards and reportedly requested the state government to provide police protection. According to the Amnesty International report, following this request, the DPC allegedly entered into a contractual security arrangement with the government of Maharashta that involved the services of 100 State Reserve Police. This SRP squad and local police were then involved in a series of incidents involving harassment, violence, arbitrary arrest, and detention. One of these incidents involved Sugandha Vasudev Bhalekar, the wife of one of the leaders of the protests. Detailing the circumstances of her arrests on 3 June 1997, she testified as follows:

> At around 5 in the morning when I was in the bathroom, several male police with batons in their hands forcibly entered the house and started beating members of (my) family who were asleep ... Being terrified, I told them from inside the bathroom that I was taking a bath and that I would come out after wearing my clothes. I asked them to call for women police in the meantime and to ask them to wait near the door. But without paying any attention to my requests, the policemen forcibly opened the door and dragged me out of the house into the police van parked on the road. (While dragging me) the police kept beating me with batons. The humiliation meted out to the other members of the family was similar to the way I was humiliated ... my one and half year old daughter held on to me but the police kicked her away.

Another incident involved Adiath Kaljunkar, a leader of another protest group. On the evening of 27 February 1997, four *goondas* (ruffians) came to his house and threatened to murder him if he continued to oppose the Enron project, as they had taken on-site contracts and would suffer losses. The local police refused to record Kaljunkar's complaint.[46]

Amnesty International's report was the first to detail the abuses of corporate as well as government power. The U.S. ambassador in New Delhi, Frank G. Wisner, put pressure on the Indian government not to terminate the Enron project, before retiring and taking a seat on the Enron board.[47]

Drugs and the 'Americanization' of International Law Enforcement

Professor Ethan Nadelmann in his book *Cops Across Borders* (1993) has traced the dominant part played by the United States in the harmonization or 'Americanization,' of national criminal justice systems in the past few decades. According to Nadelmann,

> The modern era of international law enforcement is one in which U.S. criminal justice priorities and U.S. models of criminalization and criminal investigation have been exported abroad. Foreign governments have responded to U.S. pressures, inducements, and examples by enacting new

criminal laws regarding drug trafficking, money laundering, insider trading, and organized crime and by changing financial and corporate secrecy
laws as well as their codes of criminal procedure to better accommodate
U.S. requests for assistance. Foreign police have adopted U.S. investigative techniques, and foreign courts and legislatures have followed up
with the requisite legal authorizations. And foreign governments have
devoted substantial police and even military resources to curtailing illicit
drug production and trafficking ... By and large, the United States has
provided the models, and other governments have done the accommo-
dating.[48]

Nadelmann also stresses the dominant role that drug enforcement
has played in the evolution of U.S. international law enforcement since
the 1960s. Drug trafficking is only one of several illegal activities that
transcend national boundaries, but the American war on drugs has
'provided the crucial impetuses for a host of actions and agreements
that otherwise would never have occurred.'[49]

The first giant step towards the Americanization of international law
enforcement occurred in 1961 when the U.N.'s Single Convention on
Narcotic Drugs brought under one instrument all the prior international narcotics pacts, except one which the United States did not
approve of. The single convention extended international control to
include the cultivation of plants grown as the raw material of natural
narcotic drugs, putting cannabis plant and coca bush under the same
international control system as opium. It also prohibited the practices
of opium smoking, opium eating, coca-leaf chewing, hashish smoking,
and the use of the cannabis plant for any non-medical purposes.[50] The
convention thus announced the beginning of a global drug prohibition
regime constructed on the U.S. model.

Since 1961 the international response has been to build on the prohibitionist framework provided by the single convention. In 1971
another U.S. initiative saw the setting up the U.N. Fund for Drug
Abuse Control and became another tool for the implementation of
U.N. legislation. In 1972 the single convention was amended by a pro-
tocol that strengthened its provisions related to preventing the illicit
production of, traffic in, and use of narcotics. More significantly, the
1988 Convention Against Illicit Traffic in Narcotic Drugs and Psychotropic Substances came into force in November 1990. This convention
calls on party states to take specific law enforcement measures to
improve their ability to identify, arrest, prosecute, and convict those

who traffic in drugs across national boundaries. Such measures include the establishment of drug-related criminal offences and sanctions under domestic law, making such offences the basis for international extradition between party states, and providing for mutual legal assistance in the investigation and prosecution of covered offences, as well as the seizure and confiscation of proceeds from and instrumentalities used in illicit trafficking activities.[51] The United Nations, ironically, considering its mission, had thus encouraged the rapid expansion of drug-control bureaucracies in more than a hundred countries in order to perpetuate an American crusade that, as we have seen, was overtly racist in origin and covertly racist in operation.

Given the massive and increasing demand for drugs worldwide, drug trafficking will continue to be a growth industry. The fluidity and spontaneity in the drug market and the corruptibility of government officials not just in the United States but in every other nation ensures that the war on drugs can never be won under the present global prohibition regime.

There must be a serious evaluation of current prohibitive drug control policies in order to reduce the damage done by drugs and drug trafficking to both rich and poor countries. As David Bewley-Taylor argues in *Creating Constraint* (1996): 'Alternative strategies must be considered if both national and international approaches to drug use are to have any chance of success ... drug laws must be in accord with the culture, customs, and conventions that exist in any particular society.'

The prospects for such a rethink, however, are grim, he continues, 'while nations remain constrained by a framework of U.N. drug control conventions and an international norm based upon the failed doctrine of U.S.-oriented drug prohibition.[52] So long as countries are constrained by U.N. conventions and committed to U.S.-style drug prohibition, there is little chance of a diminution in the damage done by illegal drugs.

The Perception of Organized Crime as an International Security Threat

The influence of the United States has thus helped to ensure that most countries have come into step with an international prohibition-based drug control regime built around the framework established by U.N. conventions. But the war on drugs, according to the U.N.'s own admission, has failed. In 1992 a U.N. report noted that 'the illegal use of drugs has grown at an alarming rate over the past twenty years, cross-ing all social, economic, political, and national boundaries.'[53]

Recent U.N. estimates have indicated that coca cultivation has dou-bled since 1985, and drug prices generally have fallen. This failure is confirmed by the estimates of other institutions. Although the United Nations has consistently put the eradication of opium at centre-stage, the Lindesmith Center found in 1998 that opium production had been rising sharply.[54] Prompted by the 1961 convention's legacy of failure, Anthony Henman asked, 'How is it that an instrument designed to reduce the use of illicit drugs can ultimately have ushered in an age when the consumption of these substances has increased beyond even the most alarmist projections? ... Is it not obvious,' he continued, 'that the misconceived obsession with extirpating the use of certain drugs – those deemed illicit – greatly increases the profitability of their pro-duction?'[55] As money laundering scandals continue to show, the massive profits available from the distribution as well as production of illegal drugs has encouraged the development of significant inter-national criminal associations and networks among professionals, such as lawyers, accountants, corrupt officials, career criminals, and simple opportunists. The violence and corruption that has accompa-nied the global proliferation of networks involved in the drug trade since the 1961 U.N. convention brings to mind Chamberlin's 1931 warning that the intentions of American idealists may have supplied 'the pavement for the hell of organized crime.'[56]

By the post–Cold War era a new generation of American idealists were setting the international agenda and could not countenance con-ceptualizations of organized crime that implied a critique of U.S. laws and institutions. On the contrary, they needed the international com-munity to accept a conceptualization of organized crime that both excused the failure of national and international efforts against drugs and justified the expansion of these efforts. U.S. politicians, govern-ment officials, journalists, and academics thus sought ways to reduce the world's complexities to the same type of good versus evil proposi-tions that served so well during the Cold War. The menace of trans-national or global organized crime not only helped explain away the failure in the drug war but was as easy to communicate as contain-ment.

A Washington, DC, conference of high level U.S. law enforcement and intelligence community personnel led the way in September 1994 by internationalizing America's pluralist revision of the Mafia conspiracy theory. They began to propagate a very simple idea. Because forces outside of mainstream national cultures now threatened national institutions everywhere, U.S. organized crime-control techniques should be employed everywhere. These techniques were necessary to combat what the conference title referred to as *Global Organized Crime: The New Empire of Evil*.

According to the executive summary of the conference, 'The dimensions of global organized crime present a greater international security challenge than anything Western democracies had to cope with during the cold war. Worldwide alliances are being forged in every criminal field from money laundering and currency counterfeiting to trafficking in drugs and nuclear materials. Global organized crime is the world's fastest growing business, with profits estimated at $1 trillion.'

The keynote speaker at the conference, FBI Director Louis Freeh, stressed that 'the ravages of transnational crime' were the greatest long-term threat to the security of the United States and warned that the very fabric of democratic society was at risk everywhere. CIA Director R. James Woolsey noted that 'the threats from organized crime transcend traditional law enforcement concerns. They affect critical national security interests ... some governments find their authority besieged at home and their foreign policy interests imperiled abroad.'[57]

Claire Sterling, an American journalist based in Italy, also spoke at the conference and reiterated the thesis of her recent book *Thieves' World* (1994). In this she had argued that a new global network of organized crime – a 'Worldwide Mafia International' had emerged since the fall of communism. In this network or 'Pax Mafiosa,' the Sicilian Mafia, the American Cosa Nostra, the Russian Mafia, Colombian drug cartels, Japanese Yakusa, and Chinese triads were working together and constituted 'the most massive and insidious criminal assault in history.'[58] This new global threat of organized crime required a tougher and more collaborative international response, more specifically it required more thorough information sharing between police and intelligence officials in different countries and improved methods of transcending jurisdictional frontiers in pursuing and prosecuting malefactors.[59]

Two months after the Washington conference, the United Nations held the World Ministerial Conference on Organized Transnational Crime and provided an international forum for the global pluralist theory of organized crime. The conference was held in Naples and attended by high level governmental representatives from 138 countries. The rhetoric and analysis was essentially the same as that employed by Freeh, Woolsey, and Sterling. According to the U.N.'s press release, participants at the conference recognized the growing threat of organized crime, with its 'highly destabilizing and corrupting influence on fundamental social, economic and political institutions.' This represented a challenge demanding increased and more effective international cooperation. 'The challenge posed by transnational organized crime,' the document continued, 'can only be met if law enforcement authorities are able to display the same ingenuity and innovation, organizational flexibility and cooperation that characterize the criminal organizations themselves.'[60] Essentially this was the same line as that articulated by American commentators from the 1950s onwards and given presidential support by Richard Nixon in the early 1970s.

U.N. Secretary-General Boutros Boutros-Ghali set the tone of the conference and gave probably the best exposition of the new conventional wisdom on organized crime with his opening address:

'This is a particularly opportune moment for us to reflect together on ways and means of strengthening action to combat organized crime. Indeed, throughout the world, transnational crime is spreading. It encompasses all regions and all continents. Organized crime has thus become a world phenomenon. In Europe, in Asia, in Africa and in America, the forces of darkness are at work and no society is spared ...

Once, transnational crime was organized along relatively simple lines and involved a limited number of activities. Today it is profoundly diversified and widespread. During the past few years, its fields of operation have been constantly expanding. To its traditional spheres of activity, such as prostitution, the arms trade and trafficking in drugs, organized crime has now added money laundering, the trade in nuclear technology and human organs and the transporting of illegal immigrants. And these are only a few examples of the new markets which feed and enrich contemporary transnational crime.

... Organized crime on a transnational scale tends today to be impersonal and anonymous. Operating in several countries, making profits from the proceeds of its activities throughout the world, and taking advantage of new technology to insinuate itself insidiously into the machinery of national economies, it scoffs at frontiers and becomes a universal force. Traditional crime organizations have, in a very short time, succeeded in adapting to the new international context to become verita-

ble crime multinationals. Thus, illegality is gaining inexorably. It is corrupting entire sectors of international activity ...

... Transnational crime ... undermines the very foundations of the international democratic order. Transnational crime poisons the business
climate, corrupts political leaders, and undermines human rights. It
weakens the effectiveness and credibility of institutions and thus undermines democratic life.

When order is in retreat, and when law, morals and democracy are
under attack, all kinds of criminal ventures and deviant behavior may be
spawned. This is what we are bound to work together to prevent. The
danger is all the more pernicious because organized crime does not
always confront the State directly. It becomes enmeshed in the institutional machinery. It infiltrates the State apparatus, so as to gain the indirect complicity of government officials ...

We also know, however, that when the States decide to take effective,
voluntary steps to combat transnational crime, and when they decide to
cooperate with each other and harmonize their efforts, legitimate society
regains all its power and strength. It is on behalf of this effort to promote
the rule of law and to combat transnational crime that we are meeting
here in Naples.[61]

Boutros-Ghali was followed by series of speakers echoing the same
themes: the threat posed by organized crime to societies and governmental institutions across the globe and the need for more international cooperation to meet this threat. The seriousness of the perceived
threat was emphasized in the language of many of the speeches. For
example, Elias Jassan, Secretary of Justice in Argentina, described organized crime as 'a new monster ... the Anti-State' and Silvio Berlusconi,
Prime Minister of Italy, described crime organizations as 'armies of
evil' who could be defeated 'only by international collaboration.'[62]
There was no significant dissent from this line at the conference – discussion of organized crime at the highest international level had been
frozen by images that effectively excluded discussion.

U.S.-approved organized crime control strategies were emphasized
by most speakers and this deferential consensus was most clearly
reflected in another background document for this conference, which
singled out 'the 1970 Racketeer Influenced and Corrupt Organizations
(RICO) statute as an example of 'dynamic' legislation able to 'adapt
itself to ... developments.' The document then elaborated, 'In the
United States, the RICO statute is generally considered to be the start-

ing point of a new process of awareness of organized crime by the United States Government and its criminal justice system. Its effectiveness has been demonstrated in the many indictments and convictions of members of organized crime groups that have resulted since the legislation was passed.'[63]

U.S. Attorney-General Janet Reno reiterated this theme in her speech to the conference. She suggested that her fellow leaders should identify the strategies and tactics that contributed to recent successes against organized crime. Other governments should, she continued, 'pledge to expand the implementation of such useful measures in their own legal systems and ensure that their recommendations were quickly put into place.'[64] The language was carefully chosen to avoid sounding too arrogant, but it can be safely assumed that she was mainly referring to American successes against such gangsters as 'Fat' Tony Salerno, Tony 'Ducks' Corrallo, John Gotti, and others associated with America's Cosa Nostra crime families. It can also be assumed that the useful measures she was referring to included American organized crime control measures such as laws facilitating the use of covert methods to obtain evidence and the seizure of assets belonging to suspected or convicted criminals.

Western governments had been clearly moving towards the American organized crime control model even before the conference. To those that were lagging President Bill Clinton issued this warning in October 1995: 'Nations should work together to bring their banks and financial systems into conformity with the international money laundering standards. We will work to help them do so. And, if they refuse, we will consider appropriate sanctions.' Clinton called for a joint declaration on international crime, including a 'no sanctuary' clause to facilitate extradition, 'so that we could say together to organized criminals, terrorists, drug-traffickers, and smugglers: You have nowhere to run and nowhere to hide.'[65] Clinton was clearly demanding that the global organized crime control model come into line with the American organized crime model as soon as possible.

Such ambitions were undoubtedly boosted in December 2000 when government officials from 140 countries gathered in Palermo, Sicily, to sign or consider signing the U.N. Convention Against Transnational Organized Crime. Among other things, it was hoped that the convention would complement the 1988 Convention Against Illicit Traffic in Narcotic Drugs and Psychotropic Substances – and finally make global drug prohibition a reality.

The new convention's analysis of the problem and many of its proposed solutions were clearly based on the U.S. model. The purpose of the convention is 'to promote cooperation to prevent and combat transnational organized crime more effectively.' Following U.S. government practice, draftees of the convention decided to define the problem of organized crime in terms of criminal hierarchies. Article 2 described an organized crime group as 'a structured group of three or more persons, existing for a period of time and acting in concert with the aim of committing one or more serious crimes or offences established in accordance with this Convention in order to obtain, directly or indirectly, a financial or other material benefit.'[66] As we saw in Chapter 5, however, the shift in U.S. thinking that led to grouping evidence related to organized crime around categories of criminals rather than around categories of criminal law only contributed to the dumbing of discourse on the problem.

States signing up to the convention will be committing themselves to organized crime control on the U.S. model with its heavy emphasis on undercover policing operations, witness protection programs, and asset forfeitures. As we have seen, the intense use of these methods has only succeeded in making America's organized crime control problems more complex. Such tactics and techniques can be justified in certain cases, but their use in the U.S. war on drugs has only helped to perpetuate a lawless crusade. Governments contemplating increasing the use of such tactics should at least ensure more rigorous supervision than the Americans have so far managed.

As in the case of the Mafia conspiracy theory and its American pluralist offspring, some evidence does support the global pluralist theory articulated at the Washington and Naples conferences. No one disputes the existence of gangster groups all over the world. Enough serious research has been conducted in the United States and elsewhere to reveal at least some of the ways various Triads, Mafiosi, Camorrista, and other groups have survived and adapted to intermittent enforcement efforts and more frequent periods of internecine bloodshed. More recent groupings of Colombian and Mexican drug traffickers and outlaw bikers have proved just as likely to use violence and intimidation in the pursuit of business activities that are often damaging and destructive in themselves.[67]

There are, however, problems with the global pluralist theory of organized crime that make it dangerously inadequate. The first is that

Mafia-type groups only participate in illegal markets, despite countless claims to the contrary, they rarely, if ever, control them. If they had tried to control illegal markets, according to R.T. Naylor, they would have 'run afoul not only of institutional and legal barriers, but also of the inherent lack of trust that inevitably threatens relations between groups whose modus operandi is based on fraud and force, and where fealty can operate only within a limited social and geographical space.'[68]

Despite frequent assertions by U.S. government officials, the Colombian drug 'cartels,' for example, never 'controlled' the cocaine market by restricting supply. Cartel was an inappropriate description in the first place since the price of cocaine has been steadily and uncontrollably declining since the 1970s.[69] Colombian cocaine syndicates are better described as loosely tied criminal organizations that can subdivide, disperse, and reunite in new and unpredictable formations.[70]

Instead, as noted in Chapter 7 and as most conscientious researchers have confirmed, fragmentation and competition rather than monopolization characterize drug and other illegal markets. Looking at the European situation, Vincenzo Ruggiero and Nigel South, found, for example, that flux is the norm in illegal markets, which 'seem populated by small firms, some of which are peripheral and ephemeral, in a highly mobile and active scenario.'[71]

Governments, whether individually or jointly, would have few problems combatting organized crime if it really was dominated by a relatively small number of supercriminal organizations. They would eliminate the leadership of these organizations and that would be the end of the problem. However, as the Americans have found, orchestrating the downfalls of Al Capone, Lucky Luciano, Tony Salerno, John Gotti, and the rest did not see the end of the messy reality of American gangsterism, let alone the much more pervasive, multifaceted, and nebulous problem of organized crime.

The second problem with the global pluralist theory is that, like the Mafia conspiracy theory, it uses semantics to camouflage the involvement of respectable institutions in organized criminal activity. Throughout Boutros-Ghali's speech in Naples, for example, the implication was always that respectable institutions were threatened by organized crime. Organized crime, he said, 'poisons the business climate,' it 'corrupts political leaders,' and it 'infiltrates the State apparatus.' Understood in this way, the only response to the organized crime 'forces of darkness' is a harmonized international effort on behalf of 'legitimate society.'[72] However, as we have seen, government agencies and key institutions, such as corporations, have frequently gained from and sometimes helped to sustain many kinds of organized criminal activity.

Finally, the history of U.S. organized crime itself demonstrates the inadequacy of global pluralist analysis, as doubtless could the history of organized crime in any of the countries represented at the U.N. transnational organized crime conferences. As has been shown throughout this book, organized criminal *activity* was never a serious threat to established or evolving economic and political power structures in the United States but more often a fluid, variable, and open-ended phenomenon that complemented those structures. Seen in this light, the wisdom of using the pretext of organized crime control to give extra powers to the officialdom that supports these structures should at least be questioned.

Governments are, however, hardly likely to support any analysis that makes them part of the problem. At the Naples conference, every government speaker represented a nation with a great deal of dirty linen to conceal – some, such as the Indonesian Minister of Justice, more obviously than others.[73] The American concept of organized crime as a threat to legitimate society gave all of them a way of formulating organized crime control policy without examining past and current evidence of government, corporate, or professional involvement in systematic criminal activity. So, like those New Yorkers who cheered the racket-busting efforts of Thomas Dewey in the 1930s, they were happy to go along with the construction of a giant labyrinthian trap for criminal rats, to learn whether or how soon they can get out of it.'[74]

The U.S. 'rat-trap' organized crime control strategy of targeting and immobilizing specific criminals or criminal networks has already been successfully exported to many parts of the world and will continue to provide short-term successes for diligent policing and prosecuting agencies. This will certainly ensure sensational arrests and convictions of major international crime figures, and this in itself is no bad thing. The 'rat-trap' strategy will, however, be as inadequate in addressing the problems of international organized crime in the twenty-first century as it was in the United States during the twentieth century.

The international community could develop alternative organized crime control strategies based on re-examining counterproductive drug control policies and giving adequate resources to efforts that reduce the damage done by systematic criminal activity. However, the international community is unlikely to make much progress towards reducing the destructive impact of organized crime in all its many and varied forms while its understanding of the problem is based on an analytical framework that only serves to justify unworkable laws and whitewash flawed systems. Thus, most countries thus seem set to continue down the costly and hazardous American road detailed in the foregoing pages.

Notes

Introduction

1 U.N. General Assembly, *Ninth United Nations Congress on the Prevention of Crime and the Treatment of Offenders: Discussion Guide* (New York: United Nations, 1993) 9.

2 E.R. Hawkings and Willard Waller, 'Critical Notes on the Cost of Crime,' *Journal of Criminal Law and Criminology* 26 (1936): 684–5.

3 See, e.g., the Introduction by Andrew A. Bruce in John Landesco *Organized Crime in Chicago* (Chicago: University of Chicago Press, 1929), which included the following description of Chicago: 'It is a city of the slums and of the river wards and of the lake front of Michigan Boulevard. To it have come hundreds and thousands of the poor of Europe who, in most cases have arrived without friends and without money. In its slums and river and railroad wards have congregated the native-born "down and outs" of a large part of the American continent. It is a noticeable fact that in these less favored areas, in these abiding places of the transients and of the "down and outs," and of the newly arrived immigrant, are to be found the breeding places of the gangs, of the Mafia, and of the professional criminal.' (6).

4 The following works did much to demolish the intellectual credibility of mafia mythology: Joseph Albini, *The American Mafia: Genesis of a Legend* (New York: Irvington, 1971); William Moore, *The Kefauver Committee and the Politics of Crime* (Columbia: University of Missouri Press, 1974); Alan A. Block, *East-Side–West Side: Organizing Crime in New York, 1930–1950* (Cardiff: University College Cardiff Press, 1980); Dwight Smith, *The Mafia Mystique* (New York: Basic Books, 1975); Humbert Nelli, *The Business of Crime: Italians and Syndicate Crime in the United States* (New York: Oxford University Press, 1976); Gordon Hawkins, 'God and the Mafia,' *Public Inter-*

est 14 (Winter 1969): 24–51. Howard Abadinski, *Organized Crime* (Chicago: Nelson-Hall, 1985); and Jay Albanese, *Organized Crime in America* (Cincinnati: Anderson, 1989) are also valuable introductions.

5 Gary W. Potter, *Criminal Organizations: Vice, Racketeering, and Politics in an American City* (Prospect Heights, Ill.: Waveland Press, 1994), 7.

1   Old World Antecedents and the Rise of American Power

1 Clinton Rossiter, 'Introduction' in Edward S. Corwin, *The 'Higher Law': Background of American Constitutional Law* (Ithaca, NY: Great Seal, 1957), vii.
2 Karl Friedrichs, *The Philosophy of Law in Historical Perspective* (Chicago: University of Chicago Press, 1958), 34.
3 Michael E. Tigar and Madelaine R. Levy, *Law and the Rise of Capitalism* (New York: Monthly Review Press, 1976), 10–22.
4 Quoted in Ramsey Macmullen, *Corruption and the Decline of Rome* (New Haven: Yale University Press, 1988), 91.
5 Quoted in ibid., 92.
6 Ibid., 142–60.
7 Quoted in ibid., 162.
8 J.M. Roberts, *The Pelican History of the World* (Harmondsworth: Penguin, 1980), 400.
9 Raymond Moley, 'Behind the Menacing Racket,' *New York Times*, 23 Nov. 1930, 1.
10 Elizabeth Taylor, *Kings Caple in Archenfield* (Little Logaston, Woonton Almeley: Logaston Press, 1997), 23.
11 Andrew McCall, *The Medieval Underworld* (London: Hamish Hamilton, 1979), 107–8.
12 Charles Tilly, 'War Making and State Making as Organized Crime,' in Peter Evans, Dietich Rueschemeyer, and Theda Skocpol, eds., *Bringing the State Back In* (Cambridge: Cambridge University Press, 1985), 173.
13 Ibid.
14 Ibid., 183.
15 In Sicily, e.g., where the term 'mafia' began to be used in the late nineteenth century. In 1900 Gaetano Mosca, one of the first experts on crime in Sicily, described mafia as 'a particular type of behaviour in a certain context of social relations: it is used in Sicily to refer to ... a complex of small groups each with its own specific aims and purposes ... that had nothing fixed or bureaucratic about them.' John A. Davis, *Conflict and Control: Law and Order in Nineteenth-Century Italy* (Basingstoke: Macmillan, 1988) 296.

16 Richard Cobb, *Paris and Its Provinces, 1792–1802* (London: Oxford University Press, 1975), 186.

17 Ibid., 192.

18 Christopher Hibbert, *The Roots of Evil: A Social History of Crime and Punishment* (Harmondsworth: Penguin, 1966), 66.

19 Uwe Danker, 'Bandits and the State: Robbers and the Authorities in the Holy Roman Empire in the Late Seventeenth and Early Eighteenth Centuries,' in Richard J. Evans, ed., *The German Underworld: Deviants and Outcasts in German History* (London: Routledge, 1988), 99.

20 Roberts, *Pelican History,* 492, 529.

21 Edoardo Grendi, 'Counterfeit Coins and Monetary Exchange Structures in the Republic of Genoa during the 16th and 17th Centuries,' in Edward Muir and Guido Ruggiero, *History from Crime* (Baltimore: Johns Hopkins University Press, 1994), 170–205.

22 Roberts, *Pelican History,* 529; Fernand Braudel, *The Structures of Everyday Life* (London: Fontana, 1981), 475.

23 Hugh Thomas, *The Slave Trade: The History of the Atlantic Slave Trade, 1440–1870* (London: Papermac, 1997), 239; E.P. Thompson, *Whigs and Hunters* (London: Allen Lane, 1980), 114; Geoffrey Alderman, *Modern Britain, 1700–1983: A Domestic History* (London: Croom Helm, 1986), 13–14.

24 Virginia Cowles, *The Great Swindle: The Story of the South Sea Bubble* (London: Collins, 1960), 119–23.

25 Thomas, *Slave Trade,* 241.

26 Quoted in Robert Minton, *John Law: The Father of Paper Money* (New York: Association Press, 1960), 149.

27 Cowles, *Great Swindle,* 68.

28 Quoted in Minton, *John Law,* 248.

29 Thompson, *Whigs and Hunters,* 294.

30 Ibid., 197–217.

31 Peter Wilson Coldham, *Emigrants in Chains: A Social History of Forced Migration to the Americas, 1607–1776* (Stroud, England: Alan Sutton, 1992), 20.

32 Quoted in Samuel Walker, *Popular Justice: A History of American Criminal Justice* (Oxford: Oxford University Press, 1980), 42.

33 Coldham, *Emigrants,* 13; Gerald Howson, *It Takes a Thief: The Life and Times of Jonathan Wild* (London: Cresset, 1987).

34 Bernard Bailyn, *Voyagers to the West: Emigration from Britain to America on the Eve of the Revolution* (London: I.B. Taurus, 1986), 262.

35 Bailyn *Voyagers,* 295; Coldham, *Emigrants,* 27–8.

36 Bailyn, *Voyagers,* 302–8.

37 William J. Chambliss, 'State-Organized Crime – The American Society of Criminology, 1988 Presidential Address,' *Criminology*, 27 (1989), 185–7.

38 Daniel M. Friedenberg, *Life, Liberty, and the Pursuit of Land: The Plunder of Early America* (Buffalo: Prometheus Books, 1992), 21.

39 Kenneth Andrews, *Trade, Plunder and Settlement: Maritime Enterprise and the Genesis of the British Empire*, 1480–1630 (Cambridge: Cambridge University Press, 1984), 182.

40 Marcus Rediker, 'Life under the Jolly Roger,' *Wilson Quarterly* (Summer 1988), 165–6.

41 Thomas, *Slave Trade*, 370.

42 Ibid., 143, 239.

43 Ibid., 794.

44 All quotes from Bernard Bailyn, *The Ideological Origins of the American Revolution* (Cambridge, Mass.: Bellnap Press, 1977), 135–6.

45 Winthrop quoted in Loren Baritz, 'God's Country and American Know-How,' in Allen F. Davis and Harod D. Woodman, *Conflict and Consensus in American History*, 9th ed., vol. 2 (Boston: Houghton-Mifflin, 1997), 503.

46 Hugh Brogan, *History of the United States*, (London: Longman, 1985), 80–4.

47 Charles E. Goshen, *Drink, Drugs, and Do-Gooders* (London: Collier-Macmillan, 1973), 5–6.

48 Maldwyn A. Jones, *The Limits of Liberty: American History, 1607–1980* (Oxford: Oxford University Press, 1983), 16.

49 David E. Stannard, *American Holocaust: The Conquest of the New World* (New York: Oxford University Press, 1992), 268.

50 Angie Debo, *A History of the Indians of the United States* (London: Pimlico, 1995), 293.

51 Freidenberg, *Life, Liberty*, 27.

52 Gustavus Myers, *History of the Great American Fortunes* (New York: Modern Library, 1936), 35; Brogan, *History*, 61.

53 Freidenberg, *Life, Liberty*, 26.

54 Brogan, *History*, 60.

55 Brogan, *History*, 122; Ronald Wright, *Stolen Continents: The Indian Story* (London: Pimlico, 1992), 110; Richard Van Alstyne, *Empire and Independence: The International History of the American Revolution* (New York: Wiley, 1965), 17; Freidenberg, *Life, Liberty*, 109–36.

56 Quoted in Marc Egnal, *A Mighty Empire: The Origins of the American Revolution* (Ithaca, NY: Cornell University Press, 1988), 225–6.

57 Quoted in Brogan, *History*, 125.

58 Edmund Morgan, *The Birth of the Republic, 1763–89* (Chicago: University of Chicago Press, 1977), 73; Brogan, *History*, 124–5; Bailyn, *Voyagers*, 176–7; Van Alstyne, *Empire*, 24–5.

59 Oliver M. Dickenson, *The Navigation Acts and the American Revolution* (Philiadelphia: University of Pennsylvania Press, 1951).

60 Egnal, *Mighty Empire*, 234.

61 Dickenson, *Navigation Acts*, 230–1.

62 Thomas, *Slave Trade*, 477.

63 Dickenson, *Navigation Acts*, 242–50.

64 Egnal, *Mighty Empire*, 4–7; Friedenberg, *Life, Liberty*, 152–3.

65 Quoted in Howard Zinn, *A People's History of the United States* (Harlow: Longman, 1994), 85.

66 M.J. Heale, *The American Revolution*, (London: Methuen, 1986), 13. Jones, *Limits of Liberty*, 43–4; Morgan, *Birth*, 49–58; Brogan, *History*, 166–8.

67 Morgan, *Birth*, 76.

68 John Gough, *John Locke's Political Philosophy* (Oxford: Clarendon Press, 1973), 9.

69 Allan Nevins and Henry Steele Commager, *America: The Story of a Free People* (Oxford: Oxford University Press, 1966), 105–6; Morgan, *Birth*, 125–34.

70 Michael Parenti, *Democracy for the Few* (New York: St Martin's Press, 1983), 60–75; J. R. Pole, *Foundations of American Independence* (London: Fontana, 1973), 197. Friedenberg, *Life, Liberty*, 323.

71 Zinn, *People's History*, 95.

72 Brogan, *History*, 264–5.

73 Alexander Hamilton, James Madison, and John Jay, *The Federalist Papers* (New York: New American Library, 1961), 51: 322.

74 C. Peter Magrath, *Yazoo: Law and Politics in the New Republic* (Providence: Brown University Press, 1966), 3.

75 John T. Noonan, *Bribes: The Intellectual History of a Moral Idea* (Berkeley: University of California Press, 1987), 437; Magrath, *Yazoo*, 5–7.

76 Noonan, *Bribes*, 437.

77 Magrath, *Yazoo*, 15.

78 Ibid., 18.

79 Noonam, *Bribes*, 439.

80 Myers, *Great American Fortunes*, 217.

81 Magrath, *Yazoo*, 96.

82 Zinn, *People's History*, 99.

83 Morton J. Horwitz, *The Tranformation of American Law, 1780–1860* (Cambridge: Harvard University Press, 1977), 253.

84 Myers, *Great American Fortunes*, 101.

85 Noonam, *Bribes*, 442–3.

86 Myers, *Great American Fortunes*, 93–148 gives a detailed account of Astor's often criminal business methods.

87 Angie Debo, *History of the Indians of the United States* (London: Pimlico, 1995), 119.

88 Ibid., 122–3.

89 Gregory Nobles, *American Frontiers: Cultural Encounters and Continental Conquest* (Harmondsworth: Penguin, 1997), 130.

90 Richard White, *'It's Your Misfortune and None of My Own': A New History of the American West* (Norman: University of Oklahoma Press, 1991), 339.

91 Helen Hunt Jackson, *A Century of Dishonor: The Early Crusade for Indian Reform* (New York: Harper, 1965; first published, 1881), 338–40.

92 Robert Wiebe, *The Opening of American Society: From the Adoption of the Constitution to the Eve of Disunion* (New York: Knopf, 1984), 344–5.

93 White, *It's Your Misfortune*, 115.

94 Quoted in Melissa L. Meyer, '"We Can Not Get a Living as We Used To": Dispossession and the White Earth Anishinaabeg, 1889–1920,' *American Historical Review* 96 (2) (1991), 394.

95 Carol Wilson, *Freedom at Risk: The Kidnapping of Free Blacks in America* (Lexington: University Press of Kentucky, 1994), 1–9.

96 Charles M. Wiltse, *The New Nation, 1800–1845* (London: Macmillan, 1965), 160.

97 James Lal Penick, *The Great Western Land Pirate: John A. Murrell in Legend and History* (Columbia: University of Missouri Press, 1981).

98 Thomas, *Slave Trade*, 597.

99 Daniel Mannix and Malcolm Cowley, *Black Cargoes* (London: Longman, 1963).

100 Wiebe, *Opening*, 347.

101 Edward Pessen, 'Corruption and the Politics of Pragmatism: Reflections on the Jacksonian Era,' in Abraham S. Eisenstadt, Ari Hoogenboom, Hans L. Trefousse, eds., *Before Watergate: Problems of Corruption in American Society* (Brooklyn: Brooklyn College Press, 1978), 79.

102 David R. Johnson, *Policing the Urban Underworld: The Impact of Crime on the Development of the American Police, 1800–1887* (Philadelphia: Temple University Press, 1979), 23–4.

103 Timothy Gilfoyle, *City of Eros: New York City, Prostitution and the Commercialization of Vice* (New York: W.W. Norton, 1992), 45.

104 Friedenberg, *Life, Liberty*, 328.

105 Myers, *Great American Fortunes*, 282.

106 Charles Dickens, *American Notes for General Circulation* (Harmondsworth: Penguin, 1985; first published, 1842), 286–7.

107 Matthew Josephson, *The Robber Barons* (New York: Harcourt, Brace, 1934), 135.

108 Myers, *Great American Fortune*, 285.
109 Ken Dornstein, *Accidentally on Purpose: The Making of a Personal Injury Underworld in America* (New York: St Martin's Griffin, 1998), 31.
110 Johnson, *Illegal Tender: Counterfeiting and the Secret Service in 19th Century America* (Washington, DC: Smithsonian Institution, 1995) xiv, 37.
111 Ibid., 41.
112 Johnson, *Policing the Urban Underworld*, 51–9.
113 Charles N. Glaab and A. Theodore Brown, *A History of Urban America* (New York: Macmillan, 1976), 78; Gus Tyler, ed., *Organized Crime in America: A Book of Readings* (Ann Arbor: University of Michigan Press, 1967), 89–108.
114 Gilfoyle, *City of Eros*, 85–91.
115 Johnson, *Policing the Urban Underworld*, 155; Gilfoyle, *City of Eros*, 69.
116 Glaab and Brown, *History of Urban America*, 187.
117 Charles Garrett, *The La Guardia Years: Machine and Reform Politics in New York City* (New Brunswick, NJ: Rutgers University Press, 1961), 1–33; Alfred Connable and Edward Silberfarb, *Tigers of Tammany: Nine Men Who Ran New York* (New York: Holt, Rinehart and Winston, 1967), 114–213.
118 Gustavus Myers, *Tammany Hall* (privately published, 1901); Herbert Asbury, *The Gangs of New York* (New York: Knopf, 1927), 177.
119 Robert M. Fogelson, *Big-City Police* (Cambridge: Harvard University Press, 1977), 3.
120 Wiebe, *Opening* 374.
121 Letter in the *New York Times*, 13 Dec. 1860 quoted in Kenneth Stampp, ed., *The Causes of the Civil War* (New York: Touchstone, 1991), 76–7.
122 Sherman quoted in John F. Marszalek, *Sherman: A Soldier's Passion for Order* (New York: Macmillan, 1993), 236.
123 James M. McPherson, *Battle Cry of Freedom: The Civil War Era* (New York: Oxford University Press, 1988), 808–11; William Miller, *A New History of the United States* (London: Paladin, 1970), 192.
124 Eliza F. Andrews, *The War Journal of a Georgia Girl (1908)*, excerpted in Thomas A. Bailey and David M. Kennedy, eds., *The American Spirit* (Lexington: D.C. Heath, 1991), 448–9.
125 Brogan, *History*, 353.

2 Whitewash: Racism, Xenophobia, and the Origins of Organized Crime in the United States

1 Quoted in Leon F. Litwack, 'Black Liberators' in Thomas E. Frazier, *The Underside of American History*, vol. 2, *Since 1865* (New York: Harcourt Brace Jovanovitch, 1982), 32.

2 Quoted in Herbert Shapiro, *White Violence and Black Response: From Reconstruction to Montgomery* (Amherst: University of Massachusetts Press, 1988), 5.
3 Quoted in Pete Daniel, 'The Metamorphosis of Slavery, 1865–1900.' *Journal of American History* 66 (June 1979) 90.
4 Allen Trelease, *White Terror: The Ku Klux Klan Conspiracy and Southern Reconstruction* (Westport, Conn.: Greenwood Press, 1971, 1995), 139–40.
5 Robert Higgs, *Competition and Coercion: Blacks in the American Economy, 1865–1914* (Cambridge: Cambridge University Press, 1977), 9.
6 Forest G. Wood, *Black Scare: The Racist Response to Emancipation and Reconstruction* (Berkeley: University of California Press, 1970, 85.
7 Statute quoted in Stetson Kennedy, *Southern Exposure* (New York: Doubleday, 1946), 23–4.
8 Stanley F. Horn, *The Invisible Empire: The Story of the Ku Klux Klan 1866–1871* (Cos Cob, Conn.: John E. Edwards Reprint, 1969), 10–12.
9 Wyn Craig Wade, *The Fiery Cross: The Ku Klux Klan in America* (New York: Simon and Schuster, 1987); Trelease, *White Terror* George C. Rable, *But There Was No Peace: The Role of Violence in the Politics of Reconstruction* (Athens: University of Georgia Press, 1984).
10 Quoted in Albion Winegar Tourgee, *The Invisible Empire* (Baton Rouge: Louisiana State University Press, 1989), 64.
11 Christopher Waldrep, 'Substituting Law for the Lash: Emancipation and Legal Formalism in a Mississippi County Court' *Journal of American History* (March 1996), 1450.
12 Trelease, *White Terror*, 290; Jonathan M. Wiener, *Social Origins of the New South: Alabama, 1860–1885* (Baton Rouge: Louisiana State University Press, 1978), 64.
13 Wade, *The Fiery Cross*, 75.
14 Wiener, *Social Origins*, 64.
15 Trelease, *White Terror*, 189–90.
16 *Report of the Joint Select Committee to Inquire into the Condition of Affairs in the Late Insurrectionary States (Ku Klux Klan Conspiracy)*, 19 Feb. 1872, Report no. 22, pt. 1, 42nd Congress, 2d. Session, 18.
17 Ibid., 448.
18 Ted Tunnel, *Crucible of Reconstruction: War, Radicalism and Race in Louisiana, 1862–1877* (Baton Rouge: Louisiana State University Press, 1985), 154–5.
19 Carolyn E. DeLatte, 'The St Landry Riot: A Forgotten Incident of Reconstruction Violence,' *Louisiana History* 17 (Winter 1976), 46–7.
20 Tunnel, *Crucible of Reconstruction*, 157.
21 Trelease, *White Terror*, 241.
22 Rable, *But There Was No Peace*, 88–90.

23 Eric Foner, *Reconstruction: America's Unfinished Revolution* (New York: Harper and Row, 1988), 426; Trelease, *White Terror*, 287.

24 Foner, *Reconstruction*, 442.

25 Albert P. Blaustein and Robert L. Zandgrando, eds., *Civil Rights and African Americans: A Documentary History* (Evanston, Ill.: Northwestern University Press, 1991), 233–42.

26 Trelease, *White Terror*, 416–18; Stephen Cresswell, 'Enforcing the Enforcement Acts: The Department of Justice in Northern Mississippi, 1870–1890,' *Journal of Southern History* no. 3, (August 1987) 432; Rable, *But There Was No Peace*, 189.

27 Tunnell, *Crucible of Reconstruction*, 190–3.

28 Michael Perman, 'Counter Reconstruction: The Role of Violence in Southern Redemption,' in Eric Anderson and Alfred A. Moss, Jr, eds., *The Facts of Reconstruction: Essays in Honor of John Hope Franklin* (Baton Rouge: Louisiana State University Press, 1991), 132.

29 Michael Perman, *The Road to Redemption: Southern Politics, 1869–1879* (Chapel Hill: University of North Carolina Press, 1984).

30 C. Vann Woodward, *The Origins of the New South, 1877–1913* (Baton Rouge: University of Louisiana Press, 1951); Matthew Josephson, *The Politicos, 1865–1896* (New York: Harcourt, Brace, 1938, 1966), 226–31.

31 Woodward, *Origins of the New South*, 46.

32 Quoted in Vincent P. Desantis, 'Rutherford B. Hayes and the Removal of the Troops and the End of Reconstruction,' in J. Morgan Kousser and James M. McPherson, *Region, Race, and Reconstruction: Essays in Honor of C. Vann Woodward* (Oxford: Oxford University Press, 1982), 436.

33 James S. Pike, *The Prostrate State: South Carolina under Negro Government* (New York: Harper Torchbooks, 1968; first published 1874), xiv–xv.

34 Wade, *Fiery Cross*, 115–16.

35 Ibid., 138.

36 Quoted in Irving Sloan, 'Balance and Imbalance: "New History Texts and the Negro,"' in David G. Bromley and Charles F. Longio, Jr, *White Racism and Black Americans* (Cambridge: Schenkman, 1972), 343.

37 W.E. Burghardt DuBois, *Black Reconstruction in America* (New York: Russell and Russell, 1963; first published, 1935), 583.

38 Hortense Powdermaker, *After Freedom: A Cultural Study in the Deep South* (New York. Russell and Russell, 1968; first published, 1939), 86.

39 Benjamin Quarles, *The Negro in the Making of America* (New York: Macmillan, 1964), 150.

40 Nicholas Lemann, *The Promised Land: The Great Black Migration* (London: Macmillan, 1991), 19.

41 Edward L. Ayers, *Vengeance and Justice: Crime and Punishment in the*

19th Century American South (New York: Oxford University Press, 1984), 226 n6.

42 Ibid., 191.

43 Ayers, *Vengeance*, 193; Ray Ginger, *Age of Excess: The United States from 1877 to 1914* (New York: Macmillan, 1975), 33.

44 Quoted in Mark T. Carleton, *Politics and Punishment: The History of the Louisiana State Penal System* (Baton Rouge: Louisiana State University Press, 1971), 45.

45 Ayers, *Vengeance*, 196.

46 Ibid., 196.

47 This section on peonage relies most heavily on the work of Pete Daniel, *The Shadow of Slavery: Peonage in the South, 1901–1969* (Chicago: University of Illinois Press, 1972). See also Neil R. McMillen, *Dark Journey: Black Mississippians in the Age of Jim Crow* (Urbana: University of Illinois Press, 1989).

48 Daniel, *Shadow of Slavery*, 129.

49 Ibid., 49–54.

50 Ibid., 59.

51 William J. Cooper, Jr and Thomas E. Terrill, *The American South: A History* (New York: Random House, 1990) 481–4; Daniel, *Shadow of Slavery*, 37–8; Kennedy, *Southern Exposure*, 50.

52 Daniel, *Shadow of Slavery*, 11.

53 C. Vann Woodward, 'The Mississippi Horrors,' *New York Review of Books*, 29 June 1989, 15–17.

54 Alfreda M. Duster, ed., *Crusade for Justice: The Autobiography of Ida B. Wells* (Chicago: University of Chicago Press, 1970), 47–52.

55 Stewart E. Tolnay and E.M. Beck, *A Festival of Violence: An Analysis of Southern Lynchings, 1882–1930* (Urbana: University of Chicago Press, 1995), 74–5.

56 Foner, *Reconstruction*, 597–8.

57 All quotes taken from Charles E. Silberman, *Criminal Violence, Criminal Justice* (New York: Vintage Books, 1978), 167–8.

58 Quoted in Robert C. Bannister, Jr, 'Race Relations and the Muckrakers,' in John M. Harrison and Harry H. Stein, eds., *Muckraking: Past, Present and Future* (University Park: Pennsylvania State University Press, 1973), 57.

59 Dewey W. Grantham, *The Life and Death of the Solid South* (Lexington: University Press of Kentucky, 1988), 59–78.

60 Bannister, *Race Relations*, 46.

61 Donald J. Lisio, *Hoover, Blacks and Lily Whites: A Study of Southern Strategies* (Chapel Hill: University of North Carolina Press, 1985), 194–5.

62 Frederick M. Thrasher, *The Gang: A Study of 1,313 Gang in Chicago* (Chicago: University of Chicago Press, 1960; first published 1927), 142.

63 Clarence Lusane, *Pipe Dream Blues: Racism and the War on Drugs* (Boston: South End Press, 1991), 31.

64 Jeffrey Clayton Foster, 'Rocky Road to a "Drug Free Tennessee": A History of the Early Regulation of Cocaine and the Opiates, 1897–1913,' *Journal of Social History* 29 (1996) 550.

65 Ibid., 552.

66 Quoted in John Helmer, *Drugs and Minority Oppression* (New York: Seabury Press, 1975), 12.

67 Andrew Sinclair, *Prohibition: The Era of Excess* (London: Faber and Faber, 1962), 49.

68 Charles Crowe, 'Racial Violence and Social Reform – Origins of the Atlanta Riot of 1906,' *Journal of Negro History* 53 (1968), 249.

69 Denise A. Herd, 'Prohibition, Racism and Class Politics in the Post-Reconstruction South,' *Journal of Drug Issues* (Winter 1983), 84.

70 Sinclair, *Prohibition*, 51.

71 Quoted in David F. Musto, *The American Disease: Origins of Narcotic Control* (New York: Oxford University Press, 1987), 305; and John J. Rumbarger, *Power, Profits and Prohibition* (Albany: State University of New York Press, 1989), 177–8.

72 William F. Holmes, 'Moonshining and Collective Violence: Georgia, 1889–1895,' *Journal of American History* 67 (Dec. 1980), 589–611.

73 Quoted in Edith Abbott, *Historical Aspects of the Immigration Problem: Selected Documents* (Chicago: University of Chicago Press, 1926), 449–50.

74 Ibid., 603.

75 Quoted in Larry K. Harsfield, *The American Response to Professional Crime, 1870–1917* (Westport, Conn.: Greenwood Press, 1985), 90.

76 Edward Crapsey, *The Nether Side of New York; or the Vice, Crime, and Poverty of the Great Metropolis* (Montclair, NJ: Patterson Smith, 1969; first published, 1872), 156–7.

77 Ibid., 9–10.

78 Ibid., 96.

79 Ibid., 144.

80 Ibid., 162–3.

81 Ibid., 82.

82 F.P. Dewees, *The Molly Maguires: The Origin, Growth, and Character of the Organization* (Philadelphia: J.B. Lippincott, 1877) excerpted in Abbott, *Historical Aspects*, 671–82.

83 For the development of mafia mythology, see Dwight Smith, *The Mafia Mystique* (New York: Basic Books, 1975); Richard Gambino, *Blood of My Blood: The Dilemma of the Italian-Americans* (New York: Anchor Books, 1975).

84   George E. Cunningham, 'The Italians, a Hindrance to White Solidarity in Louisiana, 1890–1898,' *Journal of Negro History* 50 (Jan. 1965), 35.

85   Humbert S. Nelli, *The Business of Crime: Italians and Syndicate Crime in the United States* (New York: Oxford University Press, 1976), 50.

86   Ibid., 51.

87   Ibid., 62.

88   Ed Reid, *Mafia* (New York: Signet, 1954), 149.

89   Salvatore J. LaGumina, *Wop! Anti-Italian Discrimination in the United States* (San Francisco: Straight Arrow Books, 1973), 74–83.

90   Frederic Sondern, *Brotherhood of Evil: The Mafia* (London: Panther, 1961), 50; Jay Robert Nash, *World Encyclopedia of Organized Crime* (London: Headline, 1992), 280; John H. Davis, *Mafia Kingfish: Carlos Marcello and the Assassination of John F. Kennedy* (Markham, Ont.: Signet, 1989), 56.

91   David Chandler, *Brothers in Blood: The Rise of the Criminal Brotherhoods* (New York: E.P. Dutton, 1975), 175–94.

92   Nelli, *Business of Crime*, 64.

93   J. Alexander Karlin, 'The Italo-American Incident of 1891 and the Road to Reunion,' *Journal of Southern History* (May 1942), 242–6.

94   Gambino, op.cit., 118.

95   Gambino, op.cit., 282.

96   Jack Lait and Lee Mortimer, *Chicago Confidential* (New York: Crown, 1950), 163.

97   Jack Lait and Lee Mortimer, *USA Confidential* (New York: Crown, 1952), 77.

98   Lait and Mortimer, *Chicago Confidential*, 176.

99   Lait and Mortimer, *USA Confidential*, 15.

100 Lait and Mortimer, *Chicago Confidential*, 38–44.

101 Lait and Mortimer, *Washington Confidential* (New York: Crown, 1951), 117.

102 Lait and Mortimer, *USA Confidential*, (1952) 316.

103 William Moore, *The Kefauver Committee and the Politics of Crime* (Columbia: University of Missouri Press, 1974), 85.

104 Book Review Section in *New York Times*, 25 July 1948, 5 March 1950, 16 March 1952.

105 Reid, *Mafia*, 25.

106 Ibid., 1.

107 Quoted in Michael L. Kurtz, 'Organized Crime in Louisiana History: Myth and Reality,' *Louisiana History* (Fall 1983), 356.

108 Stephen Fox, *Blood and Power: Organized Crime in Twentieth-Century America* (New York: Penguin, 1990), 64.

109 Freda Adler, Gerland O.W. Mueller and William S. Laufer, *Criminology* (New York: McGraw-Hill, 1995), 304. A new edition of this textbook with

the same opening sentence on the history of organized crime was published in 2000.

3   Organized Crime and Corporate Power, 1865–1950

1 Ray Ginger, *Age of Excess* (New York: Macmillan, 1975), 25; Roy F. Nichols, *The Stakes of Power* (New York: Hill and Wang, 1961), 176–80.
2 Martin Sklar, *The Corporate Reconstruction of American Capitalism, 1890–1916: The Market, the Law and Politics* (Cambridge: Cambridge University Press, 1988), 29–30.
3 For a discussion of the work of James Weinstein, Gabriel Kolko, and Robert Wiebe, see R. Jeffrey Lustig, *Corporate Liberalism: The Origins of Modern American Political Theory, 1890–1920* (Berkeley: University of California Press, 1982), 304.
4 Quoted in Sigmund Diamond, *The Reputation of American Businessmen* (Gloucester, Mass.: Peter Smith, 1970), 56.
5 Stewart H. Holbrook, *The Age of the Moguls* (New York: Arno Press, 1981; first published 1953), 21; J. Lane Wheaton, *Commodore Vanderbilt: An Epic of the Steam Age* (New York: Knopf, 1942), 241; Gustavus Myers, *History of the Great American Fortunes* (New York: Modern Library, 1936), 307.
6 Charles F. Adams, Jr and Henry Adams, *Chapters of Erie and Other Essays* (New York: Augustus M. Kelley, 1967; first published, 1871), 30.
7 Myers, *Great American Fortunes*, 411–2.
8 Adams and Adams, *Chapters of Erie*, 135–7.
9 Ibid., 95.
10 Drew quoted in Bouck White, *The Book of Daniel Drew* (New York: Arno Press, 1973; first published, 1910.), 278. Although there is some doubt about the authenticity of this book, there is little doubt that these observations reflect late nineteenth-century business culture accurately.
11 Ibid., 270–1.
12 Holbrook, *Age of Moguls*, 56.
13 Myers, *Great American Fortunes*, 413–19.
14 Ibid., 311.
15 John D. Hicks, *The Populist Revolt: A History of the Farmers' Alliance and the People's Party* (Lincoln, Neb.: Bison Books, 1961), 65.
16 Howard Crosby, 'The Dangerous Classes,' *North American Review*, 136 (1883), 348–9.
17 Quoted in Thomas K. McCraw, *Prophets of Regulation* (Cambridge, Mass.: Bellnap Press, 1984), 27.
18 Myers, *Great American Fortunes*, 410; Lustig, *Corporate Liberalism*, 99–106.

19 Collis P. Huntington quoted in John Hutchinson, *The Imperfect Union: A History of Corruption in American Trade Unions* (New York: E. Dutton, 1972), 20; Milton H. Smith quoted in Ginger, *Age of Excess*, 20; Peter N. Caroll and David Noble, *The Free and the Unfree: A New History of the United States* (Harmondsworth: Penguin Books, 1982), 288.

20 Sidney Lens, *Labor Wars: From the Molly Maguires to the Sitdowns* (New York, Doubleday, 1973), 43–4; Myers, *Great American Fortunes*, 441–2; Matthew Josephson, *The Robber Barons* (London: Eyre and Spottiswoode, 1962), 163–4.

21 Josephson, *Robber Barons*, 117; Ginger, *Age of Excess*, 20; James William Coleman, *The Criminal Elite: The Sociology of White Collar Crime* (New York: St Martin's Press, 1985), 24.

22 Ida Tarbell, *The History of Standard Oil Company*, vol. 2 (New York: McClure, Phillips, 1904), 57–9.

23 Quoted in Ginger, *Age of Excess*, 20.

24 Ibid., 32.

25 William Miller, *A New History of the United States*, (London: Paladin 1970), 246; Daniel Yergin, *The Prize: The Epic Quest for Oil, Money and Power* (London: Simon and Schuster, 1991), 54–5.

26 Tarbell, *History of Standard Oil*, 287.

27 Ibid., 265–75.

28 Ibid., 297–9.

29 Ibid., 256–7.

30 Wayne G. Broehl, *The Molly Maguires* (Cambridge: Harvard University Press), 84, 96; Melvyn Dubofsky, *Industrialism and the American Worker, 1865–1920* (Arlington Heights, Ill.: Harlan Davidson, 1975), 35–8, Anthony F.C. Wallace, *St Clair: A Nineteenth-Century Coal Town's Experience with a Disaster-Prone Industry* (Ithaca: Cornell University Press, 1988), 275.

31 James Walker Coleman, *The Molly Maguire Riots: Industrial Conflict in the Pennsylvanian Coal Region* (New York: Arno Press, 1969), 35–7, 70–94.

32 Broehl, *Molly Maguires*, 115–18.

33 Anthony F.C. Wallace, *St Clair*, 332–3.

34 Broehl, *Molly Maguires*, 152–69.

35 Lens, *Labor Wars*, 29–33, Wallace, *St Clair*, 346.

36 Joseph G. Rayback, *A History of American Labor* (New York: Macmillan, 1966), 132; Dubofsky, *Industrialism and the American Worker*, 38.

37 Wallace, *St Clair*, 354–6.

38 Ibid., 358.

39 Ibid., 358–66.

40 Philip S. Klein and Ari Hoogenboom, *A History of Pennsylvania* (New York: McGraw-Hill, 1973), 289.

41 Wallace, *St Clair*, 366.

42 Joseph A. Page and Mary-Win O'Brien, *Bitter Wages* (New York: Grossman, 1973), 54.

43 Lens, *Labor Wars*, 26; Broehl, *Molly Maguires*, 353.

44 Allan Pinkerton, *Thirty Years a Detective* (New York: G.W. Carleton, 1886), 14.

45 Burton J. Bledstein, *The Culture of Professionalism: The Middle Class and the Development of Higher Education in America* (New York: W.W. Norton, 1977), 100.

46 Ibid., 100–4.

47 Hutchinson, *Imperfect Union*, 141.

48 Quoted in Graham Adams, *Age of Industrial Violence, 1910–1915* (New York: Columbia University Press, 1966), 159–60.

49 19. Lens, *Labor Wars*, 172; Thomas R. Brooks, *Toil and Trouble: A History of American Labor.* (New York: Delta, 1971), 129–30; Adams, *Age of Industrial Violence*, 146–75.

50 Rhodri Jeffreys-Jones, 'Violence in American History: Plug Uglies in the Progressive Era,' offprint from *Perspectives in American History* 8 (1974), 515; Rhodri Jeffreys-Jones, *Violence and Reform in American History* (New York: New Viewpoints, 1978), 81.

51 Hutchinson, *Imperfect Union*, 94.

52 Herbert Asbury, *The Gangs of New York* (New York: Knopf, 1929), 358–68.

53 Jenna Weissman Joselit, *Our Gang: Jewish Crime and the New York Jewish Community, 1900–1940* (Bloomington: Indiana University Press, 1983), 107–12.

54 Hutchinson, *Imperfect Union*, 30–41.

55 New York State Organized Crime Task Force, *Corruption and Racketeering in the New York City Construction Industry: Final Report to Governor Mario M. Cuomo*, Dec. 1989, 59–61.

56 Harold Seidman, *Labor Czars: A History of Labor Racketeering* (New York: Liveright, 1938), 241–2.

57 Philip S. Foner, *History of the Labor Movement in the United States*, vol. 3 (New York: International Publishers, 1947), 169.

58 Henry Demerest Lloyd, *Wealth against Commonwealth* (Westport, Conn.: Greenwood Press, 1976; first published, 1894), 169–70.

59 For a history of pro-labour and working-class film before the dominance of big business and 'Hollywood,' see Steven J. Ross, *Working-Class Hollywood: Silent Film and the Shaping of Class in America* (Princeton, NJ: Princeton University Press, 1998).

60 Jeremy Felt, 'Children at Work,' in Thomas R. Frazier, *The Underside of*

American History, vol. 2, *Since 1865* (New York: Harcourt Brace Jovanovich, 1982), 36–7.

61 Myers, *Great American Fortunes*, 368–9.

62 Gabriel Kolko, *Main Currents in Modern American History* (New York: Harper and Row, 1976), 93.

63 David Rosner and Gerald Markowitz, eds., *Dying for Work: Workers' Safety and Health in Twentieth Century America* (Bloomington: Indiana University Press, 1989), xi.

64 Nell Irvin Painter, *Standing at Armageddon: The United States, 1877–1919* (New York: W.W. Norton, 1987), 251.

65 Leonard Dinnerstein and David M. Reimers, *Ethnic Americans: A History of Immigration and Assimilation* (New York: Dodd, Mead, 1975), 44.

66 *The Independent* 70 (9 Feb. 1911), 306–9.

67 Jerold S. Auerbach, *Unequal Justice: Lawyers and Social Change in Modern America* (London: Oxford University Press, 1976), 44; Anthony Woodiwiss, *Rights v Conspiracy: A Sociological Essay on the History of Labour Law in the United States* (New York: Berg, 1990), 94.

68 Upton Sinclair, *The Jungle* (Harmondsworth: Penguin, 1982; first published 1906), 115–20.

69 Louis Filler, *Crusaders for American Liberalism: The Story of the Muckrakers* (New York: Collier, 1961), 162.

70 Page and O'Brien, *Bitter Wages*, 52–3.

71 Coleman, *Criminal Elite*, 138. Louis Filler, *Crusaders*, 337–8.

72 John Whiteclay Chambers II, *The Tyranny of Change: America in the Progressive Era, 1900–1917* (New York: St Martin's Press, 1980), 133; Irving Bernstein, *The Lean Years: A History of the American Worker, 1920–1933* (Baltimore: Penguin, 1966), 235–7.

73 Chambers II, *Tyranny of Change*, 132.

74 Page and O'Brien, *Bitter Wages*, 56.

75 Ibid., 54.

76 Lincoln Steffens, *The Shame of the Cities* (New York: Hill and Wang, 1963; first published 1904), 1–21.

77 'David Graham Phillips Attacks a National Boss: April 1906,' Document excerpted in Richard Hofstadter, *The Progressive Movement, 1900–1915* (Englewood Cliffs, NJ: Prentice-Hall, 1963), 108–12.

78 Washington Gladden, *Recollections* (Boston: Houghton Mifflin, 1909), 404, quoted in Robert H. Bremner, *The Depths of Poverty in the United States* (New York: New York University Press, 1956), 133.

79 Edward A. Ross, *Sin and Society: An Analysis of Latter-Day Iniquity* (Boston: Houghton Mifflin, 1907), 29–30.

80 Ibid., 26.
81 Ibid., 123.
82 Quoted in Yergin, *The Prize*, 108.
83 Gabriel Kolko, *The Triumph of Conservatism: A Reinterpretation of American History, 1900–1916* (Chicago: Quadrangle, 1967), 114–7; Frank Pearce, *Crimes of the Powerful* (London: Pluto Press, 1976), 88.
84 David Burnham, *Above the Law: Secret Deals, Political Fixes, and Other Misadventures of the U.S. Department of Justice* (New York: Scribner, 1996), 228–9.
85 Yergin, *The Prize*, 109.
86 Pearce, *Crimes of the Powerful*, 88.
87 Quoted in Martin J. Sklar, *The Corporate Reconstruciton of American Capitalism, 1890–1916: The Market, the Law, and Politics* (Cambridge: Cambridge University Press, 1988), 418.
88 Quoted in Kolko, *Triumph of Conservatism*, 260.
89 Maldwin A. Jones, *Limits of Liberty, American History 1607–1982* (Oxford: Oxford University Press, 1989), 390; Kolko, *Triumph of Conservatism*, 267.
90 Louis Filler, *Crusaders for American Liberalism: The Story of the Muckrakers* (New York: Collier Books, 1961),.337–8.
91 Quoted in Danny Schecter, *The More You Watch the Less You Know* (New York: Seven Stories Press, 1997), 445.
92 Ross, *Sin and Society*, 124.
93 Samuel Walker, *Popular Justice: A History of the American Criminal Justice System* (Oxford: Oxford University Press, 1980), 169–70.
94 Henry Barrett Chamberlin, 'The Chicago Crime Commission – How the Businessmen of Chicago are Fighting Crime,' *Journal of Criminal Law and Criminology* (Nov. 1920), 397.
95 Frederick Lewis Allen, *Only Yesterday* (New York: Bantam, 1959), 109–10.
96 Page and O'Brien, *Bitter Wages*, 59–63.
97 Daniel M. Berman, *Death on the Job: Occupational Health and Safety Struggles in the United States* (New York: Monthly Review press, 1978), 29; William Graeber, 'Hegemony through Science: Information Engineering and Lead Technology, 1925–1965,' in Rosner and Markowitz, *Dying for Work*, 145–7.
98 Ellis Hawley, *The Great War and the Search for a Modern Order: A History of the American People and Their Institutions, 1917–1933* (New York: St Martin's Press, 1979), 67, William E. Leuchtenburg, *The Perils of Prosperity, 1914–32* (Chicago: University of Chicago Press, 1970), 99.
99 Daniel Jordan, 'The Mingo War: Labor Violence in the Southern West Virginia Coal Fields, 1919–1922,' in Gary M. Fink and Merl E. Reed, eds., *Selected Papers, Southern Labor History Conference, 1976* (Westport, Conn.: Greenwood Press, 1977), 105–6.

100 Jerold S. Auerbach, *Labor and Liberty: The La Follette Committee and the New Deal* (New York: Bobbs-Merrill, 1966), 116–9.

101 Edwin H. Sutherland, *White Collar Crime: The Uncut Version* (New Haven, Conn.: Yale University Press, 1983), 43.

102 Keith Sward, *The Legend of Henry Ford* (New York: Russell and Russell, 1968), 398–9.

103 Estes Kefauver, *Crime in America* (London: Victor Gollancz, 1952), 166; Fred Cook, *Mafia!*, (London: Coronet, 1973) 98–9.

104 Quoted in Hutchinson, *Imperfect Union*, 115.

105 G.L. Hostetter and T.Q. Beesley, 'Twentieth Century Crime,' in Gus Tyler, ed., *Organized Crime in America* (Ann Arbor: University of Michigan Press, 1967), 49–57.

106 Murray I. Gurfein, 'The Racket Defined,' in Tyler, *Organized Crime*, 186.

107 Walter Lippmann, 'The Underworld as Servant,' in Tyler, *Organized Crime*, 61.

108 Paul Conkin, *The New Deal* (London: Routledge and Kegan Paul, 1967), 35–64.

109 See Jonathan Kwitny, *Vicious Circles: The Mafia in the Marketplace* (New York: W.W. Norton, 1979) for a survey of gangster activity in business and unions during the 1960s and 1970s.

110 *Chicago American*, 22 March 1934: Milton Mayer, 'The Case of Roger Touhy,' in Albert Harper, ed., *The Chicago Crime Book* (London: Tandem, 1967), 76.

111 Ovid Demaris, *Captive City* (London: Sphere, 1971), 139.

112 Ibid., 123.

113 Ibid., 122.

114 Ibid., 122; Kefauver, *Crime in America*, 55–7.

115 Demaris, *Captive*, 29–30.

116 Otto Friedrich, *City of Nets: A Portrait of Hollywood in the 1940s* (London: Headline, 1986), 61–8; Malcolm Johnson, 'Into Hollywood,' in Tyler, *Organized Crime*, 196–205.

117 Dan E. Moldea, *Ronald Reagan, MCA and the Mob* (New York: Penguin, 1987), 27.

118 Ibid., 24.

119 *New York Times*, 1 Nov. 1943.

120 Friedrich, *City of Nets*, 65; Charles Rappleye and Ed Becker, *All American Mafioso: The Johnny Rosselli Story* (New York: Doubleday, 1991), 89–90.

121 Johnson, 'Into Hollywood' in Tyler, *Organized Crime*, 203.

122 Virgil Peterson, *Barbarians in Our Midst* (Boston: Little Brown, 1952), 232–7.

123 Carlos Clarens, *Crime Movies: From Griffith to the Godfather* (London: W.W. Norton, 1980), 219; Rappleye and Becker, *All American*, 120.

124 Howard Kimeldorf, *Reds or Rackets? The Making of Radical and Conservative Unions on the Waterfront* (Berkeley: University of California Press, 1988), 124–5.

125 Ibid., 75.

126 Alan Block, *East Side – West Side: Organizing Crime in New York* (Cardiff: University College Cardiff, 1980), 184.

127 Kimeldorf, *Reds or Rackts?*, 125.

128 William Keating, *The Man Who Rocked the Boat* (London: Four Square, 1958), 80–5.

129 Alan A. Block, 'Organized Crime: History and Historiography,' in Robert Kelly, Ko-Lin Chin, Rufus Schatzberg, eds, *Handbook of Organized Crime in the United States* (Westport, Conn.: Greenwood Press, 1994), 63.

130 Hoffa quoted in Hutchinson, *Imperfect Union*, 253–4.

131 Arthur M. Schlesinger, Jr, *Robert Kennedy and His Times* (London: Futura, 1979), 179.

132 Arthur A. Sloane, *Hoffa* (London: MIT Press, 1991), 33.

133 Steven Brill, *The Teamsters* (New York: Pocket Books, 1978), 204.

134 Permanent Subcommittee on Investigations of the Committee on Government Affairs, United States Senate, 1981, *Oversight Inquiry of the Department of Labor's Investigation of the Teamsters Central States Pension Fund*, in Block, ed., *The Business of Crime: A Documentary Study of Organized Crime in the American Economy* (Boulder: Westview: 1991), 207–44; James Neff, *Mobbed Up: Jackie Presser's High-Wire Life in the Teamsters, the Mafia, and the FBI* (New York: Dell, 1989), 403–5. Dorfman remained close to the centre of a web of risky loans and kickbacks until 1983 when he was murdered just before facing a series of extortion and bribery trials.

135 Quoted in John McClellan, *Crime without Punishment* (New York: Popular Library, 1963), 155; Hutchinson, *Imperfect Union*, 252.

136 Alan A. Block and William J. Chambliss, *Organizing Crime* (New York: Elsevier, 1981), 77.

137 Richard Hofstadter, *The Paranoid Style in American Politics and Other Essays* (New York: Vintage, 1967), 190–4; Robert Harrison, *State and Society in Twentieth Century America* (London: Longman, 1997), 202.

138 Paul. F. Lazerfield and Robert K. Merton, 'Mass Communications, Popular Taste and Organised Social Action,' in Wilbur Lang Schramm, ed., *Mass Communications* (Urbana: University of Illinois Press, 1970), 505–6.

139 Ruth Vasey, *The World According to Hollywood, 1918–1939* (Exeter: University of Exeter Press, 1997), 194–5.

140 Edwin H. Sutherland, *White Collar Crime: The Uncut Version* (New Haven: Yale University Press, 1983), 8.
141 Ibid., 7.
142 Ibid., 79–152.
143 Ibid., 229–30.
144 Gilbert Geis and Colin Goff, 'Introduction' in Sutherland *White Collar Crime*, x.
145 Frank E. Hartung, 'White-Collar Offenses in the Wholesale Meat Industry in Detroit,' *American Journal of Sociology* 56 (1950), 25–32; Marshall B. Clinard, *The Black Market* (New York: Rinehart, 1952).
146 Alan Brinkley, *The End of Reform* (New York: Knopf, 1995), 266.

4 America's Moral Crusade and the Organization of Illegal Markets, 1789–1950

1 Gordon S. Wood, *The Radicalism of the American Revolution* (New York: Knopf, 1992), 335. See also Michael Woodiwiss, *Crime, Crusades and Corruption, Prohibitions in the United States, 1900–1987* (London: Pinters, 1989) for a more detailed account of America's moral crusade.
2 Clifford Roe, *Horrors of the White Slave Trade: The Mighty Crusade to Protect the Purity of Our Homes* (London: privately published, 1911), 319.
3 Andrew Sinclair, *Prohibition: The Era of Excess* (London: Faber and Faber, 1962), 117–23.
4 K. Austin Kerr, ed., *The Politics of Moral Behavior: Prohibition and Drug Abuse* (Reading, Mass.: Addison-Wesley, 1977), 73, 96, 154; John J. Rumbarger, *Profits, Power and Prohibition: Alcohol Reform and the Industrializing of America, 1800–1930* (Albany: State University of New York Press, 1989), 175–83.
5 Rufus King, *The Drug Hang-Up: America's Fifty Year Folly* (New York: W.W. Norton, 1972), 24; David Musto, *The American Disease: Origins of Narcotic Control* (New York: Oxford University Press, 1987), 104–11.
6 Frank Browning and John Gerassi, *The American Way of Crime* (New York: G.P. Putnam's Sons, 1980), 467; Edward Brecher, *Licit and Illicit Drugs* (Boston: Little, Brown, 1972), 48–50.
7 Robert Wiebe, *The Search for Order, 1877–1920* (New York: Hill and Wang, 1967), 96.
8 Quoted in David J. Langum, *Crossing Over the Line: Legislating Morality and the Mann Act* (Chicago: University of Chicago Press, 1994), 38.
9 'May the United States Prevent the Importation of Vice?' *Outlook* 92 (29 May 1909), 250–1.

10 All quotes taken from Langum, *Crossing Over the Line*, 42–4.

11 Timothy Gilfoyle, 'Moral Origins of Political Surveillance: The Preventitive Society in New York City, 1867–1918,' *American Quarterly,* 38 (1986), 264; Claire Marie Renzetti, 'Purity vs Politics: The Legislation of Morality in Progressive New York, 1890–1920,' doctoral dissertation, University of Delaware, 1993, 135.

12 Quoted in Langum, *Crossing Over the Line*, 273, n7.

13 Norman H. Clark, *Deliver Us from Evil: An Interpretation of American Prohibition* (New York: W.W. Norton, 1976), 4.

14 Josiah Strong, *Our Country: Its Possible Future and Its Present Crisis* (Cambridge: Harvard University Press, 1963; first published, 1885), 132.

15 Sinclair, *Prohibition*, 173–4.

16 New York Society for the Prevention of Crime, Annual Report, 1896 quoted in Paul W. Rishell and Albert E. Roraback, *A History of the Society for the Prevention of Crime* (unpublished and undated document held in Box 9, SPC Collection, Rare Books and Manuscript Library, Columbia University, New York), 29.

17 Gilfoyle, 'Moral Origins of Political Surveillance,' 643.

18 Quoted in Rishell and Roraback, *A History of the Society,* 21.

19 Charles W. Gardner, *The Doctor and the Devil: A Startling Exposé of Municipal Corruption* (New York: Warren Publishing Company 1894), 41.

20 Frank Moss, *The American Metropolis: From Knickerbocker Days to the Present Time* (1897), quoted in Ken Dornstein, *Accidentally on Purpose: The Making of a Personal Injury Underworld in America* (New York: St Martin's Griffin, 1998), 48.

21 Auerbach, *Unequal Justice*, 17–8.

22 Renzetti, *'Purity vs Politics,'* 65.

23 Rev. Charles Parkhurst, 'Needed Municipal Reforms,' *The North American Review* 158 (Feb. 1894), 202.

24 Theodore A. Bingham, 'The Organized Criminals of New York,' *McClures Magazine* 34 (1909–10), 62–7.

25 Samuel Walker, *Popular Justice: A History of American Criminal Justice* (New York: Oxford University Press, 1980), 171.

26 Gilfoyle, *'Moral Origins of Political Surveillance,'* 256–7.

27 Alfred Connable and Edward Silberfarb, *Tigers of Tammany: Nine Men Who Ran New York* (New York: Holt, Rinehart and Winston, 1967), 197–269.

28 Robert M. Fogleson, *Big City Police* (Cambridge: Harvard University Press, 1977), 59.

29 Ibid., 49.

30 Fogelson, *Big City Police*, 168–9.

31 V.O. Key, 'Police Graft,' *American Journal of Sociology* 40 (March 1935), 631.

32 John F. Kramer quoted in John Kobler, *Ardent Spirits: The Rise and Fall of Prohibition* (New York: G.P. Putnam's Sons, 1973), 222; Roy Haynes quoted in Charles Merz, *The Dry Decade* (Seattle: University of Washington Press, 1969), 123–4.

33 Merz, *Dry Decade*, 56–61.

34 Harry G. Levine and Craig Reinarman, 'From Prohibition to Regulation: Lessons from Alcohol Policy for Drug Policy,' in Ronald Bayer and Gerald M. Oppenheimer, eds., *Confronting Drug Policy: Illicit Drugs in a Free Society* (Cambridge: Cambridge University Press, 1993), 171.

35 Al Smith quoted in Charles E. Goshen, *Drink, Drugs and Do-Gooders* (London: Collier-Macmillan, 1973), 34.

36 Andrew Sinclair, *Prohibition*, 219–29.

37 *Telegram*, quoted in Kobler, *Ardent Spirits*, 234–5.

38 Hank Messick and Burt Goldblatt, *The Mobs and the Mafia* (London: Spring Books, 1972), 52; John Kobler, *Ardent Spirits*, 316–21.

39 Gifford Pinchot, quoted in Brian Inglis, *The Forbidden Game: A Social History of Drugs* (London: Hodder and Stoughton, 1975), 147.

40 John Kobler, *Capone: The Life and World of Al Capone* (London: Coronet, 1973), 81–9.

41 Patrolman quoted in Richard C.Lindberg, *To Serve and Collect: Chicago Politics and Police Corruption from the Lager Beer Riot to the Summerdale Scandal* (New York: Praeger, 1991), 163.

42 Chicago *Tribune* quoted but not dated in James O'Donnell Bennett, 'Chicago Gangland,' a pamphlet in the National Commission on Law Observance and Enforcement (hereinafter called the Wickersham commission), *Official Records*, vol. 4, 372.

43 Humbert Nelli, *The Business of Crime* (New York: Oxford University Press, 1976), 164–5.

44 Kobler, *Ardent Spirits*, 260.

45 Ibid., 245.

46 Herbert Asbury, *The Great Illusion: An Informal History of Prohibition* (New York: Doubleday, 1950) 254; Kobler, *Ardent Spirits*, 266.

47 Leonard Katz, *Uncle Frank: The Biography of Frank Costello* (London: Star, 1973), 63–4.

48 Mark Haller, 'Bootleggers and American Gambling, 1920–1950,' in Commission on the Review of the National Policy Towards Gambling, *Gambling in America* (Washington, DC: U.S. Printing Office, 1976), Appendix 1, 115.

49 Kenneth Allsop, *The Bootleggers* (London: Arrow Books, 1976), 76; See also

Craig Thompson and Raymond Allen, *Gang Rule in New York* (New York: Dial Press, 1940), 100.
50 Eisen, quoted in F.D. Pasley, *Al Capone: The Biography of a Self-Made Man* (London: Faber and Faber, 1966), 292.
51 Asbury, *The Great Illusion*, 185.
52 Association Against the Prohibition Amendment, 'Scandals of Liquor Law Enforcement,' 1929 in Wickersham commission, *Report on the Enforcement of the Prohibition Laws of the United States*, 71st Congress, 3rd Session, H.D. 722, vol. 5, 211.
53 Thomas A. Repetto, *The Blue Parade* (New York: Free Press, 1978), 279.
54 Association Against the Prohibition Amendment, *'Scandals,'* 197–218; Asbury *The Great Illusion* 176–85.
55 Samuel Hopkins Adams, *The Incredible Era: The Life and Times of Warren Gameliel Harding* (New York: Capricorn, 1964), 339.
56 Mabel Willebrandt, *The Inside of Prohibition* (Indianapolis: Bobbs-Merrill, 1929), 200.
57 Wickersham commission, 1931, vol. 3, 356.
58 Quoted in Hutchinson, *Imperfect Union*, 67–8.
59 Wickersham commission, 1931, Final Report, 51.
60 Pasley, *Al Capone*, 301.
61 Quoted in Mary McKintosh, 'The Growth of Racketeering,' *Economy and Society* (Nov. 1973), 61.
62 Kobler, *Life and World of Capone*, 192.
63 Frederick Lewis Allen, *Only Yesterday* (New York: Bantam Books, 1959; first published, 1931), 185–6.
64 Kobler, *Life and World of Capone*, 128.
65 Mark H. Haller, 'Illegal Enterprise: A Theoretical and Historical Interpretation,' in Nikos Passas, ed., *Organized Crime* (Aldershot: Dartmouth, 1995), 225–53.
66 Allsop, *Bootleggers*, 40, 193–207.
67 For the most comprehensive account of Chicago businessmen's activity against Capone, see Dennis E. Hoffman, *Scarface Al and the Crime Crusaders: Chicago's Private War against Capone* (Carbondale and Edwardsville: Southern Illinois University Press, 1993).
68 Eliot Ness and Oscar Farley, *The Untouchables* (London: Hodder, 1967). See Laurence Bergreen, *Capone: The Man and the Era* (London: Macmillian, 1994), for a good account of Ness's career and decline after the Prohibition era.
69 Kobler, *Life and World of Capone*, 312–30.
70 James D. Calder, 'Al Capone and the Internal Revenue Service: State-

Sanctioned Criminology of Organized Crime,' *Crime, Law and Social Change* 17 (1992) 1–23.

71 Frank J. Wilson and Beth Day, *Secret Agent: Twenty-Five Years with the U.S. Treasury Department and Secret Service* (London: Frederick Muller, 1966), 54.

72 Calder, 'Al Capone,' 1.

73 Morris Sheppard and Clarence Darrow quoted in Asbury, *The Great Illusion*, 316–17.

74 Senator Robert Wagner of New York, a speech made in the Senate of the United States, 17 Feb. 1931, reprinted in USA Constitutional Documents, *Repeal the Eighteenth Amendment* (Washington, DC, 1931).

75 Norman H. Clark, *Deliver Us From Evil* (New York: W.W. Norton, 1976), 194–201; David E. Kyvig, *Repealing National Prohibition* (Chicago: University of Chicago Press, 1979), 94; Raymond Fosdick and Albert L. Scott, *Towards Liquor Control* (New York: Harper and Brothers, 1933). John D. Rockefeller, Jr, financed the research for Fosdick and Scott's book and wrote the Foreword.

76 Leuchtenburg, *The Perils of Prosperity*, 261–3; Walter La Feber, Richard Polenberg, and Nancy Woloch, *The American Century: A History of the United States since the 1890s* (New York: McGraw-Hill, 1992), 176.

77 Quoted in Kobler, *Ardent Spirits*, 350–1.

78 Harry Levine, 'The Birth of American Alcohol Control: Prohibition, the Power Elite, and the Problem of Lawlessness,' *Contemporary Drug Problems* 12 (1985), 72.

79 David E. Kyvig, *Repealing National Prohibition* (Chicago: University of Chicago Press, 1979), 178, 186.

80 V.O. Key, *Southern Politics* (New York: Vintage, 1949), 235.

81 Mark Haller, 'Bootleggers as Businessmen: From City Slums to City Builders,' in *Law, Alcohol and Order*, 143–5; *The Independent on Sunday*, 14 Feb. 1993; James H. Grey, *Booze: The Impact of Whisky on the Prairie West* (Toronto: Macmillan of Canada, 1972), 138–9.

82 Raymond Fosdick and Albert A. Scott, *Towards Liquor Control* (New York: Harper, 1933) 30.

83 Ruth Rosen, *The Lost Sisterhood: Prostitution in America, 1900–1920* (Baltimore: Johns Hopkins University Press, 1982), 32, 33, 137, 172.

84 Charles Winick and Paul M. Kinsie, *The Lively Commerce: Prostitution in the United States* (Chicago: Quadrangle, 1971), 27–8.

85 Milton Mackaye, *The Tin Box Parade* (New York: McBride, 1934), 30, 300; Connable and Silberfarb, *Tigers of Tammany*, 282–5.

86 Polly Adler, *A House Is Not a Home* (London: Ace Books, 1957), Carol Erwin,

The Disorderly Orderly House (London: Panther Books, 1965), 270–8; Mary McInkosh, *The Organization of Crime* (London: MacMillan, 1975), 72–3.

87 David J. Langum, *Crossing Over the Line: Legislating Morality and the Mann Act* (Chicago: University of Chicago Press, 1994), 170–1.

88 Henry Chafetz, *Play the Devil: A History of Gambling in the United States from 1492 to 1955* (New York: C.N. Potter, 1960), 387.

89 John Landesco, *Organized Crime in Chicago: Part III of The Illinois Crime Survey, 1929* (Chicago: University of Chicago Press, 1968), 445–83.

90 Mark Haller, 'Organized Crime in Urban Society: Chicago in the Twentieth Century,' *Journal of Social History* (Winter 1971–2), 213.

91 Francis A.J. Ianni, *Black Mafia* (London: New English Library, 1976), 118–19; Mark Haller, 'The Changing Structure of American Gambling in the Twentieth Century,' *Journal of Social Issues* 35 (1979), 95–7. Peter Reuter, *Disorganized Crime: The Economics of the Visible Hand* (Cambridge, Mass.: MIT Press, 1983), 47.

92 Daniel Bell, *The End of Ideology* (New York: Free Press, 1960), 143; Dayton David McKean, *The Boss: The Hague Machine in Action* (Boston: Houghton Mifflin, 1940), 48–9.

93 Atherton's report published in full in the *San Francisco Chronicle*, 17 March 1937.

94 William Moore, *The Kefauver Committee and the Politics of Crime, 1950–1952* (Columbia: University of Missouri Press, 1974), 18–19.

95 Fred Cook, *Mafia!* (London: Coronet, 1973), 123–4; Haller, 'Organized Crime,' 99.

96 Moore, *Kefauver Committee*, 115.

97 *New York Times*, 5 July 1935.

98 William Ivy Hair, *The Kingfish and His Realm: The Life and Times of Huey Long* (Baton Rouge: Louisiana State University Press, 1991), 295.

99 Katz, *Unde Frank*, 102–3.

100 Cook, *Mafia!* 124–8.

101 La Guardia quoted in Garrett, *The La Guardia Years* (New Brunswick, NJ: Rutgers University Press, 1961), 162.

102 Lisa Ann Vardzel, 'Newport, Kentucky: A Study of Organized Crime, 1920–1952,' master's dissertation, Pennsylvania State University, 1989, 24–33; Hank Messick and Burt Goldblatt, *The Mobs and the Mafia* (London: Spring Books, 1972), 149–54.

103 Dean Jennings, *We Only Kill Each Other* (Greenwich, Conn.: Fawcett, 1968); Burton Turkus and Sid Feder, *Murder Inc.* (London: Victor Gollancz, 1952), 187–9; Rena M. Vale, 'A New Boss Takes Los Angeles,' *American Mercury*, May 1941, 299–307.

104 Ed Reid and Ovid Demaris, *The Green Felt Jungle* (London: Heineman, 1965), 27–9.
105 William Eadington, 'The Casino Gaming Industry: A Study of Political Economy,' *Annals of the American Academy* (July 1984), 25–9.
106 Moore, *The Kefauver Committee*, 33.
107 Commission on the Review of the National Policy Towards Gambling, *Gambling in America*, Appendix I, 46, Rowley quoted in *Newsweek*, 17 Feb. 1947.
108 Ernest Haveman, 'Gambling in the United States,' *Life*, 19 June 1950.
109 Virgil Peterson, *Gambling: Should It Be Legalised?* (Springfield, Ill.: Charles Thomas Publisher, 1945), quoted in *Gambling in America*, Appendix IV, 55.
110 Norton Mockridge and R.H. Prall, *The Big Fix* (New York: Holt, 1954), 224.
111 New Orleans, *States*, 8 Dec. 1945.
112 *Report of the Special Citizens' Investigating Committtee* (SCIC), New Orleans, April 1954, vol. 2; quote on 28.
113 New Orleans, *Item*, 26–30 May 1949.
114 New Orleans, *Item*, 14 Sept. 1949.
115 *The Attorney General's Conference on Organised Crime*, 15 Feb. 1950, Washington, DC, Department of Justice, 1950, 26–7.
116 Memo prepared for the Kefauver committee, marked *DeLesseps S. Morrison* in file for the Louisiana crime hearings, *Kefauver Papers*, University of Tennessee, Knoxville.
117 Edward M., Brecher, *Licit and Illict Drugs*, (Boston: Little Brown, 1972), 50.
118 King, *The Drug Hang-Up*, 25.
119 Jonna Weissman Joselit, *Our Gang: Jewish Crime and the New York Jewish Community, 1900–1940* (Bloomington: Indiana University Press, 1983) 146.
120 Robert Lacey, *Little Man: Meyer Lansky and the Gangster Life* (London: Arrow, 1991), 61.
121 Quoted in James A. Inciardi, *The War on Drugs: Heroin, Cocaine, Crime, and Public Policy* (Palo Alto: Mayfield, 1986), 99.
122 David F. Musto, *The American Disease: Origins of Narcotic Control* (Oxford: Oxford University Press, 1987), 190–4; Edward J. Epstein, *Agency of Fear, Opiates and Political Power in America* (New York: Putnam's, 1977) 23–34.
123 Musto, *The American Disease*, 207–8.
124 John C. McWilliams, *The Protectors: Harry J. Anslinger and the Federal Bureau of Narcotics, 1930–1962* (Newark: University of Delaware Press, 1990), 32–3.
125 *Guardian*, 26 June 2000.
126 Musto, *The American Disease*, 1987, 223.
127 McWilliams, *The Protectors*, 52–3.
128 Donald Dickson, 'Bureaucracy and Morality: An Organizational Perspec-

tive on a Moral Crusade,' *Social Problems* 1968 16 143–56; Michael Woodiwiss, *Crime, Crusades and Corruption: Prohibitions in the United States, 1900–
1987* (London: Pinter, 1988), 31–2; Musto, *The American Disease*, 222.
129 McWilliams, *Protectors*, 86–9.
130 Ibid., 92–5.
131 State of California, Special Study Commission on Organized Crime, *Third
Progress Report*, Sacramento, 31 Jan. 1950, 100.

5 Organized Crime and the Dumbing of American Discourse, 1920 to the Present

1 John Higham, *Strangers in the Land: Patterns of American Nativism, 1860–1925*
(New York: Atheneum, 1974), 327.
2 Quoted in Gus Tyler, *Organized Crime in America: A Book of Readings* (Ann
Arbor: University of Michigan Press, 1967), 110.
3 Harry E. Barnes, 'The Racket as Ideal,' in Tyler, *Organized Crime in America*,
178–9.
4 Raymond Moley, 'Behind the Menacing Racket,' New York Times, 23 Nov.
1930, Section 5, 2.
5 James C. Young, 'Crime Gangs Organized as Big Business,' *New York Times*,
4 April 1926.
6 F.D. Pasley, *Al Capone: The Biography of a Self-Made Man* (London: Faber and
Faver, 1966).
7 Moley, 'Politics and Crime,' *Annals of the American Academy of Political and
Social Science* 25 (1926), 78–84.
8 Frederick M. Thrasher, *The Gang: A Study of 1,313 Gang in Chicago* (Chicago:
University of Chicago Press, 1960; first published, 1927) 416.
9 Frank Tannenbaum, *Crime and the Community* (New York: Ginn and Company, 1936), 115.
10 Edwin Sutherland, *The Professional Thief* (Chicago: University of Chicago
Press, 1937), 209.
11 Moley, 'Politics and Crime,' 83.
12 Thrasher, *The Gang*, 414–17.
13 Moley, *Behind the Menancing Racket*, 2.
14 Thrasher, *The Gang*, 458–62.
15 Quoted in Dwight C. Smith, 'Wickersham to Sutherland to Katzenbach:
Evolving an "Official" Definition for Organized Crime,' *Crime, Law and
Social Change* 16 (1991), 140–1.
16 Henry Barrett Chamberlin, 'Some Observations Concerning Organized
Crime,' *Journal of Criminal Law and Criminology* 22 (1931–2), 668.

17 Alfred Lindesmith, 'Organized Crime,' *Annals of the American Academy of Political and Social Science*, 217 (1941), 119–27.
18 Quoted in Lawrence M. Friedman, *Crime and Punishment in American History* (New York: Basic Books, 1993), 340.
19 Barnes, 'Racket as Ideal,' 179.
20 Tannenbaum, *Crime and the Community*, 46.
21 Walter Lippmann, 'The Underworld as Servant,' in Tyler, *Organized Crime in America*, 59–69.
22 Chamberlin, 'Some Observations,' 669.
23 August Vollmer, *The Police and Modern Society* (Berkeley: University of California Press, 1936), 99–118.
24 Moley, 'Politics and Crime,' 83.
25 Tannenbaum, *Crime and Community*, 476.
26 Quoted in James D. Calder, *The Origins and Development of Federal Crime Control Policy: Herbert Hoover's Initiatives* (Westport, Conn.: Praeger, 1993), 69.
27 Quoted in Smith, *Wickersham*, 138–42.
28 Ibid., 141.
29 Quoted in Friedman, *Crime and Punishment*, 274.
30 Quoted in Richard Gid Powers, *G-Men: Hoover's FBI in American Popular Culture* (Carbondale and Edwardsville: Southern Illinois University Press, 1983), 9.
31 Quoted in Robert Sherrill, *Saturday Night Special* (New York: Penguin, 1975), 47.
32 Sandford Ungar, *FBI* (New York: Atlantic, Little and Brown, 1975), 72–82.
33 Andrew Begman, *We're in the Money: Depression America and Its Films* (London: Harper and Row, 1972), 13.
34 Hank Messick and Burt Goldblatt, *Gangs and Gangsters: The Illustrated History of Gangs* (New York: Ballantine Books, 1974), 160–4.
35 Athan G. Theoharis and John Stuart Cox, *The Boss: J. Edgar Hoover and the Great American Inquisition* (New York: Bantam, 1990), 150.
36 Ibid., 157–8.
37 Sherrill, *Saturday Night Special*, 48–9.
38 For gangsters films see Colin McArthur, *Underworld USA* (London: Secker and Warberg, 1972); Carlos Clarens, *Crime Movies* (London: W.W. Norton, 1980); John Baxter, *The Gangster Film* (London: Zwemmer, 1970); Frank Pearce, 'Art and Reality in Film and Society,' *Sociological Review*, Monograph 26, 1979. For 1930s radio see J. Fred MacDonald, *Don't Touch That Dial! Radio Programming in American Life, 1920–1960* (Chicago: Nelson-Hall, 1979).

39 New York *Daily Mirror*, 8 June 1936.

40 Benjamin Strolberg, 'Thomas E. Dewey: Self-Made Myth,' *American Mercury* (June 1940), 140–7.

41 Quoted in Todd Gitlin, 'Television Screens: Hegemony in Transition,' in Donald Lazere, ed., *American Media and Mass Culture: Left Perspectives* (London: University of California Press, 1987), 250.

42 *First Interim Report of the Special Crime Study Commission on Organized Crime* (Sacramento: California Board of Corrections, 1 March 1948).

43 There was, however, a long way to go before mainstream opinion was reconciled to such an interest-serving understanding, particularly as the 1947 conference was followed by a series of revelations that showed that Californian police officers were as actively involved in the organization of illegal enterprise as any of their colleagues nationwide. See Michael Woodiwiss, *Crime, Crusades and Corruption: Prohibitions in the USA* (London: Pinter Press, 1988), 90–4.

44 Hoover, quoted in *Final Report of the Special Crime Study* (Sacramento: State of California, 1953), 74–6.

45 Williams, quoted in Dwight Smith, *The Mafia Mystique* (New York: Basic Books, 1975), 123–4.

46 Quoted in Kathryn Meyer and Terry Parssinen, *Webs of Smoke: Smugglers, Warlords, Spies, and the History of the International Drug Trade* (Oxford: Bowman and Littlefield, 1998), 284.

47 Douglas Clark Kinder, 'Bureaucratic Cold Warrior: Harry J. Anslinger and the Illicit Narcotics Traffic,' *Pacific Historical Review* 50 (May 1981), 171.

48 David F. Musto, 'The Rise and Fall of Epidemics: Learning from History,' in G. Edwards, J. Strang, and J. H. Jaffe, eds., *Drugs, Alcohol, and Tobacco: Making the Science and Policy Connections* (Oxford: Oxford University Press, 1993), 283.

49 U.S. Congress, Senate Special Committee to Investigate Crime in Interstate Commerce (hereinafter called the Kefauver committee), 82nd Congress, *Third Interim Report*, Washington, DC, 1951, 147–150.

50 Jack Lait and Lee Mortimer, *New York Confidential*, 2nd ed. (New York: Crown, 1951), 220.

51 Kefauver, *Crime in America*, 28.

52 Kefauver Committee, *Hearings*, part 10, 501.

53 Lester Velie, 'Rudolph Halley: How He Nailed America's Racketeers,' *Colliers Magazine* (19 May 1951).

54 Kefauver Committee, *Hearings*, part 7, *Moretti Testimony*, 334, 348.

55 William Moore, *The Kefauver Committee and the Politics of Crime* (Columbia:

University of Missouri Press, 1974), 113. Moore's book is indispensable to all students of the Kefauver commitee.

56 Frederic T. Martens and Michele Cunningham-Niederer, 'Media Magic, Mafia Mania,' *Federal Probation* (June 1985), 61.

57 Lait and Mortimer, *USA Confidential* (New York: Crown, 1952), 27.

58 Lait and Mortimer, *Chicago Confidential*, (New York: Crown, 1950)1, 182.

59 Ibid., 196.

60 Lait and Mortimer, *Washington Confidential*, (New York: Crown, 1951), 107.

61 Lait and Mortimer, *USA Confidential*, ix, 29.

62 Fred Cook, *Mafia!* (London: Coronet, 1973), 84–5.

63 Alan Block, *East Side – West Side: Organizing Crime in New York, 1930–1950* (Cardiff: University College Cardiff, 1980), 3–9.

64 Martin Short, *Crime Inc.: The Story of Organized Crime* (London: Thames Methuen, 1984), 156.

65 This verdict is based on the following two primary sources. New York State, Commissioner of Investigations, Report of Investigation, 17 Sept. 1954, held in the Thomas E. Dewey Papers, Rush Rhees Library, University of Rochester, New York. Memo prepared by George Martin of the *Scranton Times*, 19 Aug. 1955 and filed in the Estes Kefauver Papers, University of Tennessee Library, Knoxville.

66 Frederick Sondern, *Brotherhood of Evil: The Mafia* (London: Panther, 1961), 81.

67 Although Nicholas Gage in the *New York Times* and Tony Scaduto, *Lucky Luciano* (London: Sphere, 1976), made a strong case doubting the authenticity of *The Last Testament*, some academics still mine the latter as a source of the gangster's thoughts.

68 Brian Freemantle, *The Octopus: Europe in the Grip of Organised Crime* (London: Orion, 1995), 262–7.

69 See, for example, Block's discussion of a 1987 U.S. Department of Justice's history of La Cosa Nostra in Alan A. Block, *Perspectives on Organizing Crime: Essays in Opposition* (London: Kluwer, 1991), 19–21.

70 Meyer and Parssinen, *Webs of Smoke*, 285.

71 The Luciano letter is held in the Thomas E. Dewey Papers, Department of Rare Books and Special Collections, University of Rochester Library.

72 Mickey Spillane quoted in Dwight Smith, *Mafia Mystique*, 264–74.

73 For the best researched account of these investigations and other aspects of New York organized crime history, see Block, *East Side – West Side*.

74 Publicity information on films held in the library of the British Film Institute.

75 Pearce, 'Art and Reality,' 266.

76 David Caute, *The Great Fear: The Anticommunist Purge under Truman and Eisenhower* (London: Secker and Warburg, 1978). For the purge of academics during these years, see W. W. Schrecker, *No Ivory Tower: McCarthyism and the Universities* (New York: Oxford University Press, 1986).

77 Daniel Bell, *The End of Ideology* (New York: The Free Press, 1962), 138–50.

78 Andrew Tartaglino testimony from U.S. Senate hearings before the Permanent Subcommittee on Investigations of the Committee on Government Operations, *Federal Drug Enforcement*, 94th Congress, 1st Session, 9, 10, and 11 June 1975, Part 1, 134–44.

79 Researchers have to apply to the Permanent Subcommittee of Investigations of the Senate Governmental Affairs Committee for these documents. That committee is generally unwilling to open 'investigative files relating to individuals and containing personal data, personnel records, and records of executive nominations' until they are fifty years old.

80 According to a quote from FBN agent Charles Siragusa, retold in Clare Sterling's *The Mafia*, published in 1990: 'Mr Anslinger, with his usual keen foresight, saw an influx of heroin coming into the United States when World War II ended.' Short in *Crime Inc.* included the above and another flattering Siragusa quote about his boss. Anslinger was hailed as the first man to see the 'evil of organized crime in the United States,' 160.

81 Bell, *End of Ideology*, 140; *New York Times*, 15 Nov. 1957, 27 Nov. 1957, 10 Nov. 1958, 28 Feb. 1960, 29 Nov. 1960.

82 Robert F. Kennedy, *The Enemy Within* (London: Popular Library, 1960), 229.

83 Robert F. Kennedy, 'The Baleful Influence of Gambling' (1962), article reprinted in Robert D. Herman, ed., *Gambling* (New York: Harper and Row, 1967); *New York Times*, 26 Sept. 1963.

84 Robert F. Kennedy, 'What's Wrong with the $2 bet?' *Look* (3 July, 1962).

85 Smith, *Mafia Mystique*, (1975), 229–30.

86 Robert Leuci, quoted in Sidney Zion, *Loyalty and Betrayal: The Story of the American Mob* (San Francisco: Collins, 1994), 124.

87 Valachi's testimony is extensively quoted in Gordon Hawkins, 'God and the Mafia,' *Public Interest* (Winter 1969); Norval Morris and Gordon Hawkins, *The Honest Politicians Guide to Crime Control* (Chicago: University of Chicago Press, 1970), 203–35.

88 Kennedy quoted in Peter Maas, *The Valachi Papers* (London: Panther, 1972), 9; Commission on the Review of the National Policy Towards Gambling (U.S. Government Printing Office, 1976); *Gambling in America*, Appendix I, 63.

89 President's Commission on Law Enforcement and the Administration of

Justice, *The Challenge of Crime in a Free Society* (Washington, DC: Government Printing Office, 1967), 187–209.

90 John Dombrink and James W. Meeker, 'Organized Crime in the Twilight of the mob': Groups, Enterprise, and Legal Innovation; in John A. Conley, ed., *The 1967 President's Crime Commission Report: Its Impact 25 years Later,* (Cincinnati: Anderson, 1994), 107.

91 Quoted in Morris Ploscowe, ed, *Organized Crime and Law Enforcement,* vol. 1 (New York: Grosby Press, 1952), 242.

92 *Time,* 22 Aug. 1969.

93 Mario Puzo, *The Godfather Papers* (London: Pan, 1972), 28–31.

94 Cook, quoted in Smith, *Mafia Mystique,* 276–7.

95 *New York Times,* 1 Aug. 1972; *New York Times,* 15 Aug. 1971; Smith, *Mafia Mystique,* 302.

96 Kennedy, *Enemy Within,* 253.

97 Television commercial, quoted in Edward J. Epstein, *Agency of Fear: Opiates and Political Power in America* (New York: G.P. Putnam's Sons, 1977), 62.

98 Text of Nixon's Message to Congress proposing a campaign on organized crime reprinted in the *New York Times,* 24 April 1969, 30.

99 For a full discussion of the background to the Organized Crime Control Act see Alan A. Block and William J. Chambliss, *Organizing Crime* (New York: Elsevier, 1981), 193–217. Levy quoted in Sam Pizzigati, 'The Perverted Grand Juries,' *Nation,* 19 June 1976.

100 Frank Donner, *The Age of Surveillance* (New York: Knopf, 1980), 358.

101 Ehrlichman testimony in *Federal Drug Enforcement,* Hearings before the Permanent Subcommittee on Investigations of the Committee on Government Operations, US Senate, 94th Congress, Second Session, July 27, 28, 29, 1976, Part 4, (Washington DC; U.S. Government Printing Office, 1976), 794.

102 Quoted in Rufus King, *The Drug Hang-Up: America's Fifty Year Folly* (New York: W.W. Norton, 1972), 308. It should also be noted that since Mitchell's time researchers have found that a genuine link between drug addiction and the extent of street crime does exist but this link is now more usually used as an argument for legalization or decriminalization.

103 Max Singer, 'The Vitality of Mythical Numbers,' *Public Interest* (Spring 1971).

104 Epstein, *Agency of Fear,* 174.

105 Letter to Congress, 14 July 1969, excerpted in K. Austin Kerr, ed, *The Politics of Moral Behavior: Prohibition and Drug Abuse* (Reading, Mass.: Addison-Wesley, 1977), 227–33.

106 *New York Times*, 15 July 1969.
107 Albert Goldman, *Grass Roots* (New York: Harper and Row, 1979), 100; Richard C. Schroeder, *The Politics of Drugs* (Washington DC: Congressional Quarterly, 1980), 123; Lawrence A. Gooberman, *Operation Intercept: The Multiple Consequences of Public Policy* (New York: Pergamon Press, 1974).
108 The Drug Abuse Council, *The Facts about 'Drug Abuse'* (New York: The Free Press, 1980) 38; Schroeder, *The Politics of Drugs*, 130.
109 Ethan A. Nadelmann, *Cops across Borders: The Internationalization of U.S. Criminal Law Enforcement* (University Park: Pennsylvania State University Press, 1993), 141.
110 Ibid., 145.
111 Arnold Trebach, *The Heroin Solution* (New Haven, Conn.: Yale University Press, 1982) 237; King, *Drug Hang-Up*, 307–22.
112 Quoted in *Newsweek*, 9 Feb. 1970.
113 King, *Drug Hang-up*, 311; *New York Times*, 25 June 1973.
114 Richard Nixon quoted in *New York Times*, 21 March 1973; Richard Kleindienst, quoted in David J. Bellis, *Heroin and Politicians* (London: Greenwood Press, 1981), 72.
115 *New York Times*, 25 June 1973; Joe Eszterhas, *Nark!* (San Francisco: Straight Arrow Books, 1974).
116 Charles Goodell, *Political Prisoners in America* (New York: Random House, 1973), 199.
117 Epstein, *Agency of Fear*, 223.
118 John Finlator, *The Drugged Nation* (New York: Simon and Schuster, 1973), 322–3; August Bequai, *Organized Crime* (Lexington: Lexington Books, 1979), 146; King, *Drug Hang-up*, 319.
119 Ehrlichman testimony in Federal Drug Enforcement, 804.
120 National Commission on Marijuana and Drug Abuse, *Drug Use in America: Problem in Perspective* (Washington, DC: Government Printing Office, 1973), 3.
121 Ibid., 27.
122 *New York Times*, 19 March 1973.
123 J. Anthony Lukas, *Nightmare: The Underside of the Nixon Years* (New York: Penguin, 1988), 112.
124 James William Coleman, *The Criminal Elite: The Sociology of White Collar Crime* (New York: St Martin's Press, 1989), 53. Lukas, *Nightmare*, 123.
125 David Burnham, *Above the Law: Secret Deals, Political Fixes, and Other Misadventures of the U.S. Department of Justice* (New York: Scribner, 1996), 222.
126 Coleman, *Criminal Elite*, 53.
127 Joseph A. Page and Mary Win-O'Brien, *Bitter Wages*, 191–2. See also Frank

Pearce and Steve Tombs, *Toxic Capitalism: Corporate Crime and the Chemical Industry* (Aldershot, England: Dartmouth, 1998), 266–8.

128 Quoted in Gerry Spence, *With Justice for None* (New York: Penguin, 1989), 311. 'Naderism' in Nixon's comment referred to Ralph Nader, a leading opponent of corporate crime.

129 Conyers testified to the House Judiciary Subcommittee No. 1 during *Hearings on the Fort Worth Five and Grand Jury Abuse*, 1973, and this was added to House of Representatives, Committee on the Judiciary, Subcommittee on Immigration, Citizenship and International Law, Hearings on H.J. Res 46, H.R. 1277 and Related Bills: Federal G.J. (Washington, DC: Government Printing Office, 1976), 344–56.

130 The fate of the Watergate conspirators is summarized in *Newsweek*, 14 June 1982, and in Tom Passavanat and Conan Putnam, 'Watergate Inc.: An Anniversary Audit,' *Playboy,* June 1982.

131 *New York Times*, 19 Aug. 1973.

132 Danny Schechter, *The More You Watch the Less You Know* (New York: Seven Stories, 1997), 166.

133 *New York Times*, 3 May 1971, 29 June 1971.

134 Jack Newfield, 'The Myth of Godfather Journalism,' *Village Voice*, 23 July 1979.

135 Ovid Demaris, *The Last Mafioso* (London: Corgi, 1981), 452–3.

136 Ronald A. Farrell and Carole Case, *The Black Book and the Mob: The Untold Story of the Control of Nevada's Casinos* (Madison: University of Wisconsin Press, 1995), 60–78.

137 Quoted in Alan A. Block (ed.), *The Business of Crime: A Documentary Study of Organized Crime in the American Economy,* (Boulder: Westview Press, 1991), 258.

138 James Goode, *Wiretap: Listening in on the American Mafia* (New York: Simon and Schuster, 1988), 64–5.

139 Mark Tran, 'Mafia Families Feel the Heat as the Teflon Don Comes to a Sticky end,' *Guardian*, 3 April 1992, 5; Rod Nordland, 'Goodbye, Don,' *Newsweek*, 13 April 1992, 28–33.

140 *The Gotti Tapes: Including the Testimony of Salvatore (Sammy the Bull) Gravano* (London: Arrow, 1992), 118.

141 Ibid., 106–13.

142 Ronald Goldstock quoted in Nordland, 'Goodbye, Don,' 33.

143 Dennis Wagner and Pat Flannery, 'Gravano Busted,' *Arizona Republic*, 25 Feb. 2000. www.geocities.com/imokproductions/gravanobust.html; Edward Barnes, 'Ecstasy in Arizona: a cop and bull story,' *Time* (Canadian ed.), 5 Dec. 2000, www/canoe.ca/TimeCanada0006/06_time17.html

144 *New York Times*, 24 Nov. 1986.

145 G. Robert Blakey quoted in *New York Times*, 22 Oct. 1990.

146 Hank Messick, *Secret File* (New York: G.P. Putnam's Sons, 1969), 11.

147 David Burnham articles in *New York Times*, 25 April 1970, 26 April 1970; *The Knapp Commission Report on Police Corruption* (New York: George Braziller, 1972).

148 Peter Maas, *Serpico* (London: Fontana, 1977).

149 John A. Gardiner and David Olson, 'Wincanton: The Politics of Corruption,' in William J. Chambliss, ed., *Crime and the Legal Process* (New York: McGraw-Hill, 1969); *Gambling in America*, Appendix 1, 82; John A. Gardiner, *The Politics of Corruption: Organized Crime in an American City* (New York: Russell Sage, 1970).

150 William J. Chambliss, *On the Take: From Petty Crooks to Presidents* (Bloomington: Indiana University Press, 1978); Block and Chambliss, *Organizing Crime*, 96–114.

151 Peter Reuter, 'Police Regulation of Illegal Gambling: Frustrations of Symbolic Enforcement,' *Annals of the American Academy*, July 1984, 43–4.

152 *Wall Street Journal*, 16 March 1982.

153 *Gambling in America*, Appendix 1, 156–7; J. Edgar Hoover, 'Gambling and Corruption,' *FBI Law Enforcement Bulletin*, Aug. 1971.

154 Lacey, *Little Man: Meyer Lansky and the Gangster Life* (London, Arure, 1991), 301.

155 George Sternlieb and James W. Hughes, *The Atlantic City Gamble: A Twentieth Century Fund Report* (Cambridge: Harvard University Press, 1983), 132–53; *New York Times*, 22 Oct. 1990, B7.

156 Quoted in *U.S. News and World Report*, 14 March, 1994, 46.

157 *New York Times*, 27 Feb. 1970.

158 *New York Times*, 6 April 1971; Richard Kunnes, *The American Heroin Empire* (New York: Dodd, Mead, 1972), 80–2, 116–17; Abrahman S. Blumberg, 'Drug Control: Agenda for Repression,' in Richard L. Rachin and Eugene H. Czajkoski, *Drug Abuse Control* (Lexington: Lexington Books, 1978), 13.

159 The Knapp Commission Report on Police Corruption, 91–3.

160 Ibid.

161 Robin Moore, *The French Connection* (London: Hodder and Stoughton, 1969), 1.

162 *New York Times*, 1 Feb. 1973, 19 Nov. 1971, 3 Dec. 1971, 4 Dec. 1971.

163 David Durk and Ira Silverman, *The Pleasant Avenue Connection* (New York: Harper and Row, 1976), 33.

164 Robert Daley, *Prince of the City* (London: Granada, 1980), 30–1.

165 *New York Times*, 9 Aug. 1981.

166 *Los Angeles Times*, 24 May 1982, 7.

167 *Narcotics Control Digest*, 27 March 1991.

168 Alan A. Block, 'Failure at Home and Abroad: Studies in the Implementation of U.S. Drug Policy,' in Alfred W. McCoy and Alan A. Block, eds., *War on Drugs: Studies in the Failure of U.S. Narcotics Policy* (Boulder: Westview Press, 1991), 58.

169 *U.S.A. Today*, 2 Nov. 1982; *Narcotics Control Digest*, May 1984; *National Law Review*, 22 Aug. 1983; *U.S. News and World Report*, 6 Feb. 1984; *Washington Post*, 4 Nov. 1982; *New York Times*, 28 Aug. 1982, 3 April 1986; *Narcotics Control Digest*, 12 June 1985, 16 Oct. 1985, 30 Oct. 1985, 19 March 1986.

170 *Narcotics Control Digest*, 26 Feb. 1992.

171 Ibid., 11 March 1992.

172 Ibid., 24 April 1991.

173 Quoted in Burnham, *Above the Law*, 202.

174 Malcolm Gladwell, 'Rotten to the Corps,' *Guardian*, 6 Oct. 1993; *New York Times*, 21 March 1994, B3.

175 Steven R. Donziger, ed., *The Real War on Crime: The Report of the National Criminal Justice Commission* (New York: Harper Perennial, 1996), 164.

176 Mike Davis, *City of Quartz: Excavating the Future in Los Angeles* (Vintage: London, 1990), 272–7.

177 Alexander Cockburn, 'The War at Home,' *New Statesman and Society*, 22 March 1991, 14–15.

178 Davis, *City of Quartz*, 20.

179 Mike Rothmiller and Ivan G. Goldman, *L.A. Secret Police: Inside the LAPD Elite Spy Network* (New York: Pocket Books, 1992), 20.

180 Ibid., 170.

181 Matt Lait and Scott Grover, 'LAPD Corruption Probe Grows to Shootings, New Allegations (*latimes.com*, 22 Oct. 1999); Christopher Reed, 'Grief Provides No Hiding Place for LAPD's Chief,' *Observer*, 4 June 2000.

182 *New York Times*, 2 Dec. 1975, 24 Dec. 1975, 28 Dec. 1975, 27 March 1977, 28 March 1978.

183 David W. Rasmussen and Bruce L. Benson, *The Economic Anatomy of a Drug War: Criminal Justice in the Commons* (Lanhan, Md.: Rowman and Littlefield, 1994), 110; Stephanie Mencimer, 'Black Robe – There's One Group of Criminals Judges Still Go Easy On: Themselves,' *Washington Monthly* (April 1992).

184 Robert W. Greene, *The Sting Man: Inside Abscam* (New York: Dutton, 1981), reviewed in the *Washington Post*, 29 May 1981.

185 *Los Angeles Times*, 11 March 1982.

186 Reagan's speech printed in full in *Drug Enforcement* (Spring 1983); *New York Times*, 15 Oct. 1982.

187 Kaufman Commission, *Hearing 1, Organized Crime: Federal law Enforcement Perspective*, 29 Nov. 1983.

188 Gary W. Potter, *Criminal Organizations: Vice, Racketeering, and Politics in an American City* (Prospect Heights, Ill.: Waveland Press, 1994), 7.

189 Kaufman Commission, *The Impact: Organized Crime Today* (Washington, DC: Government Printing Office), 171–9.

190 Curbing the Narcotics Traffic: Recommendations of the Organized Crime Commission, reprinted in the *Narcotics Control Digest* (19 March 1986).

6   Industrial and Corporate Racketeering, 1950 to the Present

1 Mary Beth Norton, David M. Karzman, Paul D. Escott, Howard P. Chudacoff, Thomas G. Patterson, William M. Tuttle, Jr., *A People and a Nation: A History of the United States*, vol. 2 (Boston: Houghton Mifflin, 1994), 922–3.

2 James William Coleman, *The Criminal Elite: The Sociology of White Collar Crime* (New York: St Martin's Press, 1989), 14.

3 Norton et al., *A People*, 1047.

4 Ibid., 923.

5 Ibid., 12–13.

6 Tom Kemp, *The Climax of Capitalism: The U.S. Economy in the Twentieth Century* (London: Longman, 1990), 126.

7 Ibid., 126–7.

8 William Keating, *The Man Who Rocked the Boat* (London: Four Square, 1958), 180–5.

9 John Hutchinson, *The Imperfect Union: A History of corruption in American Trade Unions* (New York: E.P. Dutton, 1972) 102.

10 Keating, *Man Who Rocked*, 107.

11 *Waterfront Corruption*, Report Made by the Permanent Subcommittee on Investigations of the Committee on Governmental Affairs United States Senate, 27 March 1984, excerpted in Alan A. Block, *The Business of Crime: A Documentary Study of Organized Crime in the American Economy* (Oxford: Westview Press, 1991), 162–9.

12 Ibid., 161.

13 Robert F. Kennedy, *The Enemy Within* (New York: Popular Library, 1960), 243–50.

14 John L. McClellan, *Crime without Punishment* (New York: Popular Library, 1963), 31.

15 Ibid., 32.
16 Kennedy, *Enemy*, 207.
17 Ibid., 209.
18 Ibid., 209–12.
19 Quoted in Hutchinson, *Imperfect Union*, 182.
20 Steven Brill, *The Teamsters* (New York: Pocket Books, 1978), 71.
21 Walter Sheridan, *The Fall and Rise of Jimmy Hoffa* (New York: Saturday Review Press, 1972), 73.
22 Ibid., 75.
23 Kennedy, *Enemy*, 159.
24 Brill, *Teamsters*, 30–1.
25 James Neff, *Mobbed Up: Jackie Presser's High-Wire Life in the Teamsters, the Mafia, and the FBI* (New York: Dell, 1989).
26 Ibid., 261.
27 Ibid.
28 Peter Siskind, 'Rank and File Rebellion,' *Lies of Our Times*, Nov. 1991.
29 U.S. Bureau of Labor Statistics, *Union Members in 1996*, http://www.itcilo.it/english/actr ... earn/global/ilo/seura/usunion.htm
30 Russell Mokhiber, *Corporate Crime and Violence: Big Business Power and the Abuse of the Public Trust* (San Francisco: Sierra Club Books, 1988), 214–15.
31 Gilbert Geis, 'The Heavy Electrical Equipment Antitrust Cases of 1961,' in Gilbert Geis, *White-Collar Criminal: The Offender in Business and the Professions* (New York: Atherton Press, 1968), 105.
32 Ibid., 107–8.
33 Steven Box, *Power, Crime, and Mystification* (London: Tavistock, 1983), 31.
34 Geis, 'Heavy Electrical Equipment,' 106.
35 John E. Conklin, *Illegal But Not Criminal* (Englewood Cliffs, NJ: Prentice-Hall, 1977), 46.
36 D. Stanley Eitzen, *Social Problems* (Boston: Allyn and Bacon, 1983), 405.
37 Frank Hagen and Peter Benekos, 'What Charles Keating and "Murph the Surf" Have in Common: A Symbiosis of Professional and Occupational and Corporate Crime,' *Criminal Organizations: International Association for the Study of Organized Crime*, 7 (1992), 24.
38 Paul Z. Pilzer and Robert Deitz, *Other People's Money: The Inside Story of the S & L Mess* (New York: Simon and Schuster, 1989), 100–1.
39 Kitty Calavita and Henry Pontell, 'Savings-and-Loan Fraud as Organized Crime: Towards a Conceptual Typology of Corporate Illegality,' *Criminology*, 31 (1993), 519–48.
40 Stephen Pizzo, Mary Ricker, and Paul Muolo, *Inside Job: The Looting of*

America's Savings and Loan (New York: McGraw-Hill, 1989), 209, 193; Hagan and Benekos, 'What Charles Keating and "Murph the Surf" Have in Common,' 10.

41 Kitty Calavita and Henry Pontell, '"Other People's Money" Revisited: Collective Embezzlement in the Savings and Loan and Insurance Industries,' *Social Problems*, 38 (1991), 99.

42 Pizzo, Ricker, and Muolo, *Inside Job*, 392–404.

43 Hagan and Benekos, 'What Charles Keating,' 3; 'Keating Loses Appeal over Repaying Money,' *USA Today*, 28 May 1996.

44 Calavita and Pontell, 'Other People's Money, 94; John Kenneth Galbraith, *The Culture of Contentment* (Harmondsworth: Penguin, 1992), 61.

45 Charles McCarry, *Citizen Nader* (London: Jonathan Cape, 1972), 8–9.

46 Coleman, *Criminal Elite*, 41; Gerry Spence, *With Justice for None* (New York: Penguin, 1989), 201.

47 Mokhiber, *Corporate Crime*, 373–82; Gerry Spence, *With Justice*, 200–1.

48 Mokhiber, *Corporate Crime*, 150.

49 Marshall B. Clinard, *Corporate Corruption: The Abuse of Power* (New York: Praeger, 1990), 103.

50 Coleman, *Criminal Elite*, 46; Morton Mintz quoted in Mokhiber, *Corporate Crime*, 157.

51 Mokhiber, *Corporate Crime*, 151.

52 Judge Miles W. Lord quoted in Spence, *With Justice for None* (New York: Penguin, 1989), 202–3.

53 Coleman, *Criminal Elite* 35

54 Spence, *With Justice for None*, 305.

55 Clinard, *Corporate Corruption*, 98.

56 Mokhiber, *Corporate Crime*, 279.

57 Clinard, *Corporate Corruption*, 98.

58 Adam Raphael, *Ultimate Risk: The Inside Story of the Lloyd's Catastrophe* (London: Transworld, 1994), 109.

59 Clinard, *Corporate Corruption*, 99; Raphael, *Ultimate Risk*, 124.

60 Clinard, *Corporate Corruption*, 100.

61 Alan A. Block and Frank R. Scarpitti, *Poisoning for Profit: The Mafia and Toxic Waste in America* (New York: William Morrow, 1985), 39–40; Mokhiber, *Corporate Crime*, 269.

62 Clinard, *Corporate Corruption*, 114.

63 Coleman, *Criminal Elite*, 37.

64 Clinard, *Corporate Corruption*, 115; *Newsweek*, 7 March 1983, 24–31; Raphael, *Ultimate Risk*, 162.

65 Coleman, *The Criminal Elite*, 39.

66 Donald J. Rebovich, *Dangerous Ground: The World of Hazardous Waste Crime* (New Brunswick: Transaction, 1992), xiv–xv.

67 Clinard, *Corporate Corruption*, 115–16; Frank Pearce, 'US Capital versus the Third World,' in Frank Pearce and Michael Woodiwiss, *Global Crime Connections* (Basingstoke: Macmillan, 1993), 188.

68 Laureen Snider, 'The Politics of Corporate Crime Control,' in Pearce and Woodiwiss, *Global Crime*, 213; Coleman, *The Criminal Elite*, 7; David Burnham, *Above the Law: Secret Deals, Political Fixes, and Other Misadventures in the Department of Justice* (New York: Scribner, 1996), 211–46.

69 Coleman *The Criminal Elite*, 7; Snider, 'The Politics,' 212; Steven Box, *Power, Crime, and Mystification* (London: Tavistock, 1983), 28.

70 Mokhiber, *Corporate Crime*, 215–220.

71 Coleman, *The Criminal Elite*, 15.

72 Pearce, *Crimes of the Powerful* (London: Pluto Press, 1976), 78.

73 Burnham, *Above the Law*, 42.

74 Clinard, *Corporate Corruption*, 14–15.

75 Snider, *The Politics*, 215–6.

76 Burnham, *Above the Law*, 220.

77 Laureen Snider, 'The Regulatory Dance: Understanding Reform Processes in Corporate Crime,' *International Journal of the Sociology of Law* 19 (1991), 220.

78 Frank Pearce and Steve Tombs, *Toxic Capitalism: Corporate Crime and the Chemical Industries* (Aldershot, England: Dartmouth, 1988) 267.

79 Burnham, *Above the Law*, 234.

7 Drugs: Private Enterprise and Government Bounty

1 Susan George, *The Debt Boomerang: How Third World Debt Harms Us All* (London: Pluto Press, 1992), 34.

2 Richard A. Spears, *The Slang and Jargon of Drugs and Drink* (London: Scarecrow Press, 1986), 486–7.

3 Bruce Bullington, 'America's Drug War: Fact or Fiction,' in Ross Coomber, ed., *The Control of Drugs and Drug Users: Reason Or Reaction* (Amsterdam: Harwood Academic Press, 1998), 113.

4 Steven R. Donziger, ed., *The Real War on Crime: The Report of the National Criminal Justice Commission* (New York: Harper Perennial, 1996), 15.

5 Ibid., 201.

6 Richard Schroeder, *The Politics of Drugs* (Washington, DC: Congressional Quarterly, 1980), 121.

7 Joel Brinkley, 'Drug Smugglers Say Hard Part Is What to Do with the Money,' *New York Times*, 29 Nov. 1984.

8 Albert Goodman, *Grass Roots* (New York: Harper and Row, 1979), 100.

9 *Las Vegas Review Journal*, 29 March 1985.

10 Robert McBride, 'Business as Usual: Heroin Distribution in the United States,' *Journal of Drug Issues* (Winter 1983); Steven Wisotsky, 'Exposing the War on Cocaine: The Futility and Destructiveness of Prohibition,' *Wisconsin Law Review* (1983); Anthony Henman, Roger Lewis, and Tim Malyon, *Big Deal: The Politics of the Illicit Drugs Business* (London: Pluto, 1985).

11 Hank Messick, *Secret File* (New York: G.P. Putnam's Sons, 1969) 24–36; Donald Goddard, *Easy Money* (New York: Farrar, 1978), 361.

12 *Detroit Free Press*, 30 March 1972; *New York Times*, 18 Feb. 1983, 7 Oct. 1984; Wisotsky, *Exposing the War on Cocaine*, 1401.

13 Study by Malcolm W. Klein of the University of Southern California cited in *Narcotics Control Digest*, 26 Feb. 1992.

14 Officer Roland Garcia, 'Black Street Gangs' Organization and Subculture,' paper delivered in the early 1990s – no other information available. A phone call to the LAPD's Gang Squad on 24 Aug. 1999 confirmed the essential accuracy of Officer Garcia's description. Gang members now make themselves less easy to identify by dropping the colours and most of the hand signals.

15 Burham Wazir, 'LA's Gangland Wars Rage Again,' *Observer*, 30 May 1999, 25.

16 Leon Bing, *Do or Die* (New York: Harper Perennial, 1991), Luis J. Rodriguez, *Always Running* (New York: Touchstone, 1991), Sanyika Shakur, *Monster* (New York: Penguin, 1993).

17 Information from the Intelligence Squad of the Portland Police Department Intelligence. Duncan Campbell, 'Still on the Road,' *Guardian*, 14 June 2000, G2; Yves Lavigne, *Good Guy, Bad Guy: Drugs and the Changing face of Organized Crime* (Toronto: Ballantine Books, 1991), 362–84; Margaret Beare, *Criminal Conspiracies: Organized Crime in Canada* (Scarborough, Ont.: Nelson, 1996), 80–1.

18 David Downes, 'Prison Does Wonders for the Jobless Figures,' *Guardian*, 25 Nov. 1997, 17.

19 Anti-Defamation League (1999), *From the Prisons to the Streets: The Nazi Low Riders Emerge in California*, http://www.adl.org/issue-combating-hate/nazi-low-riders.html

20 For prison gangs, see David B. Klanick, *The Inmate Economy* (Lexington, Mass.: Lexington Books, 1980); *Sunday Times*, 22 Jan. 1978; *High Times*, April 1981; *Washington Post*, 7 April 1982; *New York Times*, 20 Jan. 1982; *Narcotics Control Digest*, 16 Oct. 1985; *San Francisco Chronicle*, 18 March 1985; *New York Times*, 20 Jan. 1986. Eric Schlosser, 'The Prison Industrial Complex,' *Atlantic Monthly*, Dec. 1998, 51–77.

21 Robert S. Fong and Salvador Buentello, 'The Detection of Prison Gang Development: An Empirical Assessment,' *Federal Probation*, March 1991, 66; Jennifer Gonnerman, 'Gangs behind Bars,' *Village Voice*, 21 Oct. 1997, 41–7.

22 Donziger, *Real War*, 45–96.

23 Schlosser, 55.

24 *New York Times*, 24 Oct. 1982.

25 Patricia Adler, *Wheeling and Dealing: An Ethnography of an Upper-Level Drug Dealing and Smuggling Community* (New York: Columbia University Press, 1993), 191.

26 Peter Reuter and John Haaga, *The Organization of High-Level Drug Markets: An Exploratory Study* (Santa Monica, Rand, 1989), discussed in Adler, *Wheeling and Dealing*, 1919–22.

27 Philip Mattera, *Off the Books: The Rise of the Underground Economy* (London: Pluto, 1985), 55–61.

28 *Business Week*, 18 March 1985.

29 Henman et al., *Big Deal*, 2–3; President's Commission on Organized Crime (hereinafter called the Kaufman commission), *Interim Report to the President and the Attorney General, The Cash Connection: Organized Crime, Financial Institutions, and Money Laundering* (Washington, DC: Government Printing Office, Oct. 1984).

30 Quoted in Penny Lernoux, 'The Miami Connection,' *Nation*, 18 February 1984.

31 See Peter Truell and Larry Gurwin, *False Promises: The Inside Story of BCCI, The World's Most Corrupt Financial Empire* (Boston: Houghton-Mifflin, 1992) for the most comprehensive account of BCCI's criminal activities and its connections to the American intelligence community.

32 Beare, *Criminal Conspiracies*, 113–14.

33 Ibid., 115.

34 Jeffrey Robinson, *The Laundrymen* (London: Pocket Books, 1998), 388–9.

35 Quotes from *New York Times*, 6 March 1986.

36 Quote from *New York Times*, 5 March 1986.

37 *Guardian*, 5 Aug. 1986, 15 Sept. 1986, 21 Oct. 1986.

38 Milt Freudenheim, 'Booming Business: Drug Use Tests,' *New York Times*, 3 Jan. 1990.

39 Ibid.

40 *Drugs in the Workplace* (Nov. 1989).

41 *Narcotics Control Digest* (29 Dec. 1986); Clarence Lusane, *Pipe Dream Blues: Racism and the War on Drugs* (Boston: South End Press, 1991), 105–8.

42 *Guardian*, 28 June 1991, 22.

43 David Burnham, *Above the Law: Secret Deals, Political Fixes, and Other Misadventures in the Department of Justice* (New York: Scribner, 1996), 190.

44 Richard Grant, 'Drugs in America: Zero Tolerance,' *Independent on Sunday,* 20 June 1993, 14–16; Terrance G. Reed, 'American Forfeiture Law: Property Owners Meet the Prosecutor,' *Policy Analysis* (29 Sept. 1992), 1–29.

45 Bush quoted in Marc B. Stahl, 'Asset Forfeiture, Burdens of Proof and the War on Drugs, *Journal of Criminal Law and Criminology,* 83 (Summer 1992), 275.

46 'An Asset for Your Asset Forfeiture Efforts!' Advertisement in *National Fraternal Order of Police Journal* (Fall/Winter 1992), 47.

47 Mitch Miller and Lance H. Selva, 'Drug Enforcement's Double-Edged Sword: An Assessment of Asset Forfeiture Programs,' *Justice Quarterly,* 11, 1994, 313–25.

48 *Pittsburg Press,* 14 Aug. 1991.

49 Steven B. Duke, America's Lost War: Rethinking Our Tragic Crusade against Drugs (New York: Putnam's, 1993), 144.

50 *Pittsburg Press,* 11 Aug. 1991; *Brunswick Times,* 21 June 1993.

51 *New York Times,* 3 Sept. 1993.

52 Jack Briggs, 'Forfeiture!' *Los Angeles Reader,* 18 Dec. 1992, 12.

53 *FEAR Chronicles,* June 1992.

54 Briggs, 'Forfeiture!,' 11–12.

55 Burnham, *Above the Law,* 190.

56 Gary Marx, *Undercover: Police Surveillance in America* (Berkeley: University of California Press, 1988), 163.

57 Information on FEAR's website: http://www.fear.org/whatsnew.htlm, updated on 3 May 2000.

58 Bureau of Justice Statistics, Drugs and Crime Facts, 1994 (Rockville, MD: ONDCP Drugs and Crime Clearinghouse, 1995) 21; Diana Gordon, *The Return of the Dangerous Classes* (New York: W.W. Norton, 1994), 143.

8   American Power and the Dumbing of Global Discourse, 1945 to the Present

1 Paul Kennedy, *The Rise and Fall of the Great Powers* (London: Unwin Hyman, 1988), 358–60.

2 Christopher Simpson, *Blowback: America's Recruitment of Nazis and Its Effects on the Cold War* (New York: Weidenfield and Nicolson, 1988), 83–4. See also William Blum, *The CIA: A Forgotten History* (London: Zed Books, 1986).

3 John Ranelagh, *The Agency: The Rise and Decline of the CIA* (London: Hodder and Stoughton, 1988), 119.

4 New York State, Commissioner of Investigations, *Report of Investigation*, 17 Sept. 1954, held in the Thomas E. Dewey Papers, Rush Rhees Library, University of Rochester, New York.

5 Alfred W. McCoy, *The Politics of Heroin: CIA Complicity in the Gobal Drug Trade* (Chicago: Lawrence Hill Books, 1991), 60–1.

6 Roger Lewis, 'Serious Business: The Global Heroin Economy,' in Anthony Henman, Roger. Lewis and Tim Malyon, *Big Deal: The Politics of the Illicit Drugs Trade* (London: Pluto Press, 1985), 10–11.

7 McCoy, *Politics of Heroin*, 122–92; Joathan Kwitny, The Crimes of Patriots (New York: Touchstone, 1988), 47. It is also important to note that the American intelligence community's involvement with the Afghanistan resistance fighters and corrupt Pakistani military officials during conflict with the Soviet Union from the late 1970s also helped the Golden Crescent area in Southwest Asia become a major producer of the world's supply of opium. See McCoy, *Politics of Heroin*, 441–60.

8 Kwitny, *The Crimes*, 52; Drug scandals have continued to characterize the U.S. armed services. In May 1996, twenty-one sailors, including a lieutenant commander, were arrested for participating in a drug smuggling operation in Italy. In April 2000, a US army colonel, formerly in charge of running the U.S. military's anti-drug effort in Colombia, admitted that he had covered up his wife's heroin smuggling and money laundering activities. See *Guardian*, 30 May 1996, 4 April 2000.

9 Mark Tran, 'Gang Rivalry Led to Funeral Attack,' *Guardian*, 31 July 1990, 7.

10 Simpson, *Blowback*. Simpson's work uncovers U.S political warfare practices of the early postwar era and their consequences. He shows how the United States recruited Nazis, ex-Nazis, and fascist collaborators from Eastern Europe and the Soviet Union, many of whom were war criminals responsible for the massacre of thousands, to serve as intelligence analysts, spies, covert operations specialists, guerrilla warfare candidates, and assassination experts, all in the name of anti-communism. This recruitment process was either unknown to the media or effectively covered up. Klaus Barbie was one of those on the U.S. payroll during these years.

11 R.T. Naylor, *Hot Money and the Politics of Debt* (London: Unwin Hyman, 1987), 165–86; M. Linklater, I. Hilton, and N. Ascherson, *The Fourth Reich: Klaus Barbie and the Neo-Fascist Connection* (London: Hodder and Stoughton, 1984), 16–19, 215–319; Noam Chomsky, *Turning the Tide: U.S. Intervention in Central America and the Struggle for Peace* (London: Pluto Press, 1985) 198–207.

12 U.S. Senate Subcommittee on Terrorism, Narcotics, and International Operations of the Committee on Foreign Relations, *Drugs, Law Enforcement*

and Foreign Policy (Washington, DC: Government Printing Office, 1989), 36.

13 Bernard Weirnaub, 'Reagan Condemns Nicaragua – Plea for Aid to Rebels,' *New York Times*, 17 March 1986, 1; Joel Brinkley, 'Drug Agency Rebuts Reagan Charge,' *New York Times*, 19 March 1986, 3.

14 See Peter Dale Scott and Jonathan Marshall, *Cocaine Politics: Drugs, Armies, and the CIA in Central America* (Berkeley: University of California Press, 1998), 98–103, for a detailed account of the alleged Sandinista drug connection story.

15 Quoted in Alexander Cockburn and Jeffrey St Clair, *White Out: The CIA, Drugs, and the Press* (London: Verso, 1998), 391–2.

16 Ibid., 385.

17 Quoted in Noam Chomsky, *The Chomsky Reader* (London: Serpent's Tail, 1987), 318.

18 William Blum, *The CIA: A Forgotten History* (London: Zed Books, 1986), 68.

19 Daniel Yergin, *The Prize, The Epic Quest for Oil, Money, and Power* (London: Simon and Shuster, 1991), 470.

20 For other accounts of Operation Ajax see also John Ranelagh, *The Agency*, 261–4; Coleman, *Criminal Elite*, 69–70.

21 Stephen Schlesinger and Stephen Kinzer, *Bitter Fruit: The Untold Story of the American Coup in Guatamala* (Garden City, NY: Doubleday, 1982); Blum, *CIA*, 77–89; Ranelagh, *Agency*, 264–8.

22 Coleman, *Criminal Elite*, 71.

23 Morton H. Halperin, Jerry J. Berman, Robert L. Borosage, and Christine M. Marwick, *The Lawless State: The Crimes of the U.S. Intelligence Agencies* (Harmondsworth: Penguin, 1976), 15–29; Ranelagh, *Agency*, 514–20; Anthony Sampson, *The Sovereign State: The Secret History of ITT* (London: Coronet, 1974) 242–56; Coleman, *Criminal Elite*, 70–2; Blum, *CIA*, 232–43.

24 William Chambliss, 'State-Organized Crime,' in Nikos Passas, ed., *Organized Crime* (Aldershot: Dartmouth, 1995), 274–5.

25 David Kauzlarisch and Ronald Kramer, *Crimes of the American Nuclear State* (Boston: Northeastern University Press, 1998), 93.

26 Ibid., 117.

27 Ibid., 118–42.

28 Ibid., xi.

29 R.T. Naylor, 'Loose Cannons: Covert Commerce and Underground Finance in the Modern Arms Black Market,' *Crime, Law, and Social Change*, 22 (1995), 3.

30 Ibid., 11.

31 Coleman, *Criminal Elite*, 50.

32 Naylor '*Loose Cannons*,' 17–18.

33 Ibid., 20–1.

34 Tom Kemp, *The Climax of Capitalism: The U.S. Economy in the Twentieth Century* (London: Longman, 1990), 201.

35 Marshall B. Clinard, *Corporate Corruption: The Abuse of Power* (New York: Praeger, 1990), 144.

36 Ibid., 147.

37 Clinard, *Corporate Corruption*, 141.

38 Ibid., 141–2.

39 David C. Korten, *When Corporations Rule the World* (London: Earthscan, 1995), 129.

40 Frank Pearce and Steve Tombs, *Toxic Capitalism: Corporate Crime and the Chemical Industries* (Aldershot, England: Dartmouth, 1988), 197.

41 Clinard, *Corporate Corruption*, 140; Pearce and Tombs, *Toxic Capitalism*, 200.

42 Pearce and Tombs, *Toxic Capitalism*, 200.

43 Fred Pearce, 'Legacy of a Nightmare,' *Guardian*, 13 Aug. 1998, *Online*, 3.

44 Pearce and Tombs, *Toxic Capitalism*, 212.

45 Korten, *When Corporations Rule*, 129.

46 Amnesty International, *INDIA: The 'Enron Project' in Maharashtra: Protests Suppressed in the Name of Development*, London, July 1997.

47 Nick Cohen, 'Influent, Affluent. Mostly Effluent,' *Observer*, 6 Sept. 1998, p. 18.

48 Ethan Nadelmann, *Cops across Borders: The Internationalization of U.S. Criminal Law Enforcement* (University Park: Pennsylvania State University Press, 1993), 470.

49 Ibid., 466.

50 David Stewart, 'Internationalizing the War on Drugs: The U.N. Covention against Illicit Traffic in Narcotic Drugs and Psychotropic Substances,' *Denver Journal of International Law and Policy,* 18 (1990), 387–404.

51 Ibid., 389–91.

52 David R. Bewley-Taylor, 'Creating Constraint: The United States and International Drug Control, 1945–1964,' doctoral dissertation, University of Wales, Swansea, 1996, 265–6. Bewley-Taylor's thesis has been extended and published as *The United States and International Drug Control, 1909–1997* (London: Pinter, 1999).

53 *The United Nations and Drug Abuse Control* (U.N. International Drug Control Programme, UN Department of Public Information, 1992), 7.

54 Recent estimates quoted in Mark Tran, 'Drug War Just an Exercise in Futility,' *Guardian, 11 June 1998, 19*. See also Paul B. Stares, *Global Habit: The Drug Problem in a Borderless World* (Washington, DC: Brookings Institute, 1996).

55 Anthony Henman, 'Cocaine Futures,' in Henman, *Big Deal*, 157–8.

56 Henry Barrett Chamberlin, 'Some Observations Concerning Organized Crime,' *Journal of Criminal Law and Criminology*, 22 (1931–32), 669.

57 Quotes taken from Linnea Raine and Frank J. Cilluffo, *Global Organized Crime: The New Empire of Evil* (Washington, DC: Center for Strategic and International Studies, 1994), ix. FBI Director Freeh has elsewhere defined organized crime as 'a continuing criminal conspiracy having a firm organizational structure, a conspiracy fed by fear and corruption.' Quoted in Mona Stephens, 'Global Organized Crime,' paper read at the Woodrow Wilson School Policy Conference 401A Intelligence Reform in the Post-Cold War Era, 6 Jan. 1996.

58 Quoted in the *Guardian*, 29 June 1993, 13.

59 R.T. Naylor, 'From Cold War to Crime War: The Search for a New National Security Threat,' *Transnational Organized Crime* (Winter 1995), 38.

60 U.N., Background Release, *World Ministerial Conference on Organized Trasnational Crime to be held in Naples, Italy, from 21 to 23 Nov.*, 17 Nov. 1994.

61 U.N., Background Release, *Statement by the Secretary-General on the Occasion of the World Ministerial Conference on Organized Transnational Crime*, Naples, 21 Nov. 1994.

62 All quotes taken from U.N. Background Release, *Proposed Formulation of Global Convention against Organized Crime Discussed at World Ministerial Conference*, 22 Nov. 1994.

63 U.N. Economic and Social Council, *Appropriate Modalities and Guidelines for the Prevention and Control of Organized Transnational Crime at the Regional and International Levels, Background Document*, E/CONF.88/5, 19 Sept. 1994.

64 See n61.

65 Clinton quoted in the *Guardian*, 23 Oct. 1995, 8.

66 U.N. General Assembly, *Report of the Ad Hoc Committee on the Elaboration of a Convention against Transnational Organized Crime on the work of its first to eleventh sessions*, A/55/383, 2 Nov. 2000, 25.

67 See, for example, Letizia Paoli, 'The Pentitis Contribution to the Conceptualization of the Mafia Phenomenon,' in Vincenzo Ruggiero, Nigel South, and Ian Taylor, eds., *The New European Criminology: Crime and Social Order in Europe* (London: Routledge, 1998), 264–86; Peter Dale Scott and Jonathan Marshall, *Cocaine Politics: Drugs, Armies, and the CIA in Central America* (Berkeley: Univeristy of California Press, 1998).

68 Naylor, 'From Cold War to Crime War,' 37–56, 51.

69 Ibid., 40–1.

70 Michael Massey, 'Desparate Over Drugs,' *New York Review of Books*, 30 March 1989, 23.

71 Vincenzo Ruggiero and Nigel South, *Eurodrugs: Drug Use, Markets and Trafficking in Europe* (London: UCL Press, 1995), 86.
72 See n62.
73 For an account of the 'genocidal' aftermath of the Indonesian invasion of East Timor and the West's complicity, see Hugh O'Shaughessy, 'Secret Killing of a Nation,' *Observer*, 7 April 1991, 11.
74 Benjamin Strolberg, 'Thomas E. Dewey: Self-Made Myth,' *American Mercury*, June 1940, 140–7.

Index

professionalism 124; racketeering
4, 107–16, 124–30, 148–64, 293;
regulating 6, 136, 140–3, 147, 153,
165, 335–9; 'revolving door'
arrangements 338–9, 353; safety
negligence 112–13, 117, 122–3,
132–3, 146–7, 329–30, 335–9, 374–7;
strikebreaking 105–6, 120, 124–5,
127, 157–8, 160, 163; union
relationship 8, 12, 106, 118–22,
317, 319–20, 324–5; and U.S. foreign policy 369–74; violence used
8, 106, 120, 123–9, 140, 149, 166–9,
377–8
Corridan, John (Catholic priest) 161
corruption: in the American
Revolution 31–3, 36–9; in British
government 25–6; in Customs
Service 58, 191; in the DEA 301–2;
in early U.S. 43–7; in FBN 225,
256–7, 301; in government 5, 79,
191–2, 194, 222, 265, 278–82, 306–7,
329; in justice system 38, 61, 110–
11, 114, 147, 154–6, 158–9, 305–6; in
justice system (from bootlegging)
184, 192; in justice system (from
drug trafficking) 299–300; in justice system (from gambling
rackets) 207; in justice system
(Roman Empire) 16–17; in leading
families 16–17; in local government 84–5, 94–6, 111, 160, 161, 196,
207, 242 (see also political machinery); in local government (from
bootlegging) 189–91; in local government (from gambling rackets)
207–8, 293–4; in Narcotics Division
301; in police 58, 64, 156, 163, 196,
216–17, 239, 241–2, 419; in police
(from bootlegging) 184, 189–91; in

police (from drug trafficking)
219–20, 225, 296–301, 302–3, 305,
359–60; in police (from gambling
rackets) 207–8, 210–11, 215–17,
292–4; and power 16–17, 43–6; in
prisons 26, 84–5, 347–8; in profes-
sional classes 6, 43, 61, 95, 314; in
Roman Empire 15–18; skimming
214, 295, 300; in unions 12, 127–30,
150, 151, 159–64, 314–24. See also
graft system
Corruption and the Decline of Rome
(McMullen) 17
Cosby, W.D. (justice of peace) 86
Cosmopolitan Magazine 138–9
Costello, Frank (gangster) 210–11,
217, 249
counterfeiting 10, 22–3, 60, 234
Courtney, Thomas C. (lawyer) 154–5
Cowley, Malcolm (writer) 57
Crafts, Wilbur Fisk (Reverend) 93
Cranston, Alan (senator) 329
Crapsey, Edward (writer) 95–6
CRASH 305
Creating Constraint (Bewley-Taylor)
380
Crédit Mobilier 114
Creek tribe 36, 44, 49
Crime and the Community
(Tannenbaum) 230
Crime Does Not Pay series 239–40
Crime Inc. (Short) 251
Crime of Carelessness, The (film) 133
Crimes of the American Nuclear State
(Kauzlarisch and Kramer) 372
Criminal Organizations (Potter)
11–12, 308–9
Croker, Richard (Tammany boss) 64
Crosby, Clyde (of Teamsters Union)
318–19